Healing War Trauma

Healing War Trauma details a broad range of exciting approaches for healing from the trauma of war. The techniques described in each chapter are designed to complement and supplement cognitive-behavioral treatment protocols—and, ultimately, to help clinicians transcend the limits of those protocols.

For those veterans who do not respond productively to—or who have simply little interest in—office-based, regimented, and symptom-focused treatments, the innovative approaches laid out in *Healing War Trauma* will inspire and inform both clinicians and veterans as they chart new paths to healing.

Raymond Monsour Scurfield, DSW, LCSW, is a Vietnam veteran (who was a social work officer on one of the Army's two psychiatric teams), professor emeritus of social work at the University of Southern Mississippi, and the founding director of the VA's National Center for PTSD in Honolulu, Hawai'i.

Katherine Theresa Platoni, PsyD, maintains a private practice in Centerville, Ohio, is a colonel in the Medical Service Corps of the United States Army Reserve, and serves as Army Reserve Psychology Consultant to the Chief in the Medical Service Corps. She is a veteran of four deployments, including Operation Desert Storm, Operation Iraqi Freedom, and Operation Enduring Freedom.

ROUTLEDGE PSYCHOSOCIAL STRESS SERIES
Charles R. Figley, Ph.D., Series Editor

42. *The Compassion Fatigue Workbook: Creative Tools for Transforming Compassion Fatigue and Vicarious Traumatization,* by Françoise Mathieu, M.Ed.
43. *War Trauma and Its Wake: Expanding the Circle of Healing,* by Raymond Monsour Scurfield, D.S.W., and Katherine Theresa Platoni, Psy.D.
44. *Healing War Trauma: A Handbook of Creative Approaches,* by Raymond Monsour Scurfield, D.S.W., and Katherine Theresa Platoni, Psy.D.
45. *Helping Traumatized Families,* by Charles R. Figley, Ph.D., and Laurel Kiser, Ph.D.
46. *An EMDR Practitioner's Guide to Treating Traumatic Stress Disorders in Military Personnel,* by Mark C. Russell, Ph.D., and Charles R. Figley, Ph.D.

Healing War Trauma
A Handbook of Creative Approaches

Edited by
Raymond Monsour Scurfield and
Katherine Theresa Platoni

Routledge
Taylor & Francis Group

NEW YORK AND LONDON

This book is part of the Psychosocial Stress Series, edited by Charles Figley.

First published 2013
by Routledge
711 Third Avenue, New York, NY10017

Simultaneously published in the UK
by Routledge
27 Church Road, Hove, East Sussex BN3 2FA

Routledge is an imprint of the Taylor & Francis Group, an informa business

© 2013 Taylor & Francis

The right of Raymond Monsour Scurfield and Katherine Theresa Platoni to be identified
as the authors of the editorial material, and of the authors for their individual chapters, has
been asserted in accordance with sections 77 and 78 of the Copyright, Designs and Patents Act 1988.

Library of Congress Cataloging in Publication Data
Healing war trauma : a handbook of creative approaches / Raymond Monsour Scurfield
and Katherine Theresa Platoni, eds.
    p. cm. — (Routledge psychosocial stress series)
    Includes bibliographical references and index.
    1. Post-traumatic stress disorder—Treatment. 2. Veterans—Mental health.
    3. Psychic trauma—Treatment. I. Scurfield, Raymond M. II. Platoni, Katherine Theresa.
    RC552.P67H427 2013
    616.85'212—dc23
    2012015352

ISBN: 978–0–415–80705–0 (hbk)
ISBN: 978–0–415–63777–0 (pbk)
ISBN: 978–0–203–15381–9 (ebk)

Typeset in Minion
by Swales & Willis Ltd, Exeter, Devon

Printed and bound in the United States of America by Sheridan Books, Inc. (a Sheridan Group Company).

Contents

Notes on Contributors

Janice E. Buckley was born in Illinois but now lives in Snohomish, Washington, and considers it home. In 2004, she established the Washington chapter of Operation Homefront. This non-profit organization brought financial help and comfort to the families left behind and to the wounded that returned home. In 2009, Ms. Buckley wanted to focus her entire efforts on wounded warriors and their families, so she changed the name of her organization to "Heartbeat—Serving Wounded Warriors." Janice@heartbeatforwarriors.org.

Ron Capps is the founder and director of the Veterans' Writing Project. He served in the Army and Army Reserve for 25 years, including a combat tour in Afghanistan. Ron developed and leads the writing therapy program at the DoD National Intrepid Center of Excellence, and is the lead instructor for the National Endowment for the Arts Operation Homecoming program at NICoE. He also teaches writing at The George Washington University. ron@veteranswriting.org.

Lily G. Casura is an honors graduate of Harvard University. In February 2006 she created HealingCombatTrauma.com, an award-winning website that provides therapeutic resources and information to combat veterans with PTSD. A graduate of the Center for Mind-Body Medicine's practitioner and advanced level trainings, and the National Center for PTSD's clinical training program, Casura is the author of *Gentle Medicine* (Self Health Press) and also curated the "Art and War" series for Ovation television online. HealingVeterans@gmail.com.

Mary Cortani is a U.S. Army veteran and a certified Army Master Instructor of Canine Education, as well as an American Kennel Club certified Canine Good Citizen® Evaluator. Mary has taken her love of dogs, her personal experiences in the U.S. Army, and her corporate career skills, to assist our veterans returning from recent military operations and others who have suffered traumatic injuries, resulting in disabilities. Mary founded Operation Freedoms Paws in January 2010 and, as of May 2011, Operation Freedoms Paws became a 501(c)(3) non-profit organization. Mary has been training dogs for over 35 years. She is also the head trainer for Monterey County Search and Rescue Dogs, Inc., and a K9 Coach Plus. mcortani@operationfreedomspaws.org.

Robert Csandl is co-founder and Executive Director of Treatment Trends, Inc. He works primarily with criminal justice-involved addicts. Robert earned a Master's Degree in Human Services, is a licensed professional counselor, is a practitioner of mindfulness, and conducts training throughout Pennsylvania and the entire country. Robert is a Vietnam veteran who served during Operation Market Time, June 1965 through July 1967. robertcsandl@treatmenttrends.org.

Lori R. Daniels, PhD, LCSW, works for the Portland (Oregon) Veteran Center as a military sexual trauma psychotherapist and a Hartford/VA geriatric social work research scholar. She has held positions within residential and outpatient specialized PTSD treatment programs; as an Assistant Professor of Social Work at Hawaii Pacific University; and as a Consultant with the National Center for PTSD. Dr. Daniels has been treating military-related PTSD since 1989. lorizdisc@gmail.com.

Eric Forbell has 15 years of experience in developing complex software systems of varying scales. He is currently a principal engineer at USC's ICT, leading a variety of efforts, including the SimCoach project, to bring virtual characters to the web and thereby break down barriers to behavioral healthcare. forbell@ict.usc.edu.

J. Galen Buckwalter, PhD, is a Research Scientist at the USC ICT. Dr. Buckwalter has an active career in the academic and private sectors. His academic career focuses on virtual reality, psychoneuroendocrinology, statistical methodology, and personality. jgbuckwalter@ict.usc.edu.

Joyce Hartwell Pelletier, MEd, NCC, LCPC, has a private practice in Portland, Maine, and has over 35 years of experience as an educator, guidance counselor, and clinical therapist. Joyce counsels those who face life crises, psychological problems, spiritual issues, trauma, or family difficulties, and responds to critical incidents as part of the Crisis Care Network. Her co-authored book, *Recovering from Traumatic Stress: A Guide for Missionaries*, was released by William Carey Library in 2010. She can be contacted at info@sunriseseminars.com, or visit www.joycepelletier.com.

Daniel L. Kirsch, PhD, is President of the American Institute of Stress. He is board certified by the American Academy of Pain Management. He is a member of the International Society for Neurotherapy and Research, and of Inter-Pain in Germany. He is an Editor of the *Journal of Neurotherapy* and of *Practical Pain Management*. He has worked with the U.S. Army Combat Stress Control Teams for Iraq and Afghanistan, and was in Kuwait in 1992. dkirsch@stress.org.

Stephanie Laite Lanham, MSN, PMHNP-BC, native of Camden, Maine, and mother of 3 sons, is owner of HOPE Mental Health, P.C., and has over 35 years combined medical and psychiatric experience. She has written two books on trauma recovery, *Veterans and Families' Guide to Recovering from PTSD* (republished 4 times) and, co-written with Joyce Hartwell Pelletier, *Recovering from Traumatic Stress: A Guide for Missionaries*. Contact info@sunriseseminars.com or stlrnc@aol.com.

Belinda Lange, PhD, is a Senior Research Associate in the MedVR Group at the USC ICT and holds a Research Assistant Professor position in the School of Gerontology at the USC. Her research interests involve the use VR for physical and cognitive rehabilitation, and virtual human character interactions for health. Lange@ict.usc.edu.

Colleen Mizuki, MA Counseling Psychology, is an instructor in the mind-brain-body system and mindfulness for the USAR Yellow Ribbon Reintegration Program. She has co-facilitated for the Coming Home Project and is a Board Member and Assistant Director of Research for the American Institute for Veteran Research and Policy. Ms. Mizuki is one of the first 16 people trained in the mindfulness-based Mind Fitness approach for military populations through the Mind Fitness Training Institute. mizukicolleen@yahoo.com.

Emily Nash, LCAT, is a licensed creative arts therapist in New York. She founded, and is Co-Director of, the Therapeutic Arts Alliance of Manhattan (TAAM). Emily has been a leader in the field of trauma work and therapeutic theatre for 30+ years. She was Director of Training and Supervision, pilot Project America. Emily currently maintains a private practice in New York, and co-leads the creative arts therapy program at Veterans' Sanctuary in Allentown, PA. emilylnash@aol.com.

Katherine Theresa Platoni, PsyD, maintains a private practice in Centerville, Ohio, is a colonel in the Medical Service Corps of the United States Army Reserve, and serves as Army Reserve Psychology Consultant to the Chief in the Medical Service Corps. She is a veteran of four deployments, including Operation Desert Storm, Operation Iraqi Freedom, and Operation Enduring Freedom.

David Rabb is Director of Psychological Health, 63rd Readiness Support Command at Moffett Field. He started as a Marine Corps infantryman, and has completed 22 years in the USAR, including as Commander of the 785th Medical Company, Combat Stress Control, and has deployed to Iraq and, currently, Afghanistan. He has been employed in the VA since 1985 and, currently, his VA position is Executive Assistant, Veteran Health Administration—Under Secretary for Health Diversity Advisory Board. davidrabb17@aol.com.

Janet Raulerson is the sister of Janice Buckley and lives on Whidbey Island in Washington state. She is a volunteer, as well as a board member, at Heartbeat, while working as a registered nurse at Seattle Children's Hospital. Ms. Raulerson became involved with Heartbeat in 2005, shortly after its inception, and is a strong supporter of the military community. Amphibs1998@yahoo.com.

Albert (Skip) Rizzo, PhD, Clinical and Neuro-Psychologist, is Associate Director of the University of Southern California (USC) Institute for Creative Technologies (ICT). Skip conducts research on the design, development, and evaluation of VR systems which target the areas of clinical assessment, treatment, and rehabilitation, spanning the psychological, cognitive, and motor clinical domains. rizzo@ict.usc.edu.

Kenji Sagae, PhD, is a Research Scientist at the USC ICT and a Research Assistant Professor in the USC Computer Science Department. His main area of research is natural language processing, focusing on data-driven approaches for analysis of syntax, semantics, and discourse. sagae@ict.usc.edu.

Raymond Monsour Scurfield, DSW, LCSW, is a Vietnam veteran (who was a social work officer on one of the Army's two psychiatric teams), professor emeritus of social work at the University of Southern Mississippi, and the founding director of the VA's National Center for PTSD in Honolulu, Hawai'i. raymond.scurfield@usm.edu.

David Traum, PhD, is a principal scientist and leader of the natural language dialogue group at ICT, and research faculty in Computer Science at USC. Dr. Traum's research focuses on dialog communication between human and artificial agents. He is author of over 200 technical articles, and is President Emeritus of SIGDIAL. traum@ict.usc.edu.

Sherrill Valdes, LCSW, BCD was the Social Work Service Supervisor at the Veterans Affairs Healthcare System Broward Outpatient Clinic, Sunrise, Florida. She retired from this position, after 31 years of service, in May 2012. Specializing in the treatment of trauma, in 1987, she was awarded Social Worker of the Year for Broward County. In 2005, she was the recipient of the Secretary of Veterans Affairs Hand and Heart Award. skvaldes@aol.com.

Josh Williams is a writer and a project manager for ICT's Medical Virtual Reality Research Group, and has designed and created content for multiple cross-disciplinary interactive virtual human efforts, including the U.S. Army Accession Command's SGT Star, the Museum of Science Boston's InterFaces museum guides, and the DcoE's SimCoach project. williamsj@ict.usc.edu.

Mary Beth Williams, PhD, is in private practice in Warrenton, VA. A large component of that practice is working directly with veterans of many wars (WWII to Afghanistan) and helping veterans complete the claims process for VA benefits. She is a former school social worker, and is the author of numerous books including *The PTSD Workbook*, with Soili Poijula, which is presently being revised for summer publication and being translated into German, and *Life After Trauma: A Workbook for Healing*, with Dena Rosenbloom. mbethwms@infionline.net.

John P. Wilson, PhD, Professor of Psychology, Cleveland State University, and a Fulbright Scholar, is internationally recognized as a PTSD expert clinician, consultant, researcher, and author. He is a founding member and past president of the International Society for Traumatic Stress Studies, the author of over 11 books and 20 monographs, and consultant to numerous organizations, including the U.N., the White House, the Commonwealth of Australia, the World Health Organization, and the Red Cross. His numerous honors include a Presidential Commendation (President Jimmy Carter) for his work with Vietnam Veterans. j.p.wilson@csuohio.edu.

Stephanie Wise, MA, ATR-BC, LCAT, is a registered and Board-certified member of the American Art Therapy Association, a licensed creative arts therapist in New York, and Co-Director of the Therapeutic Arts Alliance of Manhattan (TAAM). She was Director, Programs, for The ArtReach Foundation during the pilot Project America. She is currently Clinical Assistant Professor in Art Therapy, Marywood University, Scranton, PA, and co-leads the creative arts therapy program at Veterans' Sanctuary in Allentown, PA. slwise51@gmail.com.

Michael Zacchea served in Iraq from 2004 to 2005 as an advisor to the Iraqi Army. He was wounded in the 2nd Battle of Fallujah, Operation Phantom Fury. As a result of his wounds, Mike was medically retired. Mike became very active in veterans' advocacy during his recovery from his wounds. He runs a program for disabled veterans at the University of Connecticut, and has been featured in numerous national media venues discussing the war and related issues. His email is Mjzacchea@gmail.com or Michael.zacchea@business.uconn.edu.

Series Editor's Foreword

This is the second of two books that focus on returning war veterans' readjustment. The first, *War Trauma and Its Wake*, was published earlier in this Routledge Psychosocial Stress Series. That book, and the one you have in front of you, were edited by Dr. Raymond Scurfield and Dr. Kathy Platoni, each of whom is both a war healer and a veteran. That makes them especially qualified to help us better appreciate the nature of war's effects on everyone in its wake, and the strategies which appear to be especially helpful. Their *War Trauma and Its Wake* book contributes to this Routledge series, as well as to the fields of traumatology, military behavioral health, and war and combat trauma, by transforming their challenging adversities within the military into tangible advantages.

This book, *Healing War Trauma: A Handbook of Creative Approaches*, takes the next step in providing a comprehensive reference source for the busy practitioner: it is a handbook for helping those suffering from war-related trauma including, but not limited to, war veterans and their families. This book builds on the first book by offering a number of innovative approaches to helping the survivors of war.

The familiar symptoms of PTSD are especially troublesome for those dealing with war-related traumatic stress injuries. Current methods that work with typical clients often do not work as well with war-related issues, due, in part, to the isolation most clients feel prior to seeking help. The use of standard CBT protocols by the Veterans Administration medical system only works with half its patients who choose to enter such treatment. The innovative methods offered in this volume will certainly be invaluable in helping to heal trauma stemming from wartime service.

The chapters that follow provide an extraordinary array of approaches for helping those broken by war. In so many ways, they provide practitioners a great resource in their work of helping. Now, more than ever, as American involvement in wars significantly diminishes, this handbook provides practitioners with practical strategies to match the presenting war-related problems with one or more of the innovative treatment approaches so desperately needed in the healing process. An illustration of the commitment that war veterans have to those who also serve is the quote on the bracelet that the second editor, Kathy Platoni, has worn since her last deployment as a psychologist and Army colonel: "Who will go for us? Here am I. Send me." No matter the cause they served, we human beings owe a debt to those who served their country and came back in need of help, and all others who carry the burdens of war. And, as I noted in my foreword for the editors' previous book: when we understand how best to help those impacted by war, we become more effective in caring for all traumatized people and communities.

Charles R. Figley, PhD
Tulane University
New Orleans, Louisiana

Preface

As a Vietnam veteran, I (Scurfield) have been very concerned about, and interested in, the welfare and fate of our current-day service members who have served their country as part of the global war on terror, particularly regarding those who have served in the wars in Iraq and in Afghanistan, and those who have yet to serve.

In addition, I have been dismayed by how little *our country* and *our communities* and *our citizens*, by and large, truly appreciate the experiences and sacrifices of our service members and their families. There remains a historic and current dichotomy between those who are familiar with and concerned about those who serve, and those who have no knowledge or awareness about what OEF (Operation Enduring Freedom) or OIF (Operation Iraqi Freedom) or Operation New Dawn (OND) stand for, and/or who tend to lump together all service members and veterans into one monolithic and, indeed, amorphous category. For those who have served, this issue in and of itself frequently comes to the boiling point of intolerance for the unequalled ignorance of far too much of the American populace.

Expanding the Circle of Healing

The underlying ethos of *Healing War Trauma: A Handbook of Creative Approaches* is to expand the circle of healing to incorporate increasingly more persons, institutions, communities, and approaches, so as to hopefully optimize the contributions to the healing of our service member and veteran population that are so urgently needed. Scurfield and Platoni are both children of World War II veterans. Scurfield's clinical experiences as a Vietnam veteran, and with veterans of wars from WWII onward, spanning a 29 year military and VA career, coupled with Platoni's distinguished career with the U.S. Army Reserves (to include Operation Desert Storm; Joint Task Force Guantanamo Bay, Cuba; Iraq; and Afghanistan), offer a perspective grounded in understanding and serving multiple generations of war veterans. This underlies the premise(s) and the means by which creative approaches to healing from war are so vital to the reintegration of our service members, veterans and their families.

In the first two chapters, Scurfield and Platoni (along with Chapter 2 co-author COL David Rabb, an OIF and OEF veteran *who was serving our country on deployment to Afghanistan at the time of this writing*) provide the context and backdrop for appreciating the imposing task that confronts military personnel, veterans, and their families—those whose lives have been so markedly impacted by war. Chapter 1 identifies *essential factors to consider in assessing and treating* war-related trauma. Chapter 2 provides a detailed description of *the survival modes that service members utilize to be able to function in and survive war—and what they subsequently bring home* from the war. This information is based upon their extensive clinical and personal experiences, both while deployed and after returning home as veterans of the Vietnam (Scurfield) and Iraq and Afghanistan (Platoni and Rabb) Wars.

In Chapter 3, Mike Zacchea, a physically disabled OIF veteran and a vigorous and articulate advocate on behalf of veterans, describes "the battle after the battle" that service members historically have faced after return from wartime service—the seemingly unceasing struggles to demand that our country do right by its veterans, who have given their all in service to our country. He describes both important positives and cautions about such advocacy in terms of the impact on participating veterans.

Culture-Specific and Community-Based Approaches

The fourth chapter, by John Wilson, pioneering war-related PTSD writer, theoretician, researcher, and clinician, is the "gateway" chapter to various healing approaches. Wilson describes extraordinary experiences involving cultural rituals, particularly those that American Indian warrior tribes have developed over centuries to help returning warriors heal and reintegrate back into their tribes. Wilson, with whom Scurfield has a collegial and friendship relationship dating back to 1979–80, is a Vietnam era veteran with a rich history of PTSD work in various cultures. He describes modern adaptations of such rituals, and the polarity of positives and cautions about integrating them into modern PTSD treatment.

Sherrill Valdes describes the remarkable interactive healing benefits of carefully planned ceremonies embedded within extensively developed community partnerships that involve the reunion of warriors of different eras, their families, and communities.

> "It takes a village to heal warriors—and it takes the warrior to teach the village how."

Sherrill represents practitioners who put the welfare of our veterans first, representing all that is good about the U.S. Department of Veterans Affairs (VA) (as do many practitioners with whom I had the pleasure to work in a 25 year VA career in west Los Angeles; Washington, DC; Tacoma, WA; Honolulu; and Gulfport, MS). Equally compelling, Robert Csandl, a Vietnam veteran, illustrates how the spirit, innovative vision and tireless efforts of a dedicated veteran advocate of one era (Vietnam), along with a dedicated group of equally committed persons, can be the driving, inspirational, force to bring about the community partnerships necessary to create markedly needed community-based healing resources for veterans of all eras.

Expressive-Experiential Approaches

Many expressive and experiential treatment approaches have evolved over the decades. Four authors exemplify some of these creative and diverse applications with veterans. Stephanie Wise and Emily Nash provide detailed descriptions of their rich and impactful utilization of creative-expressive arts with veterans, as does OEF veteran Ron Capps, with an impressive, semi-structured approach to enhance veterans' writing. Lori Daniels—with whom Scurfield first worked in 1988, at the American Lake VA Post-Traumatic Stress Treatment Program, Tacoma, WA, and subsequently as colleagues with the Pacific Center for PTSD in Honolulu—describes her innovative approach to resolving war-related nightmares.

Mind–Body Approaches

Going beyond "talk" therapies includes yet another grouping of extremely knowledge-able authors, who each describe wonderfully diverse mind–body approaches. Colleen Mizuki enlightens readers about the therapeutic and practical benefits of mindfulness-based practices, and co-editor Kathy Platoni shares her extensive knowledge and profi-ciency in hypnotherapy and pain management. Finally, Dan Kirsch describes what might be the best kept secret in mental health treatment—a remarkably simple, yet sophisti-cated, non-invasive, user-friendly intervention that utilizes mild electrical stimulation of the brain with astounding results, and that is backed by an extensive body of research.

Animal Assisted and Outdoor Approaches

Humans have nourished a connection with various animals over the millennia. The therapeutic benefits of such connections have, in relatively recent times, become more formalized and developed in specialized ways. Also, we have all heard of the special con-nections between dogs and their handlers in the military overseas. We are honored to have such amazingly talented and dedicated people as Mary Cortani, Army veteran, and sisters Janice Buckley and Janet Raulerson, who share their inspiring stories in chapters on canine and equine assisted therapies respectively, as developed for wounded warri-ors. Janice and Janet also describe the exciting Scuba Warriors program—an example of outdoor-based interventions. For other outdoor-based approaches, see the chapter by Reyes in our first book, *War Trauma and Its Wake*.

Technological and Web-Based Approaches

OEF, OIF and OND service member veterans and their families are part of by far the most techno-savvy generation of those who have served our nation. In recognition of their familiarity with the use of computers and web-based technology, two chapters describe the harnessing of technology for enhancement of treatment, healing, and networking support for military personnel and veterans. Lily Casura, founder and one-woman ring-leader and originator of the Healing Combat Trauma website, offers a rare, in-depth, insider's view of the challenges, successes, and ongoing journey required to establish and shepherd the evolvement of what is likely *the* most extensive non-governmental infor-mational and social media/communication website serving military personnel, veterans, their families, and providers. Al (Skip) Rizzo and a distinguished group of colleagues out of the University of Southern California describe the state-of-the-art technological Sim-Coach project: the astonishing development of intelligent virtual humans as an interface and facilitator of inquiring service members, veterans, and their families, enabling them to access a wide range of needed services. Scurfield has been honored to have been a PTSD consultant to this project.

Other Creative Approaches: Resolving Guilt, Employment and Spirituality

Finally, three creative approaches do not fit in any of the preceding groupings. These approaches illustrate the variety of underlying knowledge, method, and the application of other creative approaches to healing war trauma. First, there is an innovative technique, Determining the Percentages of Responsibility, that Scurfield has developed over 25 years in order to address the very salient and painful legacy of survivor guilt and issues surrounding an exaggerated sense of responsibility. This remarkably impactful technique is described in detail, and includes Platoni's application with OEF and OIF veterans.

Second, there is an innovative, comprehensive, approach to facilitating veterans to seek, obtain, and retain employment. Written by Mary Beth Williams, a longtime friend and colleague, this chapter provides very practical information that is packaged in a most creative and useful format to inform clinicians and other providers about an employment-focused approach grounded in dynamics relevant to service members and veterans about what, unfortunately, is an often-neglected aspect of mental health treatment.

Finally, for service members, veterans, and family members with a religious and/or spiritual orientation and belief system, Lanham and Pelletier's closing chapter is an affirmation and revelation. It describes the impact of wartime service on such beliefs, and a thoughtful Christian-based approach that includes the pairing of relevant scripture readings with various PTSD symptoms and post-war issues. This chapter reflects the authors' impressive work over the years, and is a most complementary "companion chapter" to that written by Army Chaplain LTC (RET) Charles Purinton in our related book, *War Trauma and Its Wake: Expanding the Circle of Healing* (Scurfield and Platoni, 2012). Chaplain Purinton describes spiritual and religious-based interventions with service members while deployed in Iraq and Afghanistan.

Finding a Co-Editor

My (Scurfield's) original intention was to be the sole editor of *Healing War Trauma: A Handbook of Creative Approaches*, and of the first book, *War Trauma and Its Wake: Expanding the Circle of Healing*. I intended to write a number of the chapters and find several other authors for the topics for which I did not have sufficient knowledge. I also reflected on being in my late 60s, and a Vietnam veteran. I had had some meaningful interactions with, and knowledge about, OEF/OIF/OND service members, including through my wife Margaret's several roles as an MSW with the U.S. Navy, especially as director of several Fleet and Family Service Center programs. However, I decided to have a co-author who was as versed in the OEF/OIF/OND Wars as I was regarding the Vietnam War. I asked my colleague and good friend, Kathy Platoni, to be co-editor. There was only one small problem—at the time, Kathy was deployed to Afghanistan with a combat stress control detachment, and remained in the throes of dealing with the horrific murders at Ft. Hood several months earlier. Five of her fellow soldiers/friends, who were part of her unit and its sister unit and in the process of readying for deployment, were killed, with 13 wounded, several critically. Even so, I emailed Kathy to ask if she was interested. While we both knew there would be significant challenges, she agreed. This and our recently published first book are the gratifying result.

One Huge Book or Two "Separate but Related" Books?

Perhaps the greatest obstacle that we faced in finalizing our original book proposal to Routledge/Taylor & Francis was the large number of chapters (approximately 38) we envisioned. Due to marketing and pricing considerations, we were advised to limit any book proposal to a maximum length of roughly 500 pages. The outcome was to resubmit our original book proposal as two proposals for "separate but related" books.

We decided to focus our first book on an "expanding circle of healing" that describes both the unique and distinctive impact of war and military service on a number of populations and four innovative treatment approaches that emphasized active duty populations. We were also fortunate to find a significant number of OEF and OIF veterans who were experts in many of the chapter topics and who were willing to author those chapters. The book title, *War Trauma and Its Wake: Expanding the Circle of Healing*, reflects such an expansion of healing to various populations and approaches:

- *Special populations of warriors*: Reserve forces, National Guard, women and Canadian military forces
- *Special populations of wounded warriors*: those with traumatic brain injuries and PTSD, seriously wounded and injured warriors, veterans troubled with suicidality, warriors victims of military sexual trauma (MST), and veterans involved with the criminal justice system.
- *Special populations of civilians impacted by war*: the civilian populations of Iraq and Afghanistan, respectively (and an Afterword describing the personal experiences of a surviving spouse of an OEF service member killed-in-action).
- *Innovative approaches to healing*: combat operational stress control and psychological debriefings conducted in Iraq and Afghanistan, outdoor and adventure-based approaches, innovative civilian-military expressive arts programs, and the role and services of military chaplains in Iraq and Afghanistan.

Captain Christian Hallman and Those Killed at Ft. Hood, Texas

In closing, we want to acknowledge those who will never have the opportunity to read our books or reap the fruits of the sacrifices of the hundreds of thousands of service members who deployed to Iraq and/or Afghanistan, and the sacrifices of their families. These are service members KIA (killed-in-action), or who otherwise lost their lives during service to our country or following their return. These include the five colleagues of Platoni murdered and the others seriously wounded at Ft. Hood, Texas, while they were preparing to deploy (for more detail, please refer to our Acknowledgments). Ironically and tragically, Captain Christian Hallman died while in the midst of co-writing Chapter 15 of *War Trauma and Its Wake*. Our hearts and well-wishes and prayers go out to all such casualties of war, including their families, whose impact from such deaths will, of course, be lifelong and profound.

Closing

Perhaps the two worst experiences that can befall service members or veterans following their return from war *are to be berated/vilified for their military service* and/or *to be forgotten*—their lives and sacrifices disregarded or never fully appreciated. This and our companion book are here to shout out loudly: *you are not forgotten—you are remembered, you are appreciated. And your surviving family members are remembered and appreciated!* It is our honor and privilege to dedicate this book to all who have been impacted by war, as well as to those who care about them and/or wish to be more informed. Our mission is to pay it forward, please. Hooah!

Raymond Monsour Scurfield
Pass Christian, Mississippi

Katherine Theresa Platoni
Beavercreek, Ohio

Acknowledgments

This book is dedicated, first and foremost, to all of the men and women who have served and are serving our country as a service member, and to their families. Also, it is a privilege to have been able to recruit such a gifted and dedicated array of authors to contribute to the expanding circle of healing that each and every service member, veteran, and family member, so richly deserves.

One of those service members so deserving "just happens to be" my co-editor, Kathy Platoni. Kathy is a cherished and invaluable colleague, friend and sister war veteran, with whom I have embarked on this incredible journey to produce two major books about war trauma, its impact, and healing. Kathy's extensive knowledge of combat operational stress control and the military, her family military history, her courage in facing her ongoing health struggles—which are military-related—and her remarkable network of colleagues and friends around the country, are inspirations to this aging (but not out-to-pasture yet) Vietnam vet. I wanted this book to be a true collaborative effort "from Vietnam to Iraq and Afghanistan;" Kathy has been invaluable in having that happen. Hooah!

I would be remiss not to acknowledge Charles Figley, fellow Vietnam vet and a long-time valued colleague and friend, since the earliest days of the VA vet center program over 30 years ago. His contributions to the field of post-traumatic stress, and especially to war-related traumatic exposure and recovery, are legendary. He was very encouraging of my writing this book and our "companion" book, *War Trauma and Its Wake: Expanding the Circle of Healing*. Charles even allowed my request to "steal" the title of his precedent-setting book, *Trauma and Its Wake* (Volume 1, 1985), which was one of the first major edited works to cover a spectrum of trauma populations (I was privileged to write the overview chapter on treatment). Above all, Charles does all that he does with an amazing grace and humility that infuses his wisdom and accomplishments.

Then, there is the amazing Routledge/Taylor & Francis editor, Anna Moore. Anna has been an *absolute delight* to work with; we are indebted to her knowledge and also her incredibly positive attitude.

And, to my soulmate of 31+ years—my wife Margaret—and our three adult children, Helani, Armand, and Nick: you are the essence of what makes my life a most precious and joyful journey. You have been with me through the many relocations I put y'all in, moving from one wonderful opportunity after another to serve veterans (mostly with the Department of Veterans Affairs)—from West Los Angeles to Washington, DC, to Tacoma, WA, to Honolulu, and then to the place where Margaret was raised and which

I have adopted as my home—the Mississippi Gulf coast. But, through it all, including Hurricane Katrina, we were, and are, *a family*. And our faith as practicing Catholics has been a life source that underlies everything. Truly, we are blessed.

—Ray Scurfield

This book is dedicated, first, to my beloved husband, LTC (RET) John David Hutchinson, whose home front heroism has been my life force for 24 years. Thank you for standing your watch over the American populace, above the clouds, as an Air Force aviator for 25 years. For the last 14 months, and since my redeployment from Afghanistan, this extraordinary man has, without complaint, tolerated my inexplicable commitment to avoid sleep and to drink gallons of coffee in order to write and edit this book. Never once has he complained about the infinite sacrifices he has made, from managing the house, bills, grocery shopping, bill paying, snow shoveling, dog washing . . . a list as long as I–70 going west. Waiting 35 years for him was the best decision I have ever made. I continue to marvel at all you are and all you do, dear spousal unit!

Second, I wish to dedicate this book to my sister, Lynnette Santolla and my nephews and nieces, Michael Santolla, Christopher Santolla, Nihad Santolla, and Jennifer Santolla, for waiting for me to find you for more than five decades. You are my touchstones in this life. I must also include in this my dearest cousins of all time, Adelmo Platoni, his wife Patricia, and Janette Platoni, who terminated prejudice and anti-Semitism within my own family, so as to permit my inclusion within the family fold, despite a lifetime of opposing ethnicities.

I wish to thank Dr. Ray Scurfield, who trusted sufficiently in my abilities to take me on as a partner in the writing of this book. While I worked tirelessly to try to come home from war, he helped me to gather up the pieces of my life, encouraging me when I had nothing left in my addled brain, and fortifying my empty soul with the belief that producing this book was well within my capabilities. For "CPT Ray," thanks are but a miniscule token of my colossal gratitude for a debt that has yet to be paid. Thanks to you, my mentor and ultimate teacher, I will come home again and continue to write my war stories. You are no less than a national treasure.

I wish to thank Anna Moore, Associate Editor of Routledge, our publishers, profusely, for not only believing in the massive undertaking involved in the writing of this book, but for her undying efforts to make this entire project possible . . . and for her with legendary patience. That this has come to fruition owes much to her efforts. This calls for eternal gratitude.

Those that I wish to thank for their unceasing support through the writing of this book—and for their belief that we would actually see this to its logical conclusion—comprise an elongated list of friends and family members, sometimes one and the same. And I wish to thank the thousands of soldiers and their families who have allowed me into their confidences, and the trenches of their private wars, through the course of my four deployments, particularly those assigned to the 3rd Infantry Division (2/69th Armored Regiment), the 4th Infantry Division (Bravo Company, 3rd Platoon, 1–12th Infantry); among them SGT Ryan Vallery, SSG Matt McIvor, SGT "Tre" Trejo, CPT Dave Seay, CPT Lee Gray, MAJ Steve Gribshaw, CPT Joe Walker, CPT Christopher Preece, Beth Hudson, and SPC Sean Hudson. They willingly overlooked my rank, gender, and my small stature to allow me entry into the camaraderie and espirit de corps of combat arms, which few outsiders are privileged to enter. At the hand of these most extraordinary educators, I have mastered the lesson that is the readiness and inclination to lay down one's life for brother-sister soldier, as the most supreme life force. You are my heroes, one and all. I cannot go without mentioning those extraordinary soldiers and comrades at arms whose unending ministry of presence prevented me from losing faith in humanity, time and time again, and who reminded me that there are some who truly know *what right looks like*: CPT Sean Gargan, MAJ Cora Courage, LTC Val Reyes, LTC Jeffrey Drexler, Dr. Marilyn Shea, Dr. Debra Sowald, Dr. Barry Goldstein, Dr. Ed and Emily Harf, CPT John Fry, SSG Dick Hurtig, former Army SGT Michelle Wilmot, SGT Trey Cole, Victoria Bruner, and CPT Dana Hollywood. There are a host of others who fall into this category, without whose unceasing support I would truly have not survived a year of austerity, sans the bare minimum of supplies with which to conduct business in Afghanistan, from edible food to the most basic of supplies to run our combat stress control clinic to, God love you, toilet paper. With the creation of a nationwide supply chain, envisioned and created by my husband (Operation Runtbo), the numbers of care packages and supplies rivaled a strategic military airlift. Making a hell-hole livable for the multitudes with their angelic deeds were Mom Bev Peyton of OPERATION THANK YOU; Dr. Dan Kirsch; Chaplain Dave Fair; MP Godmother, LTC(RET) Glenda Hull, and her merry band of patron saints and "adoptive parents," Shirley Blayne, Edith Roach, Vicki Snodgrass, Jan Hull, SGM (RET) Joe Attaway, CSM Connie Commenia-Hill, MAJ (RET) Bud Montgomery, COL (RET) Don Franklin, LTC (RET) John Noland, SGT (RET) Monica McCravy, Theresa Ogelsby, and Corrie Ballard; COL (RET) Kathleen Hayes; CPT(RET) Millie Hand-Biawitz; Maria DiMenna; Sally Webster; COL (RET) Dick and Carolyn Redman; Kellie Sharpe; Frank and Sara Jane Lowe; Dr.Ed Rugh, and his miracle-working staff, MAJ Linda Bronski, Jay, John, and Trisha Buza; Dr. Judy Green; Dr. Bob Glaser; Mark Collison; Charlotte Davis; Johanna Smith; Alison Lighthall; Ariel Gurvey; Charlotte Davis; Deborah Michalak; Charles Hand; Deb Hatchett; Barbara Hughes; Jamie Keyes; MSG Dave and Kay Johnson; Vicky Snodgrass; John and Margie Baren; Steve Bennett; Terry Borger; Phyl Friend; Hoosiers Helping Heroes; Jacob's Light; the VFW of Turlock, CA; Albertson's Foods; and Ray's Supermarket. I am knee deep in debt to each for a balance that can never be paid. I wish to thank and bless my extraordinary rescue dogs, Priscilla and Maggie, successors of those beloved pets who died during my last deployment (Suzie and Skippy), whose love and presence during the most difficult of times remains boundless, even at o'dark thirty. Lastly, I wish to pay tribute to my cherished friends and fallen comrades, who lost their lives so tragically during one of the most heinous criminal acts in military history, the Ft.Hood Massacre. The enormity of these catastrophic losses has redefined my life: *Major Libardo Eduardo Caraveo, 467th Medical Detachment (CSC); Captain John Gaffaney, 1908th Medical Detachment (CSC); Staff Sergeant Amy Krueger, 467th Medical Detachment (CSC); Captain Russell Seager, 467th Medical Detachment (CSC); and Lieutenant Colonel Juanita Warman, 1908th Medical Detachment (CSC).* The Hero Bracelet inscription upon which their names are engraved: "Who will go for us? Here am I. Send me."

—Kathy Platoni

1 Innovative Healing Approaches to War Trauma

Raymond Monsour Scurfield (Vietnam)

Limitations and Concerns Regarding CBT Approaches

The purpose of this book is to introduce a wide range of innovative therapeutic approaches to healing from war trauma. We have intentionally minimized the presence of evidence-based manually-driven cognitive-behavioral treatment (CBT) protocols, even though they have brought a great degree of relief to a substantial number of military personnel and veterans and offer a significant degree of reliability and consistency to interventions across settings and practitioners.

The major strengths of most CBT approaches typically also are major limitations. There is a very narrow psychiatric symptom focus, oftentimes primarily—if not exclusively—on the "core" DSM-IV-TR criteria for PTSD. It is, therefore, often the case that vital factors intrinsic to military trauma are ignored or downplayed: factors essential to developing an expanded circle of healing. Typically, CBT protocols are applied in individual treatment sessions, involve a regimented intervention that requires strict adherence, and do not appeal to a number of veterans unwilling to be involved in intensive exposure-based approaches. Also, a significant number who do enter such treatment do not complete the full protocol.

Two such protocols, adapted from sexual assault treatment protocols and adopted by the U.S. Department of Veterans Affairs, are Cognitive Processing Therapy (CPT) (www.ptsd.va.gov/public/pages/cognitive_processing_therapy.asp) and Prolonged Exposure Therapy (PET) (http://www.ptsd.va.gov/public/pages/prolonged-exposure-therapy.asp). It has been reported that 70% of veterans who enter VA CBT treatment protocols complete the prescribed treatment regimens, and that 70% of those who complete the regimens indicate "treatment success" (Spira, 2011). This also means that about 50% of the veterans (e.g., 70% of those who start and complete the protocols and 70% of the 70% who actually complete the protocols with successful results) who choose to enter such CBT protocols in the VA do *not* have "successful" treatment results. Of course, such statistics do not indicate what percentage of the total VA patient population of veterans with PTSD and associated war-related mental health conditions do not, or choose not to, even enter such CBT protocols. This is a substantial group of veterans, with significant mental health conditions, who need treatment approaches that they find sufficiently appealing for them to seek these forms of treatment in the first place. Also, an even larger group of veterans do not utilize mental health treatment services provided by the VA, yet have war-related PTSD and/or other related mental health conditions.

Brock and Passey (2012) report that CBT protocols are frequently insufficient for many and too overwhelming for some, and that prolonged exposure has not been helpful for those service members and veterans with predominant feelings of shame or guilt, or for those with uncontrolled rage around their traumatic memories. Finally, those with significant dissociation or full blown flashbacks are poor candidates for PE until such symptoms are better controlled.

The Rationale for This Book

Veterans suffering from war and service-related PTSD and associated mental health conditions that do not, or are not able to, benefit sufficiently from involvement in most CBT protocols are the primary rationale for this book. One size does not fit all. This includes CBT protocols, no matter how impressive their evidence bases. Also, many service members and veterans with war-related PTSD/associated conditions frequently have great ambivalence, if not unwillingness, to seek treatment in the first place. The limitations and concerns regarding prolonged exposure approaches, and the ambivalence or resistance to seeking needed treatment, make it all the more compelling that there be the widest array of treatment approaches available; this makes it more likely that one or more treatment approaches will be found to be sufficiently appealing to the veteran for him or her to engage in treatment in the first place, and/or to engage in treatment to an extent adequate to garner the therapeutic benefits desired and needed.

Admittedly, there is minimal evidence-based scrutiny of the approaches described in this book—Alpha-Stim technology (Kirsch, Chapter 12) and Mindful-Practices (Mizuki, Chapter 10) are notable exceptions—yet these various approaches have been described, through considerable subjective indicators (the testimony and positive self-report of participating veterans, observations of participating clinicians, etc.), as very positive and impactful. Hopefully, one by-product of this book will be the stimulation of more empirically-based examination, to include qualitative research strategies, of the various healing approaches described.

The availability of innovative healing approaches continues to be significantly hindered by the clamor of many empiricists who insist upon (only) utilizing manual-based CBT protocols. There is the very real danger that the emergence of "new" therapeutic approaches that have yet to be empirically tested will continue to be stifled. Moreover, we have heard from VA colleagues that a number of VA and other clinicians do *not* prefer to have CBT protocols "prescribed" or mandated as "the" trauma-focused intervention, and that it can be very restrictive and exhausting to have such manually-based, narrow symptom-targeted protocols comprise the primary emphasis of their trauma-focused endeavors. Finally, there is concern that individualized treatment creativity, to address the idiosyncratic aspects of individual patients, is not fully sanctioned.

An Expanded Circle of Healing

Special Populations Impacted by War: The First Element of an Expanded Circle of Healing

Special populations impacted by war are one of two primary emphases of our first book, *War Trauma and Its Wake: Expanding the Circle of Healing* (Scurfield & Platoni, 2012) (described in the Preface). Trauma-focused intervetions require specific knowledge and understanding of the distinctive dynamics and challenges that face several populations of warriors (Reserve forces, et al.), wounded warriors (physically wounded, et al.), and civilians (Iraqi and Afghan civilians, and surviving spouses of service members killed in action). And yet, most CBT treatment protocols do not address, either significantly or in a systematic way, the distinctive, if not unique, issues, dynamics, and challenges that characterize these various special populations. The implication seems to be that it is unimportant to understand, or to attend to, such overlooked characteristics.

We beg to differ.

Individualized assessment and interventions need to account for the distinctive and unique dynamics, characteristics, and healing challenges that typify various special populations. Service member one and two, or veteran one and two, are *not* identical. Each requires *consideration of the veteran's unique or distinctive characteristics, related to his or her special population status, to be built into* treatment protocols and other interventions.

Supplemental and Alternative Healing Approaches

The second characteristic of an expanded circle of healing is to ensure that *a full range of healing interventions is available* (Scurfield, 2006a and b).[1] We have been impressed with the many paths to healing that are in addition to CBT office-based talk therapy. For example, several Army installations (e.g., Joint Base Lewis-McChord, Ft. Carson and Ft. Bliss) have the Warrior Adventure Quest (WAQ) program. WAQ combines high adventure, extreme sports, and outdoor recreational activities appropriate to the geographic locale; these include rock climbing, mountain biking, river rafting, paintball, scuba diving and ropes courses, followed by leader-led after action debriefings. Such "action-oriented" approaches have an intuitive appeal to many service members, and are geared to assist service members in transitioning their military operational experiences into a "new normal," enhancing military readiness, reintegration, and adjustment to garrison or "home" life.

VA and community organizations both have implemented beyond-the-office interventions. For example, over 20 VA medical centers offer gardening programs, including a 12 acre parcel at the West Los Angeles VA where veterans propagate fruits, vegetables, and flowers in recognition of "working the earth" as good therapy (Adelman, 2009). The non-profit Farmer-Veteran Coalition helps returning veterans find jobs, training, and places to mend on America's farms (http://www.farmvetco.org/). *Healing War Trauma* includes an expressive and creative arts approach embedded in the veteran peer group (Wise and Nash, Chapter 7), an experiential approach to treating traumatic war dreams (Daniels, Chapter 9) and writing as a healing medium for veterans (Capps, Chapter 8). Finally, there are wonderfully impactful canine assisted (Cortani, Chapter 13), equine assisted and scuba diving programs for veterans (Buckley and Raulerson, Chapter 14).

The Salience of Military Peer Relationships to Surviving War and Post-War Healing

The vital peer connections among military personnel reflect the *profound interpersonal* aspects of healing that are distinctive and crucial to war veterans. Combat or war zone trauma is never an individual experience that occurs in isolation. Rather, it is *inextricably embedded within the context of the small, operational, military unit* in which profound bonds of comradeship occur among peers and with their small unit command. Once in harm's way, it is well understood, by those who have been there, that *by far the most compelling factor* that overrides everything else is *the welfare and safety of one's fellow and sister comrades in the small operational military unit*. This often takes precedence even over one's own safety and, indeed, over the commitment to fighting for one's country (Scurfield, 2006a).

After returning home, there is the deeply held bond and identity *of being a veteran* that has been bonded through war and military service, and there is the accompanying belief that non-veterans cannot possibly understand or fully appreciate the military and veteran experience. These fuel the very strong initial tendency that, if a veteran is going to talk with anyone about his or her war experience, *it almost universally will be with others who have fought in that same war* or served in that same era. For many veterans, this is where the expansion of the healing circle *stops*. And the same is true for military families—the bonds and belief that understanding can only come from other military families who have "walked in their boots" (ibid.).

This peer bonding and identity is *the first and, for many, the most powerful element in an expanding circle of healing relationships*. Hence, it is essential to consider how we can make peer groups available as part of what we can offer to help heal from war trauma. Unfortunately, many CBT protocols for war-related PTSD do not pay any meaningful attention to the healing milieu of the military and veteran peer group.

Veterans of Other Generations, Eras and Theaters

Beyond veterans-to-veterans of the same era and war, an additional powerful level is veterans-to-veterans of different eras. For example, this can occur in a therapy group, with veterans of different eras participating, in which veterans of earlier wars readily become mentors with those "new" Iraq and Afghanistan veterans who are facing many of the very same kinds of post-war challenges and issues (Scurfield, 2006a). Chapters in this volume by Zacchea (Chapter 3), Valdes (Chapter 5), Csandl (Chapter 6), and Wise and Nash (Chapter 7) are examples of healing approaches that meaningfully involve veteran peers.

Beyond the Veteran-to-Veteran Circle

Beyond the veteran-to-veteran circle, an expanded circle of healing recognizes that, for a substantial number of service members and veterans, *there are additional sets of fractured, alienated and/or voided relationships that, inevitably, have been affected*. The indelible impact of combat is a legacy embedded within that can contain, to varying degrees, alienation, loss, grief, anguish, and, for some, bitterness, resentment, and/or hatred. *And so, who else, if anyone*, does the veteran most need to allow entrance into his or her circle of healing in order to further enhance a more complete post-war recovery?

> Today there is a new feeling of strength and self-direction among the People.
> It would be good if the Circle of Powers were made whole again.

It would be good to see again Men and Women, Elders, priests, deacons and
   Sisters
All equal in sharing in the circle of gifts for helping the people.
It would be good to sit down together, to listen to the Elders, to listen to each other's
   hearts, to consider, to choose, to pray, for a way of traveling together.
Best for the whole people.

("The Circle Restored," in Twohy, 1987, p. 245)

Scurfield describes elsewhere an expanded set of relationships (2006a). Three sets of
relationships are briefly summarized here, in order to facilitate consideration of the
incorporation of such a paradigm into an expanding circle of healing.

Relationships with Non-Veterans

The next step beyond veteran-to-veteran is for veterans to include those who are *significant others in their current lives,* such as a partner, parent, child, or other relation, and
close friends. However, oftentimes this can be quite difficult to accomplish.

> A wife of an Iraq War veteran described how difficult her adjustment has been to
> "what the war did to her husband." She couldn't help feeling left out since her hus-
> band seemed to prefer being with other soldiers than with her, and she is very aware
> of the distance between them that she cannot seem to bridge: "I know there's a lot of
> things that he can talk to his (soldier) friends about . . . But I'm sitting here thinking,
> Why can't he talk to me?"
>
> (Corbett, 2004, p. 41)

Why is this so? Because the identity of being a veteran oftentimes *transcends, overshad-
ows,* or *is at least as strong as* an identity that is based on gender, age, marital or familial
roles, race, ethnicity, religion, and socio-economic status. And yet, the VA healthcare
system, geared to serve the veteran, offers *a miniscule* fraction of services to family members. Also, almost all veteran treatment programs never move beyond the veteran-to-
veteran circle, for example to include a mixed treatment or support group comprised
of both veterans and non-veterans, in order to facilitate discovery of the universality of
humanity and trauma experience.

The Relationship That Military Personnel and Veterans Have with the U.S. Government and American Society

> The government sends us to war, the military uses us in war, and society forgets us
> after war.
>
> (Scurfield, 2006a, p. 186)

A natural extension of allowing *non*-veterans into one's healing circle concerns the very
distinctive and extraordinary relationship between military personnel and veterans,
on the one hand, and our government, political leaders and society on the other. Our

government, military leaders, and society sanction service members, as our patriotic duty, to do something that is otherwise both forbidden by society and severely punished: to maim and kill other human beings (albeit in defense of our country), as well as to put ourselves in harm's way for our country and the cause of freedom. This singular, compelling, factor is interwoven with a sacred covenant between our society and the veteran: *our country promises a life-long commitment to honor, support and assist active duty military and veterans in recognition and various forms of benefits in return for this extraordinary risk* (Scurfield, 2006a, 2007).

This covenant is crucial to a successful post-war readjustment for many war veterans: to believe that our country will fully honor the promises that were made while service members were being recruited and after they entered active duty. However, for too many, this is experienced as an empty promise, a trusted relationship diluted or voided. *This is a central issue* of betrayal for many veterans and families. Hence, a crucial and valid therapeutic element is for clinicians to address veterans' relationship with their country, and part of the solution is for veterans to experience caring persons and organizations that are sincere and go beyond empty promises and walking the walk. Finally, we must consider in what meaningful ways we can enable veterans to become active, positive, change agents and/or contributing citizens (see Zacchea, Chapter 3).

The Relationship Between Trauma Negatives and Potential Positives

Many veterans and family members remain fixated and preoccupied with hurt, loss, the horrors of war, and negative experiences post-deployment. It is essential to give appropriate attention to opposite and seemingly contrary thinking in regard to such sufferings and loss: the potentially positive aspects of war-and post-war related traumatic experiences. Typically, these positives have been *embedded within* negative preoccupations. Hence, they are largely, if not completely, overlooked or minimized by many survivors, unless a (cognitive) reframing is facilitated to enable self-acknowledgment that the positive aspect also is true and relevant to them (Scurfield, 2006a).

One example of such a companion polarity: a common negative preoccupation is that veterans can be hyper-sensitive and hyper-reactive to "being treated like a number" by the VA and other agencies. On the other hand, veterans can develop strong convictions about being treated with dignity and respect, and are willing to responsibly take a stand to hold bureaucracy accountable for humanely and responsively providing services.

The People and Land of the Country in Which You Fought

At yet another level of the healing circle, two return trips to peace-time Vietnam have taught Scurfield an invaluable lesson (Scurfield, et al., 2003; Scurfield, 2004, 2006a, b). Such returns are a unique opportunity to both witness and to experience *the capacity of an entire land and people* to have survived and regenerated—a land and people once ravaged by war. And this learning and opportunity will be just as relevant to veterans of Iraq and of Afghanistan in the coming years. There are two extraordinarily powerful chapters in our first book that describe the impact of war on the people of Iraq (Dawoody) and Afghanistan (Badkhen).

In the summer of 2010, Scurfield consulted with a former Baghdad war correspondent who was accompanying a group of physically disabled OIF veterans back to Iraq. One of the vets had had both of his lower extremities traumatically amputated by an IED. He said, "I want to go back so that this time I can walk out of Iraq on my own—not carried out on a medevac litter."

Closing

We pray that our working together will help to actualize an expanded circle of healing that is readily accessible to many more of our nation's current (and previous era) wounded warriors and their families. It is our fervent hope that this will result in fewer OEF, OIF, and OND (Operation New Dawn) veterans finding it necessary to return to Iraq or Afghanistan 30 or 40 years from now—as is the case with so many veterans today visiting Vietnam—in order to be able to more fully recover from their wounds of war.

This book introduces a number of innovative approaches to assist in the healing from war trauma, including remembering and appreciating the sacrifices and journeys of the peoples of Vietnam, Iraq, and Afghanistan and the military and civilian casualties of so many other wars before, and yet to come.

Pax mentis and *Semper fi.*

Note

1. Our first book, *War Trauma and Its Wake*, also identifies several creative military and resiliency initiatives, including resiliency trainings and debriefings, suicide prevention, outdoor/ adventure-based interventions, the use of the creative arts with active duty military, and the role of military chaplains.

References

Adelman, J. (Associated Press). (2009, Dec. 19). "Veterans Find a Welcome Kind of Peace. Former Troops now Work in the California Produce Fields." Accessed at www.sunherald.com.

Badkhen, A. (2012). "Afghan Civilians: Surviving Trauma in a Failed State." In R. M. Scurfield & K. T. Platoni (Eds.). *War Trauma and Its Wake: Expanding the Circle of Healing.* New York, NY: Routledge.

Brock, S., & Passey, G. (2012). "Canadian Military and Veteran Experience." In R. M. Scurfield & K. T. Platoni (Eds.). *War Trauma and Its Wake: Expanding the Circle of Healing.* New York, NY: Routledge.

Corbett, S. (2004, February 15). "The Permanent Scars of Iraq." *The New York Times Magazine:* 34–35, 38–41, 56, 60, 66.

Dawoody, A. (2012). "Iraqi Civilians and the Recycling of Trauma." In R. M. Scurfield & K. T. Platoni (Eds.). *War Trauma and Its Wake: Expanding the Circle of Healing.* New York, NY: Routledge.

Scurfield, R. M. (2004). *A Vietnam Trilogy: Veterans and Post Traumatic Stress, 1968, 1989 & 2000.* New York, NY: Algora Publishing.

Scurfield, R. M. (2006a). *War Trauma: Lessons Unlearned from Vietnam to Iraq.* New York, NY: Algora Publishing.

Scurfield, R. M. (2006b). *Healing Journeys: Study Abroad with Vietnam Veterans.* New York, NY: Algora Publishing.

Scurfield, R. M. (2007, March 11). "Military Problems go Beyond Walter Reed Army Medical Center." Hattiesburgamerican.com.

Scurfield, R. M., Root, L., Wiest, A., Coiro, F. N., Sartin, H. J., Jones, C.L., & Fanugao, M. B. (2003, Fall). "History Lived and Learned: Students and Vietnam Veterans in an Integrative Study Abroad Course." *Frontiers: The Interdisciplinary Journal of Study Abroad, IX*: 111–138.

Spira, J. (2011, March 10). "Treating Polytrauma: Post Traumatic Stress Disorder with Co-Morbid Post-Concussive Symptoms or Pain Disorders." Workshop presented at the Institute on Violence, Abuse and Trauma, 8th Annual Hawaii Conference on Preventing, Assessing and Treating Child, Adolescent, and Adult Trauma, Honolulu, HI.

Twohy, P. J. (1987). *Finding A Way Home: Indian and Catholic Spiritual Paths of the Plateau Tribes.* Spokane, WA: University Press.

Part I

Surviving Both War and the Battles Back Home

COL David Rabb (OIF/OEF)

Introduction

The price of freedom is often underestimated. If you don't believe me, as I am writing this Introduction while deployed in Afghanistan, ask any deployed service member or combat veteran. With the war in Iraq over, and the war in Afghanistan coming to a steady conclusion, it is time to refocus, reset, and reconnect on an individual, family, community, and national level. The two chapters in this section focus on what it takes to survive war and, after retuning from war, how veterans have had to engage in advocacy efforts, and the impact on them personally.

The chapter by Scurfield, Platoni and Rabb (Chapter 2) describes the journey to war and its impact after returning home. The authors, through their collective experiences, which range from Vietnam and the Gulf War to Iraq and Afghanistan, offer their "boots on ground" war experiences to delve deeper into the hearts, minds, and souls of today's veterans. The 12 most common survival modes during war, which are subsequently brought back home, serve as a guidepost for readers, as they call upon their courage, compassion, and connections to support themselves or returning service members and combat veterans in their transition home—however long that may take.

The chapter by Mike Zacchea (Chapter 3), an OIF veteran, offers an in-depth analysis and historical perspective of the challenges and struggles of veterans in advocacy. He examines today's challenges and struggles and those that might yet be encountered during reintegration into society. He boldly asks the provocative question, "Should veterans be recognized as a special class of citizen that has a unique claim to federal benefits?" He also describes various motivations, actions, rewards, and occupational hazards of becoming a veteran advocate. Finally, he exhorts a call to support, through respect, awareness, and understanding, the bond between veterans' social contract with our nation and our nation's obligation.

When our perils are past, shall our gratitude sleep?

—George Canning

2 Survival Modes, Coping, and Bringing the War Home

From Vietnam to Iraq and Afghanistan[1]

Raymond Monsour Scurfield (Vietnam),
COL Katherine Theresa Platoni (ODS and OIF/OEF),
and COL David Rabb (OIF/OEF)

> I had the misfortune to have a mental breakdown three years ago and, as part of that heal-ing process, discovered that my service and my cousin's services to this country were full of soul-rendering terror. I now remember sitting on the back steps at our house in Texas and listening to my cousin, "Dub," wake up the neighborhood with his screaming. I could not imagine what was causing his blood-curdling screams. Somehow along the way, Dub and I both managed to put up a wall around this issue.
>
> There is nothing honorable in killing. Nothing is as horrible as the inner soul-render-ing scream that comes with the first time. Then the numbness comes to silence it. Numb-ness is a narcotic to the soul. Numbness takes over your life and has a death grip on you until (if) you finally reach a point of total security with being home among family and friends. There is nothing to glorify what we do in war.
>
> (McDonald, 2004)

Yes, veterans perfect the ability, while deployed, to function at a level where emotions are unavailable. But later, after becoming emotionally accessible once again, the feelings and thoughts come flooding back. And so, how do service members survive during war and what ingrained emotions, patterns of thinking, and behaviors do they bring back home following deployment? What are the potential positive and/or negative ramifica-tions of various survival strategies on Iraq, Afghanistan (and Vietnam and other) veter-ans, post-deployment?

In addition to addressing the above issues, we must consider the reactions of those civilians who find themselves intolerant of, confused by, or fearful of those veterans who seem unable or unwilling to "let go" of being a war veteran—those who cannot come all the way home. Former combatants can return from deployment very resentful of civilians who have no clue, or even, seemingly, no care whatsoever, of what it took *out* of you to be over there and what it ingrained *within* you—and which you have brought home with you.

> We long to fit in and to find what represents some kind of normalcy, but our old selves are no longer hanging in the closet.
>
> (OIF veteran)

And then comes the bitter realization that there is a second battleground that must be fought on the homefront, a tragic commentary of the mounting burdens of war and our government's unwillingness to dedicate the resources necessary to provide service members and veterans with that which is necessary to heal from the physical and emotional wounds of war.

We now turn to discuss 12 of the most common survival modes that make it possible to survive and function while deployed to a war zone. Such ingrained modes of functioning are then brought, in varying degrees, back home and into veterans' families and communities. *It is vital to note that not everything can be blamed on the war, nor should the impact of the war be ignored or downplayed* (Scurfield, 2006a).

Fight, Flight, or Freeze

Fight: there is a seeking out, engaging and destroying the enemy (if you find them), withdrawing and retreating to return to relentless combat missions day after day. Flight: conversely, in the face of overwhelming odds, you choose to strategically retreat to fight another day (Scurfield, 2004). A third response is a survival mode of "freezing," or an immobility response that activates when neither fight nor flight will ensure one's safety. (This has been well documented in animals and in some traumas such as sexual assault.) Another set of writers postulates "fright" as a fourth survival mode.[2] However, we have not personally observed these last two phenomena while deployed; we believe that freezing and fright are relatively rare survival modes among combatants in a war zone.

Fight, flight, and freeze are instinctual survival strategies that have been genetically imprinted in human beings over the millennia. These are instinctual responses that have ensured the survival of the human species from the days of the earliest human beings and up through modern times.

> Always in overdrive until the crash and burn—a vicious cycle and endless spin. For example, riding in convoys was so extremely dangerous at any point along the way because of IEDs (improvised explosive devices) or small arms fire that your survival instinct was fully mobilized. Your hyper-arousal state almost never would go away—because you just knew that any second could be your last. So, you played over and over in your head what you would do if your vehicle was hit or you found yourself in the middle of an ambush . . . you just cannot de-escalate—and are always at the brink . . .
>
> (Platoni, 2006, unpublished)

Bringing It Home

Conversely, there is a potential post-war downside to this dual survival strategy. A number of veterans, after leaving the war zone, or even while still there, have found themselves inundated with feelings of guilt, shame, grief or unremitting rage over what they had to do to survive in the war zone—or what they did not do. This may be bothering the service member or veteran now; it may come back to haunt her or him months or years from now. During and returning from war, there is the feeling that they never finish the job. This can be manifested as overwhelming shame and guilt for not having taken care of business—or having survived when fellow and sister troops did not.

Dehumanizing the Enemy

Training for war ingrains the new military recruit in the classic strategy of fostering detachment by dehumanizing the enemy. "They are not human beings like we are; they are horrible, evil, heartless, immoral." And racism and extreme ethnocentrism are key dehumanizing strategies; there is a promotion of racial and ethnic negative stereotypical attitudes and language directed towards the enemy—krauts, japs, slant-eyes, gooks, towel-heads, A-rabs, Muslim radicals, hajis:

> "You just sort of try to block out the fact that they're human beings and see them as enemies," he said. "You call them hajis, you know? You do all the things that make it easier to deal with killing them and mistreating them."
>
> (Hebert, 2004)

One Iraq veteran described a parallel between what happened to Vietnam veterans and what seems to be happening with a number of Iraq veterans, beginning with the realization that the original mission or justification given for the war proved to be false.

> There was a progression of thought that happened among soldiers in Vietnam. It started with a mission [in Vietnam]: contain Communism. That mission fell apart, just like it fell apart now—there are no weapons of mass destruction. Then you are left with just a survival instinct. That, unfortunately, turned to racism. That's happening now, too. Guys are writing me saying, "I don't know why I'm here, but I hate the Iraqis."
>
> (Goodman, 2004)

It is much easier to seek out an enemy that *you have dehumanized* in order to kill, rather than an enemy regarded as human, good, and an honorable adversary fighting for a just cause (Scurfield, 2004).

Bringing It Home

And you can become cut-throat, cold, uncaring, developing an intense hatred and loathing that *remains* with you for a very long time. For example, we have met a number of World War II veterans who *still* have a vitriolic hatred towards or discomfort being around Japanese or Germans—*any* Japanese or Germans. And there still are way too many Vietnam veterans who continue to maintain a vitriolic hatred towards the Vietnamese: any Vietnamese, be they living in Vietnam or here in the U.S. Of course, such profound hatred can inevitably poison attitudes towards those who are of differing races, creeds, religions, and ethnic heritages, and a gross intolerance of differences. One OEF/OIF vet stated that, when she saw American troops being dehumanized by Iraqis or watched them cheering and celebrating when Americans were blown-up or killed, this fueled a rage towards Iraqis—towards *any* Iraqis—that could not be contained.

Detachment, Numbing, Denial, and Acceptance

One learns to be self-protective against the horrors of what is being witnessed by convincing oneself that "it don't mean nothin'," no matter what happens. One learns self-anesthetizing, not feeling the anxiety, fear, shock, horror, depression, loss, and grief that otherwise might become overwhelming. This prevents one becoming emotionally overwhelmed (Scurfield, 2004).

> In Vietnam and in OEF/OIF, the operative mantra was "fuck it, it don't mean nothin'." Anything to shut down the impact and meaning of terrible things—yet searching for meaning and purpose to sustain yourself . . .
>
> (OIF service member: "This abuse I am getting from my commander is just crap—screw it or fuck it—it doesn't mean a damn thing.")
>
> In OEF/OIF, as the wars have progressed, so have the methods of destruction. As insurgents adapted to the U.S. strategies of fighting, the advent of deadly roadside bombs (e.g., IEDs/VBIED) and rocket attacks became prevalent. One of the biggest fears of troops was traveling on roads, not knowing if you were going to be hit by an IED or step on a pressure plate "land mine" while on patrol. The potential of being one convoy or one step away from dying was always there. A steady undercurrent of uncertainty and doubt in the psyche was often present . . . Even the myriad rocket attacks that frequently missed their mark in Kandahar always had the possibility of hitting soldiers as they scurried into concrete bunkers. In order to live day-to-day with multiple threats, we had to maintain a healthy sense of denial and/or an attitude that faced death down. What happens, happens. You can't live under a rock and effectively perform your mission. At some point one must accept the possibility of death to make it through.
>
> (Rabb, unpublished)

Bringing It Home

There is a potential downside. One gets so good at detachment, denial, and emotional numbing that this accompanies one back to the civilian world. For example, a number of family members have described their veteran family member as not able to show or, perhaps, even feel normal emotions like everyone else, and that they are emotionally inaccessible.

Tunnel Vision

There is preservation of an intensely focused state of mind in order to guarantee full attention to the tasks at hand. One learns to focus one's energies and attention on completing the immediate task or objective to the exclusion of every thing else (Scurfield, 2004).

> On convoys I would force myself to think of nothing else but to repeat to myself endlessly and visualize and revisualize how to operate my M-16 and my 9 millimeter, how to pull the gunner in from the turret to save that person's life, how to call

in a 9-line MEDEVAC[3] (the nine steps for calling in a medevacuation chopper)—repeating these steps to the exclusion of all else. I was constantly repeating, over and over and over again, what to do to sustain everyone's life in the vehicle.

Sleep remained elusive and seemed such a waste of time with so much work to do to salvage the emotional lives of the multitudes. And even if there was time to sleep, it was all I could do to slam shut the relentless thoughts that might keep me awake, trying so hard to find a shut-off valve for all of it, the endless anguish that built up everyday; to read until I couldn't keep my eyes open anymore . . .

Doing critical event (critical incident) debriefings in the war zone with the members of a unit that had suffered death: while *there is so much going on* in the room (various members tearful, or one or two breaking down and others remaining outwardly very stoic and you, yourself, feeling the pain), you've got to keep focusing yourself *on the debriefing*—and *not* on the losses, so you could get through the debriefing.

(Platoni, unpublished)

Intuitively, tunnel vision can be a source of strength and of weakness. A combat veteran may find that with tunnel vision comes a sense of detecting patterns or blocking out unnecessary and frivolous information to quickly arrive at a decision point or action. When situations of life and death are of concern, snap decisions and the ability to sort through the gray to be able to make black and white choices are not required—they are demanded. Over a period of time, the comfort level of one's ability to make such decisions creates a sense of confidence and assurance. It can be hard retreating or changing course of action once the decision has been made. In war, rapidly processing information and making selections are prized abilities, and can lead to successful results.

Bringing It Home

When transitioning to civilian life, this same ability can produce positive and negative or even grave results. Back home, you might find that tunnel vision helps to get through tough times. Conversely, tunnel vision may have become so ingrained that there is great difficulty or even impossibility in turning it off—a feeling that *there is no on and off switch.* This can be devastating to everyday decision-making, to relationships, or to enabling one to be able to enjoy life fully.

The External Discharging of Emotions

One *has* to find an outlet for the inevitable cumulative build-up of stress, frustration, grief, fear, and rage that are inevitable in a war zone. Typically, this is expressed through rage towards the enemy, which can be very functional, and it can fuel an internal anger and resolve to persevere. Conversely, there may be an absence of regular opportunities to discharge such pent-up emotions; this is especially likely in a war waged by guerillas, insurgents, or terrorists. Thus, accumulated emotions can erupt strongly and unexpectedly, possibly towards innocent or apparently innocent civilians, and even towards other

Americans. This is because *these pent-up emotions have to go somewhere.* If not expressed outwardly, such feelings may well be redirected inwardly or be suppressed, keeping them pushed down and pushing them down and pushing them down . . . (Scurfield, 2004).

> You know, along with the constant threat from a hidden enemy, there was the abuse from command. Sometimes I was powerless to hold back. I bore so much anger and resentment towards my commander for what so many of us had encountered—vicious personal assaults and the commander's absolutely gross ignorance of his damaging behaviors upon a selected few singled out for punishment. For example, I tried to assist another officer who was going to be involuntarily extended less than 24 hours before he was scheduled to leave—and he was in a state of absolute rage and tears. I tried to get information from the commander and XO about finding an immediate replacement for him rather than extending him because he was in no condition to be extended. And I just blew up. And another office wrote me up and turned his report over to the commander—because I had exploded in anger about the situation because they were doing such great harm to this officer. I was punished severely for doing the right thing and taking care of my soldiers.
>
> (Platoni, unpublished)

Bringing It Home

Back home, discharging one's emotions can be helpful in releasing unexpressed feelings. On the other hand, months and years later, you can find yourself yearning to be set free of deep-seated emotions—but without an available outlet that won't be hurtful to yourself or to others. This can make it very difficult to share what is going on with your family members or close friends. You might keep it all bottled up within—and then you explode in anger, frustration, or grief. And so, like in the war zone, there might be a continuation of *compartmentalization and a shutting off* of what is too painful to bring to conscious awareness, yet is critical to survival. Or, you isolate yourself in an attempt to avoid having deep emotions and memories triggered, or as a strategy to prevent venting emotions against others. And these feelings may detonate at quite expected moments or at the most unsuspecting of innocent targets.

"Comparing" War Traumas

Own it as it was, and celebrate your noble service, sacrifices, and contributions as they were. Some troops who are wounded, suffer losses, or have other traumatic experiences while deployed, will "compare" (both while on deployment and afterwards) their trauma with what others have experienced. One comparison is to tell yourself that you did not suffer nearly as much as many others. This can be used as a positive; for example, some wounded troops focus on how much worse some others were injured (or were killed), or what others faced in combat, as motivation to help them to persevere and get through the tough times, and to count their blessings and see the glass as half full rather than half empty. Conversely, this can result in denying or not admitting to yourself how much you were impacted, and feeling that you do not deserve to have negative or troubling reactions. Such comparisons may lead to feelings of guilt, shame, or severe self-criticism because of perceived weaknesses: of not being "strong" enough because others are having troubles, even though you went through so much less (either minimizing or maximizing your own war trauma).

The opposite form of comparison is to tell yourself, "I suffered much more than many others." Focusing on how much worse off you are can lead to bitterness, blame, anger, depression, self-pity, or may cause you to be very judgmental of others. There can also be a distorted sense of entitlement because you went through so much more than others. The reality is that *any comparisons are no-win propositions*:

> Your traumatic experiences were your traumatic experiences, period. It was and is meaningful to you, and comparing your traumas to anyone else's trauma is not fair to anyone and is a way for you to deny the full impact of your traumatic experience. (And, of course, there is no way to objectively compute the personal impact of trauma—especially to others.)
>
> (Scurfield, 2006a)

Belief in Fate, Randomness, a Higher Power

Many military personnel rely on their long-standing faith in a higher power or Supreme Being to sustain them through the horrors of war and find their faith and beliefs strengthened. Conversely, others find their beliefs severely challenged or decimated in the face of the horrors and inhumanity and the conundrum of having to kill in order to save the lives of oneself and others. The first question that a number of troops often ask after something bad/horrific has happened to themselves or to comrades is, "Why me, God?" Or, "Why did this have to happen, God?" Or, "What kind of God would allow such brutality against humanity?" One's faith becomes shaken, unable to sustain the service member when forced to confront killing. And yet, still others will ask, "Why me, God?" but will then accept that this is a burden that they must bear, and a God with whom they need to reconnect:

> When we lost 10 soldiers outside of Ramadi, Iraq, who were incinerated when their Bradleys (tank) ran over fuel-cell-piercing IEDs and no one could do anything about it, I screamed silently inside for days. How could a higher power allow for such human wreckage (to include wreckage of the soul) to occur?! And yet . . . God and our buddies were ALL that we had to hang onto!
>
> (Platoni, unpublished)

Some religious moral imperatives also can seem irrelevant, paradoxical, or impossible to follow when confronted with the horrors of war. "Thou shalt not kill" (especially women, children and the elderly), "Thou shalt not commit adultery," and "What you do to the least of my brethren you do unto me." Chaplains are a source of great comfort and counsel to many troops (see Purinton, 2012). On the other hand, some combat veterans perceive a marked conflict in the role of chaplains, viewing them as "blessing our troops to kill" and emphasizing how "God is on our side," and, of course, not on the enemy's side.[4] And these can include disbelief how a God or higher power would allow people, and even oneself, to do what is done to each other in a war zone (Scurfield, 2004, 2006a).

Bringing It Home

Such issues can be carried back home *and* be sources of emotional distress, exacerbated by excessive guilt and self-blame or the blaming of others or a loss or crisis of faith. For those who believe, the soul may return home, damaged, with critically wrenching and unanswered questions that violate the spirit.

> Nevertheless, frequently chaplains were viewed in a positive light because not only did they carry with them the Cross that represented faith, forgiveness and hope; they carried a confidentiality specific to their role. They were seen as safe harbors before or after going out into the high tides of war and uncertainty. After traumatic events, such as seeing ones buddies severely injured or killed, some service members figuratively found their backs against the wall and had to make a decisive choice in moving forward. Would they return to duty and back to the fight fueled by faith or fueled by fear?
>
> Indeed, chaplains oversaw church and memorial services, yet their main contributions, I believe, were in assisting troops [to] deal with their personal and existential questions.
>
> In many ways the service members' faith was seen as and accounted for a major protective factor in supporting resiliency; they could take comfort in knowing that they were not alone. For instance, many service members found value in scriptures such as "Be anxious for nothing, but in everything by prayer and supplications, with thanksgiving, let your request be made known to God; and the peace of God, which surpasses all understanding, will guard your heart and minds through Christ Jesus" (Philippians 4:6–7).
>
> (Rabb, unpublished)

And, for service members who were able to have their faith be a protective factor in supporting resiliency, and who found value in scripture, prayer, and/or discussions with a chaplain, this could continue as a source of sustenance and strength back in the civilian world (Purinton, 2012).

Be Enraged

The one feeling commonly allowed to emerge in a war zone is the one most conducive to survival—rage directed at the enemy. However, this outlet is not readily available if your duty does not involve wielding weapons against the enemy (i.e., medical personnel, administrative specialists, chaplains) nor in guerilla warfare or where insurgents use covert operations, stealth, surprise, and quick retreat. With few clear and present targets at which to vent rage and frustrations, it is easy to become increasingly agitated and frustrated, especially in the face of losses of life, limb, and devastating injuries. One may become undependable, unstable, or inappropriately act out against others, in order to expunge the rage (Scurfield, 2004, 2006a).

The severe challenge of *what is the responsible thing to do while immersed in a hell-hole*—to stand up and be enraged and refuse to tolerate when you see acts of malfeasance occurring in your midst (coming from command against subordinates, or when some unit members get carried away with rage kill towards what might be innocent Iraqis). You could remain silent, looking the other way—and take guilt and shame with you back home because you just wanted to go home and not write anything up and sweep it under the rug and go home—and later back home you are paying a price for it). This tells you a lot about your own soul.

(Platoni, unpublished)

Bringing It Home

And this unsatisfied, pent-up rage, agitation, frustration and overwhelming desire to act upon impulse can be taken back home, with dire consequences:

> Sometimes the enemy is inside the gates, and sometimes that rage is transferred to those that you love the most, a convenient and available target. It's all too easy to be *immersed* in anger.
>
> (Platoni, unpublished)

> Sometimes the anger and rage are so overwhelming and self-destructive, that to get better one must "self-destruct" or "be destroyed." When service members and veterans are not in the mode of "self-destruct," they are allowing the process to happen and they retain their locus of control . . . they are not victims. When service members and veterans avoid taking steps to heal or seek help they have the potential of letting the anger and rage destroy them and their relationships through self-medicating, getting into trouble with the law, divorce, domestic abuse, suicidal or homicidal ideations. Over time, the internal conflict, hurt, pain, anger and frustration culminates into creating victims. Service members and veterans require a safe holding environment where they can release the pain and hurt without feeling they are a threat to themselves and others . . . this place is often not found (sufficiently) in individual therapy sessions. Rather, it can be more easily found in groups and communities where other service members and veterans have gone through or are going through similar struggles.
>
> (Rabb, unpublished)

Social Isolation and Alienation

Another common behavior to promote detachment is to isolate oneself from others and not let anyone get close emotionally. The profound bonding that occurs among most brother and sister troops in a war zone is a two-edged sword. It helps one to survive what otherwise is un-survivable. On the other hand, losing a close buddy can be devastating, and so a number of troops *decide not to let anyone get too close* because it hurts too much when they die or are maimed. And this attitude gets carried home:

There was always this approach—avoidance dynamic and conflicting pressures—becoming the best of friends, promising you would take care of each other and make sure the other got back home safely—and yet putting on the brakes in a relationship because any day you might wake up and they might not be in the cot next to you or eat next to you ever again . . .

(Rabb, unpublished)

This is particularly salient for Reserve and National Guard personnel, as they are separated by miles and units, leaving assigned units and returning to the civilian world and apart from the support of their closest comrades with whom they bonded in the war zone.

Bringing It Home

And then, back home, a lot of veterans find themselves only wanting to be around other veterans—if they want to be around anyone—because of their discomfort around almost anyone who isn't a vet or with anyone who did not fight in the same war as they did. Still other vets find themselves avoiding meaningful discussions or interactions with other veterans, because it brings back too many disturbing memories and too much pain: "When I came home after the war, I felt that Vietnam vets were the only people I could relate to. But, they were the last ones I wanted to be with" (Vietnam veteran, cited by Scurfield, 2004).

Drinkin' and Druggin' (Self-Anesthetizing)

Substance use and abuse are common tactics for those men and women in a war zone who try to temporarily escape reality, suffering, or are avoiding psychological, emotional, physical, or spiritual pain, and also afterwards, to achieve detachment and relief. The military, as an organization, historically has made cheap or even free alcohol readily available; oftentimes, the unspoken understanding is that one can have a drinking problem as long as one shows up and does the job. To compound this problem, there is unmatched ingenuity and enterprise among troops in somehow being able to procure or manufacture intoxicating substances—even (or, perhaps, especially), in the middle of nowhere (Scurfield, 2004). In Iraq this included buying black market Valium near the Iranian border, or soldiers snorting/huffing the compressed air used to clean sand out of computers. Also, some "underemployed" troops, and those between missions outside of the wire, occupied their time with snorting, shooting, speedballing, or otherwise ingesting any substances they were able to acquire while in the wartime theater.

Bringing It Home

And so, vets who may have entered the war zone with substance use problems might *leave* with a bigger problem, and other veterans, who did not deploy having substance-use problems, can leave the war zone with them. This can become or continue as a habit back home—or vets revert back to such substances, especially when things get rough or they're feeling down: a self-anesthetization to not feel. This tendency is exacerbated by a dominant characteristic of the wars in Iraq and Afghanistan—multiple deployments sandwiched around short periods of down-time back home.

Excessive Risk-Taking, Thrill, and Sex Addiction

It can become easy, while deployed, to be immersed in and "addicted" physiologically, psychologically, and behaviorally to the thrill, the risk, the danger, the adrenaline rush, of living on the edge 24/7. And sex is always available in a war zone, always. For a minority of troops, sex can be, and is, bought with local civilians or, for some, the intensity and loneliness of life in the war zone can spark sexual encounters that are mutually sought—or forced. Also, troops can become action junkies, and this can be a powerful elixir to help survive, or it can lead to increasingly more dangerous attitudes and behaviors. This deeply ingrained "rush" becomes extremely difficult to simply turn off when returning to civilian life.

> After a while, oftentimes there is the feeling that "my number is coming up," so caution is thrown to the wind and any opportunities are sought to maintain that high so you don't start to feel or think. This can be temporarily satiated, for some troops, by finding sex with multiple partners and other actions to keep that mind-numbing adrenaline rush at an all time high—to put yourself in positions where you just don't think or feel—and cutting yourself off from anything under the surface.
>
> Many times, we would find *any* available opportunity to *go out on missions* as a way to maintain that overwhelming adrenalin rush—you were doing there what you were sent there to do—putting yourself in harm's way—while at the same time maintaining that high state of arousal. And then you come home and find yourself looking for life in the fast lane and trying to replicate the adrenalin rush—while coming up empty.
>
> (Platoni, unpublished)

Bringing It Home

This can be a devastating blow to the psyche and to the body. However, some are able to satisfy some or most of this high risk/adrenaline habit through successful post-war employment in high-risk, high-thrill occupations, such as emergency medical, fire and rescue, law enforcement, off-shore drilling, and contract positions in support of military operations (not to mention being a psychotherapist with combat veterans). Others try to continue to live life on the edge/the wild side—extremes of food, drink, speed, website pornography, whatever extremes are available—and/or stay immersed in danger and/or in memories/feelings about the war. Too many veterans continue "being there while living here."

Yes, living on the extremist edge of disaster, thirsting for danger, is a *really* hard habit to break. After experiencing significant trauma, it can be hard living with it; conversely, it can be hard to live without it: for example, an alarming number of recently returned Iraq and Afghanistan Army and Marine veterans have been killed in single-occupant vehicle accidents.

> We absolutely have a problem. The kids come back and they want to live life to its fullest, to its wildest. They get a little bit of time to let their hair down, and they let their hair all the way down and do everything to excess. They drink to excess. They eat to excess. They party to excess. And then, some drive. They want something that goes fast and keeps up that high they felt during the war . . . speed fills some indescribable urge for excitement that they've felt since returning from war . . . Going fast is like a drug—the newest crack out there.[5]

Bizarrre or Gallows Humor

In the midst of horror and chaos, resorting to what otherwise would be seen as gross or inappropriate humor can be at least a partial antidote to the relentless horrors of war. Humor and irreverence can be very healthy and adaptive during challenging times. They help to stop you from crying, or becoming overwhelmed by what you're facing day after day after day. Instead, you can get a deep belly laugh, a moment of absurdly hilarious respite, a closeness of comradeship with the only people who could possibly get it or tolerate such humor—your war buddies (Scurfield, 2004):

> Hey John. We seem to have an extra leg among all these body parts from the last mass casualties we received. Since I can't figure out which body it belongs to, I'm going to give this here guy a third leg. That'll give the body handlers stateside a little surprise when they open up the body bag.
>
> (Vietnam veteran)

Or, the ability to find raucous laughter in the mundane, and seek to celebrate the most ridiculous of inane acts at the most inopportune times, becomes an excellent survival skill:

> Every night at the chow hall at our FOB [Forward Operating Base] in Iraq, we utilized every opportunity to act out inappropriately (such as when someone was not looking, we put all of the condiments on their tray so that they would have to carry four tables worth of salt, pepper and ketchup around with them). And we would make fun of each other mercilessly. We engaged in the most ridiculous of behaviors every night—the evening's prime time entertainment. In addition to being a source of release, this was much to our great advantage in terms of mobilizing soldiers and marines to seek out our combat stress control services. They laughed with us and then they knew we were one and the same as them.
>
> (Platoni, unpublished)

In Afghanistan:

> I had to send one of the combat stress control teams from a FOB out to another
> FOB to facilitate a critical event debriefing for a unit that had one KIA and three
> WIA two days prior. That afternoon, when my team had to fly out to a nearby COP
> (Combat Outpost), I learned that another IED had hit another armored vehicle that
> was in the area and there were two more U.S. KIAs. When my team finally made it
> to their destination the team leader contacted me at my headquarters to tell me that
> her team had made it to their destination. She said that her ground convoy that was
> only supposed to take 30 to 45 minutes took over four hours because the convoy
> had to take an alternate route. When I asked how was she doing, she said, "I'm in
> one piece!" I praised her in her unique choice of words. We both laughed, which
> relieved a lot of tension in a difficult situation.
>
> (Rabb, unpublished)

This respite provides *temporary* relief *but, of course, it does not erase* the horrors, feelings,
and indelible images from your mind or from your heart—it just puts them on the back
burner and you soldier on.

Bringing It Home

This kind of humor can be carried back home in either a positive or negative
way. You may be able to have an irreverent attitude; an enjoyable or refreshingly
unexpected or amusingly sarcastic or humorous attitude that at least some others
find to be a welcome breather, especially during tough times. It really helps you to
cope with difficult situations, and sharing such humor with others who have been
there is invigorating and bonding. Or, you can become pejorative, cynical, nasty,
insulting, critical, and derogatory towards others in the face of mounting frustrations—and you could not care less. Or, perhaps, you fall somewhere in between.

Going Outside the Box: Reunification and Sustainment, Post-Deployment

It is well known that coming back from war is more difficult than leaving for war. This
is due partly to the fact that there is exponentially more intensive and sustained condi-
tioning accumulated through basic and advanced trainings and readiness operations to
prepare military personnel to go *to* war than *will ever* occur in deprogramming military
personnel back *from* war. This is coupled with 24/7 reinforcement after arriving in the
war zone: exposure to danger and engaging in the survival modes described earlier further ingrain war into one's head, body, and soul. Yet, no military or other governmental
resource ever has—nor ever will—provide an adequate effort at "deprogramming" to
permit much better readjustment to the civilian world.

Also, everything one left behind when going off on deployment has changed. Troops
"going outside the box" now must contend with the effects of having survived deployment, adapting to the physical rigors and emotional strain of the battlefield and the

uncertainty and chaos that accompany it; their ways of thinking have shifted and appear "out of sync" with family, friends, and co-workers. And yet, as much as service members have changed, so have their families—especially for families of Reserve and National Guard personnel whose lives bounce back and forth between the civilian and military worlds. It also happens with families of regular military forces; they have learned new avenues for coping and have had no choice but to attempt (not always successfully) to become more independent or mature in order to overcome struggle and survive.

Below, are common thoughts and feelings heard from troops who have gone outside the box—reflecting the disjointedness between adapting to deployment and returning home.

> "I made it back, alive!" "Being back feels weird." "I already feel like I don't belong." "They don't understand what I have been through." "They survived without me." "I don't want to be around civilians." "I have changed." "We have changed." "I can't do this anymore." "I feel blessed." "I wish I was back there." "I need to find another job." "I feel like an alien in my own country and/or home." "Please send me back." "Civilians just don't get it."

On the other hand, some common thoughts and feelings that we have heard from family members/significant others of military personnel returned from deployment are:

> "It's great to have him/her back home." "He/she has changed for the (worse/best)." "I don't get why we are arguing so much." "He/she can't really appreciate what I have been through." "I don't believe what he said." "I don't feel safe." "In some ways, it is easier for me/us when he/she was away." "I wish he/she would take more initiative." "I will not let you around your kids." "I'm outta here."

Going outside the wire and making the transition from the war zone to the home zone will require some, if not considerable, recalibration and resetting behaviors. Hence, it is important that families of all military personnel—and, perhaps, particularly those of Reserve and Guard Forces—are educated as to the common reactions of military members to reintegration and returning to their civilian lives, and about the mistaken belief of members that they are "going crazy" because of the thoughts that pass through their minds. Transition is a process that may require considerable time, remembering that no one, whether in uniform or a family member, is on the same timeline. Following their return, several months may be required to overcome the hurdles of transition and full readjustment to civilian life. For many, 12 or more months may be necessary for the reintegration process, if we accept the rule of thumb that military personnel must experience a full cycle of events that were missed during deployment (i.e., birthdays, holidays) before they can come full circle and feel reconnected with their previous lives. The transition may take longer, based on experiences in the box and the ability to find meaning and balance. Based on the authors' work in the VA with WWII, Vietnam era, and Persian Gulf era veterans, we are cognizant of the fact that this course can take years, if not a lifetime, before some combat veterans are able to fully return home in the truest sense. And, tragically, some never do . . .

The Positive Impact of War and Deployment

The preceding discussion has emphasized the potential and actual negative impact, both short and longer-term, of serving in a war zone. There is another side: the remarkable positives, the extraordinary valor, strengths, comradeship, heroism, and humanity that can characterize what goes on in wars. These can be brought home and become a powerful positive within many veterans and their families.

One very common positive is that military personnel, veterans, and their families often are blessed with the development of resilience, strength, and a very positive identity as a military member, veteran, or military family member. They do not just tolerate or adapt to their military family member's service—they are deeply proud of the service their spouse, parent, or sibling has *willingly donated to* our country, and the sacrifices made both by the active duty military person or veteran and by the family. This experience of being part of a deployed military or veteran's family can help equip both the troops returned from deployment, the veterans, and the families with a profound strength, courage, pride, perspective, and grace. *They truly know and value the costly price of freedom.*

This was revealed in the stories of the veterans, described by Scurfield (2004, 2006b), who participated in experiences such as the dedication of the national Vietnam Veterans Memorial in Washington, DC, helicopter ride therapy, and outward bound therapy, and those who returned on healing journeys to Vietnam in 1989 (Scurfield, 2004) and in 2000 (Scurfield, 2006b). In the words of a Vietnam veteran 20 years after the war (Scurfield, 2006b), "maturity, self-esteem, teamwork, accomplishment, pride, excitement, and adventure certainly are as much a part of the war zone experience as anything else. For these, I am extremely gratified." In the words of an Iraq OIF veteran while still in Iraq:

> These two deployments have taught me a degree of patience and tolerance that I never thought possible. I have been forced to live in terribly deprived conditions and with ungodly levels of frustration and uncertainty, far more than in any arena of my life as I knew it before OEF and OIF. I have learned to live without the most basic comforts of life for months on end, without privacy and with endless restrictions and limitations. To this end, I have learned to appreciate why freedom has a tremendously high cost. I am grateful to be among the bravest and the finest in this struggle to bring democracy to the people of Iraq, so that someday they may be able to live a better life.
>
> (Platoni, 2006, unpublished)

In the words of an Afghanistan OEF service member *currently deployed* (December, 2010):

> The deployment has caused me to think about how much we have going for us in the United States. When I talk with an Afghan child, and ask him or her, "What will you do when you grow up?" they are puzzled, and might say, "I will live here in the village, grow old and die." Being deployed here, to Afghanistan, allows me to think about how much opportunity we have back home in the United States. Many of the

children here in Afghanistan have never seen a big screen TV or listened to a car radio. I have learned to value what I have, and not take life for granted.

(Specialist Edwin Angulo, age 20)

I now value being able to listen to other soldiers' stories and really appreciating what our war fighters go through . . . how lucky I am to be in the job that I'm in and not being at an outlying FOB having to fight insurgents and seeing my buddies get hurt or killed. I cherished what I have.

(Sergeant Susana Murillo, age 20)

I'm better able to regulate my emotions . . . having to deal with being at war and what's happening around me and then having to call and connect with my family back home . . . I have to manage to stay positive.

(Sergeant First Class Jose Chavarin, age 30)

Living in the moment is the most important thing that I have learned being deployed. You don't know when your time is up, or when it will be the last time you see your buddies. Respecting the time you have in the moment is so important—it's all I have.

(1st Lieutenant Francisco Rivera, age 34)

I value my life and the struggles and sacrifices that Americans have made before me to get us to where we are as a society. America isn't perfect—it's a work in progress— but it is all we strive for and all we got, despite the political quagmire, unemployment or underemployment, economic turmoil, discrimination, and civil unrest . . . By far, in any stretch of imagination, it outpaces living in any other country.

(Colonel David Rabb, aged 52)

When service members return home from war, they bring with them both challenges and benefits that need to be recognized. If we look not too far in our past from WWII to today, we can take away lessons that can guide us in responding to today's OEF/OIF/ OND veterans. As in many wars, depending on the age of the combatant, going to war marks the demarkation from youth to adulthood as it relates to rites of passage. It can be a time of discovery and self-reflection. Nowhere else in American society can such a huge number of individuals from all walks of life enter into a system that can provide them with a new dimension of discipline, self-respect, selfless service, integrity, and professional growth.

For persons who entered the military and deployed to war, they will have experienced a personal feat that will mark their contribution and ownership to freedom and democracy. They will have earned the title of "combat veteran," which few people in our society can claim. On the other hand, the authors have known service members that felt disenchanted or guilty for being in the military during time of war yet not being deployed: they actually wanted to be deployed overseas.

It can be argued (and persuasively) that nowhere else in any sector of our society are there so many people of character that espouse what "right looks like." Solid NCOs and officers in one's ranks can make a difference to those young service members who are looking for good role models that might have been absent while growing up. Nowhere else in our society is there a place where so many people of different races, gender, ages, religious beliefs, and economic levels are melded together in the common endeavor that encompasses missions that can make the difference to our national security and pride. But, more importantly, nowhere in our society are young (and not-so-young) men and women—shaped in leadership, refined by fire (existing in a hostile environment), and steeped in perseverance—enabled to transform into new selves. For better or worse, deploying into a war zone will change the person . . .

Responding and supporting how they come back into the orbit of civilian life is the responsibility, not only of the military, but also of the government and civilians that sent them off to war in the first place. Combat and other veterans who have been deployed require the space and time to heal, and recognition for their service, without unrealistic expectations that they should return and fit into their old lives as they did before (Tick, 2005). As is the case with traditional and tribal societies, we need to create safe places, rituals, and treatments that allow for a rebooting process to occur.

Finally, while deployed in Afghanistan, COL Rabb also wrote the following, when asked to identify positive impacts from being deployed:

> Another great thing about going on deployment is that you get to see how the large U.S. military system works . . . how it comes together to accomplish its wartime mission. There are so many parts of the puzzle that service members get to see that they would not normally have an opportunity to see if they were not deployed, or served only during peace time. In a culture that prides itself on the public display of valor, achievement, and tradition, going on deployment and coming back with a war patch, ribbons, combat action badge, unit achievement awards, guidons, and streamers, symbolizes the significance of service and accomplishments to the individual service members and their units.

Closing

These first two chapters provide an essential context for appreciating the negative and positive impact of war, both short and longer-term, and the expanding circle of healing required to truly "bring our troops home." The next chapter discusses the *post*-military battles that many veterans discover are required to protect and achieve social justice and benefits for their military service.

Notes

1. Ten of these 12 survival modes are excerpted in part from Scurfield (2004, 2006a) and from Kathy Platoni's "Warning Signs, Triggers, Survival and Coping Strategies for Iraq War Veterans," unpublished manuscript, which is partly adapted from content in Scurfield (2006b).
2. See Levine (1997). Also, in responding to danger it may be appropriate to consider a sequential set of four distinct fear responses that more accurately characterize the acute stress response in humans. The initial freeze response, more typically referred to as hypervigilance (being on guard or hyper-alert) includes "stopping, looking, and listening," an advantageous survival strategy associated with fear. (In the animal kingdom, prey that freezes in place is more likely to avoid detection.) This is followed by an attempt to flee and, subsequently, to fight. This reordering offers a more appropriate set of fear responses: "flight and fight," in lieu of "fight or

flight." Lastly, "panic-like" symptoms emerge, attributed to the survival response that occurs when faced with an overwhelming threat; hence, "fright." This is illustrated by the passivity or immobility demonstrated by victims of violence or sexual assault. This becomes adaptive when there is little or no chance of escaping or winning the battle. The new expanded order to be considered is, therefore, "*freeze, flight, fight, or fright.*" See Bracha, et al. (2004). See Rigg (2012) regarding continuing instinctual survival reaction.

3. MEDEVAC is the commonly used acronym for "Medical Evacuation."
4. Frank and realistic dialogue is absolutely necessary to address such real, not just imagined, conflicts in a war-zone, and such dialogue may well have to go beyond private one-to-one conversations and occur in the very circle that is the sustaining life-blood of military combatants—the small unit peer group. For a more detailed discussion of the conflicts between faith and behavior in a war zone, see Scurfield, 2004, 2006b.
5. From October 2003 to September 2004, when troops first returned in large numbers from Iraq, 132 soldiers died in vehicle accidents, a 28% jump from the previous 12 months. Two-thirds of them were veterans of Iraq or Afghanistan. There had been a 23% increase in deaths from vehicle accidents in the past seven months (Zoroya, 2005).

References

Bracha, H. S., Ralston, T. C., Matsukawa, J. M., Williams, A. E., & Bracha, A. S. (2004, October). "Does 'Fight or Flight' Need Updating?" *Psychosomatics, 45:* 448–449.

Goodman, D. (2004, Oct. 11). "Breaking Ranks: More and More U.S. Soldiers are Speaking Out Against the War in Iraq." Accessed at: http:://www.motherjones.com/news/feature/2o00o4/11/10_400.html.

Hebert, B. (2004, May 21). "'Gooks' to 'Hajis.'" *The New York Times.*

Levine, P. (1997). *Walking the Tiger: Healing Trauma. The Innate Capacity to Transform Overwhelming Experiences.* Berkeley, CA: North Atlantic Books.

McDonald, J. P. (2004, Nov. 12). "Letter to the Editor." *Sun Herald,* Biloxi: D2.

Platoni, K. (2006, August). "The War Room." *The Ohio Psychologist:* 10–11.

Platoni, K. (n.d.) "Warning Signs, Triggers, Survival and Coping Strategies for Iraq War Veterans." Unpublished manuscript.

Purinton, C. (2012). "Military Chaplains' Role in Healing: 'Being Here and There.'" In R. M. Scurfield & K. T. Platoni (Eds.). *War Trauma and Its Wake: Expanding the Circle of Healing.* New York, NY: Routledge.

Rigg, J. (2012). "Traumatic Brain Injury and Post Traumatic Stress: The 'Signaure Wounds' of the Iraq and Afghanistan Wars." In R. M. Scurfield & K. T. Platoni (Eds.). *War Trauma and Its Wake: Expanding the Circle of Healing.* New York, NY: Routledge.

Scurfield, R. M. (2004). *A Vietnam Trilogy: Veterans and Post-Traumatic Stress, 1968, 1989 & 2000.* New York, NY: Algora Publishing.

Scurfield, R. M. (2006a). *War Trauma: Lessons Unlearned from Vietnam to Iraq.* New York, NY: Algora Publishing.

Scurfield, R. M. (2006b). *Healing Journeys: Study Abroad with Vietnam Veterans.* New York, NY: Algora Publishing.

Tick, E. (2005). *War and the Soul: Healing Our Nation's Veterans from Post-Traumatic Stress Disorder.* Wheaton, IL: Quest Books.

Zorya, G. (2005, May 2). "Survivors of War Take Fatal Risks on Roads." *USA Today.* Accessed online 5 Feb. 2005.

Further Reading

Anonymous. (2004, Dec. 6). "Editorial." *Sun Herald,* Biloxi: B2.

APA Help Center. (2005). *The Road to Resilience.* American Psychological Association Featured Topics.

Corbett S. (2004, Feb. 15). "The Permanent Scars of Iraq." *The New York Times Magazine*: 34–35, 38–41, 56, 60, 66.

Herman, J. (1997). *Trauma and Recovery: The Aftermath of Violence—from Domestic Abuse to Political Terror.* New York, NY: Basic Books.

Ninh, B. (1996). *The Sorrow of War.* New York, NY: Penguin Group.

Rothschild, B. (2000). *The Body Remembers: The Psychophysiology of Trauma and Trauma Treatment.* New York, NY: W.W. Norton & Company.

Scurfield, R. M. (2002, Jan./Feb.). "The Normal Abnormal" [Coping in the aftermath of the Terrorist Acts of September 11th]. *Psychology Today, 35*(1): 50.

Swales, P. (2005). *Coping with Traumatic Stress Reactions: A National Center for PTSD Fact Sheet.* Iraqi War Clinician Guide, Appendix J.

Twiggs, T. N. (2008, Jan.) "PTSD: The War Within." *The Marine Corp Gazette, 92*(1): 59.

3 Veterans' Advocacy
Social Justice and Healing Through Activism

LTC (RET) Michael Zacchea (OIF)

> The willingness with which our young people are likely to serve in any war, no matter how justified, shall be directly proportional as to how they perceive the Veterans of earlier wars were treated and appreciated by their Nation.
>
> (George Washington)

The essence of veterans' advocacy can be summed up by a simple proposition: that American citizens who have taken up arms to support and defend the Constitution of the United States against all enemies, foreign and domestic, deserve to be distinguished from American citizens who have not sworn the oath and laced up the boots, in the form of a social contract that guarantees reintegration opportunities, healthcare, benefits, and compensation not necessarily available to non-serving citizens (see Scurfield, 2006a, 2007, regarding the sacred covenant between our nation and our veterans).

On May 28, 2011, Azriel Relph described, in excruciating detail, the stories of three Marines returning from combat tours in Iraq and Afghanistan, replete with ineptitude, chaos, and pathos, ending in tragedy (Relph, 2011). These stories are anything but atypical. One Marine, wounded in Iraq, had become an advocate for veterans with the advocacy organization Iraq and Afghanistan Veterans of America (www.IAVA.org); unable to overcome his own struggles with post-traumatic stress, he committed suicide earlier in 2011. Another Marine struggled with joblessness and homelessness. The third Marine was unable to get treatment from the VA for his PTSD. He lives virtually paralyzed and unable to deal with an American society divorced from the sacrifice of the two-thirds of the 1 percent of Americans fighting the wars—an American society both apathetic to the conduct of the decade-long wars (Dao, 2011a) and indifferent to the plight of returning veterans (Haberman, 2010).[1] This chapter describes the battles that veterans too often have had to face *after* being discharged from active duty: the history surrounding the issue of whether or not veterans deserve to be considered a special population with special benefits owed for their service, and the historic struggle for veterans' benefits and fair treatment from World War I up until the present wars in Iraq and Afghanistan. This description serves as the context and rationale for the subsequent discussion of why and how veterans themselves become involved in advocacy; clinical implications, cautions, and suggested guidelines for veterans engaging in advocacy; and the continuing struggle to achieve meaningful and deserved rights, benefits and understanding. Since its inception, American society has been wrestling with the difficult problem of reintegrating its citizens returned from combat into the larger population. Not only has our nation not resolved the problem of veterans returning from war, it continues to repeat the very same mistakes.

The Crisis: Lies, Lies and Damn Statistics

The sheer statistics are staggering. According to the VA policy watchdog and advocacy organization, Veterans for Common Sense (2011), some 2.6 million Americans have served on active duty in the military since September 11, 2001. Of that number, some 2.2 million, or 85 percent, have served in the combat theaters of the Middle East or central Asia. More than 6,000 have been killed in action. More than 45,000 have been wounded in action. Nearly 57,000 have been medically evacuated for injuries or illness unrelated to combat. There have been more than 108,000 battlefield casualties. More than 940,000, or 42 percent, have experienced multiple deployments to a combat theater—a predictor of PTSD, in that multiple studies have shown there is a causal relationship between the number of combat deployments and the likelihood of suffering PTSD (Litz & Schlenger, 2009).

More than 1.3 million, or more than 60 percent, of those are now eligible for health-care and reintegration benefits through the VA (Veterans for Common Sense, 2011). Of those, more than 711,000 (49 percent) have sought healthcare treatment through the VA, 367,000 (fully 52 percent) have sought mental healthcare treatment. More than 211,000 (30 percent) of all patients seeking care have been diagnosed by the VA with PTSD. Of those, more than 624,000 have filed disability claims (88 percent of patients seeking mental healthcare through the VA). The landmark Rand Corporation study estimated that as many as 20 percent of all Iraq and Afghanistan veterans suffer from PTSD, and as many as 25 percent suffer from a TBI (traumatic brain injury) (Tanelian & Jaycox, 2008). Finally, 25 percent of veterans of the wars in Iraq and Afghanistan report having a service-connected disability (Bureau of Labor, 2011).

Even more troubling are the statistics for veterans post-combat/post-military. Within the population of Iraq and Afghanistan veterans who have accessed the VA for health-care, more than 4,000 have died within two years of returning from a combat tour (Glantz, 2011)! One-fifth (20 percent) of all the suicides in the U.S. have been committed by veterans (*Orlando Sentinel*, 2011). One-fourth (25 percent) of all Americans who experience homelessness in any given year are veterans (U.S. Interagency Council on Homelessness, 2010). The unemployment rate for veterans of the past decade of wars is greater than the civilian rate (U.S. Congressional Report, 2011) and, for first-term soldiers aged 20–24, the unemployment rate is more than twice that of civilians of the same age group. In some states, the unemployment rate for this group is more than triple the national civilian unemployment rate (Maze, 2011). Despite its sacrifices, this generation of veterans has suffered far more, economically, compared to non-veteran civilians in the past decade, particularly as a result of the recession that began during the second term of Republican President George W. Bush. Job insecurity also precipitates homelessness—this generation of veterans has seen the most rapid descent into home-lessness of any generation of veterans (Eckholm, 2007). As the toxic stew of multiple combat tours, PTSD, and TBI ferment (often undiagnosed) (Alvarez, 2008), veterans' disability, a deteriorating economy, homelessness, and unemployment have become persistent and pervasive problems. This potent combination is taking a devastating toll on this most recent generation of veterans (Grogan, 2008). It has created a wealth-trap for veterans that will have long-lasting, far-reaching, multi-decade, generational effects (Alvarez, 2008).

Wars cost money (Daggett, 2008). Blood is a big expense. Stiglitz and Bilmes (2008), in their book, *The Three Trillion Dollar War*, estimate the direct cost of paying for veterans' benefits and healthcare for this generation of Iraq and Afghanistan veterans, and the indirect costs in terms of lost productivity, will be *one trillion dollars per decade for the next four to five decades*. And there is the very real risk that the American people—and their elected representatives—may tire in 2050 of paying for a war that began in 2001 (Klein, 2011).

What's at Stake?

If you are inclined to agree with George Washington, the stakes are high: nothing less than the security and defense of our country. From a social obligation and humanitarian perspective, the responsibility of a nation towards its citizens, sons and daughters, veterans and their families constitutes a social contract between the nation and less than two-thirds of one percent that take up arms in the defense of the nation. The central question is: should veterans be recognized as a special class of citizen, or should veterans be treated in the same way as the rest of the common citizenry (Ross, 1969)? President Roosevelt stated in 1935, "Able-bodied veterans should be accorded no treatment different from that accorded to other citizens who did not wear a uniform during the war. There is, before this Congress, legislation providing old-age benefits and a greater measure of security for all workers . . . in all this the veteran shares (ibid.)."

In short, our nation's treatment of its veterans is an historic and socio-political debate not yet satisfactorily resolved. As recently as November 10, 2011, Senator Jim DeMint (R-SC), himself a non-veteran, cast the lone vote against the recent VOW to Hire Heroes Act,[2] which gave employers tax credits for hiring Iraq and Afghanistan veterans. Senator DeMint asserted, as justification for his unpopular vote, "All Americans deserve the same opportunity to be hired. I cannot support this tax credit because I do not believe the government should privilege one American over another when it comes to work" (Wong, 2011). Many veterans themselves strongly believe that they are especially entitled to some consideration above that of the average citizen, who took no risks, sacrificed not a whit, and suffered nothing for the Constitution. Returning from foreign lands and bloody battlefields by the millions, veterans historically have been inclined to come together to form political and social advocacy groups to demand, from politicians and society, the benefits promised by a grateful nation.

Veterans' Advocacy and the Historic Struggle for Benefits and Fair Treatment: From World War I to the Twenty-First Century

Veterans' advocacy in the modern era dates to World War I. There was a rapid and massive expansion of what had been a rather small professional army. The draft inducted more than 2.8 million men into the military and more than 1.39 million saw combat in 13 battles (Ayres, 1919). There were more than 116,000 dead in the European theater and more than 670,000 wounded in action, many grievously (VA Factsheet, "America's Wars," 2011).

The Beginning of Modern Veterans' Benefits

Modern veterans' benefits began with the so-called Bonus Expeditionary Army in the wake of WWI. The practice of awarding a "bonus" to veterans of the nation's wars began with the Revolutionary War, after which a private (an entry level rank) received 100 acres and 80 dollars at the war's conclusion. The veterans of the Mexican-American War, the Indian Wars, and the Spanish-American War all received a bonus authorized by Congress. A mere 18 years after the conclusion of the Spanish-American War, in 1919, Congress voted a bonus of only 60 dollars to the American Expeditionary Forces. Veterans were so distraught by the rank disparity between treatment of the Spanish-American War veterans and WWI veterans—who, after all, had survived the worst combat the world had yet seen—that they formed the American Legion (www.legion.org) in March 1919, even while still in post-war Paris. The organization was formed as a political movement and lobbying organization for veterans' rights and benefits. It was instrumental in lobbying for, and creating, the Veterans' Bureau in 1921, which would become the U.S. Department of Veterans Affairs 65 years later.

The newly-formed American Legion advocated an additional bonus shortly after its creation. Finally, in 1924, and over the veto of Republican President Calvin Coolidge, who stated, "We owe no bonus to able-bodied veterans of the World War" (Ross, 1969), Congress legislated a bonus for war veterans, authorizing the issue of more than 3.6 million bonds with a 20-year maturity (ibid.). The American Legion and its allies in Congress later pushed to honor the certificate as a means of relief for veterans struggling during the Depression, opposed by the Republican President Hoover. In 1932, some 45,000 veterans and their families from around the country "marched" on Washington, DC. President Hoover had two regiments commanded by General Douglas MacArthur rout the peaceful veterans at bayonet point; several hundred veterans were wounded. The immediate effect of this attack against the popularly-called "Bonus Expeditionary Force" was a renewed, sympathetic, focus on the plight of veterans of the Great War (Cox, 2011). The Veterans' Bureau merged with the Bureau of Pensions and the National Home for Disabled Volunteer Soldiers to become the Veterans' Administration in 1931.

World War II

Of course, no one knew that some 16 million Americans would serve in uniform in WWII (VA Factsheet, "America's Wars," 2011). The political establishment, led by Democratic President Franklin Roosevelt, could not accept the possibility of millions of combat veterans protesting any maltreatment. The political debate centered around two issues: where did the New Deal end and veterans' rights and benefits as a separate class of citizen distinct from the average private citizen begin; and, secondly, which government agency would administer veterans' benefits?

Eventually, in 1944, a series of legislative Acts resolved the issues for WWII veterans, who came to be known as The Greatest Generation. The Mustering Out Act of

1944 created a schedule of cash bonuses for service members. The Veterans' Preference Act of 1944 established federal preferences and employment rights among other federal administrative benefits (Ross, 1969). Finally, the crowning legislation was the passage of the Servicemen's Readjustment Act, commonly known as the GI Bill. The GI Bill involved sweeping changes that included low interest, zero down-payment homes or farms for veterans, guaranteed by the VA; federally funded education or vocational training; unemployment benefits for unemployed veterans for the first year they were mustered out of service; medical benefits through the VA's hospitals; and disability pensions for medically-disabled combat veterans.

The ultimate effects of these changes altered the social landscape of the United States forever. College education and home ownership became possible for millions of veterans who otherwise would not have been able to access those touchstones of the middle class. It has been estimated that, for every dollar spent on veterans' reintegration after World War II, the federal government realized a seven dollar return (IAVA, 2008).

Post–World War II

Unfortunately, as legislation has slowly carved out a niche for combat veterans as a special interest class, the federal government has narrowly construed the legislative mandate and erected hurdles to the access of veterans' rights and benefits. The Vietnam era of veterans suffered every indignity of a hostile homecoming from an unpopular war. More than three million Americans deployed to Southeast Asia from 1965 to 1975, and more than 1.5 million served in combat (VA Factsheet, "America's Wars," 2011). More than 153,000 were wounded, 58,220 were killed in action, 21,000 were permanently and totally disabled, and more than 830,000 suffered symptoms of PTSD. Advocacy efforts, led by the Vietnam Veterans of American (www.vva.org) formed in 1978, gave voice to an entire generation of hundreds of thousands of veterans who had been politically and socially marginalized because of the unpopularity of the war. Important issues included exposure to Agent Orange, a carcinogenic defoliant, chronic PTSD, attendant long-term unemployability and the homelessness of veterans.[3]

The three most recent conflicts—the Persian Gulf War (1990–1991) and the Iraq (2003–2011) and Afghanistan wars (2001–present)—have seen countless scandals regarding veterans' healthcare and disability benefits. Tens of thousands of Gulf War veterans suffer from a mysterious malady that has been coined "Gulf War Syndrome" (Michel, 2008). Similarly to its denial regarding exposure to Agent Orange, the VA controversially opposed the existence of any such disease (Engel & Maugh, 2008). Approximately 210,000 veterans from the U.S., Canada, and the United Kingdom have been diagnosed with symptoms of Gulf War Syndrome (Research Advisory Committee, U.S. Congress, 2008). The VA refused to recognize the legitimacy of the constellation of symptoms and disabilities that were common to sufferers of Gulf War Syndrome, including joint pain, muscle pain, chronic fatigue, severe headache, memory loss, respiratory disorder, skin rashes, and circulatory disorders (Littlepage, 2010). The VA's stance unfortunately placed the burden of proof upon the veteran, rather than stipulating those symptoms as de facto proof of Gulf War Syndrome. For the purposes of awarding disability benefits, this approach would save the VA *tens of billions* of dollars over the life of affected veterans. The National Gulf War Resource Center (www.ngwrc.

org), organized in 1995, helped to expose the whole truth about Pentagon policies that severely impacted veterans and their families (National Gulf War Resource Center, n.d.), and overcame the VA's resistance to recognizing Gulf War Syndrome. The VA, as a result of their work with the National Gulf War Resource Center, eventually presumed that certain symptoms were Gulf War Syndrome, thereby relieving the veteran of the burden of proof.

Critics' View of the VA's Legacy

Many critics, including the former chairman of the House Veterans' Affairs Committee, Rep Bob Filner (D-CA) (Leopold, 2008), veterans and their supporters describe the VA's legacy of the past decade as one of denial, obfuscation, incompetence, and bald-faced mendacity (Kors, 2008). In July 2008, Government Accounting Office auditors found that the VA had not properly accounted for more than 6.9 billion dollars listed as "miscellaneous," approximately 15 percent of its annual budget (Coulter, 2008). In August 2008, the Bush administration attempted to prevent the registration of veterans at VA facilities, claiming that this would violate federal elections law (Rosenfeld, 2008). In October 2008, investigators discovered more than 500 recent benefit claims in shredder bins in 47 VA offices around the country (Waldman, 2008). The VA also conspired to conceal the epidemic of suicides among veterans of the recent wars (Hanchette, 2008). Freedom of Information Act inquiries revealed that the VA records more than 1,000 suicide attempts per month by Iraq and Afghanistan veterans (ibid.). During Congressional testimony, Dr Ira Katz, the Deputy Undersecretary of Mental Health Affairs and a Bush appointee, testified that there were only 790 suicide attempts *per year* (ibid.). However, in an email to Dr Michael J. Kussman, Undersecretary of the Veterans' Health Administration, Dr Katz acknowledged that the VA records more than 1,000 suicide attempts *per month* and an average of *126 successful suicide attempts per week* (MacFarqhar, 2008).

Recent Successes for Veterans' Advocates

In June 2008, a coalition of veterans' organizations, led by the Iraq and Afghanistan Veterans of America (IAVA), pushed for a new GI Bill for the newest cohort of war veterans (Simon, 2008). The bill was supported by virtually all the national veterans' organizations, including the American Legion, the Veterans of Foreign Wars, AMVETS, Disabled Veterans of America, and Paralyzed Veterans of America. This bill was originally sponsored by Virginia Senator James Webb (D-VA), a Vietnam veteran, Navy Cross recipient, and former Secretary of the Navy for President Reagan. Despite unfortunate and inexplicable opposition, led by Vietnam veteran and former POW, Senator John McCain (R-AZ), it was signed into law in June 2008 (Glantz, 2009).

The Post-9/11 Veterans' Educational Assistance Act, better known as the Post-9/11 GI Bill, includes tuition payments, a books and supplies allowance, and monthly living stipends that are only available to veterans who served after September 11, 2001. The bill was controversially amended in 2010 by the Republican-led Congress, on the one hand expanding coverage for veterans, while at the same time reducing benefits by pro-rating coverage for partial school-months.

In May 2011, the 9th Circuit Court of Appeals made a landmark ruling in the precedent-setting case of *Veterans for Common Sense, et al.* v. *Shinseki*, the retired General and former Army Chief of Staff who is now the Secretary of the VA. VCS sued the VA over veterans' access to mental healthcare in 2008 (MacFarqhar, 2008). VCS was able to prove in court the combination of ineptitude, negligence, and deceit that combined to make the VA a bureaucratic nightmare for returning veterans. The 9th U.S. Circuit Court of Appeals found that it still takes *an average* of *four years* for the VA to "fully provide the mental health benefits owed veterans" (Elias, 2011). In fact, veterans *successfully complete suicide attempts 18 times a day nationwide!* (ibid.). 9th U.S. Circuit Appeals Court Judge Stephen Reinhardt, writing the opinion for a three-judge panel in a recent ruling, opined, "No more veterans should be compelled to agonize or perish while the government fails to perform its obligations. Having chosen to honor and provide for our veterans by guaranteeing them the mental healthcare and other critical benefits to which they are entitled, the government may not deprive them of that support through unchallengeable and interminable delays" (ibid.).

Most importantly Judge Reinhardt cited the 5th Amendment of the Constitution, which reads in part, "No person shall . . . be deprived of life, liberty, or property, without due process of law; nor shall private property be taken for public use, without just compensation." Writing for the majority, the judge found that the VA had consistently and systematically violated millions of American veterans' Constitutional rights by depriving them of timely and efficient access to healthcare and disability compensation and benefits without "due process" (Williams, 2011). In other words, the federal government *misappropriated healthcare and benefits that belong to veterans by rights of their service, without due process, in violation of the very Constitution that they had sworn to support uphold and defend.*

Is it any wonder that so many veterans and their families are so disillusioned, feel so profoundly betrayed, and harbor such anger and rage towards our federal government?!

Why Advocacy, and Its Impact on Participating Veterans

I am not a therapist or a clinician, so I cannot claim that veterans' advocacy is a "therapeutically beneficial" activity. However, I am committed to advocacy for veterans and am comfortable writing from experience about different paths and impacts that bring veterans into the advocacy arena. I came to advocacy from a place of profound injury—physical, moral, and spiritual, based on my combat experiences in Iraq and my difficult homecoming and reintegration. I found it necessary to speak out—at first, about my own combat experiences, then, as I began to connect with other veterans of various wars, more generally about veterans' issues and reintegration.

How and Why Many Veterans Become Involved in Advocacy

In my own therapy and rehabilitation from my wounds, I developed an understanding of the enormity of the experience of war, not just for myself but for everyone that experiences it. I developed some ideas about advocacy, as well as a subsequent commitment to help people—veterans, families, Iraqis—whose lives have been shattered by wars.

Speaking from my experience, *one or more of three factors motivate veterans to become involved in advocacy:* our own personal injuries and impact from war; a commitment to the American people who deserve to know the full truth about war and its impact; and a commitment to help others who have been impacted by war.

I believe that veterans come to advocacy by one of three routes: rage, betrayal, and healing.

Rage-into-Advocacy

More than a few combat veterans are motivated, at least initially, by rage. I know I was. I suspect this may manifest the soul injury that occurs in combat, which is itself a transformation of personality and character. The rage is blind and directed at virtually everyone and everything: civilians, family, friends, authority figures (in bureaucracies, the work setting, etc.), and God. This is the rage of someone who is truly alienated from all social institutions of which he or she was formerly a part. Scurfield recognized this dynamic when he wrote, "Our government sends us to war, our military uses us in war, and society forgets us after war" (2006a). The understandable response is, given the trauma of combat, rage.

Betrayal-into-Advocacy

If a therapist or clinician accepts the premise that the veteran's relationship to country is a true relationship, then the dynamics of broken relationships may apply. As referenced previously, the military deliberately cultivates reverence for country and its symbolic presence, such as the flag (through daily flag-raising and lowering ceremonies called "Colors"). Upon return, and experiencing the hardships of reintegration, the veteran's encounters with the institutions of the nation unfailingly disappoint. The veteran experiences none of the "reverence" for country to which he/she has been acculturated and, more devastatingly, institutionally there is no quid pro quo. The failure by national institutions to demonstrate proper reverence for service and sacrifice begets profound feelings of betrayal. Scurfield mentioned that this dynamic is crucial to a successful postwar adjustment for many war veterans—the belief that our country will fully honor the promises that were made to our nation's military personnel while they were being recruited and after they entered active duty. However, a number of active duty military, veterans, and their families experience this as an empty promise—that this trust relationship has been diluted or voided by our government, our leaders and by society and that they have been betrayed (2006a).

Conversely, when the veteran encounters an individual or organization that *does* supply that reciprocal "reverence" between country and veteran, it engenders a feeling of "rightness" or "satisfaction." The veteran who goes into advocacy from a place of betrayal does so to restore the reverential relationship between veteran and country.

Healing-into-Advocacy

For veterans, healing physically, morally, and spiritually can last years or decades—the work of a lifetime. I believe that veterans are never wholly "healed," as trauma can never be undone; it can be accommodated, and its effects managed and mitigated. Veterans get into advocacy based on their healing experience, particularly if their experience has been positive. They are motivated to share their healing experience with other veterans who may be suffering similarly. Usually, a veteran advocate who comes from a healing place will promote one or two particularly effective healing modalities. These routes may have some correlation to the stages of grief and may, at least initially, be a form of the grieving process. Personally speaking, I believe that was the case for me.

In my experience, there are three kinds of veterans' involvement in advocacy: healthy advocacy, all-consuming advocacy, and advocacy that stokes and exacerbates the rage and sense of betrayal, rather than promoting healing from such.

Healthy Advocacy

I recognize as "healthy" advocates those veterans who gain a beneficial satisfaction from advocacy, and for whom it becomes a constructive means to deal with distrust and anger issues about how veterans have been mistreated or ignored. These veterans are often most effective in the long run, as they cultivate working relationships with non-veteran civilians, politicians, and business leaders to promote the message about the experiences of veterans attempting to reintegrate into a post-combat, post-military civilian role. Non-veteran civilians may be off-put by other sources of veteran advocacy, such as veterans fueled by rage and betrayal who may be prone to angry confrontations and may have an agenda of protest rather than healing.

All-Consuming Advocacy

Other veterans become so involved in advocacy efforts that the fierce urgency of the crisis consumes their lives to the detriment of other aspects of living, including family relationships and friendships. The veteran is acculturated by the military to put selfless service ahead of every consideration of personal well-being, family and friendship. All-consuming veteran advocacy extends this dynamic from the battlefield, risks keeping the veteran in a combat mindset, and creates a dynamic where any opposition becomes the "enemy," delaying reintegration into post-combat, post-military civilian roles.

Advocacy That Fuels Rage and a Sense of Betrayal

Finally, some veterans are so traumatized, both by their combat experiences and their post-deployment treatment by an indifferent or hostile nation (both at the institutional and personal level), that their advocacy is based in fueling the feelings of rage that animate their actions. Advocacy becomes a channel for the expression of rage to non-veteran civilians. Rage-based advocacy can attract veterans who feel similarly, and the expression of rage can be satisfying. The problem is that it requires repetitive, if not constant, rage reinforcement by similarly-minded veterans, creating a feedback loop in which rage fuels advocacy and, subsequently, rage. This type of advocacy is difficult to maintain, is rarely effective over the long term and, ultimately, is self-injurious to the veteran advocate.

Clinical Implications

I suggest each of these have clinical implications. Clinicians should be willing to recognize that *relationship with the country* (and its institutions) is a fundamental and profound unresolved issue for many veterans and is itself a source of *profound traumatic injury*. This is because of the social and moral contract that our nation purportedly promises to members of the military: in return for serving our country in harm's way, we expect to be provided with the timely benefits, services, and support that we have earned through our military service. The betrayal and sundering of this relationship, vis-à-vis reintegration, is at the heart of many veterans' discontent and disaffection. Therefore, the relationship between veteran and country should, and must, be a valid focus of attention in the therapy relationship (Scurfield, 2006a).

If a veteran is consumed with anger and issues of betrayal, and is "stuck" on the rage and betrayal, can the therapist help the veteran resolve or attend to these feelings therapeutically? Can the therapist help the veteran client channel such feelings into more constructive actions—such as advocacy—rather than remaining stuck and *refusing to do anything constructive* about it? For some veterans, working on behalf of, or with, similar veterans might be too personally impactful; for such veterans, working with a younger or older generation of veterans can be meaningful. For other veterans, advocacy efforts involving populations *other than* veterans is strongly advised, due to the extent to which focusing on veterans' issues might be too upsetting, all-consuming, and/or frustrating. For such veterans, working in causes that have personal appeal, such as children's or animal rights, community issues, etc., offers the advantages of engaging in meaningful activities that focus on helping others, but do not lead to exacerbation of the veteran's combat trauma issues (ibid.).

And so, when the nation fails to deliver on its promises, often for reasons of political expediency, the violation of the social contract has a profound impact on many military members, veterans and their families (ibid.). Ignoring the extent to which this profound dynamic warrants attention in the therapeutic relationship is to ignore a most critical dynamic that impacts on almost all military personnel, veterans, and their families.

Other Avenues to Facilitate Recovery

One way to help veterans develop greater knowledge and self-awareness is to suggest a variety of guided readings and movies/documentaries. For example, I needed to know *The Truth* about my experience of war. What did it mean? How could I come home? How could I make something meaningful of this soul-shattering, body-shattering experience?

Early in my recovery, I read two books that transformed how I think about homecoming and reintegration: Edward Tick's seminal *War and the Soul* (2005) and Dr. Jonathan Shay's insightful *Odysseus in America* (2002). Tick's book was extraordinarily important to me in explaining the soul injury that combat causes, and how other societies around the world dealt with the phenomenon of warrior/veteran reintegration into the larger society. Shay's book struck a chord, not just because I studied classics in college, but because I recognized my own behavior in the book. Also, I participated in making several documentaries, including *The Road to Fallujah* (Manning, 2009), the unreleased

Odysseus in America (Berkowitz), and a *PBS Now* documentary about PTSD (Sept 2008). Documentaries (and art) are important, because there is a visual truth to experience and trauma that prose is inadequate to portray.

All of the veterans' advocacy organizations have leveraged social media to reduce barriers to outreach and interaction with other veterans. Veterans can now interact via online chat rooms, Twitter, Facebook, LinkedIn, etc., at whim. Social media technology has created the opportunity for subsets of veterans—for instance, those who belonged to specific units or who participated in certain battles—to associate. This dynamic offers pros and cons: the veteran is more likely to associate with veterans of similar experience; on the other hand, such association can reinforce insularity and alienation from civilian society. This technology may prove to be a hindrance to reintegration in a post-combat, post-military civilian role.

Veterans' Special Place in America: The Struggle Continues

America's veterans have a special place in American history, because so much of its history has been shaped by America's wars. Reintegrating war veterans into the greater fabric of American society is an issue that dates to the founding of the Republic. American veterans have never been afforded any benefits which were not opposed by at least one major political party and for which they did not have to advocate—and in many cases, fight.

The advocacy of veterans groups, and the scope of legislation over the course of America's history, recognizes and rewards the special sacrifice of combat veterans who have answered the call of duty in times of war. Despite attempts to erase distinctions between citizens who have never served and those who have served in war, America's combat veterans have a unique claim upon federal rights and benefits, a claim that is now explicitly recognized as a Constitutional right by the federal government. The distinction lies in the Oath of Service, which states in part, "I solemnly swear to support and defend the Constitution of the United States against all enemies foreign and domestic, and to bear true faith and allegiance to the same."

Many hundreds of thousands of Americans have shed their blood and made the ultimate sacrifice for this oath. America's combat veterans are "blood owners" of the Constitution in ways that other citizens can never be. This distinctive, salient, and markedly impactful life experience can make some veterans committed, vocal, knowledgeable, articulate, determined, and vigilant advocates for other veterans. For another group of traumatized and particularly vulnerable veterans, veteran-related advocacy can be personally harmful and hinder healthy reintegration into civilian society. This dynamic is especially relevant when the very national institutions that were established *for* the welfare of veterans act in ways that violate veterans' well-being and summarily deprive them the rights and benefits for which they feel they paid with blood and sacrifice.

> [A]nd at 4:45 pm on Friday, July 1, 2011, the Department of Justice filed an appeal of the 9th Circuit Court's landmark ruling in the precedent-setting 2008 case of *Veterans for Common Sense, et al. v. Shinseki and the Department of Veterans Affairs* over veterans' access to mental healthcare. On Dec 13, the entire 9th Circuit Court heard arguments en banc. The Department of Justice, representing the Department

of Veterans Affairs, argument was essentially: veterans have no standing to seek redress through the judicial system.

(Courthouse News Service, December 15, 2011)

Will the struggle for fair, adequate and timely benefit and services for veterans and their families ever end? If recent history is any indication, the answer sadly is a resounding "NO." Our nation still hasn't figured it out.

Understanding

The first step for civilians, veterans, policy-makers and politicians, and therapists and clinicians alike, is understanding: an understanding that transcends parochial considerations of both politics and resource allocation and the nature and extent of veteran issues, in terms of the social contract; an understanding of how veterans' advocacy efforts affect a veteran's personal, and the veteran community's collective, well-being, and how advocacy helps create a more perfect political union; and, finally, an understanding how the relationship between the military, veterans and their families, and our country is a legitimate and vital topic for attention in therapeutic and counseling efforts and can be a legitimate healing activity in, and of, itself.

Closing

In the modern era, veterans' rights and benefits have been secured only by veterans advocating and, in some instances, fighting for them (Dao, 2011b). Veterans, expecting to come home to at least a supportive, if not grateful, nation, after fighting its wars, are often disillusioned to find a public and establishment hostile, ignorant, or apathetic to the plight and discontents of the hard work of reintegrating veterans into a productive, post-combat, post-military civilian role. It is as if the veteran expected society to stop and to wait for him or her to return home, only to find that life goes on—society has moved on without them. Now they are "left out." They realize the bitter truth: there are not many, to include members of the military and the VA, who are looking out for them. The options are to suffer in silence, to rely on those relatively small numbers of non-veteran advocates, or to become actively involved in advocacy and speak truth to power.

The arc of the history of veterans' advocacy tends towards recognizing the service and sacrifice of veterans as a distinct class separate from non-veteran citizens. It is also fair to say that, when presented with the full truth about the problem of veteran reintegration through the generations, the general population and their elected representatives are favorably disposed towards veterans' rights and benefits, as has been described in this chapter, as are veterans' organizations such as the American Legion, The National Gulf War Resource Center, Iraq and Afghanistan Veterans of America, and Veterans for Common Sense.

Much work remains to create a nation that "gets" veteran rights, benefits, and reintegration right; work that, because of the collective amnesia in our society about the full human cost of war that rises soon after every war ends (Scurfield, 2006a, 2006b)—*requires renewal with every new generation of war veterans* and advocates speaking out about the veteran experience to civilian non-veterans, clinicians and therapists and policy-makers alike. Washington's words were true in 1781, and remain true today. Each and every veteran has to discover for him or herself how much—if at all—he or she is able to participate in, and benefit from, advocacy activities as part of his or her own successful reintegration into a post-combat, post-military civilian life.

Notes

1. During a senatorial campaign debate between Senator Chuck Schumer (D-NY) and Republican candidate Jay Townsend, the subject of the wars and of veterans' affairs—the two largest federal agencies—did not come up at all.
2. For greater detail about the historical timeline of veterans' advocacy and legal remedies, please contact the author.
3. For an advocate's detailed account of the issues that faced Vietnam veterans in their struggles for benefits and recognition, see Nicosia, G. (2001). *Home to War: A History of the Vietnam Veterans' Movement.* New York, NY: Crown Publishing Group.

References

Alvarez, L. (2008, Aug. 26). "Iraq and Afghanistan Veterans' Brain Injuries Often Over-looked." *The New York Times.* Accessed at: http://www.nytimes.com/2008/08/26/us/26tbi. html?ref=veteransaffairsdepartment.

Ayres, L. P. (1919). *The War with Germany: A Statistical Summary.* (2nd Edn). Washington, DC: Government Printing Office.

Bureau of Labor (2011, March 11). *Employment Situation of Veterans: 2010.* Bureau of Labor Statistics Report. http://www.bls.gov/news.release/vet.nr0.htm.

Coulter, B. (2008, Aug 13). "VA Accounting Policy Challenged," *Burlington Union.* Accessed at http://www.wickedlocal.com/burlington/news/lifestyle/columnists/x1246330259/VA-accounting-policy-questioned#axzz1jgaIiVdb.

Courthouse News Service (2011, Dec. 15). *Veterans Fight in 8th Circuit for Better PTSD Treatment.* http://veteransforcommonsense.org/2011/12/15/veterans-fight-in-9th-circuit-for-better-ptsd-treatment/.

Cox, B. (2011, Oct 25). "What Does the Bonus Army Tell Us about Occupy Wall Street?" *The Awl.* Available at: http://www.theawl.com/2011/10/what-does-the-bonus-army-tell-us-about-occupy-wall-Street.

Daggett, S. (2008). "Costs of Major U.S. Wars." Washington, DC: U.S. Congressional Research Service.

Dao, J. (2011a, Nov. 2). "For Injured Veterans, Healing in Service to Others." *The New York Times.* Accessed at: http://www.nytimes.com/2011/11/02/giving/for-some-injured-veterans-community-service-is-a-way-to-heal.html.

Dao, J. (2011b, May 28) "After Combat, the Unexpected Perils of Coming Home." *The New York Times.* Accessed at: http://www.nytimes.com/2011/05/29/us/29soldiers.html.

Eckholm, E. (2007, Nov. 8). "Surge Seen in Number of Homeless Veterans." *The New York Times.* Accessed at www.nytimes.com/2007/11/08/us/08vets.html.

Elias, P. (2011, May 10). "Federal Appeals Court Blasts VA Mental Healthcare, Orders Dramatic Overhaul." *The Washington Post.* Accessed at: http://www.washingtonpost.com/national/federal-appeals-court-blasts-va-mental-health-care-system-orders-dramatic-overhaul/2011/05/10/AFP4MziG_story.html.

Engel, M., & Maugh, T. (2008, Nov. 18). "Proof of Gulf War Syndrome No Smoking Gun." *Los Angeles Times.* Accessed at: http://www.military.com/news/article/researchers-claim-proof-of-gulf-war-syndrome.html.

Glantz, A. (2009). *The War Comes Home: Washington's Battle Against America's Veterans*. San Francisco, CA: University of California Press.

Glantz, A. (2011, May 28). "Troubled Veterans and Early Deaths After Iraq." *The New York Times*. Accessed at: http://www.nytimes.com/2011/05/29/us/29bcveterans.html?pagewanted=1&src=recg.

Grogan, J. (2008, Aug. 25). "Ranks of Homeless Veterans Growing due to Poor Economy and Iraq and Afghanistan Wars." *The Day*. Accessed at: http://www.theday.com/article/20080824/DAYARC/308249902.

Haberman, C. (2010, Oct. 26). "For Many, Wars are Out of Sight, Out of Mind." *The New York Times*. Accessed at: http://www.nytimes.com/2010/10/26/nyregion/26nyc.html?_r=1&ref=nyregion.

Hanchette, J. (2008, Sept. 15). "VA Covers up Shocking Statistics on Iraq War Soldiers' Suicides." *Niagara Falls Reporter*. Accessed at: http://www.niagarafallsreporter.com/hanchette310.html.

Iraq and Afghanistan Veterans of America (2008). *A New GI Bill: Rewarding Our Troops, Rebuilding Our Military*. Accessed at: http://www.gibill2008.org.

Klein, E. (2011, March 25). "Start Paying for War." *The Washington Post*. Accessed at: http://www.washingtonpost.com/business/start_paying_for_war/2011/03/24/AFRAKXWB_story.html?wprss=rss_homepage.

Kors, J. (2008, Sept. 15). "How the VA Abandons Our Vets." *The Nation*, 287 (7). Accessed at: http://www.thenation.com/article/how-va-abandons-our-vets.

Leopold, J. (2008, Nov. 26). "Chairman Bob Filner Describes a Culture of Dishonesty at the VA." *The Public Record*. Accessed at: http://pubrecord.org/nation/418/rep-filner-culture-of-dishonesty-at-department-of-veterans-affairs/.

Littlepage, M. S. (2010, May 10). "VA to Review Gulf War Veterans' Claims." Accessed at: http://www.gulfweb.org/doc_show.cfm?ID=820.

Litz, B., & Schlenger, W. (2009). "PTSD in Military Service Members and New Veterans of Iraq and Afghanistan: A Bibliography and Critique." *PTSD Research Quarterly*, 20 (1). White River Junction, VT: National Center for PTSD. Accessed at at: http://www.ptsd.va.gov.

MacFarquhar, N. (2008, April 22). "In Federal Suit, 2 Views of Veterans Healthcare." *The New York Times*. Accessed at http://www.nytimes.com/2008/04/22/washington/22vets.html.

Manning, M. (2009). *The Road to Fallujah*. Conception Media, Los Angeles. See http://www.theroadtofallujah.com.

Maze, R. (2011, May 11). "New Bill Would Boost Job-Finding Help for Veterans." *Navy Times*. Accessed at: http://www.navytimes.com/news/2011/05/military-veterans-hiring-051111w-051111/.

Michel, L. (2008, Aug. 18). "Veterans Fight Lengthy War Over Benefits." *The Buffalo News*. Accessed at http://www.buffalonews.com/incoming/article111864.ece.

National Gulf War Resource Center. Accessed at http://www.ngwrc.org.

Nicosia, G. (2001). *Home to War: A History of the Vietnam Veterans' Movement*. New York, NY: Crown Publishing Group.

Orlando Sentinel (2011, June 9). "With Veteran Suicides Rising, the VA Must Improve Its Mental Health Services." Accessed at: http://articles.orlandosentinel.com/2011-06-09/news/os-ed-military-suicides-060911-20110608_1_veteran-suicides-veterans-for-common-sense-veterans-groups

Relph, A. J. (2011, May 28). "Returning Veterans Encounter VA Mental Health Meltdown." Accessed at: http://www.msnbc.msn.com/id/42995663/ns/health-health_care#

Research Advisory Committee on Gulf War Veterans' Illnesses. (2008). *Gulf War Illness and the Health of Gulf War Veterans*. Washington, DC: Government Printing Office.

Rosenfeld, S. (2008, Aug. 11). "2008's First Disenfranchised Voters: Our Injured and Homeless Veterans." Available at: www.veteransforcommonsense.org.

Ross, D. R. B. (1969). *Preparing for Ulysses: Politics and Veterans During World War II*. New York, NY: Columbia University Press.

Scurfield, R. M. (2006a). *War Trauma: Lessons Unlearned from Vietnam to Iraq.* New York, NY: Algora Publishing.

Scurfield, R. M. (2006b). *Healing Journeys: Study Abroad with Vietnam Veterans.* New York, NY: Algora Publishing.

Scurfield, R. M. (2007, March 23). "Beyond the Wrongs at Walter Reed: The Tragedy of Lessons Unlearned from Vietnam to Iraq," *Sun Herald,* Biloxi. Accessed at: http://www.opednews.com/articles/opedne_raymond__070518_professor_2c_school_of.htm.

Shay, J. (2002). *Odysseus in America: Combat Trauma and The Trials of Homecoming.* New York, NY: Scribner.

Simon, C. C. (2008, Nov. 2) "The New GI Bill: A Primer." *The New York Times.* Accessed at: http://www.nytimes.com/2008/11/02/education/edlife/GIBILL-PRIMER.html

Stiglitz, J., & Bilmes, L. (2008). "The Three Trillion Dollar War." New York, NY: W.W. Norton. www.threetrilliondollarwar.org.

Tanielian, T., & Jaycox, L. (2008). "Invisible Wounds of War: Psychological and Cognitive Injuries, their Consequences, and Services to Assist Recovery." Washington, DC: The Rand Corporation.

Tick, E. (2005). *War and the Soul.* Wheaton, IL: Quest Books.

U.S. Congressional Report. (2011, May 31). "Meeting the Needs of Veterans in Today's Labor Force." Washington, DC: U.S. Congress Joint Economic Committee.

U.S. Department of Veterans Affairs. (2011, Nov.). "America's Wars." Departments of Veterans Affairs Factsheet. Accessed at: http://www1.va.gov/opa/publications/factsheets/fs_americas_wars.pdf.

U.S. Interagency Council on Homelessness. (2010). *Opening Doors: Federal Strategic Plan to Prevent and End Homelessness.* Washington, DC: Government Printing Office.

Veterans for Common Sense. (2011, Dec. 2). "VCS Releases Updated War Statistics." Accessed at: http://veteransforcommonsense.org/2011/12/02/vcs-releases-updated-war-statistics/.

Waldman, S. (2008, Dec. 5). "Veterans' Affairs Investigation Deepens at New York Regional Office." *The Times Union.* Accessed at: http://timesunion.com/AspStories/story.asp?storyID=746995

Williams, C. J. (2011, May 11). "Court Orders Major Overhaul of VA's Mental Health System." *Los Angeles Times.* Accessed at: http://articles.latimes.com/2011/may/11/local/la-me-0511-veterans-ptsd-20110511.

Wong, S. (2011, Nov. 10). "DeMint Explains His Veterans 'No' Vote." Accessed at: http://www.Politico.com

Further Reading

Scurfield, R. M. (1992). "The Collusion of Sanitization and Silence about War: One Aftermath of Operation Desert Storm." *Journal of Traumatic Stress, 5* (3): 505–512.

Part II

Culture-Specific and Community-Based Approaches

4 Culture-Specific Pathways to Healing and Transformation for War Veterans Suffering PTSD

John P. Wilson (*Vietnam Era*)

The relationship of traumatic life events, culture, and recovery is a complex one, and most interesting to investigate and discover scientifically. As Wilson (2006) documented, traumatic life events are universal and archetypal across cultures or, simply said, of the human existence and experience. But, how different cultures in the world react to traumatized persons or traumatized cultures varies greatly in its diversity of reaction patterns, interventions, programs of care and recovery, as well as ritualistic forms of facilitating health-promoting physical and psychological recovery, psychic metabolism of painful events, and restoration of resilience and well-being to persons.

To begin and have a "laser focused" view of this very broad, diverse, and cross-cultural phenomena, some fundamental considerations are useful and of critical importance. In an overly simplified way, these concern the following issues:

- How is psychic trauma experienced within a culture-specific context? For example, do people in non-Western cultures (e.g., Congo, Angola, Vietnam, Cambodia, Iraq, and Afghanistan) experience and process war-related traumatic events in the same manner as the American survivors of the September 11, 2001 attacks on the World Trade Centers?
- How do different nations, cultures, and community-based organizations deal with trauma survivors, no matter what the origin of their traumatic experiences (e.g., war, disaster, political terrorists, technological catastrophe, or other significant forms of personal trauma such as childhood abuse, rape, violent assault, wrongful incarceration, etc.)?
- How do cultures create, establish, or maintain healing processes, including specific *rituals* to help the trauma victim regain psychological and physical health and well-being? How best to assist them in the process of recovery and psychic wholeness?

The journey of recovery has long been documented in the literature of mythology, anthropology and, to a much lesser extent, cross-cultural psychology (Wilson, 1989; Wilson & Tang, 2007; Wilson & Lindy, 2012). As these reviews reveal, there is a common post-traumatic journey for the trauma survivor who traverses a common pathway, but experiences many unexpected obstacles in the homecoming journey. These include expectations ranging from "welcoming arms" greetings to "flat-out avoidance" from significant family persons to empathic and compassionate understanding of their particular journey and hardships from others. These discrepant homecoming receptions, among many others, may result in secondary forms of traumatization. In short, the homecoming journey and recovery environment may be positive or toxic. Toxic recovery situations lead to complicated PTSD and psychological disorders (e.g., depression, alcoholism, anxiety disorders, personality and identity changes, etc.). On the other hand, positive, accepting, nurturing, and empathic environments will contribute to healing organismic recovery processes and the restoration of well-being.

The issue of psychic recovery from traumatizing life-events automatically raises the question of how nations, cultures, and ethnic groups respond to them, if at all. This question is especially relevant since previous research and reviews of the relevant literature have provided important and valuable information to assist healers and professionals in their efforts to aid the injured and those suffering in post-traumatic ways, such as existential concerns about "who am I," "what is the meaning of my suffering," and/or "what is life all about," and/or clinical concerns regarding depression, anxiety and/or rage.

Cultural rituals, by definition, are unique culturally-evolved processes or mechanisms to facilitate trauma recovery. It is my belief that cultures across the world evolve or develop their own "tailored" forms of healing rituals. Some of these specifically-created rituals include the following general list, but the list does not include hundreds of special indigenous rituals throughout the world that are important and scientific variants on other cultures and patterns of healing or recovery rituals. The rituals for healing cannot be described in a few pages in one reference volume on war-related post-traumatic processes. Nevertheless, at the broadest and most comprehensive level, we can identify cross-cultural and native (indigenous) rituals for healing and recovery. They are categorized below, and pertain specifically to American war veterans:

- Rituals for purification and healing (e.g., Native American Sweat Lodge).
- Community-based disclosures of collectively-based traumatic events (e.g., WWII, Holocaust survivors, September 11, 2001 terrorist attacks).
- Rituals of celebration of the survivor (e.g., special meals, wine, recognition and honoring events).
- Recognition ceremonies: specific ceremonies to honor the survivors' journeys and survival (e.g., Memorial Day and Veteran parades in the USA; Anzac Day in Australia).
- Ritual ceremonies to allow "talking circles," among survivors about their personal experiences (e.g., a specific opportunity for war veterans' organizations, such as the Vietnam Veterans of America, the American Legion, Veterans of Foreign Wars, Disabled American Veterans, Iraq and Afghanistan Veterans of America, etc., to gather and talk).
- Rituals of release and ways to confront anger, grief, and "letting go" of trauma-related experiences.
- Rituals of homecoming, reunion, and reintegration into culture (e.g., Pearl Harbor Survivor Association (PHSA) meetings; Special Forces Association (SFA) functions and ceremonies, etc.).
- Rituals of celebration and remembrance, recalling the "good" and "bad" (e.g., reunions of "enemy and foe," such as gatherings of WWII Japanese and American veterans in such locations as Iwo Jima, Hawaii, Tarawa, Guadalcanal, etc.).
- Rituals of "unfinished business" (e.g., survivor guilt) and forgiveness (e.g., revisiting

geographic areas of horror, such as Normandy, France, for the D-Day 1944 invasion of Allied forces; Vietnam veterans returning to peacetime Vietnam (Scurfield, 2006)).

- Rituals of desensitization to "trauma-triggering" PTSD and re-enactment symptoms (e.g., personal meetings and "background talks" and emails with fellow veterans).
- Rituals for rebirth and renewal; transformation of soul and personal identity (e.g., spiritual, religious church attendance, and AA meetings).
- Rituals for communal remembrance celebrations and re-construction (e.g., dedication of WWII, Korean, and Vietnam memorials in Washington, DC).
- Rituals of ceremonial transition of recovery from trauma and victimization (e.g., honoring occasions for personal change from self-destructive patterns to positive coping).

Native and Cultural-Specific Pathways to Healing

In terms of mental healthcare, cultures provide many alternative pathways to healing and the integration of extreme stress experiences. These can be provided by shamans, medicine men and women, traditional healers, culture-specific rituals, conventional medical practices, and community-based practices that offer forms of social and emotional support for the person suffering the adverse, maladaptive, aspects of a trauma, especially war trauma (Moodley & West, 2005). But how does culture influence an individual's reaction to trauma? How do they make sense of their experiences in situations of extreme stress?

To illustrate how culture shapes belief systems and influences the perception of traumatic events and their subsequent processing and integration into cognitive structures of meaning and attribution, let us consider the following illustrations. These are only "snapshots" of hundreds or thousands throughout the world, and provide a glimpse of what could be future comparative scientific studies analyzing psychic trauma and human cultures.

Dancing with Wolves

In May 1985, I attended an inter-tribal "powwow" on the Lakota Sioux Native American Indian reservation in South Dakota (Sisseton-Whapeton). A "powwow" is a ceremonial gathering during which there is traditional dancing, arts and crafts, ceremonial exchanges of gifts (e.g., the pot latch), and various rituals. In South Dakota and elsewhere, the "powwow" was a four-day event for Vietnam War veterans and their families. The event included Native American ceremonies and rituals to honor the veterans for their military service and sacrifices. These ceremonies included Sweat Lodge purification (i.e., Lakota Warrior "sweat" for healing), the Red Feather induction ceremony for injured war veterans, traditional communal singing and dancing, pot latch sharing of gifts, ceremonial fires with "talking circles," and communal dinners with the eating of traditional Native American foods. During this powwow, I had the opportunity to meet Lakota Sioux Vietnam combat veterans. Among them was a veteran whom I will refer to as Tommy Roundtree (not his real name). Tommy was a two-tour combat veteran, who had been highly decorated for his valor and courage in combat with the 101st Airborne Brigade between 1967 and 1969.

Tommy grew up on the Rosebud reservation of the Sioux Nation in South Dakota. He was an athletic, tall, handsome man with black hair and ruddy dark skin. In many respects, he had a "Hollywood" character that resembled that of the famous actor Errol Flynn.

When I met Tommy, he was dressed in traditional tribal clothing, his face painted in traditional Lakota ways for warriors. I was interested and curious as to the paints' significance and about tribal history. Visibly noticeable were the scars on his chest and back from when he had participated in Sun Dance ceremonies in which participants are skewered with straps to a pole located in the center of a powwow arena. The powwow arena is similar to a football stadium in Europe or America. The straps are skewered into pectoral and upper back muscles by small bones or sticks. At the climax of the Sun Dance ceremony, which involves dancing and blowing through a small bone, the celebrant, at the critical time, leans back and releases himself from the straps which link him to the pole. The skewers tear the skin and cause bleeding. The Sun Dance ceremony is a physically arduous process and requires stamina, mental concentration, and preparation, typically including a Sweat Lodge purification event prior to the actual Sun Dance itself. In traditional ways, it is thought that the ritual aids in the development of spiritual strength. When I observed Tommy's scars, he immediately told me that he had done three Sun Dances during his life, two prior to deployment to Vietnam. I told him that I had read about the ceremony and others that were part of Lakota culture. It was at this point that he said, "You know, John, I would like to talk with you about my Vietnam War experiences, but I am afraid that you will think I am crazy or psychotic if I tell you how I understand what happened to me there and since coming home from the war." I responded that I have great respect for traditional Native American culture, especially Lakotan, and would like to hear his story. He smiled nervously at me, as I looked at him straight in the eyes, and he said, "Well, okay, let's talk."

We found a quiet spot in the powwow grounds and began to talk. In the background, the pulsating beat of the tom-tom drums could be heard, along with the singing of traditional songs. Tommy explained that, prior to his deployment to Vietnam, the tribal elders prepared him in various ways for going to war. He was taught his "death song" to sing if fatally wounded. He was instructed on how to use his Native American cosmology and natural connection to the Earth and its creatures (e.g., jungle heat, insects, trees, wind, and rain) to help him stay alert and informed about danger and threats. Tommy said, "In Vietnam, I would ask the insects to be my eyes while I slept to look for the enemy; I asked the trees to signal me if the enemy is creeping towards me." He continued by saying that, during active combat with his M-16 automatic rifle, he would sometimes see a "blue protective shield" surrounding him that deflected enemy bullets away. Tommy said that, at other times during combat, he could hear his maternal grandmother speaking to him, saying not to worry and that he was going to live and be free from injuries or death. He added that his grandmother's voice told him that, if he did get shot, he should sing his "death song," so that ancestral spirits would be with him and provide care and assistance to the other world (Heaven). Tommy asked me if I thought he was psychotic or delusional. I replied that I did not believe that he was "crazy" or psychotic. I felt that he was testing me and being defensive. Later, we would talk, and he would detail how he survived Vietnam and his post-war traumatic memories and overwhelming experiences. However, I asked him how he dealt with his war trauma after coming home from Vietnam.

Tommy said, "John, I will show you our way of healing," and arranged for me to participate in a Lakota Warrior Sweat Lodge with a Sacred Pipe Carrier of the Lakota Sioux Nation. He also arranged for me to observe and participate in several other rituals and ceremonies for healing and psychological well-being during the "powwow" itself. Later, he explained that his perspective of the Vietnam War was different than that of the white Anglo-American culture; he volunteered for military service to honor agreements his ancestral grandfathers made about fighting for their "land and way of life." He continued by saying that, by keeping to the traditional ways, abstaining from alcohol, and working to help others who had adverse residual traumatic war injuries, he could live with harmony and balance in life in all his affairs—or so he hoped. This, he explained, was part of the Lakota way, the circle of life and the Great Spirit (God).

The Sweat Lodge Ceremony

After Tommy and I talked, he and some of the other powwow organizers invited me to a Sweat Lodge Ceremony. I had no idea or understanding at that time what a Sweat Lodge was, as a ritual. The organizers, all Vietnam War veterans, simply said to me, "Don't eat or drink very much (alcohol or other things) today, and come back around five o'clock." I returned later, and we drove to the countryside on the Sioux Reservation. We got out of the car and walked down a hilly slope to the place where the Sweat Lodge was located. I was surprised to see a dome-shaped tent-like structure, covered with canvas. In front of the Lodge was a fire with a large number of rocks being heated by firewood. There were other men there: about 12 combat veterans, all Native Americans, who had come to participate in the powwow. They stood by the "ceremonial" fire and talked quietly. Then, one of the men said, "Hey, here comes Crazy Buffalo," the medicine man who would lead the Lakota Warrior Sweat Lodge ceremony. I looked up and saw a short, gray-haired man come down the hill, carrying with him a tote bag. When he approached us he said, "Get ready." The men began undressing (naked) to prepare to enter the Lodge. At the same time, Crazy Buffalo took sacred objects out of his bag—a wing of an Eagle, the Sacred Pipe of the Sioux Nation, and other objects. He created an altar in front of the dome-shaped tent, on which to place the Sacred Pipe, which we would smoke together after the ceremony was concluded.

The Ceremony Begins

The medicine man, Crazy Buffalo, purified the Lodge both inside and out with smoke that came from a small bowl-like object that he held in his hand (a seashell of abalone). The bowl contained "sweet grass," and this is a traditional way of symbolically preparing the Lodge for the sacred ceremony. Once the Lodge was prepared, Crazy Buffalo asked us to enter through the small opening to the interior of the Lodge.

One by one we crawled into the pitch black interior and, once everyone was seated in a circle, the ceremony began. I had no idea what was about to take place and felt my heart pounding in my chest. It was now early evening, and the sun was growing lower in the sky against the rolling plains of South Dakota.

Crazy Buffalo spoke eloquently and with focused words of wisdom, information, and knowledge. I remember him saying, "This Lodge is our (Lakota) way of healing. Good things can happen in here if we put our minds together." He said, "Physical and mental pains can be cured if we put our minds together. We all have pain in life; pain is a part of living. You can let go of your pain in here. We all suffer in this life. We are here (sitting) on our Mother Earth on our (Lakota) land." He then sang a song in Lakotan, which I found soothing to my apprehensive mental state. I felt nervous as I was the only person who was not of Native blood. Most of the men were pure-blooded Native Americans who resembled the true Native actors in Kevin Costner's movie, *Dances with Wolves*.

The ceremony continued as Crazy Buffalo asked for the heated rocks to be brought into the Lodge. The Fire Keeper used deer antlers as tools and brought in the red-hot rocks, which were then placed into a small pit located in the middle of the Lodge. Finally, a bucket of water containing tree branches (pine boughs) was handed to the medicine man. Crazy Buffalo closed the flap covering the entrance to the Lodge. It was now totally dark. Crazy Buffalo, one of the few Sacred Pipe Carriers of the Sioux Nation, then splashed water onto the rocks four times to formally begin the ceremony. He sang as he splashed the red-hot rocks with water. Steam poured forth from the rocks. It was incredibly hot— hotter than any "sauna" or "steam bath" I had experienced during my life. My heart was pounding very fast and I felt fearful. The hairs in my nose burned. I started sweating profusely. I wanted to leave the Lodge and felt tense throughout my body. I carefully felt the edge of the "tent" to see if I could find a way to escape, as I found it hard to breathe. The veteran seated next to me (cross-legged) passed out and fell onto me unconscious. He let out a moan. At that point, Crazy Buffalo said, "Death is a part of life. If it is your time to die, you will die. If it is not your time to die, you must will to live." I propped up the Sioux warrior and thought, "You must will to live," and wondered if he would die that night. He later regained consciousness, and confessed during the ritual that he had an addiction to drugs. However, as the first of four rounds of the ritual proceeded, I continued to have fears and anxiety, and painful muscle tension, and wondered if I would survive the experience. I remember thinking, "You have to go way inside and find the strength to get through this steam and high heat." My hair was now totally soaked with sweat and I felt pain all over my body. It was at this point, in the total darkness, that Crazy Buffalo said, "If you hold onto your pain and fight it, you will have more pain. You must learn to let go." His voice was calm and soothing, but, at that point, I just wanted relief, a drink of water, and fresh air to breathe. To make matters worse, the first veteran was about to begin the ritual in which each person speaks of their pain and suffering for as long as necessary. Since I knew nothing of the ritual or its "rules" and procedures, I felt uncertain as to what would happen in this traditional purification and healing ritual. But, I clearly recall that the first combat veteran said, "Ah, grandmothers and grandfathers, Vietnam was so hard." He went on to speak of being wounded in battle several times, and how he suffers to this day from bad memories and dreams. As I sat and listened, it seemed like he had spoken for one hour, and I knew that were 11 others to follow. Once again, I wondered if I was going to survive the experience and felt anxious. Finally, the first veteran, in the traditional way, concluded his disclosures about his Vietnam combat experience by saying, "All my relations," which was the cue for the next person to speak.

The heat was overwhelming and seemed to penetrate my body at all levels. However, I began to notice that the more that I would concentrate on the words of others, to focus on their war-related pain and suffering, the less pain I had. At first, this ritual seemed strange. In this sense, it was one of many lessons I would learn about myself, others, and living life with compassion and suffering. Eventually, the first round of the Sweat Lodge came to an end.

Because I had no personal knowledge of the ritual, I thought the ceremony had concluded. I felt relief when Crazy Buffalo called out to the Fire Keeper to open the entrance to the Lodge. As the flap was opened, cool air rushed in and I felt good that I had "made it" through the ritual. Little did I know there were three more rounds to follow. The Fire Keeper replenished the bucket of water and handed it to Crazy Buffalo. I desperately wanted a drink of water and hoped that the bucket would be passed around for all of us to rehydrate our depleted bodies. But, that was not to be. Crazy Buffalo then said, "Every time I open the door to this Lodge, you will see more of what is out there [pointing to the hills of the plains and setting sun] and more of what is in here [spiritual space]." I was struck profoundly by those words, as this wise medicine man had just metaphorically balanced the concept of knowing *external reality* clearly with *spiritual groundedness*. He then said to the Fire Keeper, "24 more stones," signaling the start of the second round. I was in disbelief that we would repeat that which we had just endured. The Lakota warriors entered a new phase and, once again, I wondered if I would survive what was to come.

The Second Round

As the second round began, Crazy Buffalo spoke. "You may see visions in here. You may hear the elders speak to you. It is okay if these things happen. You may hear from dead grandmothers and grandfathers. This is our way. Don't be afraid." I wondered what he meant by visions and hearing ancestral voices and those of the elders. In this setting, it felt perfectly natural, and little did I know that, before the fourth and final round of the Lodge was concluded, I would have "visions" of two different types which Crazy Buffalo asked me about afterwards, when smoking the Sacred Pipe with him. It was at that time that he looked at me directly in the eye and asked whether I saw anything during my Lodge.

I remember at this point thinking of the Sweat Lodge ritual, and how its four rounds, in which more stones were added to the pit in the center of the Lodge, had different functions, such as purification (emotional release), thanksgiving, atonement, and more. During the second round, I continued to perspire profusely, but experienced less bodily tension. I was starting to get a sense of the ritual and its protocol, so to speak. To clarify, there are no discussions or conversations during the ritual. Each person speaks in turn around the *inner circle of the Lodge*. However, the medicine man (or woman) may say words of reflection (e.g., "Life involves pain and suffering," "We can release it if we choose to," etc.). He or she may sing songs to aid in the release of emotions or grief. Further, when a Lodge participant says something of deep personal importance or has a powerful disclosure or cathartic release, he or she may acknowledge that by saying in Lakota, "Ho!" which roughly translates as "that was a good thing and way to go." In the second round, the intensity of the heat inside the Lodge was more powerful than in the first round. By now, I was dehydrated and the sweating began to diminish and then, eventually, stop, as if I were "baked" dry. My physical tension reduced and my heart stopped pounding so quickly and completely slowed down. I noticed my body begin-ning to feel "light" in weight and my ability to concentrate on the painful stories of the participants seemed to sharpen in focus. I noticed, as I let myself listen freely without "clinical or psychological mindfulness," that I had more energy and an increasing sense of well-being. My state of fear, panic and anxiety in the first round was seemingly being transformed as the ritual unfolded. I did not understand it at that time. While initially reticent to disclose my personal concerns in the first round, I suddenly felt more com-fortable in sharing my stories of a painful nature without fear of judgment in the solem-nity of the Lodge and its darkness. I spoke of my sadness about my friends who commit-ted suicide when they could not put the horrors of Vietnam to rest. By the time the sec-ond round ended, I felt a sense of serenity and calmness emerging, and wondered how this was occurring. Once again, the flap was opened at the end of the second round. By now, the sun was about to set—an orange ball sitting on top of a distant knoll of South Dakota, descending over the Earth's surface. Crazy Buffalo requested more hot stones for the ceremonial fire as we all sat inside the Lodge, quiet and reflective with red faces and skin from the intense heat. I noticed that the men's eyes were clear and that their faces looked healthy and clean. The steam had done its job inside and out—the body was purged from emotional toxins and post-traumatic pains. There was now present in the Lodge an unspoken feeling of acceptance and understanding—one common to combat veterans after battle. Only, this time the battle was spiritual in nature—to become whole in oneself again.

The Third Round

The ritual continued with the third round—more hot stones, water for the bucket with pine boughs and incantations from Crazy Buffalo. Strangely, I now looked forward to having more heat and steam in the Lodge. How could this be? After all, I had fear and trepidation during the first two rounds and had hoped by the painful conclusion of the first round of the Lakota Warrior Sweat that the entire ceremony had ended. Now, as I sat looking outside at the Sacred Pipe on the altar and the setting sun, this was a place of healing and unique in nature. It was, and still is, a transcendent moment. I hoped that Crazy Buffalo would sing more songs in Lakota and talk to us at the start of the third round. He did; he disclosed parts of his history and struggles in life, including a near death experience from illness. He maintained a sense of presence that was reverent, calm, and peaceful. He had wisdom and insight about alcoholism, emotional trauma, and suffering. He had a gift: the ability to share psychologically profound insights in just a few words. In my life, very few people have such a gift, but when they do, they all have "healing" as a quality of character.

As the third round began, I felt physically light in my entire body—as if I had lost 30 pounds of weight. My body seemed buoyant, supple, flexible, and loose—like that of a yogi master. As the steam emerged from the hot rocks, I breathed it into my face and nose, using my hands to pull it towards me, welcoming it as a friend. "How strange," I thought, since this same steam burned me and scared me into a state of semi-panic dur-ing the first round. Now, I embraced it and enjoyed the warm sensation it provided my body, like a soft, pure cotton, silky blanket of comfort. My skin was totally dry and my hair was starting to dry out as the sweating had stopped. I thought, "I have gone from one state of being to another during this ritual. How is this happening?" It seemed weird, magical, and wonderful at the same time.

The third round seemed to pass very quickly, the total opposite of the first round. Time had altered, as did my perceptions of space and that of my body itself. At some moment, I realized in the most playful and joyous way that I was in an altered state of consciousness (ASC). I felt happy, euphoric and did not want the third round to end. Moreover, listening to the stories of the participants, I began to visualize what they were saying in three-dimensional color, almost as if I had been there at the time when the events unfolded. There was a remarkable clarity of connection to everyone, one in which I walked along with them on their life's journey. It was a psychic virtual reality. At this point in time, I did not want the Lodge experience to end. But, to test my new sense of awareness and consciousness, I moved my right hand in front of my face in the blackness of the Lodge and tried to reach it with my left hand. I could not find my right hand. I remember smiling at this sense of altered kinesthetic experience. Then, the third round ended, the door to the Lodge opened and the sun was gone. It occurred to me, at that moment, that Crazy Buffalo had chosen the time for the Lodge to begin as when the sun was casting its rays into the opening of the Lodge and now, as the fourth round was to begin, the South Dakota plains were dark and the moon was rising. How wonderful, I thought, these mythic themes. Lightness versus darkness; birth versus death; pain and transformation; individual and collective healing in a common earthy space of a long evolved tradition of healing. Where could it go from here?

The Fourth Round

The fourth, and final round, seemed to disappear in a few minutes. By now, I was fully enjoying the altered state of consciousness (ASC). We continued the ritual with individual self-disclosures related to Vietnam War experiences and their effects on our lives. Then, unexpected and strange things began to happen to me (and maybe others, but I did not inquire). I had two different sets of powerful visual experiences. In the first set of experiences, I saw white lights of small balls of energy shooting across the top of the interior of the Lodge. There were at least four or more of these "ghost-like" energy balls flying around the Lodge. I was not frightened by them, and several times tried to touch them. My sense of them was that they were not physical objects but spiritual states of consciousness emanating from the members of the Lodge. In the second vision, which I have never shared with anyone before writing this chapter, I saw a large Lakota Sioux Chief dressed in a full headdress, breast plates, and formal traditional clothing who came to me and said, "John, it is your mission in life to continue what you have started and are doing. You will have a long and hard journey but it is your calling to do this. You were called to this Lodge by us!" He then disappeared, and I felt a sense of relief and renewal. Soon, the final round ended. We all exited the Lodge and stood up in the cool clear air of the night. I felt cleansed, serene and with a peaceful mind.

Afterwards

After moving outside in the star-filled night, Crazy Buffalo shared the Sacred Pipe with us, one by one. When it was my turn, he handed the long pipe to me, packed tobacco into its bowl, and lit it, and I drew the smoke into my mouth. It tasted soft and fragrantly light. As I inhaled the smell of the "sweet grass" and tobacco, Crazy Buffalo looked me in the eye and asked me, "How was your Lodge? Did you see things?" I felt a sense of trust and unity at that moment and told him of my visions in the fourth round. I continued smoking for a short while and said little more. When I was done, I gratefully handed him the beautiful, hand-carved Sacred Pipe. I asked him what the visions meant. He looked me in the eye with a strong, powerful sense, and said, softly and calmly, "You are a medicine man." He then turned and left, restoring the Pipe, eagle wing, and sacred artifacts in his tote bag. I watched him walk away, and thought what a beautiful, holy, man it is who wears Levi jeans and simple clothes.

I returned to my hotel room after the Sweat Lodge. I had an incredible sense of serenity. I could not sleep. I tried watching television but it just seemed noisy, so I made notes about the Sweat Lodge. I did not know it, but there was a whole lot more to be revealed and taught to me by Native American medicine men over the next decade. When I left the powwow, I went to the elders to thank them for inviting me to the event. The truth was that I was not invited and that I just made my own arrangements to attend, as I had learned of the event from friends in the Pacific Northwest who were interested in traditional healing practices. I shook hands with the four ruddy-faced elders, thanking them for my experiences. They stoically looked me in the eye and said, "You were not invited. You were called to be here." I looked at each of them, and felt a tingle in my spine; a moment of life-changing experience, one that did alter my life forever. However, these few days in South Dakota on the Sioux reservation were a prelude of what was to come next.

But, before I left the powwow, I was to learn of the Red Feather Ceremony.

The Red Feather Ceremony

The Red Feather Ceremony honors "warriors" (veterans) who have made sacrifices for their country and tribal community. The Red Feather Society is a prestigious Sioux society, among many. The "Red Feather" takes its name from the ritual itself, during which inductees are given a sacred eagle feather with "red" blood from the society members. The nominee is selected for membership by the society. During the communal ritual, the veteran selected has his record of valor and service acclaimed before the group in stadium-like powwow grounds. Then, those selected for membership are eventually recognized by other members of the Red Feather Society, who draw their blood upon the sacred eagle feather, which is later given to the inductee.

Following the grand, collective honoring of the inductees, who have been free of alcohol and substance abuse for at least two years, there is a Sweat Lodge ritual during which the medicine man affirms their commitment to abstinence and then makes a task for the inductee, which in this instance was to "take care of, and look after" elder members of the tribal community. So, once officially accepted into the Red Feather Society, the combat veteran gained a new sense of respect and status within the community. In this case, he was a sober Native American combat veteran who was taking care of others, especially the elderly tribal folks. In return, he had unique honored respect and status amongst his peers, family, and community. As long as he maintained his status as a Red Feather, the community, in turn, would take care of him and his family. In this regard, the wounded became the *generative healers*. The wounded became *wise men and the teachers of the children to follow in the community*. Life had come full circle. The wounded veteran achieved a new home and meaning in life; from disabled and addicted to the most empowered, generative, social member in the community.

Orcas, Salmon and the Olympic National Park Mountains

After the 1985 powwow in South Dakota, I was invited one month later to another four-day gathering for Vietnam War veterans at the Howling Dog Ceremony in Port Angeles, Washington, located in the Pacific Northwest across from Victoria, British Columbia. This ceremony was being conducted by a mental health counselor who worked closely with traditional medicine men from tribes located in the Northwest USA and Canada. It was there that I met Andy Callicum, a medicine man and Chief of the Mawachet Tribe from Vancouver Island, Canada. The mental health counselor, Bruce Webster, was a personal friend whom I had met previously while doing consulting and training for professionals working with the Department of Veterans Affairs for the State of Washington in Olympia. Bruce lived on a beautiful property located on the oceanfront in Port Angeles (i.e., the Straits of Juan Defuca). From the beachfront, one could see killer whales and, in the distance, Victoria Island, Canada. Bruce told me about Sweat Lodges and other ritual ceremonies being employed at that time to assist Vietnam War veterans suffering from PTSD and related problems. So, after the profound personal experience in South Dakota, I was curious to see and learn more of culture-specific rituals and practices that may help individuals (war veterans, in particular) suffering from psychic trauma.

The four-day Howling Dog ceremony began with a sunrise Sweat Lodge which was constructed on the oceanfront just 10 meters or less from the surf water. The Lodge was similar to the one in South Dakota, but different in the sense that the winds blew inland off the Strait of Juan Defuca, bringing the smells of sea salt, fish, and kelp, and the richness of the waters teeming with salmon, trout, halibut, octopus, and crabs, which were mixed with perfumed smells of cedar and spruce trees; the essence of the Pacific Northwest.

On the first day, everyone gathered at the ocean front before sunrise. The Fire Keeper had prepared the stones for the sunrise Sweat Lodge and the Vietnam War veterans anxiously awaited the arrival of the medicine man, Andy Callicum. Soon, as the first light of dawn emerged over the large spruce and fir trees, someone said, "Here comes Andy." I looked up at the path leading to the beach and saw a short, black-haired man in a Levi jacket and jeans walking towards the Lodge. A veteran familiar with Andy said, "Watch, his bald eagle will soon fly over him." I was skeptical, and said to myself, "If an eagle does come by, it will be random chance."

Andy continued walking and, as he got closer to the beachfront Sweat Lodge, a magnificent bald eagle swooped down out of the mountains of the Olympic National Forest and flew over his left shoulder and over the Lodge itself. I thought, "Well, that was interesting, I wonder how many times that has occurred." [To "fast forward" the story, over the next decade, I had many encounters and experiences with Andy, and every time he came to do healing work, the bald eagle was present and flew over him before making a return flight to the wilderness of the Olympic National Forest. In a personal and professional sense, I stopped my scientific, Western, rational, deductive logic after that and just accepted what I had witnessed. Over the decades, I had the opportunity to learn from Andy and he took me "under his wing" and taught me a great deal about traditional Native American healing, but from a different cultural tradition to that of the Lakota Sioux of the American Midwest and plains states.]

During the first sunrise sweat in Port Angeles in 1985, Andy sang many songs from his tribal past and wisdom. He had a beautiful voice, which he could modulate in brilliant ways to elicit sadness, grief, or happiness. He sometimes would start a Sweat Lodge with a song that elicited crying and grief from all of us in the Lodge. His singing seemed to reach everyone in a powerful way and there was usually a purging of emotions. The strangest thing for me was that, time and time again, I found myself singing with him and knowing the Native American words (his) to songs, without any prior knowledge or information of his Native tribe or people. It just came naturally, and seemed good. Later, after many years, I directly asked him about this seemingly odd ability or occurrence, and he just laughed and said that one day he would explain it to me, but that I asked dumb questions for a "bright guy." I was puzzled at the time and later we had more serious talks and he explained to me what Crazy Buffalo had told me in South Dakota, and more. It was weird and wonderful and, among many other things, Andy taught me how to connect to life itself in every form from salmon to trees to fire-circles and orcas. I felt that I went from dancing with wolves to whales!

I returned almost every year to Port Angeles to be with Bruce and Andy. During that time, I was taught more about Sweat Lodges and other ritualistic forms of healing. For example, Andy once took me to the Elwah River to select stones for the Sweat Lodge ritual. He explained that it was important to find the proper stones for the Sweat Lodge, because selection of the wrong ones could result in an explosion in the heat of the Lodge or a ceremonial fire. I asked, "How do you know which ones to select?" He answered by pointing his fingers at certain rocks in the crystal clear river bed and said, "They will talk to you, John, but you must learn to listen carefully." On that day we gathered stones and took them back to the Sweat Lodge for introduction into the sacred fire. As we walked and talked together, Andy taught me that there were many uses and purposes of the Sweat Lodge: healing, purification, marriage, socializing, "power sweats" for major life decisions, peyote sweats and more. Over the years of our connection and friendship, I experienced all of these and more, as Andy shared his personal knowledge of native healing. To this day, I am eternally grateful to this gifted and beautiful man.

The Talking Circle Ritual

Among the many rituals to which Andy introduced me was the "Talking Circle," which could occur before or after a Sweat Lodge or other rituals. In the "Talking Circle," the participants of the Howling Dog Ceremony (1985) gathered around an open, outdoor fire. The beachfront grounds at Bruce Webster's property had a special site, near the ocean, in which there was a circle of harvested-cut logs on which to sit. In the middle was a large space for a log fire which was kept alive from early morning to after midnight with a steady supply of seasoned hardwood which gave off a wonderful woodsy smell in the breeze blowing inland from the ocean. It was an inviting place to sit, be with others and take in the beautiful environment.

The ritual of the "Talking Circle" is a most powerful one. Andy showed me the process. First, as a medicine man, he stood up at the six o'clock position in the circle and spoke to everyone gathered together in the circle. He spoke of the importance of honesty, friendship, and love. He spoke of the need for self-revelation and care for one another. Then, he moved to his left in a clockwise fashion and greeted those present, one at a time. As the participants were standing, he turned to face an individual participant, shook and held his hand, looked him in the eyes and spoke about his perceptions and feelings for the participant as a person. Then, one by one, he completed the circle, moving patiently from person to person. Once he returned to his original place, the next person was instructed to repeat the process.

As I sat to his left (seven o'clock), I next did the same set of actions, greeting the participants and expressing my feelings and perceptions with them. At first, it was difficult and anxiety-provoking, since this is an intimate collective experience by all who witness each individual encounter. However, as I progressed around the circle, the warm fire and ocean air, it became easier and much more comfortable. Eventually, I returned to my "seat" on the log and the next person got up and repeated the process. In this way, then, the "Talking Circle" meant that every person encountered each other at least twice. *It created deep connections of bonding and openness in a short period of time.* Once the entire circle was completed, we sat around the fire to continue talking with one another.

The process is informal after everyone has completed the circle of mutual greetings. It was not unusual for this "Talking Circle" to last for two hours or more. While there are a whole host of insights I could share about this ritual, among the most central and poignant is that persons suffering from psychic trauma could break through their isolation, detachment, avoidance, and defensiveness and embrace others with limited degrees of fear of shame, guilt, or rejection. Simply said, it was a freeing moment and experience.

Beyond Traditional Native American and Other Cultural Rituals

My work with Andy Callicum, Bruce Webster and other medicine men and women led to innovations in developing new rituals for Vietnam veterans, some of which were derivations of traditional Native American rituals. Andy was supportive of these efforts and I was cautious to solicit his opinions and criticisms as to their potential usefulness and value.

In particular, Bruce and I created an intensive experimental treatment program during September 1985 (we called it "The Intensive"). The program combined many modalities of treatment during the week-long experience. There were group therapy sessions, one-to-one counseling, Sweat Lodges daily, special crafted rituals, early and late involvement of spouses and family, physical exercise programs, responsibility for cooking meals and cleaning and other activities. It lasted from 6 am to midnight or longer. We already knew that most Vietnam combat veterans were alienated and did not trust the U.S. government programs for mental health treatment in VA hospitals.[1] We designed the program as multimodal in nature, in a wilderness area with geographical features similar to Vietnam in appearance, density, complexity, and "feeling"—the woods, trees, jungle, wildness.

We believed that the men would be more comfortable in this setting, being with other combat veterans. We designed a matched set of groups, randomly selected from Bruce's client roster of over 200, who were assigned to either the treatment or control group. There was pre- and post-testing on psychological questionnaires for PTSD and psychiatric symptoms, as well as other psychosocial measures (e.g., marital conflict, issues of intimacy, etc.) at three month intervals for one year. The results found significant and lasting positive changes for the treatment group on nearly all of the measures. Interestingly, however, we did not find changes in capacity for intimacy with spouses or partners (Wilson, 1989).

The Ritual Homecoming Welcome and Warrior Feast

The first of our ceremonies involved the ritual homecoming on the first day of the program. Once everyone was registered, the clients and veteran volunteer staff members were divided into two "squads" or "quasi-military groups." The clients wore an orange armband and the counselors had a blue one. The men were taken in two pickup trucks to opposite locations in the wilderness about two miles from the Camp David resort on Lake Crescent. Once there, they were instructed to walk back to the camp as a "military squad" in single file. The purpose of this event was to symbolically recreate the homecoming from Vietnam, i.e., to "rotate" home one by one just as they did years before, after their tour of duty had ended.

At the entrance to the campsite, along the sloping and descending dirt road with small stones and pine boughs that led to the main Lodge, were stationed the family, friends, and other staff members who waited in a long line to greet the men. We believed it was important to have them present in order to provide an authentic welcome and homecoming ceremony of appreciation for their service in Vietnam. We also thought that a symbolic reenactment of walking "back home," one by one, to an extended family group was an important beginning to the week-long treatment program. So, as the veterans came into the camp, the children would run out to greet their "daddy" and a sentry shouted out (at our instruction) that the veteran was home from Vietnam (e.g., "Hey, Mom, Bill is home from the war"). Then, each person who was lined up on the sloping dirt road greeted the veteran with a handshake and a hug and said, "Welcome home—thanks for serving. I am proud of you."

After the last individual had returned, a Warriors' Feast was held in the main Lodge. The men sat around a long rectangular table and were served smoked salmon, nuts, fruits, and other native foods of the Pacific Northwest. They were surprisingly solemn as they ate. The men were encircled by their loved ones, families, and friends who later joined them in a communal dinner which honored their sacrifices in the war. We instructed the family members to surround the communal dinner table as a way of embracing the loved ones suffering war trauma and, when invited, to sit and eat with the one they loved and cared about.

The Ritual of the Ceremonial Fire

On the last day of treatment, the families and significant others returned to the camp in the afternoon to rejoin the men and participate in a Ceremonial Fire. In this ritual, everyone gathered around the fire in a circle. Then one by one, in a clockwise order, each person walked up to the fire and "released" into it an object, actual or symbolic, of something negative and painful that they wished to "let go" from their life. For example, several veterans put their soft "bush" hats from Vietnam into the fire as a symbolic act of "letting go" of war trauma. After the ceremonial fire, a special Sweat Lodge was conducted for the women. While this was in progress, the men prepared a meal to serve to their wives, children, and significant others. The dinner concluded with a traditional pot latch during which gifts were provided for the staff and participants in the program. Finally, a "Talking Circle" was conducted. Everyone sat around a big log fire to continue conversation and dialogue about the week's activities.

The Ritual of Release and Transformation

Another ritual technique adapted for our program involved the planting of two fir trees at the conclusion of the session which addressed the issues of guilt, rage, anger, hatred, sorrow, grief, killing, and destruction, as related to the Vietnam experience. Each individual was given two fir saplings and instructed to find a special place to plant them. It was explained that, among some Native American groups, it is believed that Mother Earth receives that which is given to her in a spirit of harmony, balance, love, and the cycle of the seasons. Thus, by planting the trees, one could ask Mother Earth to receive them and, in the process, take away pain, despair, sadness, hatred, and other negative emotions. It was said that, in return, she would nurture the young trees and help them to grow in their natural way. Alone, and at the place he had chosen, each person was instructed to put his mental focus on the part of his body where he felt tension, pain, or negative feelings. He then placed that part of his body over a hole he dug with his hands and released the negative energy into the earth. The task that followed was to plant the tree and let Mother Earth transmute the negative emotion into an object of growing beauty. Thus, a "negative" was replaced by a "positive" to complete a cycle which had as its image the act of "receiving" by "letting go." By letting go of the negative emotion, the cycle of adaptation can become balanced again by a positive change (the growth of the tree = self) which emanates from nurturing of Mother Earth, the maternal symbol that gives freely what one needs "to get" to restore psychological and physical equilibrium.

The Salmon Feast of Thanksgiving

A salmon Feast of Thanksgiving was held early in the week. A gift of fresh king salmon (from local waters) was donated to the group and provided the basis to celebrate in a meal of thanksgiving for "all that is good in life," with the fish that is regarded as sacred to many of the native tribes of the Pacific Northwest. There was an abundance of freshly baked salmon, special sauces and vegetables and each participant was asked to fill himself with this special meal and to recognize that life contains many good things to be appreciated and shared with others.

The Mail Call Ritual

The mail call ritual involved a surprise, unexpected delivery of letters to the men each night after dinner. It was prearranged so that every veteran received a letter a day from a friend or family member during the stay at Camp David. The letters were written to encourage the men to continue their efforts to work through their stress disorder and other problems that brought them to the treatment program.

The "Unfinished Business" Ritual

Towards the end of the week, each participant was given two stamped envelopes and stationery in order to write letters to two persons, living or dead, with whom they had "unfinished business." Afterward, the letters were mailed, if the individual wished to have them sent. The purpose of this ritual was to attempt to bring closure or resolution to a previous and conflicted relationship with someone important in the veteran's life.

The Morning Ritual of Rebirth

Since all of the participants suffered from PTSD and allied conditions (e.g., anger, depression) we wanted to start each day with physical exercise. A participant was selected by his fellow combat veterans to awaken everyone at 6 am in order to go to the deep glacial lakefront. The person selected as morning attendant was the most senior participant, who had served longest in Vietnam in an elite Special Operation Forces unit (U.S. Navy Seals). Once the men were awakened and formed into a "unit," they walked to the lakefront, where Bruce and I greeted them. Then, with us acting as their "commanding military officers," we ordered them into the very cold (65°F) water for a wake-up plunge and swim. Our goal was threefold: (1) decrease PTSD-related hyperarousal; (2) stimulate good appetites; and (3) increase alertness and clarity of mind. As a part of this ritual, Bruce and I alternated diving into the cold water to "lead" the men and swim with them.

The Desensitization Ritual

Since Vietnam War veterans suffering from PTSD are chronically hyperaroused and extraordinarily sensitive to trauma-specific stimuli, we designed a desensitization ritual conducted in a group setting. The setting was a small but warm and cozy cabin located on the edge of Lake Crescent; it was like a Ralph Lauren advertisement. It was remote and isolated from the main Lodge and had a large open main room with a beautiful, rustic stone fireplace. It was here that we had planned a complex procedure that involved all of the volunteer counselors and the U.S. Park Ranger in charge of this area of the Olympic National Park. The men were gathered in the cabin and seated facing the large wood-burning fireplace that warmed the room. The topic of the "group" session was understanding hyperarousal and hypervigilance as a part of PTSD. The men were asked to talk about what "set them off" and how it related to their war experiences. During this two-hour session, certain items were distributed that were designed to elicit hyperarousal, including JP-4 helicopter fuel soaked into cotton towels, strings of M-60 bullets, empty shells from AK-47 and M-16 automatic rifles, a Vietcong flag and U.S. Army uniforms, etc. While the items were being distributed and passed around, Bruce Webster stood in front of me juggling a grenade in his hands, tossing it up in the air and catching it. Although the grenade was inert, it had a "firing pin" and the men did not know the weapon was not explosive.

In the next phase of this ritual, mental health counselors were situated outside the cabin near the doors and windows. We had placed strings of different strength firecrackers around the cabin and towards the end of the first hour they were detonated to simulate machine gun and mortar fire. Also, a U.S. National Park Ranger cooperated by wearing a black shirt and pants and an Asian sampan straw hat, similar to the Vietcong enemy in Vietnam, and he rode a motorbike, with a bell, in front of the window of the cabin, ringing the bell as he did so. This set of stimuli was designed to further create hypervigilance. Then, at the set time, I detonated the firecrackers, Bruce dropped the grenade and a loud set of combat-like noise filled the air.

As we expected, all of the men reacted instantly with exaggerated startle response and either ran out of the cabin or fell to the floor to cover and protect themselves. Upon reaction, each participant was greeted by a counselor and for hours afterwards talked about their PTSD-related hypervigilance and hyperarousal. At the end of the session, a Sweat Lodge was held with a specific focus of "what happened in Vietnam." The ritual was clinically successful and facilitated recognition of cues for hyperarousal but also helped the men identify more positive coping patterns. The Sweat Lodge "sealed the deal!" Everyone went to bed early that night.

The Graduation Ceremony

On the last day a graduation ceremony was held. Each man received a specially designed diploma from a local artist which displayed an eagle-like jet aircraft (the Vietnam Freedom Bird) emerging from Lake Crescent and the cedar forests that surround it. After all the diplomas were distributed, a final group session was held, at which time expressions of appreciation and gratitude were exchanged.

Lessons from Native Pathways

My experiences from work with Native Americans and others have taught me about the archetypes for healing and recovery from psychic trauma, grief, and human suffering.

- There are wounded victims and wounded healers, as Carl Jung (1963) informed us many years ago. Wounded victims can inform wounded healers in profound ways as to the pathways of healing.
- Wounded victims have as much to teach as their primary doctors, treaters, therapists, shamans, medicine healers, and rehabilitation specialists.
- Western (American/Western European) traditional approaches and methods for helping psychically traumatized persons have limits and constraints.
- One-to-one psychotherapy is *not* the only way to have intensive and curative therapeutic processes for distressed and traumatized persons.
- Throughout the millennia, each culture has evolved mechanisms, culture-specific rituals, and other ways to assist victims of abuse, trauma, violence, and war.
- Ethnocentrically-based approaches to trauma, abuse, and disaster are limited by their own assumptions and experiences with coping with trauma. How could Western psychotherapists understand the elegance and brilliance of Native American rituals for recovery from trauma, if they do not understand the cosmology,

traditional ethnicity of indigenous peoples and their cultural traumatization by colonial powers and political domination? Many similar analogies exist today in Angola, Cambodia, Sudan, the Balkans and other areas of ethnic and national conflict.

So, the question emerges as to what culturally specific techniques, rituals, and practices are utilitarian for these people? In this regard, the Native American tribes evolved their own distinct rituals for restoring members of their community to wellness and health. Indeed, they developed elaborate and complex ritualistic practices that were not "medical treatments" but part of a way of living to maintain healthy harmony and consistency of "ideology" and religious cosmology in the tribal community. In short, they found ways to facilitate helping people: what works best for whom in our cultural traditions?

War Veterans and Psychic Trauma: Are There Universal and Trans-Cultural Cures?

At present, despite enormous scientific and critical psychobiological research (Wilson, Friedman, & Lindy, 2004), there is no "magic bullet" for the intrapsychic journey of healing PTSD and allied mental states. However, are cross-cultural healing rituals applicable to facilitating the recovery process from disruptive PTSD and related psychiatric processes at this time? The answer is a complicated "yes" and "no," positive and negative.

The Positive Polarity

In an over-simplified sense, the positive polarity is as follows:

- PTSD and allied conditions are universal psychobiological states. Rituals and "treatment" procedures that reduce hyperarousal and facilitate psychological reframing and integration of traumatic memories will be effective in "retuning" organismic states of allostatic dysregulation (Wilson & Thomas, 2004). Allostatic changes in physiological functioning means, in the simplest way, that things do not return to normal (pre-trauma baseline) after trauma. The post-traumatic body does, and should, adapt to a new level of functioning.
- Culture-specific rituals (e.g., the Native American Sweat Ritual) contain *archetypal* psychobiological processes for organismic healing that are universal and can be found in many cultures of the world. For example, the use of extreme heat in the Native American Sweat Lodge has many variants throughout the world (e.g., Scandinavian sauna, Russian "hot bath houses" and similar procedures in South American indigenous tribes.) The nature of universal archetypal patterns of healing is that, throughout evolution, we have found or invented procedures to help those suffering from trauma. The psychobiological quality of these healing rituals often involves multisensory and biological aspects and, therefore, psychobiological processes. There are many cultures in the world that have utilized these techniques and procedures which include extreme heat or cold isolation self-flagellation, sensory deprivation, severe geographical isolation and much more. The ritualistic procedures intrinsically recognize the necessity to create culture-specific and validated

experiences to return the individual to healthy functioning. Wolfgang Jilek (1982) described such rituals and procedures in his writings for Native tribes in the Pacific Northwest of Canada. Further examples can be found in other countries and cultures (Wilson, 1989; Wilson & Tang, 2007).

• Among the many possible personal experiences in non-traditional rituals is that survivors/victims can experience themselves in new ways. Simply said, this means that both physically and psychologically they feel free, whole, integrated, and at one with themselves for the first time since the traumatic event. The ritual, of whatever creative cultural source, releases their inner spirit to once again grow and be stronger. At the end of the ritual or ceremony, the survivor experiences a "new soul" and inner being of wellness in life, often as a gift from God in a divine moment of life itself.

• The positive experience of non-traditional forms of healing and recovery, such as the Sweat Lodge, may be a gateway for veterans or others to explore new and unconventional approaches to treatment. Some examples would include massage therapy, acupuncture, herbal tea remedies, spiritual retreats in Buddhist monasteries or other spiritual retreats, ecological excursions to beautiful areas of the world and sensual encounters of a life-restoring beauty.

An illustration of the positive polarity occurred from 1985 to 1992, while Ray Scurfield was Director of the Post-Traumatic Stress Treatment Program (PTSTP) at the American Lake VA in Tacoma, WA. PTSTP staff conducted extensive outreach to reservations in Washington, Oregon, and Idaho and aspects of Native American warrior healing were integrated into the PTSTP. These included: hiring a Native American healer from the Nisqually Reservation as a consultant to provide adjunct treatment to any interested Native American veteran patients; having PTSTP veterans construct a Sweat Lodge on the hospital grounds that was used by PTSTP participants interested in such; incorporating the "Talking Stick" in some group therapy meetings to facilitate sharing; admitting a treatment cohort consisting entirely of Native American veterans and a second cohort consisting of 50 percent Native American veterans; and supporting patients to participate in powwows at several surrounding reservations (Scurfield, 1996, 2004).

The Negative Polarity

The negative polarity includes the following:

• In my professional experience, not all war veterans benefit or relate to non-traditional forms of healing rituals. This is the case even for some Native American veterans. For example, at the American Lake VA PTS Treatment Program, Ray Scurfield and staff found that a number of urban Native Americans, who had not maintained tribal and reservation ties, were much less open to participating in traditional rituals and ceremonies in contrast to more traditionally-oriented Native Americans and those residing on various reservations; and there were a number of non-Native veterans who found the traditional approaches very appealing and powerful, whereas others did not (Scurfield, 1996, 2004).

- Native American Sweat Lodge ceremonies are sometimes threatening to war veterans and others with PTSD-psychic trauma, especially if the medicine man or woman is not a bona fide and traditionally-trained person.
- Some Native American or culturally-adapted rituals create opportunities that may be experienced as "threatening" or dangerous due to opportunities for "openness" and "self-disclosures" of personal experiences.
- Persons of a non-specific cultural orientation may find the culture-specific healing ritual to be "out of bounds" by their own normative standards, which typically generate anxiety and avoidance behavioral patterns.

Closing

The legacy of war trauma to the human psyche is inestimable. Until modern times, with contemporary (twentieth-century) medicine and the slow acceptance of psychiatric and psychoanalytic insights and scientific findings, the reality of the complexity of psychic traumatization, especially for war veterans, has been an "underground" reality for them but not their family and loved ones. However, we now live in an era where the daily human consequences of prolonged war exposure cannot be avoided, denied, or relegated to a Congressional political closet. The wars of the past have finally come home in the beginning of the twenty-first century.

As our society has been developing "new" methodologies of treatment to attempt to facilitate healing among current-day veterans, there has been a curious and, indeed, inexplicable avoidance of understanding and appreciating the warrior healing rituals and ceremonies that have been in existence for hundreds, if not thousands, of years among American warrior tribes, and in numerous cultures. As we move on with many efforts to develop the "new," we would be wise to much more carefully study and learn from the wealth of experience and wisdom of our Native American warrior tribes and other traditional cultures. We do not need to reinvent the wheel and the circle to better help our modern day warriors heal from their war experiences and reintegration challenges. We need to look back and rediscover the wisdom that has been known for centuries—wisdom that, indeed, just might be the gateway to evolving the most impactful and effective approaches to healing for our nation's warriors.

So, where do we go from here?

Note

1   A notable exception was the American Lake VA PTS Treatment Program, established and directed by Ray Scurfield (1985–92). This was a program that consistently had a waiting list *of over 150* veterans seeking admission. Ray also made regular outreach contacts with veterans living on the Olympic Peninsula, and collaborated with Bruce Webster.

References

Jilek, W. (1982). *Indian Healing: Shamanic Ceremonialism in the Pacific Northwest Today*. Surrey, British Columbia, Canada: Hancock House.
Jung, C. G. (1963). *Memories, Dreams and Reflections*. New York: Vintage Books.

Moodley, R., & West, W. (2005). *Integrating Traditional Healing Practice into Counseling and Psychotherapy.* Thousand Oaks, CA: Sage Publications.

Scurfield, R. M. (1996). "Healing the Warrior: Admission of Two American Indian War-Veteran cohort Groups to a Specialized In-Patient PTSD unit." *American Indian and Alaska Native Mental Health Research: The Journal of the National Center, 6* (3): 1–22.

Scurfield, R. M. (2004). American Indian Healing Rituals. In *Vietnam Trilogy: Veterans and Post-Traumatic Stress, 1968, 1989 & 2000* (104–6). New York, NY: Algora Publishing.

Scurfield, R. M. (2006). *Healing Journeys: Study Abroad with Vietnam Veterans.* New York, NY: Algora Publishing.

Wilson, J. P. (1989). *Trauma, Transformation and Healing: An Integrative Approach to Theory, Research, and Post-Traumatic Therapy.* New York, NY: Brunner/Mazel.

Wilson, J. P. (2006). "Culture, Trauma and the Treatment of Posttraumatic Syndromes in a Global Context." *Asian Journal of Counseling, 13* (1): 107–144.

Wilson, J. P., Friedman, M. F., & Lindy, J. (2004). *Treating Psychological Trauma and PTSD* (2nd Edn). New York, NY: Guilford Press.

Wilson J. P., & Lindy, J. D. (2012, unpublished manuscript in preparation). *Personality Processes and Post-Traumatic Stress Disorder (PTSD).*

Wilson, J. P., & Thomas, R. (2004). *Empathy in the Treatment of Trauma and PTSD.* New York, NY: Brunner/Routledge.

Wilson, J. P., & Tang, C. (2007). *Cross-Cultural Assessment of Psychological Trauma and PTSD.* New York: Springer.

5   The Journey Home, Quilt, and Pillow Pal Ceremonies

A Gift of Love

Sherrill Valdes

An IED (improvised explosive device) exploded in Baghdad when it struck a car. School children were walking by . . . I ran and picked up a little girl and carried her to the ambulance . . . She died . . . blood was on my uniform. I still wear it to remember her. My wife had a baby girl . . . I love her but I cannot hold her.

(Sergeant, US Army)

I survived by embracing death . . . I knew I was not coming home.

(Sergeant, US Army)

There are many significant challenges that face military personnel returning from deployment following discharge from active duty. This chapter describes the range of reintegration challenges that face the service member, the family, and community, and provides an understanding of how such challenges impact the transition from deployment and military culture to civilian life. Distinctive readjustment issues facing the National Guard and Reserve components are highlighted. The primary emphasis is on the role of ceremonies to assist in the transition from deployment. Relevant to the Native American rituals and ceremonies described by Wilson (this volume), this chapter describes modern day innovative and powerful healing activities that address reintegration into the community: the Journey Home, Quilt, and Pillow Pal ceremonies. The key elements of each ceremony are described, as well as the beneficial impact upon the participants. Finally, the role that Vietnam veterans provide with returning Operation Enduring Freedom/Operation Iraqi Freedom (OEF/OIF) veterans is highlighted.

Background

American military forces, including National Guard and Reserve components (representing all branches of the military), have been quietly serving in combat longer than almost all service personnel in the nation's history. Statistics indicate that approximately 1.64 million U.S. troops have been deployed in support of Operations Enduring Freedom, Iraqi Freedom, and New Dawn (Iraq) (Tanielian & Jaycox, 2008). Approximately 30 percent of the military personnel deployed during OEF/OIF are comprised of Reserve component members who were deployed directly from their communities (Castaneda, et al., 2008). Many Guard and Reserve members have endured multiple combat deployments. To promote a smooth transition home, it is imperative to identify the needs of the military personnel and their families, as well as appropriate resources within their communities. Military personnel return home as changed individuals, although most have been eager to adjust to their family lives, their neighborhoods, and their communities. In 2003, when it was first learned that there would be OEF/OIF National Guard and Reservists returning from wartime deployments to their respective communities, there was substantial concern about the readjustment process.

Unfortunately, Reservists and their families typically do not have access to the formal structure that is offered to Active Duty service members who reside on various military installations. The military base community gives rise to a culture that "we are all in it together." Service members and their families embrace the culture of military installations, which provide emotional support within the military community. They both must ready themselves for any number of deployments and the accompanying long-standing separations. For Active Duty components, base or post housing, healthcare, post exchanges, commissaries, schools, and a host of resources may be available. This is not the case for the Reserve and National Guard components; only if families are located within a reasonable driving distance of military installations may some of these amenities be available to them, with the exception of housing.

Although some deployed men and women who have returned from deployment have successfully adjusted to their lives outside the wartime theater, others cope with a multitude of internal and external stressors. For many, the challenge of wartime service may have been rewarding, maturing, and growth-promoting. However, it is an indisputable reality that all military personnel have been impacted by their wartime experiences and changed by exposure to events that their civilian counterparts may never come to appreciate or understand. When members of the military return from deployment, they also face the tremendous challenges of addressing not only problems that occurred while deployed, but issues they are likely to experience upon returning home. Among these are difficulties pertaining to transitioning from active duty into the civilian community, seeking employment, and readjusting to former relationships. The demands of managing these stressors can also be traumatizing in a potentially destructive manner; for instance, enduring intrusive war-related thoughts and images, social withdrawal, and the loss of deep bonding with their fellow comrades on a daily basis. The psychological, social, and psychiatric toll of war may be immediate, acute, or chronic.

The Challenges and Biopsychosocial Assessment Data

What are the challenges confronted by Reserve and Guardsmen (and Guardswomen) stemming from deployment to the combat theater of operations, and by their families and their communities at large, when they return home? How can they generate a positive reintegration experience within themselves, their loved ones, and their communities? Additionally, how can they reintegrate their roles at home, at work, and within the community?

To address these concerns, this practitioner applied the Systems Theory Method approach. The identified system problem was defined as *reintegration of the military service member into the community*. A comprehensive biopsychosocial assessment provided the data to address the needs of the service member, and his or her family and community.[1] The use of the biopsychosocial assessment included referral to needed medical and/or psychiatric providers for consultation, diagnosis, and treatment planning. Social workers from the VA Broward Outpatient Clinic addressed the psychosocial issues and provided the ongoing therapeutic treatment.

Concerns Presented by Service Members

Initially, in 2003, service members reported that they were not offered transitional assistance programs and were unaware of available resources in the community. Most of the information they obtained came by word of mouth from other veterans. They presented biopsychosocial concerns, as well as problems with the vast array of stressors associated with pre-deployment, deployment, post-deployment cycles and possible future deployments, to include an overriding concern of possible injury or death. There were several categories of concern: *Medical problems* (i.e., musculoskeletal injuries, dermatological problems); *traumatic brain injuries* (TBI) (i.e., constant headaches, memory loss);[2] *psychological problems* (i.e., PTSD, depression); *social concerns* (i.e., unemployment, familial discord); *legal issues* (i.e., driving under the influence (DUI), domestic disputes).

Additional difficulties during the reintegration period included overcoming major changes in the dynamics and structure of the family, difficulty renegotiating the roles of the returning service members, and frustration over not being able to understand their families' experience during their absence. They also struggled between civilian versus military cultural roles; for example, the emphasis on individual versus unit cohesion, individual achievement versus mission, personal freedom versus devotion to duty, and mutually beneficial relationships versus chain of command.

Family Members: Spouses

When a service member is deployed to a war zone, the family also goes to war. The family's equilibrium is disrupted, roles and responsibilities shift, and the family structure is altered. The families indicated that they were often silent about their own adjustment while their loved ones were deployed. Some families felt disconnected from the military system and, oftentimes, from their own extended families, neighborhoods, and communities. Some isolated themselves, wanting to be at home at all times in order to be available when their service members tried to make contact via internet or telephone.

Additionally, during the deployment cycles, there may well have been struggles related to financial, employment, housing, possible relocation, medical, emotional, relational and/or behavioral problems.

> My husband and I were in the same unit when we deployed to Iraq. Our five-year-old daughter stayed with [my husband's] mother . . . when we returned from Iraq he wanted a divorce to marry another woman in the unit. I was shocked . . . I did not re-enlist . . . I wanted to be with my daughter. I stayed in Georgia and couldn't find a job . . . lost my house, career, and car. I hit bottom when I got food from the local church. I was proud of myself and my career. I never thought I would find myself in this situation.
>
> (Sergeant, U.S. Army)

The families' support systems were sometimes limited by distance and other factors, such as perceived and/or a real lack of emotional support and open communication. It was often difficult for members of military families to ask for help. When asked, they typically responded with the statement "I am fine." One wife stated, "People ask how my husband and children are doing, but no one asks how I am doing." These families were confronted with fears of the unknown and a feeling of powerlessness over their lives, yet they continued to function, knowing that their futures might hold even further deployments for their service members.

Children

Children of service members were frequently overlooked during the deployment cycles. They needed support as a result of the loss of one or both parents to deployment, changes in family structure during deployment, and/or enduring additional losses from divorce, injury, or death. Children lived with the fear of future absence or loss. "My son, who is four years old, grabs my legs and cries when he sees me in uniform . . . I have to change for my unit meetings outside my home" (Sergeant, U.S. Army). Family members carried their unique feelings and reactions, with respect to the long-standing impact of wartime deployments and concern about the additional consequences they will likely face within the family system over time.

Community

Service members deserve—and need—the support of their communities. The responsibility for supporting members of the National Guard and Reserve components and their families increased through all phases of deployment because they lived, worked, and contributed to the welfare of their communities, and did not have access to the formal and informal structure, services, and support provided to Active Duty service personnel and their families who lived on active military installations. Both the family and the community suffered collateral outfall when the reintegration process had been marked with upheaval, e.g., unemployment, involvement with the legal system, divorces, possible incarceration, substance abuse treatment, hospitalization, suicide, and family hardships. Such reintegration challenges, coupled with inadequate military and governmental resources, exacerbated the need for an increase in the overall availability of community support and resources. Thus, it was important for communities to be proactive in assisting in providing a "safety net" of support services as a means of faciliating the reintegration process for service members, their families, and community.

Reintegration: The Need to Bring Us Together

> The mission: "Survival of one depends on the survival of all."

To assist in the process of the service member's reintegration from deployment, it was important to address both the formal needs (i.e., employment, housing, counseling) and the informal needs of the service member, family, and community. For some, informal support may have been effective in relieving the impact of emotional stressors, for example, neighbors who are supporting families of deployed service members might assist with some of the demands and responsibilities of everyday living, which can contribute to a reduction in certain aspects of physical and emotional stress. Such tasks might include preparing occasional meals, handyman work, assistance with moving, financial coverage of rent or mortgage expenses, or providing an opportunity for "alone time" for the non-deployed parent. The families needed to feel connected to the community, appreciated, and emotionally supported through all cycles of deployment. Assistance with everyday responsibilities that might be considered trivial were not necessarily sought but, when given, were received and very meaningful to the families of the deployed. Service members faced the challenge of addressing an overabundance of issues subsequent to their wartime experiences, such as impressions of not "fitting in," "not being understood" by their families and their communities, wondering whether or not the community even knew or appreciated that they were at war and continuing challenges of addressing self-identity and profound losses.

Loss

Profound loss can include both tangible and intangible experiences that are not limited to death of a comrade. These include physical injuries, witnessing the horrific and gruesome nature of war, and the loss of innocence/inner peace and one's very purpose in life. Coming to terms with such losses is central to the healing process. Service members need validation that they experienced profound loss and change through their wartime service. "I gave some and some gave all" (OEF/OIF veteran). It was also important that loved ones and those for whom they fought understood that wartime experience brings deep-rooted physical and emotional sacrifice.

Their concerns about "not fitting in," "no one understanding," etc., were very much the same as they were for Vietnam veterans who returned from war. In addition, many Vietnam veterans stated that they were "never given a welcome home" and were tormented and ridiculed. When these statements made by Vietnam veterans were processed therapeutically, their experience of trauma and the loss of significant others was essential in order to begin to address such devastating life circumstances. For example, one Vietnam veteran, who has been married for 45 years and is retired from a successful business, stated, "I would not have made it if it was not for my wife's support and love for me." Another example is an infantry OIF service member who returned from Iraq and stated, "I love the men like I love my mother and father . . . I felt so alone when I returned . . . I just wanted the recognition that I did the right thing . . . I served . . . I want to forgive myself . . . There was shock and confusion." Family support, understanding, and compassion are vital to the healing and reintegration process.

Utilizing Ceremonies to Facilitate Readjustment and Healing

The use of ceremonies to facilitate readjustment and the reintegration of service members with their communities is based on the premise that a genuine and sincere validation is imperative to begin the grieving process and to accept that a profound loss may have been experienced. Without validation, the grieving process is thwarted, delayed, suppressed, and/or denied, which leads to complicated grief. As stated by Rando (1993), the phases include recognizing the loss; reacting to the separation; recollecing and re-experiencing the deceased and the assumptive world; readjusting to move into a new world; and reinvesting in life without forgetting the old. Complicated grief (Worden, 2002) is a response to loss that does not progress through the normal stages, phases, and/or tasks of mourning. Internal stressors such as intrusive thoughts and nightmares involving loss are typically avoided, denied, or minimized by veterans, as they concurrently attempt to address both the magnitude of major changes that have impacted who they have become, and adjust to reintegration with family and community.

When significant others validate the profound losses that service members have experienced, through their emotional support and/or participation in ceremony, it helps to normalize that their feelings are congruent with their experiences. Emotional support also contributes to providing a safe and accepting environment that encourages service members to address the stages, phases, and/or tasks of the mourning process.

Other factors and dynamics addressed by properly designed ceremonies included that some service members reported feeling alone, lonely, and unsafe because they no longer had the daily support or deep bonding and camaraderie of the men and women in their units available to them. Some reported feeling as if they had two families, their military comrades and their families at home. Many said that they wanted, and were happy, to be home, but felt guilty for their buddies left behind, some still deployed and others who were facing further deployments. Several difficult adjustments had to be made to become reintegrated back with family and community. For example, the weapons which kept these veterans safe in combat were considered a danger in civilian life. The "relationship bonding" and the availability of weapons provided safety in the combat theatre. Absent such, there was a feeling of not being safe; feeling lost and vulnerable. Also, they reported not being understood; not fitting in to civilian life any longer. One OEF/OIF veteran stated, "When I came back, I went out with my hometown buddies and could not relate to them . . . I wondered what I ever saw in them. I was alienated." Another OEF/OIF veteran indicated, "When I was in Iraq, I knew how to talk to people. Now I am not sure what to say . . . I think people are afraid of me." Many veterans often wondered whether or not members of the community even realized that their country was at war.

In the combat theater, the trust and bonds of loyalty with comrades often involved an expression of "unconditional" love. This provided them the courage to literally "put one foot in front of the other" in order to face whatever hardships and terrifying experiences they were yet to encounter. When they returned home, they required, and frequently expected, the same "unconditional" love and acceptance from their families and communities. Receiving absolute and unqualified love would contribute to a safe environment; this, in turn, could facilitate the unfolding of the profound grief for the many losses they endured in war, allowing the healing process to begin.

The Journey Home Ceremony

> It takes a village to reintegrate a service member and support his or her journey home, and it takes a service member to teach us how to do it.

The Journey Home: Putting the Pieces Together Again

The Journey Home Ceremony was written by Sherrill Valdes, LCSW, and Janice Postlewaite, LCSW, as a means of recognizing and validating the service members' experiences. Oftentimes, family members and loved ones are instructed to provide "space" to their returning service members. However, this practitioner found that it was more important to allow family members to express compassion and empathy towards their service members in regard to their combat deployment experiences, without necessarily knowing the details of their wartime tours of duty.

The ceremony was written in "feeling" concepts—necessary to give permission to loved ones and the community to communicate their sincere emotions towards returning war veterans. An example of "feeling" language would include a discussion of emotional states now—in the present—rather than asking for the historical recounting of emotions from their wartime experiences. The Journey Home Ceremony was conducted first, and followed by the Quilt Ceremony.

Preparations for the Ceremonies

The Journey Home Ceremony and/or Quilt Ceremony can be held with large groups, such as during monthly Battle Assemblies (drills) with Reserve units, during military ceremonies, for holiday events honoring military service members, and during sporting events. Smaller groups can include the local VA facilities, churches, schools, and military service organizations. The Quilt Ceremony could follow the Journey Home Ceremony. In the former ceremony, each OEF/OIF/OND Service Member participant is presented with a quilt. After a relationship has been established with Quilts of Valor program and the quilting guilds in your locality, the following elements are recommended to optimize the planning and impact of the ceremony:

- Select a date, time and place for the event.
- Create tasteful invitations to be sent to newly returning service members, their families, other combat veterans, quilters, and guests from local communities.
- Create a warm and inviting environment (military memorabilia, music, food, etc.).
- Arrange appropriate seating accommodations based upon invited OEF/OIF service members, veterans of other wars, and other invited guests.
- Display quilts in the front of the room.
- Select a Master of Ceremonies (emcee) for the program.

Example of a Ceremony Program

- Introduction
  - Welcome participants and thank everyone for coming.
  - Statement: "This is a ceremony especially for returning service members. Everyone present is here because they wish to acknowledge their service member and the sacrifices they have endured."
  - Statement: "You have been in harm's way and we are here to let you know that you were thought of, remembered, and sent love and wishes for protection in our thoughts and prayers."

- The Journey Home Ceremony
  - The emcee introduces the ceremony.
  - The emcee invites the service members from OEF/OIF to the front of the room.
  - The emcee invites combat veterans from former wars to be seated at the front of the room.
  - The emcee reads the Journey Home Ceremony and invites participants to join in reading parts of the ceremony.
- Quilt Ceremony
  - The emcee introduces the Quilt Ceremony.
  - The emcee invites one quilter to speak and to present each of the quilts.
  - The quilters are asked to present their quilts, one each to the returning service members.
- Conclusion
  - Everyone in the room is invited to thank the service members. (Handshakes and hugs are acceptable, if the veteran is amenable to receiving them.)

Journey Home Ceremony Narrative

The following is an example of the actual wording developed and utilized by Janice Postlewaite, LCSW, and this author during a Journey Home Ceremony.

Leader: This ceremony acknowledges, honors, and respects your dedication and courage for protecting our freedom and the freedom of others and the willingness to be in harm's way. We genuinely thank you for your service and sacrifices.

Veteran and former combat service members: Even though you are home, don't be surprised if it feels different, because it is. You have changed; you just haven't had time to reflect on yourself and you're still looking over your shoulder. People who know you, look at you differently. They are not sure who is in there . . . but I am. You are a hero, as much as you don't believe it, and I am glad you are home safe.

Women (speaking for mothers, wives, aunts, etc.): I wish I could have comforted you during the times of your emotional or physical pain and the times you questioned yourself or others. I wish I was there standing by your side giving you words of encouragement on the days you needed it most. Even though you may not know exactly how you are feeling . . . I will always accept you just the way you are.

Men (speaking for fathers, husbands, uncles, etc.): Although I couldn't protect you from the things you did, from the things you wished you could have done or the things you regret doing . . . I want you to know that my intent is to protect you now. I may not know the right words to say or the right behaviors to display, but I want to be there for you. Being scared to death in a truly dangerous situation is normal. Be patient with yourself. You have a whole raft of things to assimilate. Even though I don't tell you as often as I should . . . I am proud of you.

The community (neighbors, townships, etc.): War is complicated, and there are many opinions about combat. In the past, we might have misdirected our political beliefs or feelings onto the service member who fought in the war. We are sorry if we did that, but we don't want to do that again. Please be patient if we make mistakes, because we do thank you for your service and we have compassion for you . . . we are glad you are home safe. Welcome Home!

Recently returning combat veterans: Thank you for acknowledging my sacrifices and my commitment to our country and my comrades. There will be times when there will not be any words to describe my feelings, or what I saw, learned, or experienced over there. You may not understand me, but know that I need you. I may withdraw, but be patient with me. I have seen things that border on the edge of existence, but understand one thing . . . although I am proud to serve my country, I mourn many losses, including my fallen comrades, and I need time to heal. During this time, support me by believing in me in the same way that I believe in our freedom and our country and my comrades. My thanks go out to all our veterans and I welcome them home!

The Quilt Ceremony

This practitioner learned about the Quilts of Valor project in 2003. This program was created and implemented by Catherine Roberts, who wished to present a handmade quilt to every wounded service member hospitalized at Walter Reed Army Medical Center in Washington, DC. She coordinated and created a network of quilt-makers throughout the United States to support this project. Catherine Roberts was contacted by this practitioner and requested that she consider offering her quilts to those service members who had returned to their home communities, as many of them were also suffering from both visible and invisible wounds of war. Additionally, this clinician aspired to write a welcome home ceremony to accompany the presentation of each quilt. The relevance of this treatment intervention was explained to Ms. Roberts, and she generously agreed to support this endeavor.[3] This practitioner aimed to use the quilts in a ceremony, allowing each quilt to symbolize community support and validation. The ceremonial presentation of quilts is a powerful healing intervention that has been performed on a grassroots level for returning service members at the VA's Broward County Outpatient Clinic and the Dade County Medical Center. These presentations can also be conducted on a community level at local VAMCs and in actual Reserve Units by VAMC Social Work Services. The presentations were opportunities for participants to express compassion and acceptance for the wartime service of these local recipients, through the presentation of these gifts, which symbolize and authenticate their service and sacrifices. During the Quilt Ceremony, this practitioner detailed the process of planning, designing, and sewing the quilt together, as well as the expense involved for the civilian making the quilt, in order to emphasize the time and effort dedicated to the project. This clinician added that the quilts were "magical," because each stitch was made with love and prayers. If service members were feeling sad or lonely, they were told they could wrap themselves in the quilt and feel the love and support of those who made it. One veteran was called by his social worker to determine how he was doing. He stated that he was in his car on his way to his mother's funeral. She immediately offered him an appointment. He declined stating, "I wrapped myself in the quilt last night, and I am okay."

Quilt Ceremony Narrative

An example of a Quilt Ceremony narrative by Sherrill Valdes.

Introduction

"Sometimes, those who service in combat come home feeling lost and/or feeling that we, civilians at home, have no idea that our country is even in war. I want you to know that there is awareness. Many former veterans that come to our clinic feel a strong bond to you and your service in OEF/OIF/OND and wish they could have served again in your place. Citizens in the community often ask how they can support you. We want you to know that you were thought about during your deployment, not only by former veterans, but the citizens in your community. Today we want to express our appreciation for your service and let you know we are glad you are home safe."

Purpose of the Ceremony

"The awarding of quilts to military personnel has a long history. For example, during the Civil War, quilts were made by the families of service members. These quilts were made of individual patterns that were meaningful to each family and included special patches or designs to provide comfort and support for their loved ones. 'Service members have wrapped themselves against the cold, against the night, against the pain, and against the longing to be back home, with quilts made for them by those at home who sleep soundly and safely because of their sacrifice' (Mary Martinez, personal communication, July 7, 2009). In 2003, Catherine Roberts, a mother of a veteran who was deployed to Afghanistan, traveled to Walter Reed Army Medical Center to ask permission to make a quilt for everyone who was hospitalized. She has labored to create more than 43,000 quilts and, today, The Quilts of Valor Program is now an international endeavor.

There are many steps, as well as many loving hands involved in the making of a quilt. The process begins by the quilter designing a pattern, purchasing the best materials for the quilt, and sewing the material together. The quilter then delivers the quilt to the person responsible for stitching back panels to the quilt, in order to complete the process.

The quilt you are receiving today is also magical because it is infused with all the love and prayers of the guild members who contributed to its making, and it symbolizes the love from your loved ones and your whole community. Therefore, if you are ever feeling lost or alone, or that no one cares, wrap the quilt around yourself and you feel that love."

Quilt Presentation

During the quilting ceremony, the Master of Ceremonies invites a representative of one of the guilds to present their quilt to receiving service members. After their presentation, the quilter is asked to shake each service member's hand and to tell them how glad they are that they returned home safely.

Implementation of the Ceremonies

For many Vietnam and OEF/OIF/OND combat veterans, the holiday season remains a particularly difficult time, which includes depression, anxiety and withdrawal from loved ones. One method to achieve more social interaction was to create a setting where veterans were able to enjoy the holiday experience with others they trusted. As a therapist for the Vietnam PTSD group, this clinician became involved with the group in the planning of a holiday party. By planning the event together, making the preparations and inviting guests, it was hoped that the veterans would experience more positive feelings about the season, and that these feelings would be shared with their families and communities. Returning service members were honored guests invited to the 2004 Christmas party; the goal was to support and validate their wartime service with the use of the Journey Home Ceremony and Quilt Ceremony. During the party, the civilian guests, as well as the Vietnam veterans and OEF/OIF veterans, displayed empathy and understanding towards each other by listening, asking pertinent questions and providing appropriate feedback. Wisdom of great magnitude was passed on from the Vietnam PTSD group to the returning OEF/OIF veterans during this event:

> Even though you are home, don't be surprised if it feels different . . . you have changed, you just haven't had the time to truly reflect within yourself. You're still looking over your shoulder . . . being scared to death in (what feels like) a truly dangerous situation is normal . . . talk to each other . . . you still need to know they have your back . . . there are no time constraints on issues . . . Seek professional help.

After The Journey Home Ceremony, in which the Vietnam and the OEF/OIF returning service members thanked each other for their service and sacrifice, an informal ceremony for the presentation of the quilts began. The returning soldiers were informed of the emotional investment and commitment needed to complete each quilt, as well as the fact that the quilt-makers wanted them to use these quilts as a reminder that they were loved, appreciated, and remembered during their deployments. They were also assured that every stitch in their unique quilts was "magical," as each was infused with love and prayers for their safety.

Background and Impact of the Ceremonies and Lessons Learned

All who attended this successful holiday party were emotionally moved by the experience at a deep level of sharing.

Integrating Vietnam Veterans and OEF/OIF Veterans into the Ceremonies

The Vietnam veterans, who demonstrated such depth of understanding of the experiences of these new combat veterans, wished to continue this kind of support with other returning OEF/OIF service members. Some Vietnam veterans felt that this ceremonial event was their homecoming as well, and were thanked for the support of the civilian guests and their fellow comrades. This was despite the fact that when they initially returned from overseas, they had not received any kind of "welcome home" from their own communities or, in fact, their nation. The returning OEF/OIF service members reported feeling very sincere acceptance and appreciation and that these quilts had held a great deal of meaning for each of them.

This ceremony, a clinical intervention, was tremendously beneficial, therapeutically, for the Vietnam and OEF/OIF service members, and the quilters were appreciative of having their quilts assume such special significance to these service members. Thus, the creation of this exceptional healing, with the community, combat service members from former wars, and newly returning combat veterans, was an invaluable experience for all involved. Since 2004, several quilt ceremonies have been conducted. Clinic-wide ceremonies have been conducted in small groups of approximately 10 to 20 participants, as well as larger groups with as many as 100 participants.

Networking with Local Quilting Guilds

It was believed that the quilt presentations would be more salient if local guilds made quilts for the returning service personnel in their communities, then presented them to military men and women in ceremonial form. This practitioner contacted local guilds in Palm Beach and Broward Counties (Florida), who adopted the Quilts of Valor Program. The guilds in both counties agreed to make quilts for the VA Healthcare System's Broward County Outpatient Clinic.

In 2004, the Broward quilting guilds initiated their support for OEF/OIF service members and the VA Healthcare System through an exhibition of their Quilts of Valor Program, hosted at the Alvin Sherman Library at Nova Southeastern University, a community library. The quilts were displayed throughout the library in order to bring awareness to the community about our service members and their sacrifices, as well as to demonstrate gratitude and support to the returning veterans for their service.

Now, when an OEF/OIF/OND veteran registers at the Broward Outpatient Clinic and completes the social work service's protocol, a small ceremony ensues, with the presentation of a quilt to each veteran by his or her social worker. This initiative was implemented because it was difficult to engage some of the veterans in attending a scheduled ceremony, as many reported feeling that they had just been doing their jobs during their wartime service and did not want special acknowledgement. The ceremony appeared to be just as emotionally significant when conducted as a one-to-one presentation, as each veteran has been visibly moved by these events. The quilting guilds in the Palm Beach/Broward communities have supported this clinical intervention for the past seven years.

Feedback from the Quilters

Quilters who participate in this program are both male and female, and from all age groups, cultures, and ethnicities. Many have had a direct link to the military—either through serving themselves or through a loved one who is currently serving, or has served previously. The quilters have taken special care in their preparation of the quilts by presenting them in "presenting cases," which double as pillow cases, with a personalized information patch sewn on the inside of each quilt. These information patches identify the guilds that designed each quilt, with an acknowledgement of these gifts from the Quilts of Valor Program. Along with this patch, there is often a letter from the quilter who made the quilt, and a personal note with his or her picture enclosed.

Many quilters have stated that making the quilt is a labor of love and a way to express appreciation to service members. Prior to each quilt ceremony, quilters have expressed concern about whether or not receiving service members will like their quilts. Quilters are encouraged to open their quilts to explain the meanings and designs to each service member. At the completion of one particular ceremony, one quilter stated, "It was wonderful to present my quilt . . . I feel so humbled." Another quilter reported, "I really feel like I did something important." Most of the service members have openly provided feedback. For example, "My quilt was the best one." Another veteran stated, "No one did anything like this for me before." Regardless of the number of participants, there has never been an attendee who has not been visibly emotionally gratified by the power of the ceremony.

In Conclusion

Our experience has been that providing either the Journey Home Ceremony or the Quilt Ceremony independently constitutes a meaningful therapeutic intervention that emotionally supports the reintegration process. However, *combining* the ceremonies together is an even more powerful intervention to all who attend.

Pillow Pals: Emotional Healing for Military Children

The Journey Home and Quilts Ceremonies were designed primarily to facilitate the reintegration of adult service members, their families, friends, supporters, and communities. The success of these ceremonies led the author and others to realize that the children of military families might benefit even more from a ceremony that was designed especially for children.

Background

Rutledge (2007) reported that approximately 75 percent of all Reservists were parents and, currently, more than 700,000 children had at least one parent deployed. Children of these families often silently cope with their own experience in the readjustment process and typically report experiencing feelings such as sadness, anger, confusion, and loneliness, as well as behavioral changes reflective of these issues, both at home and in school settings.

One partnership developed by the VA within the Broward County community involves the Embracing Military Personnel and Families Program, a military initiative implemented by Lucia Romero[4] and supported by the Broward County School System. In 2011, the program planned and coordinated an event to honor the military-dependent children within the Broward County School System, by recognizing each child with a certificate to honor his or her individual sacrifices through each of the phases of deployment. This practitioner believed that the community could assist these children by supporting and addressing their individual emotional needs for understanding, appreciation, validation, compassion, and recognition of their plight. This author suggested that a "Pillow Pal" could be given in ceremony to symbolize continuous emotional support, caring, and devotion from their loved ones and the community. The ceremony addressed the challenges that children of military families endured, as well as the love and caring infused in the Pillow Pals. The purpose of the event was to embrace the children and empower them as having an important role within their families and to the military service of their parent(s).

An Introductory Pillow Pal Narrative

"The Pillow Pal is a special friend who is always close at hand to remind you that you are cared about by your family, friends, and other people that you have never met. The Pillow Pal is a friend to talk to, laugh, love, and cry with, and/or just hug. The Pillow Pal is also a magical friend, as it is filled with love so you can hold, rest, or sleep with it, as well as share both your happy and sad feelings, and the Pillow Pal always loves you. You are a precious child, a hero and the Pillow Pal is a gift of love . . . you never have to feel alone again."

Results

The children were excited to meet their Pillow Pal and receive their certificates of honor. The ceremony was well received and the room remained quiet as the children and their families listened intently to the significance of this poignant ceremony. A retired Army Sergeant First Class attended the celebration and empathized with the military families. From 2003 to 2004, she was deployed to Iraq. Her daughter was 4 and her son was 9. When she returned, she said her daughter was "traumatized." She stated, "I understand what they're going through, and I don't want them to miss out on what my daughter missed out on."

Closing

The Journey Home Ceremony, the Quilt Ceremony, and the Pillow Pal Ceremony have made a tremendous contribution to the reintegration process for military personnel, veterans, and their families. The quilts and pillow pals are symbolic of newly evolved community support and involvement in the reintegration and healing process. Implementing these three ceremonies has been an emotionally powerful intervention for all participants. The size of the ceremony is not as important as the intent of it. It is the ceremony that offers the opportunity to reach out from the heart, to bring together the humanity that truly exists in each of us.

Our most valued gifts come from the heart, as they are the most meaningful gifts that we possess and have to offer. One soldier commented that, "While we were over there being torn to pieces, these people have been stitching the pieces together and want us to cover ourselves with the quilts and begin healing." Children responded to their Pillow Pals by hugging them, naming them, and expressing gratitude for their special friends, magical gifts of love.

When our country goes to war, we are all in it together. As the military ethic states, "The survival of one depends on the survival of all." The ceremonies remind us of our most meaningful gift, the gift of love. The men and women who serve our country understand the value of genuine compassion, honesty, and emotional support for each other. If we join them with the same qualities, we will all be an integral and vital part of the journey home.

Acknowledgments

The opinions are those of the author, and do not necessarily reflect those of the Miami VA Healthcare System. Appreciation is expressed to all veterans from whom the author has learned, and to her colleagues. Gratitude is extended to the Social Work Service Chief, Claire Crocker; Chief Dr. Stephen Jankowski; Raymond Monsour Scurfield, PhD; Kathy Platoni, Psy.D.; Janice Postlewaite, LCSW; Catherine Roberts, Quilts of Valor Program; and to Zenaida Fisher for her technical assistance, support, and feedback.

Notes

1 The biopsychosocial assessment utilized was self-constructed by practitioners at the Miami VA Healthcare System. It includes the input of relevant specialists, including the client's self-assessment of strengths and weaknesses. Professionals from all the disciplines who are involved in the client's care should contribute to the assessment. Where such joint action is impossible, the social work case manager should gather necessary information and initiate, coordinate, conduct, and document the assessment. A uniform method of collecting and reporting assessment findings should be developed for use by all case managers in the agency or service system. Such methods are to be used only as tools in making a professional judgment. National Association of Social Workers (NASW). http://www.socialworkers.org/practice/standards/sw_case_mgmt.asp. Contact the author for more information about the assessment package and process utilized.

2 For a comprehensive discussion of TBI and the full range of symptoms, see Rigg (2012)

3 Mrs. Catherine Roberts, the founder and Executive Director of the Quilts of Valor Foundation (QOVF), can be contacted via email at cath@QOVF.org. As of 2011, 42,212 quilts have been made.

4 Ms. Lucia Romero, MSW, the founder and Executive Director of the Embracing Military Personnel and Families Program, can be contacted via email at lucia.romero@browardschools.com.

References

Castaneda, L., Harrell, M., Varda, D., Hall, K., Beckett, M., & Stern, S. (2008). *Deployment Experiences of Guard and Reserve Families: Implications for Support and Retention.* Santa Monica, CA: Rand Corporation.

Rando, T. A. (1993). *Treatment of Complicated Mourning.* Champaign, IL: Research Press.

Rigg, J. (2012). "Traumatic Brain Injury and Post Traumatic Stress: The 'Signature Wounds' of the Iraq and Afghanistan War." In R. M. Scurfield & K. T. Platoni (Eds.), *War Trauma and Its Wake: Expanding the Circle of Healing.* New York, NY: Routledge.

Rutledge, R. (2007, August 9). "Children of Soldiers Aren't Having Mental Health Needs Fulfilled." *World PTSD News.*

Tanielian, T., & Jaycox, L. H. (Eds.). (2008). *Invisible Wounds of War: Psychological and Cognitive Injuries, Their Consequences, and Services to Assist Recovery.* Santa Monica, CA: Rand Corporation, MG-720-CCF.

Worden, W. J. (2002). *Grief Counseling and Grief Therapy: A Handbook for the Mental Health Practitioner.* New York, NY: Springer Publishing Company, Inc.

6   Veterans' Sanctuary

The Journey to Open a Therapeutic Community

Robert Csandl (Vietnam)

Treatment Trends, Inc. has provided addiction and trauma services for over 40 years. Drawing from this organizational experience, we recognize that veterans face a constellation of risk factors for addiction as they transition home. The primary purpose of this chapter is to walk readers through the series of factors, struggles, and decision-making choices encountered, to be able to conceptualize, design, and open a 60 bed veteran-specific addiction, co-occurring, and PTSD therapeutic community for veterans and their families. Readers will be informed about the various strategic factors that must be considered, and how obstacles and challenges can be anticipated and addressed in order to establish a needed resource for veterans. In addition, there is identification of the core values and services being developed to address and treat, with honor and dignity, the bodies, minds, spirits, and hearts of veterans whose lives need mending. Veterans' Sanctuary is now a licensed drug and alcohol treatment facility.

A Deep Root in Our Community

Treatment Trends, Inc. (TTI) is a private, non-profit corporation located in Allentown, Pennsylvania, and has been operating addiction treatment programs since 1969. Our earliest programs were seeded during the grassroots movements and social activism of the 1960s. Our programs gained interest and involvement from the community as the growing specter of addiction began to affect the white middle class. This was furthered as many Vietnam veterans returned home with heroin and other drug and alcohol problems. Our start was rocky.[1] Our work pre-dated statewide licensing and dedicated funding streams. The key founders, of what was then named Confront, worked for more than a year without pay. This was accomplished by spouses working and collecting unemployment. Much of the Therapeutic Community (TC) movement was seeded earlier, with Synanon (Yablonsky, 1965) and Daytop Village having roots into the 1950s. As the TC movement grew across the country, a spirit of sharing information and struggles enriched the pioneer journey. We were all young, challenging the status quo, and filled with the celestial fire that kindled a quest to provide effective interventions. We were our own guinea pigs, trying what we were learning upon ourselves first. We grew through struggle, built treatment strategies person by person, and slowly built community support. Our addiction work led us into many areas about which we endeavored to learn. Many of the people seeking treatment had trauma histories, including physical and/ or sexual victimization. Some were men who battered women. A good portion of our clients engaged in criminal behaviors as part of their addiction. For what our young, developing, staff did not know, and for where we lacked skills, we compensated with heart.

We Shall Overcome

Our connections on the street served us well. We were trusted, we were not police, and we tried to do the right thing. Doing the right thing mattered when, one evening, 22 of us were arrested for "breach of the peace" in the old paint store where we ran our therapy groups. We did not know the importance of informing our neighbors who we were and what we were attempting to do. Their suspicion and multiple calls to the police resulted in surveillance, then arrest. The newspaper headlines were "Right Program, Wrong Place." The community rallied in support of us. Several service clubs donated money, and one worked to get us incorporated as a private non-profit (501(c)(3)). This arrest gained notoriety, leading to opportunities to help other communities start their own programs and to expand our services. We helped three nearby communities to open centers: Bethlehem, Reading, and Stroudsburg, PA. We quickly discovered the limitations of outpatient treatment when treating "addiction" versus substance abuse, prompting us to seek financial support in order to open a residential treatment center in the Lehigh Valley (1971). In 1972, we were awarded an H80 NIDA grant ($750,000) to establish a residential drug and alcohol treatment facility for non-residential after-care treatment at both the Allentown and Bethlehem Confront facilities. Our founding Executive Director, Richard Csandl, left Confront to open a residential therapeutic community, known as Lehigh Valley Drug and Alcohol Abuse Services (LVDAAS).

A Growing Mission

Ongoing challenges in implementing a resource for veterans include (a) the vigilance to insure that the mission is clear and relevant; and (b) to insure that we provide cutting edge program offerings. After birthing Treatment Trends, Inc. (TTI) in 1989, merging Confront and LVDAAS, we founded the Treatment Trends Foundation, also a 501(c)(3) non-profit, to financially support the services of TTI. The foundation immediately raised $200,000 to expand Keenan House to 85 beds and to purchase an 11-bed transitional living facility to enhance our continuum of care for recovering addicts. This facility we named the Richard S. Csandl Recovery House, in loving memory of our key founder. In 2003, Treatment Trends purchased the Halfway Home of the Lehigh Valley (36 beds) further enhancing our continuum of care. Our work became more specialized over the decades. Keenan House, our inpatient service, specialized in working with hardcore addiction, criminality, and co-occurring disorders. Confront, our outpatient program, specialized into addiction aftercare, sexual abuse, and non-offending parents of incestuous families; it also created specialized parenting programs aimed at involving parents with their children after years of incarceration. Our Halfway Home specializes in co-occurring disorders.

Organizationally, we deepened our work with criminality and earned an excellent reputation for providing quality services. As such, our programs are always full and we maintain a robust referral network across Pennsylvania. The inpatient programs have contracts with 35 counties, Corrections, Probation, and Parole, and specialty drug courts throughout the state. These contracts allow us to divert addicts and alcoholics from prison, provide services upon their release, and to offer the parole violator an alternative to prison. Past to present, our programs and services anticipated the emergent needs of our community. Our vision and work often preceded viable funding streams. Community-based treatment of veterans may prove to be another such story.

The Pains of War and the Risk Factors for Addiction

Our country is in two wars at the time of writing, and growing numbers of returning servicemen and women from Iraq and Afghanistan are struggling to successfully transition home. Many war veterans are coping with Post-Traumatic Stress Disorder (PTSD) by numbing their feelings with drink or drugs (U.S. Department of Veterans Affairs, 2011). This coping mechanism puts veterans at an increased risk of moving rapidly through the stages of drug/alcohol use, misuse, abuse, dependency, and finally drug addiction or alcoholism. As the commitment to drugs or alcohol grows with continued usage, another transition into the drug lifestyle and subculture also grows. Over time, an inevitable deterioration begins to manifest. An erosion and alienation from important relationships and emotional supports, divorce, domestic violence, crime and homelessness, and suicide, all become possibilities. Sadly, arrest can become the intervention that incapacitates the chronicity of addiction and subsequent crime. But without treatment, all the pain and original risk factors remain intact, often dooming the veteran to repetitive cycles of gain and loss, heartbreak and re-incarceration. Our prison populations are comprised of 8 to 12 percent veterans, primarily for drug and alcohol related crimes (Lavin, n.d.). The transition of coming home from war is often difficult, as our warriors struggle with injuries and acceptance of their experiences of war. Brain chemistry and brain injuries, traumatic events affronting our morality and sensibilities, and changes on the home front are a huge part of the struggle of homecoming. VA and DOD projections (Atkinson, Guetz, & Wein, 2009) indicate upwards of 35 percent of our nation's warriors will struggle with PTSD.

Wars' Long Shadow

When our nation goes to war, warriors from previous wars are also triggered and often destabilized. This is evidenced by the flood of Vietnam veterans using VA services, and warriors from WWII and Korea still suffering with PTSD. According to Dr. Ed Tick, author of *War and the Soul* (2005), we have not raised a generation of children without a war or major conflict since the Great Depression.

Noting the numerical projections of 2.8 million deployed (Tan, 2009), serving across a decade of time in the OIF and OEF wars, we see only part of the total picture. Pennsylvania has the fourth largest number of persons serving in the global war on terror. In our two counties, Lehigh and Northampton, we have over 60,000 veterans. Considering these factors, Treatment Trends, Inc. decided to utilize its clinical and organizational strength to do what we believe every community should do: develop services for our veteran community.

The path to this decision involved a confluence of experiences that acted to enhance our interest. We attended a national veterans' conference in Washington, DC, which focused on the struggles of so many veterans. One outstanding community-based veterans-specific treatment program, Samaritan Village Veterans' Program, caught our interest. The pursuit of holistic healing, and the spiritual disciplines of Mindfulness-Based Stress Reduction (MBSR), led us to retreats. One such retreat was with Thich Nhat Hanh, the Vietnamese monk involved in the Paris Peace Talks (Deer Park Monastery, 2012). This retreat offered an opportunity for involvement in a veterans' Sangha (community), which illuminated the shared pain of both the Vietnam veterans and Vietnamese monks, when one of the monks shared about the American War from his eyes as a small child. One of the participants was from Soldier's Heart, directed by Edward Tick (Soldier's Heart, 2011) which helps returning veterans with PTSD and prepares families and communities to support the healing of veterans. This Soldier's Heart link led us to Chicago, and a powerful five-day experiential PTSD healing experience with Vietnam and OIF/OEF veterans that incorporated sociodrama and psychodrama, Native American traditions, storytelling, and healing exercises. These seeded many ideas of what the treatment we offer might entail. These combined experiences solidified our commitment to creating a program.

Loving an Old Building

As we searched for an available building, we noticed a building for sale one block from Keenan House. We scheduled a walk-through and realized it was perfect for residential treatment. It was large, over 30,000 square feet. It contained a gym, a large room for physical therapy, an auditorium (seating 400+) with a stage, a large kitchen and pantry area, the ability to manage a changing male and female census, plentiful group rooms and office space, and was light and spacious. A center city location would give our residents convenience to governmental institutions, transportation, and access to clinics. The proximity to Keenan House would ease our ability to manage both facilities. It was perfect, except for one major hurdle: the zoning.

Zoning Issues and Actions

Our board of directors already knew of our interest in opening a veterans' program and a potential site brought things one step closer. An expansion of our vocational and educational programming would be valuable; however, our real dream was a Veterans' Sanctuary. To pursue this goal, we created a Veterans' Planning Committee, comprised of key staff members from each of our facilities. The initial plan involved several phases. The first phase was to renovate enough space for the administrative offices to move out of Keenan House and into the new building. In the vacated space, we would add 10 treatment beds and supplement our revenue towards the real goal. Since zoning would require an exception and a variance, we thought it imperative to inform the city of our plans and to seek their support. In spite of the mayor's resistance "at bringing more addicts in the central business district," the possibilities of the building made it an asset that could benefit our organization for decades to come. We made an offer of $450k to

St. John's Lutheran Church. With a congregational vote of 183 to 3, the Church accepted our offer. This support from the congregation has continued in many different ways. Once the purchase was finalized, we continued our principle of transparency and, again, sought the city's support of our pending zoning request. The mayor irately refused, and a war with the city began. Our veterans' planning committee faced several challenges: to develop the strategy and tactics to win a zoning decision; to come up with a plan to raise money to renovate the building; and to research the best treatment methods for Veterans' Sanctuary.

Strategies for Fighting City Hall: We Are the People!

Recognizing that laws were made by people, and they could be changed by people, we embarked on what many thought to be impossible—fighting City Hall. The pathway was clear to us. The legislative body of the city council could amend the zoning code. To prepare our strategy, our staff engaged in vigorous point/counterpoint sessions. We hired Allentown's best zoning lawyer and sought the advice of a Philadelphia legal group. Together, we drafted an amendment, adding a new definition called "Veterans' Treatment" to the zoning code, and sought the approval of each member of Allentown City Council. Also, we tactically decided that any public meetings should show the positive support for the program and veterans' treatment.

Opposition Galvanizes Unity: Tell 10 to Bring 10

As against us as the mayor indicated he was, we were equally strong in our desire to create Veterans' Sanctuary in this building. We employed the grassroots social activism tactics of "tell 10, bring 10", conducted 15 open houses, partnered with local military affairs organizations, and reached out through electronic media to obtain signatures. We asked people to inform people on their email lists, and that their friends keep extending out on their own email lists. Slowly, and tactically, we garnered the support of the citizenry to fight City Hall. We found a local champion on the city council. Our tactic was to generate overwhelming support, and not go after the mayor publicly. When asked by the largest local newspaper if the mayor supported the project, we stated this was best answered by the mayor himself. With visible and growing public support, we one by one obtained the support of all seven city councilpersons.

The city held hearings. We filled the chambers of the city council with vocal supporters, many veterans and their family members. We had gained support of critical committees, including members of the mayor's administration. Before the code amending vote, each city council member put aside formality and shared heartfelt personal experiences. One's father was a Vietnam veteran, one took a nephew broken by war to the VA, and one was a Korean War combat veteran. Through a courageous and painful process, each member came through their own tears and voted 7 to 0 to amend the zoning code to include a new definition called Veterans' Treatment; once codified into law, we could approach the zoning board. Substantial testimony occurred. With the media present, the hearing hall was filled two more times with veterans and civilians supporting the project, leading to a favorable 3 to 0 vote by the zoning board.[2]

Building a Solid Foundation: Grassroots Networking

It is essential to have the necessary community support and a structure in place to facilitate organized, systematic, and effective fundraising. Although our 40-plus years of anti-poverty criminal justice treatment work earned us the public's respect, we are not high profile. Our board of directors is comprised of very capable, concerned, community members, but they are not well connected to the circles of money or power. We created a new full-time position, Director of Development (DD), tasked to conduct a capital campaign and to approach foundations, corporations, and individuals. We believed that each person we touched can carry "goodwill" outward into the community, and act as an ambassador to open new doors and create support. Clearly, the roots of this project tap many wells in our community, such as patriotism, support for the troops deployed, and generations of veterans who served, as well as their families. All visitors are greeted with "talk and tour" sessions. Each takes about 1 to 2 hours, during which we treat each guest respectfully, with the hopes of generating interest. Often, a personal story emerged that needed to be heard and told: a story of service and honor of a loved one, a parent, or grandparent and, sometimes, sadly of a child lost to war or suicide. We are especially touched by the donations made in memory of loved ones, many lost due to war.

As a result of hearing so many compelling stories of courage and loss, we consciously decided to tailor the categories of giving into themes suited to a veterans' program.[3] Many first time visitors came again, bringing friends and family, helping to expand support for the Sanctuary. Each guest hears our story and tours the building and sees the rooms, their potential, and proposed use. With great effort, even in this economy, our fundraising is making gains. We raised 1.2 million dollars with another million needed to reach our campaign goal. We are grateful that corporations are generously giving, but also noteworthy are the hundreds of small donors who give with heart and a story. For example, an involved association of military organizations (Lehigh Valley Military Affairs Council) has repeatedly stepped forward to support us at zoning hearings, funding initiatives, and with financial support for our family education program, called Supporting the Home Front. Their members connected us to other helpful veteran organizations. The Veterans of Foreign Wars from across Pennsylvania presented us with a check, and Vietnam Veterans of America raised money and outfitted our map room. In-kind support is enormous. Several large corporations and churches repeatedly sent volunteers to paint and clean. Four quilting guilds are making quilts for each bed. Our various efforts keep our plight in the public eye, written in local newspapers, business emails, church newsletters, television interviews, service clubs, and even in a national trade journal for addiction treatment.

Politicians Love Veterans, Don't They?

An essential task is to understand and deal effectively with the political landscape. From the beginning, even as we negotiated the purchase of the building, we sought financial support from community partners, politicians, corporations, and the public. Naively, our first outreach was to politicians, believing they support veterans and economic development. Though there were bright spots, we quickly learned why their public approval rating is low. Some politicians were conflicted, wanting to help us but unwilling to spend political capital during our struggles against the city. This was disappointing, when considering all the rhetoric about how veterans are loved and appreciated for their service. Among competing demands for limited dollars, few politicians supported us with real dollars.[4] Overall, our project totals $2.6 million dollars in building renovations, creates 25 primarily middle class positions, will operate with a $2.4 million annual budget, and can serve 240 veterans a year when fully operational.

Our Final Challenges . . . a Clear Vision on a Foggy Path

All of the money and community support is ultimately of little benefit if the product being provided is not relevant to the needs of veterans, and of high quality. Veterans' Sanctuary is now licensed as an inpatient non-hospital drug and alcohol treatment facility. We hired staff and now must rise to our most critical challenges: providing quality treatment for addiction, alcoholism, and co-occurring disorders, including PTSD. We also need to develop a funding and referral network, such as our sister program, Samaritan Village Veterans' Program (Samaritan Village Veterans' Program, n.d.), which was accomplished in New York state. Our veterans' planning committee has been guiding this project for over three years. Members of the committee visited other programs, reviewed the research, and listened intently to the stories of veterans and their families. Our travels took us to out-of-state facilities, conferences, and retreats. We met passionate professionals of varied disciplines, expertise, and divergent points of view. Veterans' Sanctuary is a community-based (variable length) therapeutic community. It is dedicated to serving male and female veterans and providing educational assistance to their families. Family education is designed to teach family members skills to better support veterans in recovery and dealing with PTSD.

Treatment at the Veterans' Sanctuary includes an array of psycho-educational groups, primary treatment groups, individual counseling, and onsite psychiatric and medical services. The facility staff received extensive PTSD training and will utilize the Trauma-Informed Care model (Seeking Safety: Coping Skills for Trauma) supported with contracted art and drama therapists who have done extensive PTSD work with the Bronx VAMC in New York City. Specialized approaches include the use of EMDR (Boulware, 2006), art therapy, drama therapy, cognitive behavioral therapy (National Association of Cognitive Behavioral Therapists, 2011) and the use of ceremony and ritual to support successful transition and build recovery supports.

An Integrated Therapeutic Community and Holistic Model

The heart of the program, as described next, will blend the structured peer hierarchy milieu of the Therapeutic Community with Trauma-Informed Care and integrate other models such as the medical model, social earning theory, and the mindfulness practices of Mindfulness-Based Stress Reduction and Mindfulness-Based Cognitive Therapy. The treatment philosophy is based on the well-researched Therapeutic Community (TC) model (National Institute of Drug Abuse, 2002). The TC is founded upon the principles of social learning theory and integrates other philosophies, including the medical model. The medical model (Griffiths, 2005) recognizes that addiction is indeed a brain chemistry issue, as well as a chronic disease with progressive symptoms that need episodic interventions. Primary elements of our TC model and program include:

- The TC, considered a best practice, places emphasis on personal responsibility, accountability, and recovery. This intensive peer-based approach will assist residents in developing peer attachments and pro-social values, along with the skills necessary to reintegrate into the community. The TC will also utilize evidence-based Cognitive Behavioral Therapy to address criminality.
- Public domain addiction and criminal risk tools recommended and identified by Texas Christian University (Institute of Behavioral Research, Texas Christian University, n.d.) will be used to measure progress.
- The Sanctuary will also provide pro-health initiatives, through exercise and daily morning yoga classes, healthy nutrition education, and in-season organic vegetables.
- Voluntary vocational training certificate programs will be offered in Culinary Arts and Safe Serve, to assist in employment.
- The TC model has similarities to the military, and offers a sense of affiliation, belonging, acceptance, and hierarchal achievement. The TC emphasizes pro-social concepts of honesty, responsibility, trust, concern, consistency, and communication.
- The TC model is a peer hierarchy, and the residents will be empowered to help each other and themselves, similar to military concepts of Vet Helping Vet and Leave No Man Behind.
- The TC model, by design, challenges an individual's assumptions, beliefs, behaviors, and cognitions about the self, authority, power, and entitlements, and expects pro-social behaviors.
- Pro-social change is rewarded through status, recognition, and privileges, thus acting to sustain motivation.
- VS will also utilize emergent evidence-based practices, i.e., Mindfulness-Based Stress Reduction (MBSR) and Mindfulness-Based Cognitive Therapy (MBCT) (Hoffman, et al., 2010) which have shown effectiveness treating depression, anxiety, pain management, and impulsiveness. Empowering residents with MBSR and MBCT skills will help them to alleviate or mitigate some of the underlying conditions of addiction and relapse.
- Holistic approaches will be emphasized to encourage the healthy, balanced, lifestyles needed to sustain recovery. Yoga and Mindful Movement techniques, as well as physical fitness activities, will help residents sustain any gains they may have made in healing from war injuries. Yoda Nidra (Singh & Singh, 2010), a systematic method of inducing deep sleep, sleep hygiene education, and rehearsal practices shall be utilized against sleep disorders often seen with combat veterans.

In conclusion, Veterans' Sanctuary will utilize a continuum of care designed to meet the multiple needs of an adult substance abusing population. Treatment will be offered as prison diversion through veterans' courts, post-incarceration prisoner re-entry services, and, when appropriate, Halfway Back Addiction Treatment for the parole violator.

Obstacles to Treatment

The road to treatment has some noteworthy obstacles. Some barriers are specific to Veterans' Sanctuary, and others to male veterans. They are: (1) concepts of masculinity; (2) the denial system associated with addiction or alcoholism; (3) beliefs about the VA; and (4) funding criteria.

Concepts of Masculinity

Veterans seek help more easily for physical health issues than for addiction, alcoholism, or PTSD. The predominant notions of masculinity and "being strong," the "tough it out" mentality, the isolating "don't-show-anything-perceived-as weakness"—all fuel a denial system that contributes to risk factors for addiction or alcoholism. This act-strong-even-if-one-does-not-feel-strong mentality, coupled with PTSD, makes the numbing of feelings through drinking or drugging even riskier. Without interventions, many other complications can occur.

Denial Syndrome of Addiction

Many veterans have a constellation of risk factors that can rapidly propel the person from casual drug use or drinking into misuse, abuse, dependency and, finally, addiction or alcoholism. Once the individual marries the lifestyle of addiction or alcoholism, the troubles become even more exacerbated. All life energy goes into maintaining the drug relationship. This promotes shifts in values that often include criminal behaviors, damage to key relationships, and the development of anti-social values and friends. These shifts embed the drug culture as a lifestyle, and can easily become chronic as the individual protects the drug relationship with secrecy, deception and, often, drama. Changes in brain chemistry and untreated PTSD accelerate this process. This powerful drug relationship constitutes the well recognized denial syndrome of addiction (Howard, et al., 2002). Receiving help is often prompted by a crisis or pressure from family or friends or, all too often, arrest.

Beliefs About the VA and Access Issues

It is widely believed that the VA will take care of all veterans' issues. This is simply not true. Issues of access, benefits eligibility, timeliness, and responsiveness plague the VA. The VA employs many good people who provide really good care to those who can access their services. However, the National Guard and Reserves require 24 months of active duty to be eligible, unless deployed in support of Operation Iraqi Freedom or Operation Enduring Freedom (Afghanistan), which allows access to VA services for 5 years (we are now in year 10). Access to VA services due to locality can also be an issue for veterans who live too far away from a VA facility to access such services.

Service members have concerns about admitting to an alcohol or drug problem; admitting illegal drug use can result in discharge from military service or affect the military career. PTSD can be interpreted to mean unstable. Real or imagined, these are barriers. Other barriers include that a dishonorable discharge means VA ineligibility and that the VA's priority system restricts those without a service-connected injury, or with addiction and mental health issues, to lower priority. Unfortunately, when an active addict finally seeks help, any barriers or delays for services usually result in continued drug use, since addicts remain ambivalent about giving up their drugs or alcohol.

Funding: Citizen of the State First, Veteran Second

According to Michael Moreland, head of our VA Veterans Integrated Service Network (VISN4), "Veterans are citizens first, veterans second. Being a veteran does not make one ineligible for any state benefit you would otherwise be eligible for." In Pennsylvania, there are diverse public sector funding streams available for veterans with addictions. They include Public Welfare (Medicaid-managed care); Act 152 monies, designated specifically for inpatient non-hospital services; and the Behavioral Health Service Initiative, which is earmarked for the working poor. This funding enhances the VA's initiatives for homeless and incarcerated veterans.

When comparing public sector addiction treatment and VA addiction treatment, there are important differences. These include access, levels of care, lengths of stay, capacity, and locality. VA inpatient addiction treatment usually involves 21 days of hospital-based treatment, including detoxification or a 60-day addiction program (Lebanon VA), which is hampered by size (17 beds) and wait times. Longer inpatient treatment is provided through domiciliary care on VA hospital grounds with outpatient treatment. None are licensed by the state. *In Pennsylvania, persons receiving public assistance have more treatment choices than veterans are offered through the VA.* Public sector treatment in Pennsylvania is networked throughout almost every county in the state, which increases choices and access. Public funded treatment options include many levels of care: short, moderate and long-term inpatient non-hospital treatment, hospital-based treatment, hospital-based and non hospital-based detoxification, halfway homes, outpatient and intensive-outpatient treatment services and multiple pharmacological options. Addiction treatment is available in almost all Pennsylvania counties.

Conversely, VA addiction care is not nearly as available. Also, VA hospital-based care (Schinka, et al., 1998) ($405 per day) is much more expensive than public sector, inpatient, non-hospital care ($149 per day). Upon initiating this project, our market research indicated a population in need, as well as available funding. Both VA representatives and Pennsylvania Community Corrections told us they could keep our programs full. The VA has waiting periods for veterans with addictions to be accepted for treatment. We were also told that they could use a service such as that which we were proposing. However, the VA, with fewer addiction treatment resources, and greater obstacles to treatment, wait times, and significant numbers of veterans relapsing, *seldom uses community-based addiction treatment, despite their rhetoric of doing so.* Are community-based programs viewed as "competitors," rather than as valued collaborators and providers—even though VA resources typically are hard-pressed to meet existing demands in a timely manner?

The concern for veterans is driving many creative and emergent interventions. Veterans' Courts, as developed by Judge Robert Russell (Lewis, 2008), and the implementation of the Sequential Intercept Model (CMHS National GAINS Center, n.d.), developed by Mark Montez, MD, and Patricia A. Griffin, PhD, creates excellent interventions to move veterans from the criminal justice system into treatment. Numerous Veterans' Courts are planned in Pennsylvania, with three already operational. Diversion into addiction treatment programs, such as Restorative Intermediate Punishment (RIP) are already codified into Pennsylvania sentencing law (see the Pennsylvania Code). The Pennsylvania Board of Probation and Parole, working with the Pennsylvania Department of Corrections, have developed Halfway Back diversions to addiction treatment as an alternative to prison. These options are used extensively by parole agents, but not expressly because someone is a veteran. The Pennsylvania Department of Corrections is soon due to release a veterans-specific substance abuse treatment request for proposals. Once implemented, this will likely divert many veterans into the Veterans' Sanctuary. The challenge to all of these huge systems is to work cooperatively on behalf of veterans, and to provide the appropriate levels of care and lengths of stay for effective treatment to occur.

Closing

It is often the immersion in longer-term treatment, such as the therapeutic community, that allows sufficient time to address life's long-standing patterns, and to create new, healthier, patterns. Long-term treatment also allows the reinforcement of the pro-social behavioral changes so needed to counter behaviors resulting from, or exacerbated by, imprisonment or the deterioration resulting from chronic addiction. TC treatment also promotes the building of a network of recovering peers that helps support one another during recovery, Vet Helping Vet. Since so many returning service members have been exposed to trauma and prolonged and repeated tours, to provide competent PTSD treatment while simultaneously addressing addiction is imperative. Shepherding the transition back into civilian life, and including the families and loved ones, is indeed the challenge of the day. The historic lack of mental health and addiction interventions contributed to one in four homeless people identifying as veterans (Rourke, 2007) and 8 to 12 percent of state prisons and county jails (Lavin, n.d.) being populated by veterans.

Proactive approaches can mitigate the repetition of this as hundreds of thousands of service members return from Iraq and Afghanistan. It is our hope and belief that Veterans' Sanctuary, utilizing the peer hierarchy of the Therapeutic Community, the Sanctuary Model, the holistic practices of mindfulness and yoga, the use of expressive arts (drama and art therapy), Tick's work (2005) in the healing of PTSD, and the inclusion of families, will make a positive difference for our returning veterans. "I have been through several treatment centers; this is the first time I feel prepared to leave and start my life" (Joe T., graduate of Veterans' Sanctuary).

Postscript: Lessons Learned at Veterans' Sanctuary

After 10 months of operation, and losses of $459,000, Veterans' Sanctuary went into a "pause" mode. This action was taken because the organization could no longer absorb losses of $55,000 monthly without jeopardizing the other programs under the Treatment Trends umbrella. The "pause" resulted in the referral of all residents into other treatment centers and the laying off of a very talented staff. Our next task was to evaluate whether the project could become a "break-even" program and, if not, still provide veteran-centric services at the Sanctuary. Our analysis was simple: were there enough referrals, and were our results positive? The answers to both were yes, except there were not enough *paid* referrals. Getting enough paid referrals means systemic changes.

The lack of paid referrals is explained as systems inertia on all sides: county, state, and federal. State funding is administered through counties, who interpret their guidelines to literally mean that they are the payer of last resort. This interpretation gave rise to the assumption that all veterans have benefits and should go to the VA, a mantra that played repeatedly with referrals to Veterans' Sanctuary.

It also meant the Bureau of Drugs and Alcohol programs, through their county authorization system, subtly cost shift veterans into either the VA or Medicaid-managed care. Very tight eligibility criteria further narrowed opportunities for treatment. Veterans with 30% disability, receiving $385 per month, were erroneously deemed ineligible for public funding. Counties inadvertently discriminated against veterans, not allowing the same access to care as all other citizens in the state. By the time this bureaucratic log jam was resolved, it was too late.

The VA had a big hand in our financial losses as well. The VA referred some 15 veterans needing longer, more structured, addiction/PTSD treatment. Though Veterans' Sanctuary is a fee basis provider with a federal CCR number, making us able to accept paid federal referrals, the VA authorized only one person, and only for 29 days. The VA middle and upper management remains disconnected from the ground level social workers who clearly recognize the need for long-term, structured, residential addiction treatment that is different to their extended care treatment paradigm. This is evidenced by many referrals attempted by many very caring, VA line-workers.

The VA remains plagued by difficult access to addiction care, high relapse rates, and a hierarchy that does not believe in bed-based addiction care and that does not know how to integrate planning and services with local communities and community-based providers willing to help.

Veterans' Sanctuary is currently working on a promising direct state contract that will fully fund the program to assure timely access to care for any veteran who has served our country.

Notes

1   As the time demands of developing a brand new program grew, the core group of 10 founders rapidly reduced in size to six people, most of whom were our own family members: two brothers, Richard and Robert Csandl, and a sister, Ria Feller; her husband Mike; Robert's then wife, Marlene; and a friend, Anita Goldman.
2   Upon receiving the vote and despite an excellent, airtight, point-by-point summation by one of the zoning officers, an attorney who owned a nearby building, appealed the decision. Despite his appeal and predicated upon the favorable zoning rulings and huge amounts of public support, we proceeded with the renovations. Our attorney advised us that we renovate at our own peril and could lose the appeal. After four months, the Court of Common Pleas ruled in our favor, indicating that his appeal lacked anything substantive enough to overturn the zoning board ruling.
3   For example: Walking With Warriors ($10,000 and above); Healing Heroes ($5,000–$9,999); Transforming Lives (($1,000–$4,999); Calming Storms ($500–$999); and Respecting Sacrifices (up to $499).
4   We gratefully did receive a $162,000 start up grant for salaries and equipment purchases from US Representative Charlie Dent, and two $5,000 grants from Pennsylvania Representatives Brennan and Grucela.

References

Atkinson, M. P., Guetz, A., & Wein, L. M. (2009). "A Dynamic Model for Post-Traumatic Stress Disorder in Operation Iraqi Freedom." Accessed at: http://www.stanford.edu/group/knowledgebase/cgi-bin/2009/09/19/high-ptsd-rates/.

Boulware, C. (2006). "EMDR-Therapy: Eye Movement Desensitization and Reprocessing." Accessed at: www.emdr-therapy.com/.

CMHS. (n.d.). "Sequential Intercepts for Developing CJ-MH Partnerships." Accessed at: http://gainscenter.samhsa.gov/pdfs/integrating/GAINS_Sequential_Intercept.pdf.

Deer Park Monastery. (2012). "Thich Nhat Banh: Biography of our Teacher." Accessed at: http://dpweb.org/about-us/thich-nhat-hanh.

Griffiths, M. (2005). "Comprehensive Model of Addiction within a Bio-Psycho-Social Frame." *Journal of Substance Abuse, 10* (4): 191–197.

Hoffman, S. G., Sawyer, A. T., Witt, A., & Oh, D. (2010, April). "The Effect of Mindfulness Based Therapy on Anxiety and Depression: A Meta Analytical Review." *Journal of Consulting & Clinical Psychology, 78* (2): 169–183.

Howard, M., McMillan, C., Nower, L., Elze, D., Edmond, T., & Bricort, J. (2002, Oct–Dec). "Denial in Addiction: Toward an Integrated Stage and Process Model—Qualitative Findings." *Journal of Psychoactive Drugs, 34* (4): 371–382.

Institute of Behavioral Research, Texas Christian University. (n.d.). "Forms for TC Assessments." Accessed at: http://www.ibr.tcu.edu/pubs/datacoll/datacoll.html.

Lavin, P. (n.d.). "Incarcerated Veterans: The Facts." Accessed at Pennsylvania State Council, Vietnam Veterans of America website: http://www.vva.-pa.org/the%20facts.htm.

Lewis, L. (2008, April 29). "Court Aims to Help Veterans with Legal Troubles." Accessed at: http://www.npr.org/templates/story/story.php?storyId=90016059.

National Association of Cognitive Behavioral Therapists (2011). Accessed at: nacbt.org. National Institute of Drug Abuse (2002, August). "Research Reports: Therapeutic Communities." Publication Number 02-4877, National Institute of Drug Abuse.

The Pennsylvania Code. (n.d.). "303.12. Guideline Sentence Recommendations: Sentencing Programs." Accessed at: http://www.pacode.com/secure/data/204/chapter303/s303.12.html.

Rourke, M. (2007, Nov. 7). "Veterans Make Up 1 in 4 Homeless." *USA Today.* Accessed at: http://www.usatoday.com/news/nation/2007-11-07-homeless-veterans_N.htm.

Samaritan Village Veterans Program (n.d.) "Veterans' Services." Accessed at: http://samvill.org/pages/programs.php#veteran.

Schinka, J. A., Francis, E., Hughs, P., LaLone, L., & Flynn, C. (July 1998). "Comparative Outcomes and Cost of Inpatient Care and Supportive Housing for Substance Dependent Veterans." *Psychiatric Services, 49* (7): 946–950.

Singh, G., & Singh, J. (2010). "Yoga Nidra: A Deep Mental Relaxation Approach." *British Journal of Sports Medicine, 44,* Supplement 1: 71–72.

Soldier's Heart. (2011). Accessed at: http://www.soldiersheart.net/.

Tan, M. (2009). "2 Million Troops Have Deployed Since 9/11." *Marine Corps Times.* Accessed at: http://www.marinecorpstimes.com/news/2009/12/militry_deployments_121809w/.

Tick, E. (2005). *War and the Soul: Healing Our Nation's Veterans from Post-Traumatic Stress Disorder.* Wheaton, IL: Quest Books.

U.S. Department of Veterans Affairs. (2011). "Substance Abuse: Overview: Alcohol and Drug Misuse and Dependence." Accessed at: http://www.mentalhealth.va.gov/substanceabuse.asp.

Yablonsky, L. (1965). *The Tunnel Back: Synanon: A Penetrating Look at a Community of Ex-Drug Addicts Who Help One Another . . .* (1st Edn). New York, NY: Macmillan.

Part III

Expressive-Experiential Approaches

7 Metaphor as Heroic Mediator

Imagination, Creative Arts Therapy, and Group Process as Agents of Healing with Veterans

Stephanie Wise and Emily Nash

> Our soul self is the best part of us. It's what gets lost in trauma.
> —Veteran group member

Metaphors can serve as mirrors of our inner lives, accessing essential aspects of ourselves that may have been lost, ruptured, or deeply wounded as a result of traumatic experience. In the course of our intensive work with veterans from several wars, we came to profoundly appreciate that a crucial component of their healing journeys included a search for the souls they felt they had lost. Within this context, metaphor emerged as a valiant guide leading the way through the arc of creative exploration towards discovery of the "artist within" and soul reconnection.

Introduction

While working with veterans suffering from the devastating effects of Post-Traumatic Stress Disorder (PTSD), therapists often find themselves wrestling with how to restore the fundamental sense of self which has been so harmed by traumatic experience. Traumatized persons often become strangers to themselves. Memory may become an agent of fear and torment, stalking like a predator, attacking through flashbacks and intrusive, vicious thoughts. This can result in significant collateral damage. If those suffering from PTSD retreat from social interaction to protect themselves and those they love, they run the risk of losing valuable inter-personal relationships.

Words and cognition are, of course, crucial to understanding and communicating our experiences, but we also store the effects of trauma at a bodily level. Sometimes there are no words to adequately express such experiences. Developing a safe environment for the essential containment of affect and memory may require approaching trauma work within a multi-dimensional framework. The metaphor provides a powerful tool to do just this. "Essential to the healing capacity of the art therapist is the use of metaphor" (Moon, p. 64). Engaging metaphor as the mediator between the devastating sensorial bodily memory of trauma and the explicit verbal narrative of *what happened* allows opportunities for bridging between fragmented parts of the self to occur. Moon goes on to state, "Metaphoric images contain an inherent quality of comparison in which one thing (art object) is used to shed new light on the character of the artist" (p. 123). Working within the metaphor can engender prospects for distancing, expansion of possibilities, and explorations of meaning. Moreover, to leap directly from the sensorial to the cognitive may bypass necessary transformative work which lends substance to true healing.

Metaphoric engagement requires courage on the part of both veterans and therapists, because this type of healing journey does not rely upon formulaic devices. Rather, it requires the open-ended integration of imagination, empathy, and creative expression. Metaphor heroically reaches into the heart of the trauma, symbolically transforms the unspeakable into a more manageable "other," and provides psychic fuel for the safe return to "ordinary" living. Imagination, group process and creative arts therapy can contribute enormously to the healing processes of veterans with PTSD.

Brief Context of the Project

The ArtReach Foundation, founded in 1999 by visionary Susan Anderson, and head-quartered in Atlanta, GA, has, as its mission, "to influence and assist—through creative expressive arts therapies—the growth and development of children who have experienced the traumatic effects of war, violence, and/or natural disaster" (http://artreach-foundation.org/. Accessed January 5, 2011). Each professional artist, creative arts therapist and mental health professional involved with ArtReach programs over the years has left an imprint on the formation ArtReach Model™ through his or her contributions of artistic interventions, theoretical persuasions, and human heart. We gratefully acknowledge the collective offerings of all those team members who created the building blocks for the development of such rich programs. In our combined 13 years of working with ArtReach—Stephanie from 2005 to 2010 and Emily from 2002 to 2010—it has been an honor to help develop the work with these generous professionals. Over the decade-plus of its existence, ArtReach has provided opportunities for creative arts therapists to work internationally, as well as domestically. Most recently, ArtReach created a pilot program, known as Project America, to work with veterans stateside.

For 10 months, from June 2009 through March 2010, we conducted a pilot project with both male and female veterans representing three generations and five branches of military service (Army, Navy, Air Force, Marines, and Coast Guard Reserves) through our affiliation with the ArtReach Foundation. The project included both a train-the-trainers focus for clinicians and veteran peers, and direct work with veterans who were seeking an alternative healing experience. We brought to the project our over 40 years of combined experience as creative arts therapists specializing in art and drama, as well as our expertise in the field of trauma. This chapter shares our theoretical influences, clinical rationale, creative arts interventions, group process stories, and the transformative role that working in the metaphor played during our work with veterans in pilot Project America.

Theoretical Influences

Edward Tick, in his seminal book, *War and the Soul* (2005), captures the essence of war trauma's damaging effects and the challenges posed for therapists when working with veterans diagnosed with Post-Traumatic Stress Disorder. Tick (2005) refers to the soul not in religious terms, but as a person's core identity which, in the face of traumatic experience, suffers greatly

In my extensive work with vets, another thing I learned is that PTSD is not best understood or treated as a stress disorder, as it is now characterized. Rather, it is best understood as an identity disorder and soul wound, affecting the personality at the deepest levels.

(p. 5)

The soul "wounding" of veterans can be a deeply complex process requiring multidimensional therapeutic approaches to provide optimal outcomes. Tick (2005) brilliantly concedes, "We see why veterans' healing is so difficult to achieve and why conventional modalities often fall short" (p. 5). He suggests, "All such creative activities helped transform war stories from violence into art and from personal story into tribal myth" (p. 219). The role of creativity as agent of transformation is not readily found in traditional verbal therapeutic encounters.

War trauma often leaves the veteran in a wake of psychic isolation, emotionally separated from family, friends, and community. Judith Herman (1992), noted psychiatrist and trauma expert, speaks of its effect this way:

> Traumatic events destroy the sustaining bonds between individual and community. Those who have survived learn that their sense of self, of worth, of humanity, depends upon a feeling of connection to others. The solidarity of a group provides the strongest protection against terror and despair, and the strongest antidote to traumatic experience. Trauma isolates; the group re-creates a sense of belonging.
>
> (p. 214)

Tapping into the strength of the interpersonal bonding developed within the military can help facilitate relational connections outside of the combat realm. Working with veterans within a therapeutic group context often helps counteract the sense of isolation veterans may feel when re-entering civilian life.

Imagination, Creativity and Metaphor in Healing

Imagination is central to the continued advancement of the human race. On a macro level, imagination put into action has contributed to all great leaps of civilization. On a micro level, engagement of imagination opens up possibilities for us to change our perceptions of experience and grant us permission to re-write our stories as we need to tell them. Imagination is free from rules or proscriptions and links the spirit to many fundamentals of the human condition.

Imagination can propel and inspire creative expression through art making, dramatic enactment, writing, movement, and singing. Stephen K. Levine reminds us in *Trauma, Tragedy, Therapy: The Arts and Human Suffering* (2009) that, in using the full range of the creative arts, we make passage through layers of potentialities, exploring and playing with ideas, releasing constrictions between familiar and unfamiliar worlds.

The expressive arts therapist could then be considered as an expert in moving from the center to the margin and returning home; from the literal reality of the world to its imaginal possibilities, and back again, in order to find a new perspective (p. 37).

Much has been written about the effects of trauma on the brain, by such notable authors and neurologists as Bessel van der Kolk, MD, Oliver Sachs, MD, Jeanne Segal, PhD, and many others. We understand more and more about the effect of trauma on the pre-frontal cortex, hyperarousal, feedback loops, the hippocampus, serotonin, Broca's area, right brain/left brain functioning etc. Hard outcome measurements often typify the generally accepted point of view that there needs to be scientific medical model evidence for our understanding the veracity of healing work. However, scientific explanations may fall short in capturing the essence of the human experience. Measuring does not tell the entire story of what it means to suffer as a human. It certainly cannot reveal, at an existential level, that meaningful moment of feeling deeply understood by another person.

Exploration through the creative arts opens possibilities for other people to bear witness to our restorative journeys. The making of artworks can initiate relationships between their creator and the public—whether mental health providers, group peers, family members, or the public at large. The re-forging of relationships through creative witnessing can become central in repairing a sense of belonging and connectedness to others. Jonathan Shay (2002), author of *Odysseus in America: Combat Trauma and the Trials of Homecoming*, writes, "It is impossible to overstate the importance of the arts in creating the supportive social movements that permit trauma to have voice and the voice to be heard, believed, remembered, and re-spoken" (p. 244).

Collaborative engagement of the creative arts can expand the reach of more traditional forms of contemporary therapeutic interventions. Often the expressive qualities of images, movements, sounds, etc., speak in ways that go unabridged right to the heart of the matter. The arts resourcefully penetrate verbal defenses, bypassing our internal censors. These censors often reinforce habitual narratives which may have been masking our true emotional experiences. McNiff (2009) states that:

> The arts heal and further all forms of therapeutic practice by giving the psyche opportunities to treat itself through creative expression . . . This special quality of the arts enable[s] us to move between realms of consciousness in ways that are not possible in therapies based exclusively on verbal communication.
>
> (p. 13)

Working in the "metaphor" is an effective approach, for it enables people to engage in the therapeutic experience without becoming victimized by the process. Metaphor can be thought of as a way of describing something by comparing or describing it in words which are not normally associated with it. "The thunder was an angry lion roaring in the night," "His eyes were stars twinkling above my head," or "The earth was a velvet blanket beneath my feet" are simple illustrations of metaphoric allusions. In working with traumatized persons, respectful titrating of inter-psychic material is essential, so people do not become flooded, triggered, or in any way left feeling vulnerable. Metaphor helps promote a sense of safety, as one of the primary tools in the creative arts therapies repertoire, especially during the initial phases of internal exploration.

> When it is time for metaphor to step aside, the defused traumatic material is then more readily available for direct confrontation. Some patients may never be able to speak directly about certain issues, and the healing process is embedded in the

witnessed art making process and product. But I do believe that the deepest healing comes out of being helped to experience one's feelings consciously and eventually to process them verbally, and the use of the metaphor and art process and product often provide an essential, intermediary bridge to developing that capacity.

(Buk, 2007)

The simultaneous capacity for metaphor to create safe distancing, while transforming traumatic material, provide dual influences for containment and restructuring of the suffering. Murray Stein (1998) confirms, in *Jung's Map of the Soul*, "humans have the ability, and the need, to think in metaphors, and this may lie behind the process of transformation" (p. 65).

Working within the metaphor appears to tap into existential concerns about life and meaning, which can, ironically, enhance a present sense of interconnectedness among group members. Mooli Lahad (2000) in *Creative Supervision* refers to this dynamic as "the metaphoric way of thinking" (p. 16). We found it significant that, of all the people we have worked with over the years, veterans emerged among the staunchest supporters of metaphoric work, perhaps because of the direct joining between the healthy reconnection to the soul and the sense of renewal achieved through creativity. To quote, once more, from the wisdom of McNiff (2004): "The medicines of art are not confined within fixed borders. Wherever the soul is in need, art presents itself as a resourceful healer" (p. 5).

Nash/Wise Theoretical Framework

For over a decade, the programs and activities utilized by The ArtReach Foundation have been built upon a stream of contributions by very talented professional creative arts therapists, artists, and other mental health providers who have participated in running their groups. In 2009, during the evolution of the pilot Project America, we developed a guidebook entitled *Exploring the Sacred Space Within*, which clearly delineated and integrated specific principles and professional influences describing the theoretical underpinnings we drew upon for the pilot project. The following section briefly covers our clinical rationale.

We relied heavily upon the combined brilliant thinking of writers and clinicians Judith Herman, Jonathan Shay and Edward Tick for the formulation of the foundation of the work. In analyzing the over-arching principles of these three authors, we became aware of their roots of interconnectedness. Herman, in her book *Trauma and Recovery* (1992, p. 3), frames the healing process around four basic concepts: safety and a healing relationship; remembrance and mourning; reconnection; and commonality. Jonathan Shay, in *Odysseus in America* (2002, p. 243), developed a paradigm which includes a circle of communalization, purification after battle, and "to be home." Edward Tick, in *War and the Soul* (2005, p. 47), speaks of five essential steps for the healing of the warrior's soul. They are creation of a sacred space; purification and cleansing; the healing power of storytelling; initiation through transformative rituals; and the integration of historical responsibilities of all parties (veterans, families, communities, and nations). We then crafted a creative arts way to interweave (see below) their theories, fashioning a framework which had an inclusive and flexible approach to working with traumatized veterans.

Tick:	Creation of a sacred space
Herman:	Safety—A healing relationship
Shay:	Circle of communalization
Tick:	Purification and cleansing
Shay:	Purification after battle—communal rituals for all returning veterans free of sectarian, [religious], political or ideological partisanship
Tick:	The healing power of story telling
Herman:	Remembrance and mourning
Tick:	Initiation through transformative rituals
Herman:	Reconnection
Tick:	Shared responsibility of history by all parties (veterans, families, communities, nations)
Herman:	Commonality
Shay:	To be home

In addition to the healing framework, the inclusion of metaphor as a key player in the creative arts repertoire served to enhance the therapeutic alliance with veterans. Within the framework, metaphor took creativity beyond the mere pleasure of art making—though there is great value in those aspects of creative endeavor—and approached the traumatic material in ways that many veterans had not experienced before. The method was more indirect, subtle, and open to participation by all group members, because imagination was able to tap into universal experiences and understandings. The therapeutic engagement of metaphor operating in a symbolic realm created a gentle parallel process, linking healthy imagination as a counterbalance to the veteran's deeply frightening inner world of traumatic exposure.

Traumatic response, by its nature, induces constriction of thinking and feeling. The intention we specifically promoted was opening the engagement of the creative arts experiences from predictable directives to an ebb and flow of semi-planned metaphoric options, available to be chosen and experienced dynamically in the moment. We remained open to spontaneous revision, depending upon the needs of the group. We refer to this way of working as the "expansion of flexibility," whereby the framework feels organic and less prominent than the actual experience of the moment. The structure of the group experience was continuously shifting and fluctuating between the visual, the dramatic, writing, movement, storytelling, and the emotional communication between group members.

From our way of thinking, this fluidity of intention allowed for deeper and more relevant explorations. As a way of creating initial connections to one another, a newly formed group of veterans was asked to express, through movement and words, an aspect of themselves that they were bringing to the group. "Courage," a "heavy heart," "anxiety," and "a searching soul" were among the several offerings to the circle. From there, group members were invited to create, with paint and various drawing materials, symbols of their selves inspired by the words they had shared. This allowed for deeper revelation and, in some cases, transformation of the original offering. The symbols were then hung from the branches of a bare tree crafted by the son of one of our colleagues. Gathering around the tree, each person was asked to share a bit about their own creation and comment on what they observed in each other's work. From there, the common theme of "A Human Voyage" was collectively decided upon, which in turn led to deeply meaningful explorations through movement, written stories, and dramatization.

Therapists working this way need to have flexibility, willingness, imagination, and the experience to flow with the group needs of the moment and the overall therapeutic plan. To most effectively apply this work, therapists are best served by being immersed in the method themselves, in a hands-on way. We often say, "This is a way of being, not just a way of doing," as we try to guide the "expansion of flexibility" of the therapeutic session as seamlessly as possible.

Stories of Healing

From the moment we gather, we enter into a discovery process. Throughout our days together, we continue through the arc, following each thread. Consciously and unconsciously, we weave together a group, the fabric of a healing community. The following vignettes represent a few examples of the creative process as it took place in the actual sessions with veterans.

The Path: A Journey of Transformation

The archetypal image of a path helps open the way for meaningful creative exploration, especially for those who are consciously embarking on restorative journeys. Transformation is at the heart of the warriors' journey, and inspired us to create an arc of exploration that carried us from simple moving images to a profound rite of passage. We continually kept this concept in our minds as we worked with the ebb and flow of the needs of the participants in the room.

The day began with welcoming a new veteran to an already formed group. Still living on the base, Steve arrived in his Army uniform, sharing with us that he had just finished serving in Iraq and Afghanistan, and had served a combined 30 years in the military. He was now in the midst of a daunting, very rocky, transition back into civilian life. The other vets, who had already been through a number of workshops and were in training to become peer leaders, shared with him some of their experiences. They assured Steve that he was in a safe and healing environment. "If you release yourself into this experience," Roger told him, "you will find real benefit by the end of the day." "No one will be judging you," Brenda shared. "In here you are what you are, and that's completely accepted." Henry added, "What they do in here is exactly what people need. Sometimes it's hard to reach the places words cannot. This is a powerful tool to work with; a way to reach into yourself. They teach us the power of metaphor—the meaning behind the art."

We moved into a warm up with music that evoked the experience of journeying. The old spiritual, "Wade in the Water" immediately shifted the energy in the room, as each participant was encouraged to offer a spontaneous movement inspired by the music. Emily invited each veteran to "simply allow your body to guide you, to move as it wants to." Group members mirrored the movements of others. In doing this, each person created a simple movement which was then repeated by the other group members as a response to the initiator. Mirroring can be experienced as a profound way of being seen, appreciated, and joined.

We peeled out from the circle and then traveled in a line throughout the large and open room. Everyone eventually took a place at the head of the line, and roamed wherever they wished in sweeping serpentine formations of movement throughout the space. Kevin took the lead, playfully stepping into the rhythm of the music. Steve, so new to this process, surprised us by rushing next to move to the front of the line. Spreading his arms wide, and with graceful stride, he began to leap, glide, swoop, and fly, while leading us in circular patterns throughout the space. A dancer in fatigues! His face was joyful and radiant with pleasure. The artist hidden inside the soldier had been released. The movement journeys completed, we gathered as a group for a short ritual check-in, as we do following each new experience. Checking in with Steve, for whom this was all so new, Emily asked, "How did you find this experience?" Steve unhesitatingly responded, "Exhilarating!"

From the exuberant energies of the warm up, we moved into stillness, as Emily began a guided meditation. Each person was asked to find a place in the room to relax. They were directed back to their breath; slow, deep breathing, focusing only on inhaling and exhaling. In taking the time to consciously unclutter our minds of repetitive narratives, we can quiet the habitual voices that keep us spinning in place and expand internal openness. The veterans would often speak of the importance of "mindfulness" as a part of their healing process, and we made a point of interspersing times of activity with times of mindful rest. "It is the awareness of our capacity to be self-creative in the state of mindfulness which promotes the ability to change. The arts are natural activities of expression. Expression leads to mindfulness" (Moon, p. 116).

Steph then took the relaxation into a guided imagery; that of a path open to the possibilities of being familiar or not, colorful, realistic or fantastical—whatever the internal landscape offered to the mind's eye. She then, softly, asked participants to open their eyes, and directed them to a table of paints, brushes, and paper, as she invited them to paint individual images of their paths. Quiet music was played. The atmosphere was one of deep immersion in creative exploration.

As they finished, Steph prepared a space on the floor of the room for the paintings to be placed. One by one, each person thoughtfully placed their work where they felt it belonged. Some were drawn to resting their paintings very specifically next to others; some chose the corners, the center, above, or below. Time was taken for this ritual, as it became a meaningful connection between the very concentrated individual work and the collective sharing that followed.

Initially, the collective work was viewed in silence. People were standing, sitting, or circling around the art. Represented was a range of colorful and original paths. Steve painted a rich cerulean blue river, with moss green banks on both sides and a large dark brown fallen tree spanning the water between. Evan created a small pale blue paper cutout representing a homeless veteran. He glued a crimson heart to its chest and placed the tiny figure on his path with the word "HOPE" written in emerald green above. Bob fashioned a path of muted colors, with barely visible barren trees drawn in colored pencil. All the paths of the group were deeply personal and meaningful.

Steph asked the group members, "What do you see?" "Would you like to share something about your own painting?" "What may resonate with you in someone else's art?" The homeless veteran was immediately noticed and appreciated by many in the group. There was a wish to have him travel through the different trails. Steph encouraged this exploration, and asked the members to find words for what they felt the homeless veteran might want to say. As group members shared, it was clear they had a greater understanding of his journey in life, and their own, as well. Here are some of their reflections:

"There are all types of paths, winding in different directions."
"I see obstacles, lots of obstacles"
"You definitely have to look back, the journey takes you back."
"There are internal pathways."
"Images of water, nature, landscapes, that say we have gone through a lot."
"We are all on a path."
"They are not just about our own path."
"These paths have a lot to say, from the past to now."

We moved the conversation from their individual observations into finding common themes for the group. Three themes resonated: *Looking backwards and moving forward*; *obstacles*; and *sanctuary*. The chosen themes were then explored kinesthetically, through embodiment in group sculptures. As each person entered the space with a sculpted stance expressing their connection to the themes, common elements of each individual's painting became revealed through the living tableau. Bringing each theme to life this way took the group to deeper levels in their collective exploration, compelling the members towards the next major endeavor—the actual building of a path. Ultimately, Bill titled the following experience "A Journey of Transformation."

Steph directed the group's attention to the abundance of art materials on the tables in the room—large rolls of brown and white paper, construction paper, paints, markers, feathers, string, and hemp. She offered a simple directive: "As a group, please feel free to create a path, any path, of your choosing. Your path can take any form; whatever you as a community feel you need that somehow reflects your journey at this moment. Take time to speak with each other, share your thoughts and ideas and, when you're ready, gather the materials you want to use and begin to create."

The directive was intentionally open-ended, not offering specific ideas that would influence the creative expression of the group. We trusted that what would ultimately come into being would be a collective healing journey. A profound arc of exploration had brought the group to this moment. It was time for us as leaders to step away, allowing the group to struggle through the process on their own. We never doubted they would find their way.

Little did we realize, at the time, how literal our "stepping away" would be! It was our intention to sit unobtrusively in the back of the room. We hardly expected the request from the group that we actually leave the physical space. The group members asked to be completely on their own. A bit taken aback, we wondered if we might be abandoning our therapeutic responsibilities. We quickly realized that here was a room filled with veterans from the Marines, Army, Navy, Air Force, and Coast Guard Reserves! We had little to worry about. We were learning to what extent the collaborative work was tapping into the strengths and resilience of these veterans.

When we were invited back into the room, an hour later, we saw the space transformed. Spanning before us, covering the entire length of the room, was an elaborate paper pathway which was over 60 feet in length—a breathtaking and extraordinary

Figure 7.1 "Looking backwards and moving forward," "obstacles," and "sanctuary." Used with permission.

creation. We were greeted by rows of outstretched arms and welcoming words from Bob, as he invited us in and solemnly said, "This path contains everyone's footprint, handprint, and soulprint."

The path in front of us reflected the journey through the three themes. It began with "looking backward and moving forward," moved through "obstacles" located mid-way along the route, and ended with "sanctuary." At the start, twelve narrow paths merged into the central path like tributaries feeding into a river—each participant's symbolic expression of the journey taken before meeting together in this room. The common road led to a river running the width of the space. It was full of large boulders and obstacles that interrupted the current's flow, making passage difficult. Over the river rose a thin, rickety bridge—crossing the river was quite treacherous, but possible. Farther still, on the other side of the river, the path led into a painting of an orange, yellow, and red butterfly, made from a huge piece of brown paper, 6 feet by 8 feet: the sanctuary. In the middle of the sanctuary, attached to the butterfly, was the homeless veteran, this time larger in scale and with an orange heart placed on his chest. Here in the sanctuary, a

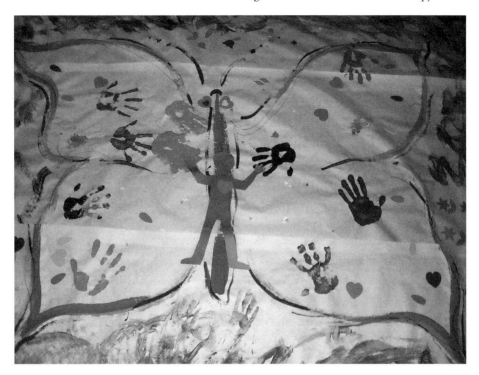

Figure 7.2 "Sanctuary for the homeless veteran." Used with permission.

place of safety and holding, the veterans said they would always find a home. They would always be welcome.

One by one, each person was invited to travel along the path. Native American flute music accompanied the passage. Bill went first. A measured step. Then another. Suddenly, he bent backwards on himself, falling over, sinking into the floor, head in his hands. Slowly regaining his balance, he began again, a few more steps forward, and he then catapulted sideways to the edge of the room, pounding the wall with his hands. With cautious determination he found his way back to the path. His movements became a bit less constricted, and his stride a bit lighter. He came to the river, but could not overcome the challenge of the boulders and strong current. He decided to take the bridge. With great care and steady gait, pausing for long intervals to balance himself, he very gradually made his way to the sanctuary, where he raised his arms in triumph and relief. An expression of joy came over his face. He turned, faced back and, with open heart, he waited to receive the next veteran about to take the journey.

In turn, each group member entered into what became a symbolic rite of passage, while the others waited, serving as witness. Evan became the homeless veteran, finding a spot under the bridge where he laid down in exhaustion and defeat. Spontaneously, others came to help him, encouraging him to carry on. Henry continually looked backwards while he moved forward, stopping often along the way to sit down and take time to think. He struggled to let go of what he had left behind—a reminder that, as he had told us often during the workshop, he had been obliged to leave behind men under his command, men he could no longer protect.

Each person reached the sanctuary, a welcomed traveler on the journey, and, when the last person completed the passage, the group stood together in silence. At that moment, in that place, the collective imagination and creative experience had transformed the room into a sacred space. We thought the best way for them to honor the experience would be to ask the veterans to write their personal reflections. Here is what Bill wrote:

> North.
> The water of life flows over my left side.
> The brambles of the path cling to the right.
> I sway and struggle to get away.
> The water cools my blood.
> I breathe in and I breathe out, facing south.
> And cross over the stream.
> Into the lightening of love.

The Return: A Dramatization

During a session in which the themes of "departure" and "return" emerged from an art exploration, very powerful living sculpts were created, embodying each of these experiences. As often happens, aspects of the living sculpture seemed ripe for further exploration. Emily asked all but two of the people inside the tableau to remain still.

Henry and Beth were facing each other, she with open arms in a forward movement towards him, he only reaching halfway and obviously conflicted. In life, Beth is married to a military man and Henry is a veteran. There was a story here, which Emily felt would be meaningful for them to bring to life through developing a dramatic enactment. She moved towards them. "Could you both come out of the freeze and imagine you are characters in a scene and give voice to whatever you feel is going on between you?" This was as much as she said, careful to not impose her idea of the actual story on them. Usually, group members will spontaneously move into characters and enact the story they need to tell.

Beth began, "Welcome home, honey." She moved to hug him. He could not respond. "Aren't you happy to see me?" she queried. He was still unable to speak. He looked towards Emily, motioning his difficulty in responding. Emily asked him what he was experiencing in his role as the husband. Henry said, "I can't respond. I'm just not feeling what I'm supposed to be feeling." Emily assured his character, "Stay with whatever you are feeling. Don't feel you need to push yourself into anything else." Always following the current of authentic emotional communication, Emily gently encouraged Beth and Henry in their roles as "wife and husband" to put into words that which most truthfully expressed what they were experiencing, in order to try to move them closer to a place of meaningful connection and new understanding.

For Henry, this situation was particularly close to his own life. The dramatization became an opportunity to explore other ways of entering into what had, since the onset of his PTSD, seemed impossible conversations. The breakdown in communication that veterans face in engaging with family and friends, when they are asked to share wartime experiences, was an ongoing theme in our groups. An opportunity through metaphoric dramatization now presented itself as another way of speaking parts of the truth to loved ones. As Beth and Henry stepped into roles as husband and wife, they were able to take the distance necessary to deepen their listening and acceptance of one another.

Emily next focused on Beth's character. Empathic communication from her might reach Henry in a way that would allow him to trust that his feelings and experiences could be safely expressed. And she, as the "metaphoric wife," might not feel so shut out or pushed away. The messy struggles relationships face in the aftermath of trauma benefit enormously from the safe exploration of relational work within the metaphor. In addition, the support of the group permits these interpersonal struggles to be practiced, through imagination and in the company of others who share similar inner conflicts, without the fears and consequences of "real life."

Emily asked Beth/Wife what she thought her "metaphoric husband" might be experiencing.

Beth/Wife: Kind of a disconnection, a strangeness around being back, a little lost . . .
Emily: Ok. With that in mind, please continue the conversation.
Beth/Wife: I guess you must be feeling really weird suddenly being back here. Kind of like you've landed on another planet or something. Is that why you won't you speak to me? You aren't happy to be back? To see me?"
Henry/Husband: I think I am but I don't know.
Beth/Wife: You really don't know? I've been waiting for this moment for so long. I'm here, Henry You can tell me everything.
Henry/Husband: That's the problem. I can't. You think you want to hear everything, but you really don't.

Beth appeared at a loss of how to respond. She looked towards Emily for guidance. Emily moved over to Beth, placed her hand on her shoulder, and explained, "I'm going to now do what we call doubling. I'm going to voice what I think you may be feeling. If it feels right, repeat it. If not, don't." Beth agreed to try to work this way in an effort to move the dialogue into deeper truth.

Emily as Wife for Beth: I'm not sure what to say, this isn't at all what I expected. But, I do want to be here for you.

Beth/Wife repeats this.

Henry/Husband: I'm not sure you can be.
Emily as Wife for Beth: I'm not sure either, but I would like you to give me a chance.

Beth/Wife repeats this.

Henry/Husband: It's just so hard for me to trust.
Emily as Wife for Beth: Well yeah, I can understand that, but it would be better if you could tell me that you can't trust, rather than just shutting down.

Beth/Wife repeated these words. She was clearly connecting with this approach, as the pitch, tone, and affect of her voice resonated with the words Emily had given her.

Henry/Husband: You would be okay with my saying that?

Beth/Wife now responded on her own.

Beth/Wife: Yes, I think so. Just as long as we could both keep talking.

Henry hesitated and appeared reluctant to speak further. Emily delicately guided him to try to stay present and allow himself to simply speak the truth in his heart.

Henry/Husband: I'm so sorry, Beth. Too much has happened and I really don't know if I am the same guy you knew before I went to war. I can't seem to trust anything or anyone anymore.

A long silence ensued. (Our work in all of the arts places high value on the importance of taking the time necessary to allow the words, images, or movements to flow at a natural pace.) Beth then continued:

Beth/Wife: Maybe you just need time?
Henry/Husband: "Do I have time? Maybe I need too much time? Maybe so much time that you will leave me?"

Beth motioned to Emily and requested a double.

Emily doubled Beth: I'm not going anywhere. I'm here.

Beth/Wife said this to Henry. The connection between them was palpable to the other group members. We were all in this moment together. Beth/Wife continued.

Beth/Wife: Can I ask you to try to let me know what's going on with you even if you just say you're having a hard day, or need some space?
Henry/Husband: I'll try. You may have to remind me.
Beth/Wife: I can do that.

Emily asked Beth if she had anything else she wanted to say to Henry. Beth immediately jumped in:

Beth/Wife: Honey, I can be real patient. And I know it will take time. And I also want to tell you that you may not think that I can handle your telling me what went on over there, but I think I can. I know I can. And really, I would like to know. So, after some time, if you are ready, you can tell me. Really, you can.

Henry's gaze softened as he took in the words Beth had expressed. He nodded his head in a motion of thanks to Beth. He understood what she had told him. Emily asked him what he was feeling. He responded that he felt calmer, lighter and more open. He pondered, and then added that maybe at some point he would be able to talk to her about what he had been through. Emily invited him to speak those words directly to Beth.

Henry/Husband: I wouldn't have thought this could happen, but I do feel closer to you. Feel like I may be able to be more open. Not now. Not yet. But maybe someday.
Beth/Wife: It's okay. We have lots of time.

Transformation: Metaphor Poems

Metaphor can serve as a transformative means of self-exploration, as well as a powerful agent of connection between group members. Early on in our work together, we invited people to write "metaphor poems," a spontaneous accessing of aspects of self through freely offering as many metaphors describing oneself that may come to mind. The process of this internal search inevitably becomes one of discovery and expansion, often moving people into parts of their inner world that may be otherwise shut down, or too difficult to traverse. Several of the veterans in our group found the process of writing these poems painful, yet liberating. The creation of the metaphor poems allowed for deep sharing of trauma stories, ultimately serving as a part of the narrative witnessing that is so crucial to the healing experience.

Bob's Poem

I was the bullet that tore the flesh and ripped the heart out of the VC,
I was the combat boots that tromped down the rice in the paddies in order to survive, for I knew walking on the dykes was deadly.
I was the shrapnel that exploded the body of a poet, a farmer, another warrior.
I was the arms holding my buddy as he died.
I was the pen that could not write to his family because my heart had bled out.
I was Anger for years, never trusting or intimate, not realizing the change within and without.
I became, as a Buddhist monk praying, meditating, seeking solace and finally able to put the garments together to become whole;
A warrior seeking peace.

Final Thoughts

Civilian clinicians, care providers, social workers, counselors, other mental health professionals, and artists working with active duty soldiers, veterans, and family members will find creative engagement a remarkable means for helping traumatized populations. Because the use of the arts is so powerful, it is recommended that professional creative arts therapists have a central role on the treatment team. Trained veterans serving as peer facilitators are crucial members of the team as well, often bridging between the therapists, the veterans, and the community as voices of authenticity and experience.
It was our very great honor to contribute to the healing journeys of those veterans we came to know, in these workshops, during Project America with The ArtReach Foundation. Integration of imagination, creative arts therapy, and group process opened

the way for the veterans to access new means of processing difficult traumatic material without experiencing triggering or flashback. New identification with "the artist within" often shifted the negative lens of personal self-concept, helping to enrich a more positive personal identity. Creativity reignited old familiar aspects of the soul which many had felt had been lost or extinguished by the oppressive inner predation of their traumatic experiences. The group became a restorative community in which each member felt accepted and valued. During the entirety of the project, metaphor stood fast—heroically containing and transforming unspeakable traumatic material as was needed, and then, when the timing was right, stepped aside as the personal narratives were ready to safely emerge.

References

ArtReach Foundation, The. (n.d.). http://artreachfoundation.org/.
Buk, A. (2007, May 4). Interview. Accessed at: Arttherapynyu.blogspot.com.
Herman, J. (1992). *Trauma and Recovery*. New York, NY: Harper Collins Publishers.
Lahad, M. (2000). *Creative Supervision*. London and Philadelphia: Jessica Kingsley Publishers.
Levine, S. K. (2009). *Trauma, Tragedy, Therapy: The Arts and Human Suffering*. London and Philadelphia: Jessica Kingsley Publishers.
McNiff, S. (2004). *Art Heals: How Creativity Cures the Soul*. Boston, MA: Shambhala.
McNiff, S. (2009). *Integrating the Arts in Therapy*. Springfield, IL: Charles C. Thomas Publishers.
Moon, B. (2008). *Introduction to Art Therapy*. Springfield, IL: Charles C. Thomas Publishers.
Shay, J. (2002). *Odysseus in America: Combat Trauma and the Trials of Homecoming*. New York, NY: Simon and Schuster.
Stein, M. (1998). *Jung's Map of the Soul*. Chicago: Carus Publishing Company.
Tick, E. (2005). *War and the Soul: Healing Our Nation's Veterans from Post-Traumatic Stress Disorder*. Wheaton, IL: Quest Books.

8 Writing by Service Members and Veterans

A Medium to Promote Healing in Self and Others

Ron Capps (OEF)

> Only, I felt, by some such attempt to write history in terms of personal life could I rescue something that might be of value, some element of truth and hope and usefulness, from the smashing up of my own youth by the war.
>
> —Vera Brittain, *Testament of Youth*

Vera Brittain was a British Army nurse during World War I. Her book, *Testament of Youth* (1933), describes how the war changed her life and the lives of those around her. It is, as she notes, an attempt to rescue something useful, something of value from the war. Writing served her, as it has served others for millennia; healing psychological wounds and providing a window of insight on war for those who were not participants.

For Brittan and for others, those insights, whether written as poetry, fiction or non-fiction, serve as testimony. They can indict or absolve the author of some action, of some memory, of some trauma; but the written work must be created first.

This chapter presents options available to therapists in utilizing writing as a therapeutic intervention or for developing a writing therapy program for traumatized war fighters and veterans. It includes a discussion of both how and why writing therapy works as a tool for allowing veterans the time and space to better understand what has happened to them, and to examine, at a distance, the events and the feelings that remain. Specific exercises are described to help individuals begin the therapeutic writing process. There is consideration of the pedagogical theories underpinning this type of work, a model structure for organizing a therapeutic writing program, and some vignettes that serve as examples.

Memories of Traumatic Events, and Writing

Memories of traumatic events fester in the mind. Indeed, memories of some traumatic experiences, especially experiences from a war, may never become fully integrated with other memories. Those memories, those stories, stand apart from other experiences in our lives because they often involve actions antithetical to what we understand as acceptable human interaction, or are so violent or damaging that they will not coalesce into a manageable form.

The violence and destruction that occur in war—killing and maiming, inhumanity and hatred—can quite often extend beyond our ability to understand. We see, but we sometimes cannot fully process what we have witnessed, because it is simply incomprehensible. And what we cannot comprehend, we cannot express. As a result, memories are compartmentalized, metaphorically stuffed into little boxes and stored under a bed in our minds, until something shakes them up. This is when problems may begin.

A personal aside may help illustrate this point. When I was mobilized for deployment to Afghanistan in 2002, I was called away from a civilian job and a cozy suburban home, ordered back to the Army I left eight years prior. I had safely compartmentalized all of the memories of earlier violence in central Africa and the Balkans into those metaphorical boxes under the bed. Mobilization rattled me enough that the lids came off of these boxes and the traumatic memories began to emerge. Within a few weeks of my arrival in Afghanistan, I began to have dreams populated by the dead and maimed, the mutilated and the dishonored. Not long afterwards, the images remained in my head during the day. I was rapidly losing control of my mind.

I was, as you might imagine, somewhat surprised to find myself face-to-face with those images. I thought I had control over the remembrance of violence, of destruction, of death. Of course, I was wrong. I had not synthesized those memories to gain full control over them.

I had tried for so long to wish those memories away. In mental health treatment, I learned that this was impossible. Not only did those memories exist, but they were capable of assuming control over my thoughts. I learned that none of us has the ability to change or undo the past or completely erase what we have seen and experienced—and, perhaps, particularly so with the memories of war trauma. In time, I learned to better manage and deal with my war trauma through writing.

Writing is, above all, an exercise of the imagination. Our minds allow us to create, with language, things that did not previously exist. Neurologists, philosophers, and artists may all have differing explanations of how this process works. But it is safe to say that the cumulative influence of our experiences allows us to shape language into words, sentences, paragraphs, dialogue, scenes, and stories.

Writing allows us to concretize, to synthesize, and to shape memories differently through expressive language, such as the use of metaphors. It offers additional avenues for expression and resolution, beyond trying to deal with trauma solely on an internal basis. Perhaps the most important skill needed is the ability to create metaphors. We can think of a metaphor as simply comparing two thoughts or ideas, such as figures of speech, or one idea envisioned as another; a type of symbol to help us better understand the underlying concept. For example, Ernst Junger (1920) described an artillery barrage: "The earth leapt up in hissing fountains, and a hail of splinters swept over the land like a shower of rain."

The ability to effectively shape a narrative, or use metaphors, is critical for expressive writing, but many traumatized veterans are inexperienced in calling upon written language as a means of understanding, at a deeper level, the impact traumatic exposure in their lives.

Comprehending the Incomprehensible: Writing About War Trauma

How do we describe, to someone who has never participated in combat, what it means to overcome fear under an artillery barrage? How can we explain something as complex as the relationships that developed among a bomber crew in combat over Europe in 1944, or a platoon of Marines defending an isolated firebase in Vietnam in 1971, or a cavalry troop dismounting to face an insurgent attack in Iraq in 2005? No matter how we try to understand these things inside our heads, they are too complex to grasp all at once. Writing allows us to structure these emotions, these events, in ways that allow us to understand them.

And so we write; we use words to give meaning to the incomprehensible. A shorter work might assist us in understanding one specific event or moment. A longer or book-length narrative allows us to separate events or feelings and to understand each of them individually and collectively. Writing also allows us to place these events in context and, hopefully, to come to grasp a greater truth—a primary goal of literary writing.

The Therapeutic Benefit of Writing

Clearly, Vera Brittain used her writing as a form of therapy. Writers have long known the cathartic value of story telling. The oldest existing stories are tales of war and return. Homer's *Iliad* is the story of Achilles and the Trojan War, and his *Odyssey* is the story of Odysseus's return to Ithaca in the eighth century BCE.[1] The idea of therapeutic writing, however, is a more recent development in medical and mental health practice.

It is important here to separate the work of a writing coach or mentor from the role of a therapist. While there are therapists who use writing as an element of their therapeutic endeavors with patients, our participants use writing as a process that has therapeutic value.

The Veterans' Writing Project (VWP) provides seminars and workshops for veterans, Active and Reserve service members, and military family members, in order to provide them with the skills required to chronicle their experiences and to translate thought and memory into the written word. The VWP's seminar leaders are all working writers, graduates of MA or MFA writing or publishing programs, and most importantly, combat veterans.

In VWP seminars and workshops, we make clear to our participants that ours is a writing program designed specifically for learning the craft of literary writing, not a form of therapy. We are writers and teachers, not medical or mental health professionals. That said, what happens in the seminars is often therapeutic for our participants; they find ways to help themselves work through emotional issues—stemming from their wartime experiences—through their writing.

Our standard seminar model opens with two questions: (1) Why do we write?; and (2) What is different about writing the military experience? The answers to these questions offer our participants a foundation upon which to create essays, stories, or poems based upon their military experiences.

Briefly, those answers are:

- We write to grant our ideas permanence and to express outwardly that which is within. The spoken word is impermanent, fleeting. The written word can make our ideas and stories concrete and, indeed, a more permanent record of our expression. We can pick up the stories and hold them, examine them, and shape them. All of these capacities are very relevant to therapeutic work.

- Writing the military experience differs from other writing in two key ways: we are writing more about the most primal of emotions and behaviors and many of the most gripping elements of our narratives risk being incomprehensible or even aversive to our readers.

Afterwards, we move on to present seminars on the basic elements of the craft of writing, including scene, setting, dialogue, narrative structure, point of view, and so on. We close with a seminar entitled "Writing about Trauma." We leave this until last for two reasons. First, because in it we give our participants the flexibility to disregard the structural "rules" we have just spent days imparting to them—writing about trauma often renders irrelevant the standard structural theories on writing. Second, because even broaching the subject of writing about trauma can be a traumatic event in itself.

In one VWP seminar held in Pennsylvania, nearly a quarter of our participants avoided this last session. Why? In most cases the veterans simply were not ready to do the work necessary to understand and manage their individual traumatic experiences.

The How and the Why

In our seminar on writing as therapy, we offer participants specific guidance on approaching their work as writers. There are five main points:

- Sit down to write for 15–30 minutes per day, every day.
- What you write about *is* important. It is not necessary to dive headlong into the middle of the traumatic event. You can work around "the edges" and slip up on it gradually, but you will have to get to it eventually.
- Explore several aspects of the event you are writing about: the event itself, how it changed you and your relationship with others (parents, friends, partner), your outlook on life before and after your wartime experiences; your job, how you view yourself, your past, present, and future. In other words, not just what happened, but what happened to you afterwards.
- Do not worry about spelling, grammar, or structure. What is important is that you write and do so for the full period of time that you have allotted yourself.
- It is *not* important whether or not you show this to anyone. The value comes in the writing itself.

Inevitably, someone will ask how writing could possibly be helpful. I have found that the central point is that writing allows participants to create space around the memory of a traumatic event, gaining perspective.

The following points detail what we have learned from working with traumatized veterans in our writing seminars:

- Through writing, you create something tangible. You can look at it. You can print it out and hold it in your hands. It is no longer something festering in the recesses of your memory.
- This airing often brings clarity of mind. You force yourself to remember the event(s) and to sort through what really happened. This also helps to give these memories coherence, in the process of putting thought to paper.

- By writing about something, you can allow yourself to assume ownership of it. This is important, because we tend to blame ourselves for things that were out of our control. This is a natural tendency. We are programmed to do this. We look at some terrible event, and something deep inside us says, "This is my fault. I should have done X, Y, or Z to stop it." Writing about an incident like this gives you a chance to absolve yourself of these feelings.
- Writing helps you put the indescribable into words. You force yourself to use metaphor to make sense of the inconceivable. This action is humanizing, because the ability to do so is uniquely human.
- By writing about significant emotional events and the trauma you have experienced, you are building a framework around the memory and placing it under your control—rather than vice versa.

Journaling: A Valuable Tool

Although we do not cover specific tools like journaling, blogging, or diary-keeping in our seminars, we believe they can often be helpful elements of a therapeutic writing program. The concept of a "journaling therapy" is growing. We have observed programs growing to create "Certified Journal Therapist" and "Certified Journal Facilitator" credentials and a "Certificate of Advanced Study in Therapeutic Writing" (Adams, 2011). However, this does not seem to have crept into more traditional, formal, behavioral or mental health-related research.

Journaling is, in itself, a valuable tool. Whether using techniques of guided (Pennebaker, 2004) or free journaling, the act of keeping a journal helps participants to organize their thoughts and shape their memories in many of the same ways as creating a literary narrative. Guided journaling is exactly that: journaling guided by a therapist. Participants/clients write in a journal for a specified period of time over a number of days. Writing prompts are given to clients ahead of time, and they are expected to respond to those prompts. What happens next is up to the participant and the therapist. Some researchers or therapists care little what the participant writes in these sessions. Their interest is in the resultant health improvements. However, a therapist working to help a client heal from war trauma and combat exposure might care a great deal about the subject matter.

Reflective journaling is a popular tool in education, particularly in adult education (Hubbs & Brand, 2005). The simple concept behind reflective journaling is that students—or participants in a seminar—reflect on a learning event by commenting (in writing) on three fundamental questions: What happened? What did I learn from it? How do I feel about it? An additional question might be: What am I going to do about it?

A few important points about journaling:

- Remember Polonius' advice to his son, Laertes, in *Hamlet*: "To thine own self be true" (Shakespeare, 1600). The idea of journaling is to put onto paper (or digits) your concerns, your memories, your thoughts. Write what you really feel and think and fear. Be brutally honest.
- Go with the flow. Pennebaker, in *Writing to Heal*, recommends beginning the work

of writing by putting words to some traumatic event, but allowing the writing to lead where it will. If you are writing about an event that occurred during the war, but find the writing pursuing some marital upheaval, this is fine. Go with it.

- How you go about this matters, but only to some extent. You can write longhand or on your computer, though you need to work at it every day for at least four days consecutively.
- Setting is important. Try to find a place where you can write in complete quiet. No distractions should tempt you away from your work. Make this place your writing space.
- If you're writing about something that you find is pushing you too far, stop. Do something else. When you restart, work on something less traumatic. Work around the edges of the trauma. You will get there eventually.

Giving Instruction

As an instructor in a writing program, or as a therapist working with a client, simply saying to someone, "Go and write" is never sufficient. The likely and proper response will be, "What about?" We need to offer prompts, cues, or instruction. In our VWP seminars and workshops, we use specific exercises to build specific skills. For example, if we are working on setting or location, we task our participants with this prompt (among others):

- Choose a setting. It can be anywhere, and at any time of your choosing. Catalogue its details. Detail its geography (even indoors): what is the physical layout of this location? Think about the time, both in terms of both period and day. Is it the fourteenth century or the twenty-first century? Is it morning? If so, what do the sun, the sky, and all the objects in the scene look like? Continue this process with people, weather, and props. Describe color, shape, temperature, sensation, and mood. Include metaphors whenever possible.

Each of our seminar sections provides a similar set of prompts for scene, dialogue, narrative structure, beginnings and endings, point of view, character, revisions, and so on. Effective therapeutic writing can start with instructions like those we have paraphrased from *Writing to Heal* (Pennebaker, 2004):

- Write for 20 minutes per day, for 4 consecutive days. More than 20 minutes is fine, but no less.
- You can write about the same event on all 4 days, or about different topics each day. Regardless, your writing should be extremely personal and important to you.
- Once you begin writing, write continuously without stopping. Do not worry about spelling or grammar. If you run out of things to say, it is okay to repeat yourself.
- Write only for yourself.
- Do not write about something you think might "push you over the edge." Deal only with events that you can handle now.
- It is completely normal to feel a little depressed or sad after an exercise like this. The feeling usually lasts a few minutes or so. Plan to leave some time after your writing session for reflection.

Pennebaker's strategy is to direct participants to write only for four days but, with the knowledge conveyed to them, that writing can become a life-long activity. These are only broad-based instructions that will need to be supplemented by specific daily (or longer) goals or objectives.

There are a number of other useful therapeutic writing prompts, such as:

- Write about the event that changed your life in a timeline. Sketch out the event, in minutes if necessary, listing your actions and those of other actors. Do not judge; just write the facts. Write within your time limits, and take as many sessions as you need to do this. Your objective is to separate your judgments and opinions from the facts. This may help you gain a clearer perspective of the events and your actions.
- Write a letter to the person (other than yourself) most affected by traumatic events. Tell them whatever it is you have most wanted to say. Is it "Thank you," or "I'm sorry," or "I forgive you," or "I hope you rot in . . ."? Whatever it is, say it directly and then explain why you feel that way. Do not mail the letter; it is for your use only in becoming accustomed to understanding how you feel and why.
- Has this traumatic event been positive for you in any way? Have you learned something about yourself because of how this event changed your life?
- In your earlier entries, are there things that were revealed in your writing that you had not previously remembered? Write about them in greater depth.
- Go back to your earlier writing. Count the number of first person pronouns (I, me, mine) you have used. Try rewriting the entry from another point of view. How did other participants view the event? Write it from that point of view.
- Write about an important, but not significantly traumatizing, event in your life. Describe in great detail the physical surroundings (setting). Describe the characters—including yourself—in detail. What are each of you are wearing? Describe the physical stature of everyone involved in this scenario; their hair color, their movements. Describe the events that led up to the action and the consequences of the event. What did you learn from this event? Does this change your point of view of the event? If so, how?
- Write about trust and confidence among your team, unit, squad, or platoon. Whom did you trust? Whom did you not trust? Did you ever feel betrayed?

Breaking Down and Rebuilding

Returning veterans face a myriad of challenges: reintegration with family and community, difficulty finding employment, homelessness, and health issues, to name only a few. A writing program cannot solve these problems, but writing can help veterans sort through and conceptualize memories as a way of helping to better manage or cope with their trauma. We view writing as therapeutic in two distinct ways: helping veterans to learn to control their memories, and helping them to bear witness to others. We might further conceptualize this as breaking down and rebuilding, or as stripping away and refinishing.

Breaking down and rebuilding is a process that veterans intrinsically understand. It is the very foundation of basic training. Civilians arrive and are quickly stripped of their identities, as they make the transition to service member. Off come the jeans and sneakers, snip snip goes the hair, away with the smirks and the attitudes and the irony. In a few days, these erstwhile civilians begin to look and walk and act like disciplined soldiers, airmen, Marines, and the like. This process is quite painful for some. There is often a great deal of corrective action levied, to include yelling and push-ups for punishment. But this results in a person who has become disciplined; strengthened, both physically and mentally, with the imposition of structure and the knowledge that he or she is bonded to others as a cohesive group, all of whom may be called upon to shed blood for their nation and for their brothers and sisters in uniform. This assumption of a new identity is part of joining a cause far greater than the self. It becomes transformative in the establishment of a reconstituted and more resilient character.

Providing veterans with the tools they need to shape a narrative that is inclusive of traumatic events can mimic the basic training process of breaking down and rebuilding. The goal is to disassemble the compartmentalization and suppression/denial of memories, by reducing the crippling anxiety and fear that they so readily produce.

Learning to Control the Memories (Breaking Down)

In our VWP seminars, we place our section on writing about trauma at the end of the seminars for a specific reason. Over the course of these seminars, which can be conducted in two days or over the course of a full, 14-week semester, we provide participants with the knowledge one would plausibly gain in a university creative writing course. The participants will have learned about showing versus telling, how dialogue and stage direction are used to display the primary character's motivation, and how setting and background can actually assume a role equal in a story to that of a character. They will have learned the rules about narrative structure and point of view. In our section on writing about trauma, however, we explain that in some cases it is acceptable to put all conventions of literary writing aside.

Literary conventions, standard ways of working and structuring written work, exist to create a high degree of unity in plot, structure, character, and the interrelationships between them. All of these can become obsolete and irrelevant in the face of traumatic experiences. As a result of trauma, one's sense of self and of the world can fracture. From that point forward, survivors view their worlds very differently.

In these cases, writers are forced to invent new ways of telling a story. That story, often the expression of a shattered self, does not always fit neatly into standard narrative forms. We instruct our seminar and workshop participants not to feel bound by convention. We tell them to write what they feel and to adapt form to story. The results may be rambling, stream of consciousness efforts, rants, or disjointed snippets with highly descriptive elements. They often require significant editing before publication but, regardless, as elements of therapy, they are invaluable to an understanding of the events that are troubling to the veteran.

One short aside: my personal writing, about my experiences in Afghanistan, began as a series of 10–15 pages long stream-of-consciousness essays, describing the sensations I had of being completely unable to control my mind, and how that affected my work in leading over 100 soldiers in combat. Several of these essays included page-long sections with no paragraph breaks or clear sentence structure—despite years of writing experience, two graduate degrees, and training as an editor. I ended up with this sort of a mess because I simply needed to get all of those emotions out of me and onto the page. Years later (I served in Afghanistan in 2002 and 2003), I am still struggling to turn those essays into something publishable. My agent and editor in New York might not like them very much, because they do not conform to literary convention, but my psychiatrist and therapist love them, because they are filled with raw, honest, emotion.

On Bearing Witness (the Rebuilding Process)

The epigram to this chapter describes Vera Brittain's writing as her attempt to make sense of what happened to her and by extension to the generation of men and women traumatized by World War I. Half a century earlier, during a speech at a Veterans' Day event held in 1884, Justice Oliver Wendell Holmes, a Civil War veteran, spoke eloquently on the idea of bearing witness:

> The generation that carried on the war has been set apart by its experience. In our youth, our hearts were touched with fire. It was given to us to learn that life is a profound and passionate thing. While we are permitted to scorn nothing but indifference, we have seen with our own eyes, and it is for us to bear the report to those who come after us.

Personally, I agree that we have a duty to bear witness. This is not always a popular viewpoint. Many veterans consider their personal histories as just that: history. They cast aside a wealth of knowledge and insights experienced with their own eyes. It is certainly feasible to hide from one's own realities in this context, and from what is held deep inside one's mind . . . but this is hardly a healthy choice.

At VWP seminars, we stress to our participants that by self-selecting writing as a medium, they have chosen to write their story and that by doing so they are bearing witness to their own truths. Even if the only objective is to put the story away in a journal or scrapbook for posterity, this remains a means of giving credence to one's personal history. Furthermore, publishing these stories allows the public to be exposed to the individual, human impact of war.

Bearing witness is one way for veterans to remain connected with military service and to other veterans. It is also an avenue for developing new circles of friends and allies, as a vital aspect of their healing. Isolation, whether physical or emotional, is a significant issue for returning veterans. Imagine serving in combat with a small group of men and women and then experiencing the dissolution of that group of close-knit service members upon return to the U.S. The absence of proximity to comrades, the lack of a sense of mission, and the diminished level of adrenaline-producing activities, can all be addressed, at least in part, by bearing witness.

Encouraging veterans to bear witness by telling their stories publicly gives them a mission. Reaching an audience may help validate their service and experience. Doing so can reinforce the notion that they remain a part of the war effort. Conversely, for others, this may provide them with a voice in expressing their views on the shortcomings of leadership or policy, or the folly or immorality of the war. To all participants in the post-war environment, this may offer a chance to memorialize their own efforts, and to provide clarity and understanding of the missions they were tasked to perform. Warriors are patriots. Departing military service, whether by choice or because of wounds or injuries, can be traumatic in and of itself. Remaining engaged, or re-engaging, can help to assuage the feelings of guilt or abandonment that frequently arise at the conclusion of one's military service, or at the end of deployment.

This is difficult work, regardless, as it challenges participants to confront painful and disturbing memories and, oftentimes, to relive them as if they were recurring. But it is important to do so. Consider these few lines from Siegfried Sassoon's (1919/2007) poem "Remorse":

> Remembering how he saw those Germans run,
> Screaming for mercy among the stumps of trees:
> Green-faced, they dodged and darted: there was one
> Livid with terror, clutching at his knees . . .
> Our chaps were sticking 'em like pigs . . . "O hell!"
> He thought—"there's things in war one dare not tell
> Poor father sitting safe at home, who reads
> Of dying heroes and their deathless deeds."

Sassoon is clearly addressing the divide between the soldier in the field and those remaining safely behind at home. But he makes an even more salient point: the very issues that this *poor father sitting safe at home* most needs to understand are those images of which the warrior's nightmares are made: issues of unending remorse and guilt, fear and unforgetting. These are components of the human costs of war.

A Personal Viewpoint

As someone who trains others in writing to heal and who does so himself, I should offer some observations from the latter's standpoint. I started writing as a way of remembering; of documenting events. I wanted to remember specific details.

I was in Kosovo and it seemed like every day something happened that I wanted to capture. I wrote about being briefly held hostage and how a Serbian thug held his pistol up against my head while screaming that he would kill me and rape my female translator; about a woman who thrust her infant into my arms and begged me to take the child away from the village and the military assault we all knew was coming; about returning to a small village I had abandoned the previous day, only to find that 42 men women and children had been massacred in my absence. I endured all of these events in a six-month period. To say that I had some issues to work through would be an understatement.

Today, a decade-and-a-half after surviving my first combat experience—a military mutiny in the Central African Republic in 1996—there are things I am still unprepared to write about. Pulling decomposing bodies out of a well in Kosovo will have to wait. Three Afghan fighters pulling me out of my vehicle and roughing me up with the barrels of their Kalashnikovs for a couple hours is a story yet to be written. Then there will be the stories of debriefing terrorists in Iraq. And then maybe I can start on what I saw and did during two years in Darfur.

Vital Points for Therapists to Consider

My combat trauma is spread out over a long period—more than a dozen years. A generation ago, this would have been quite rare. The experience of many Vietnam veterans was compressed; most Vietnam vets served one year in-country. But today it is likely that this level of combat exposure and experience is not rare at all. In October 2011, an Army Ranger was killed in Afghanistan while on his 14th combat tour (SOCOM, 2011).

At the Veterans' Center (Readjustment Counseling Service) at which I receive counseling, the Vietnam era veterans outnumber the younger Operation Enduring Freedom and Operation Iraqi Freedom veterans combined. But, in the aftermath of ten years of war in Afghanistan, we should gird ourselves for a tipping point. Between 2006 and 2010, the number of Iraq and Afghanistan veterans seeking mental healthcare quadrupled. In roughly the same time period, between 2007 and 2010, the VA's suicide prevention hotline fielded over 460,000 calls (U.S. GAO, 2011).

Here are some vital points for therapists to consider:

- In some cases, it is only through personal writing that service members will express their fears and anxieties. Both the public stigma, and the professional concern that seeking mental healthcare will cost them their security clearances and their jobs, remain salient issues.
- Memories unfold uniquely; traumatic memories unfold very uniquely. Be patient; let the writing process work.
- Trust the process. Maybe it really is enough to allow your clients to write privately.
- In group work, allow participants to choose whether to present their individual work to the group or not. Many will need to write about events and feelings yet too raw or too sensitive to share publicly.
- Even during our combat veteran-led seminars, many of our participants remain somewhat aloof, choosing carefully what to share and what to withhold from the group. Trust is earned and often remains elusive, even for the veteran seminar leader. I have experienced this during a number of seminars: a veteran joins a discussion to add something relevant, and then abruptly stops when he or she realizes that they have come to a point in the story they are not ready to share or even to open up that metaphorical box. From personal experience, I can say that there are things I had been unable to reveal with my therapist even after 15 months of therapy.

Closing

When I began to build the Veterans' Writing Project, I taped a hastily handwritten sign on the wall of my attic office, that read, "Either you control the story or the story controls you." I suppose that mental health professionals would substitute the word memory for story, but the idea remains the same. Writing therapy is all about assuming control of memories. Like other types of therapy, writing will be an effective tool for some participants, but not for others.

For those who self-select writing as therapy, the rewards can be substantial; they include a deeper understanding of self, the ability to distance oneself from traumatic incidents, and a written record with which one can bear witness to others. For clinicians, the challenges—trusting the process, earning the client's trust in both the process and the clinician, and integrating writing into a broader treatment strategy—loom large, especially given the lack of training programs and long-term research into these processes. Nonetheless, writing can and should be considered as a meaningful part of any approach to treating returned veterans and service members trying to survive PTSD.

The writing process provides an opportunity for veterans to examine an incident or series of events at a distance, to metaphorically remove the incident from the recesses of the mind, and to examine it from other points of view. I have often imagined this as similar to the art school exercise of crumpling a piece of white paper and sketching it as it lies on a table, then turning it and sketching it again as viewed from another side. This externalization of pain, of fear, of anger, allows the writer to develop perspective, sometimes for the very first time.

Writing can provide an alternative to talk therapy or serve in a complementary or supplemental role. It can serve as a necessary and accessible outlet for the more introverted of our participants, and provide practitioners with a deeper view into issues of concern to both practitioner and client. Furthermore, writing allows one to work at his or her own pace. It relieves the pressure of talk therapies by removing the interlocutor from the equation, increasing active participation in the process of unlocking what is often unspeakable. And, during this endeavor, the writer discovers that it is impossible to remain a passive observer.

As a full-time writer, I harbor literary ambitions beyond the scope of a writing therapy program. But, as a disabled combat veteran, I likely would not be a capable writer without therapy. Sadly, I had to design and implement my own writing therapy program and expand it, in order to give away to others what I learned. My program is flourishing, and I am not alone in this effort. There are other veterans' writing programs across the country—I am aware of programs in Philadelphia, Chicago, Syracuse, Oceanside, CA, St. Louis, MO, and New York. Most, if not all, of these programs are organized by writers and veterans, rather than medical or mental health professionals.

Across the country, universities host art therapy, music therapy, and dance therapy degree programs, and there are certifications available for therapists utilizing these creative arts in their work. But, to my knowledge, no writing therapy programs exist in the U.S. It is up to the medical and mental health communities to create a program to train writing therapists in the same way it trains other creative arts therapists and to integrate writing therapy into broader therapy programs. Otherwise, this valuable tool for helping our traumatized warriors and veterans will remain a blunt instrument outside the effective reach of the professional medical and mental health communities.

Note

1 It is understood that these are epic poems, which include both fact and fiction. The Trojan War is a historical event. Both poems include what I and many others believe to be extraordinarily accurate descriptions of the warrior's experience, including PTSD. But they are neither memoir nor autobiography. Many scholars believe the *Iliad* and the *Odyssey* were originally composed by a poet named Homer about 800 BCE. Other scholars believe that the poems were composed by a series of different poets over a few hundred years in the 8th century BCE and afterwards.

References

Adams, K. (2011) *The Center for Journal Therapy*. http://www.journaltherapy.com/. Accessed September 23, 2011.

Brittain, V. (1933). *Testament of Youth*. New York, NY: Penguin.

Homer (C8th BCE). *The Odyssey* and *The Iliad*. Translations include: http://classics.mit.edu/Homer/iliad. html; http://classics.mit.edu/Homer/odyssey.html.

Holmes, O. W. (1884). Speech delivered on Veterans' Day, May 30, 1884, in Keene, New Hampshire. Accessed at: http://people.virginia.edu/~mmd5f/memorial.htm.

Hubbs, D. L., & Brand, C. F. (2005). "The Paper Mirror: Understanding Reflective Journaling." *The Journal of Experiential Education*, *28* (1); Education Module, 60. Accessed October 10, 2011, at: http://image.lifeservant.com/siteuploadfiles/VSYM/7AF4374C-961E-4F5F-A526A9C0A749C054/8918D612-C29C-CE41-CE232D8A7546AF80.pdf.

Junger, E. (1920). *Storm of Steel*. Translation: Michael Hoffman. New York, NY: Penguin.

Pennebaker, J. W. (2004). *Writing to Heal*. Oakland, CA: New Harbinger.

Sassoon, S. (1919/2007). *The War Poems*. London, UK: Kessinger Publishing, LLC.

Shakespeare, W. *Hamlet*, Act I, Scene iii, 78. shakespeareonline.com. Accessed September 23, 2011, at: http://www.shakespeare-online.com/plays/hamlet_1_3.html.

SOCOM (U.S. Special Operations Command). (2011). *U.S. Army Special Operations Soldiers Killed in Combat*. Accessed September 25, 2011, at: http://www.soc.mil/UNS/Releases/2011/October/111023-01.html.

U.S. Government Accounting Office, *VA Mental Health: Number of Veterans Receiving Care, Barriers Faced, and Efforts to Increase Access*. Accessed September 25, 2011 at: http://www.gao.gov/new.items/d1212.pdf.

9   War-Related Traumatic Nightmares as a Call to Action

Lori R. Daniels

Clinicians experienced in treating combat veterans recognize the prevalence of military-related traumatic events among their clients. Most psychotherapists working with clients diagnosed with post-traumatic stress disorder (PTSD), both veterans and non-veterans, are also likely to hear clients sharing their experiences of recurrent, traumatically-based, nightmares. A survivor's experience of recurrent memories, in the form of dream images (often referencing traumatic events) is considered one of the "hallmark" symptoms of post-traumatic stress disorder, and traumatically-based nightmares often include thoughts, feelings, and actions related to a distressing event (American Psychiatric Association (APA), 2000). However, very few counseling and mental health programs (including those specifically focused on veteran PTSD recovery or combat redeployment issues) have established treatment interventions which address distressing nightmares or attempt to understand the traumatic situations revealed within a nightmare story. Instead, nightmares are almost always only addressed in counseling programs within the context of a larger diagnostic assessment of PTSD symptoms.

This chapter attempts to shift clinicians toward focusing on traumatic dreams in therapy and to perceive nightmares as useful information sources (in particular among combat veterans and "civilian" trauma survivors). This means embracing the guidance that can be obtained from a nightmare's hidden messages and allowing "nightmare therapy" work to provide direction in furthering a client's recovery efforts. This chapter will also describe creative methods of applying the information gained from "dreamwork" sessions within the context/framework of veterans' PTSD treatment interventions and recovery. Although the term "dreamwork" originated with Friedrich "Fritz" Perls (1969) as an integral aspect of Gestalt therapy, the author will be describing "dreamwork" differently than Perl's definition. Also, for the purposes of this chapter, the terms "nightmare therapy" and "dreamwork" will be used interchangeably, and indicate that the focus of the intervention is on the content of a nightmare story from the dreamer's perspective (versus extrapolated meaning and symbolism per Freud's original psycho-analytic theory; Freud, 1900).

The Need for Substantive Attention to War-Related Nightmares

Several barriers appear to contribute to a lack of substantive discussion about nightmares in war-related PTSD psychotherapy. One hindrance may simply be mental health practitioners' lack of knowledge as to how to proceed with nightmares, even if they are made aware of recurrent nightmares and the ramifications of these within their clients' lives. A second obstacle may be an inadvertent collusion with the client to avoid discussing recurrent nightmares, thereby adhering to the avoidance symptom of PTSD (APA, 2000). In both situations, a survivor is not encouraged to reveal a traumatic nightmare story in detail; this maintains avoidance of trauma material. The result is, frequently, a recurrent nightmare continuing to impact a trauma survivor's life, and relevant information regarding a traumatic incident(s) forever undetected. Furthermore, an underlying "call to action"—the clues of which are embedded in the content of combat or military-related nightmares—is missed by both client and psychotherapist. By providing mental health practitioners with a template with which to structure traumatic nightmare disclosure (such as a structured dialogue with which to address nightmares), these barriers could be addressed, and the collusion with avoidance could be overcome.

This chapter briefly summarizes a strategic method for discussing war-related traumatic nightmares. Even more so, this chapter moves that discussion to the next level—not only talking to reveal the nightmare itself (sharing a nightmare), but learning about a nightmare's hidden message and unexpressed emotional turmoil/conflict. This is followed by an appropriate response to the information uncovered by the nightmare disclosure (Brockway, 1987; King, Buckeley, & Welt, 2011). A therapist can also facilitate additional disclosures through an increased understanding of various components (e.g., images, sounds, sensations, emotions, and thoughts) of a traumatic nightmare's content. These insights can sometimes occur spontaneously when clients discuss details of a nightmare. Regardless of how insights occur, identification of thoughts, details, and emotions stemming from a nightmare can serve as a guide for follow-up behaviors by war-trauma survivors, enabling the client to finally respond to the unresolved issues being expressed within a nightmare—a traumatic dream's "call for action."

Background Regarding Traumatic Dreamwork

Evidence-based or research-supported PTSD interventions, which focus primarily on symptom management and coping skills, have evolved as the treatments of choice, and have been adopted by large-scale PTSD programs nationwide (e.g., cognitive-processing therapy, prolonged exposure therapy). These manualized interventions, none of which were initially developed for treating combat-related dreams, do have merit and have demonstrated (via quantitative measures) some reduction in PTSD distress (Alvarez, et al., 2011). Yet, very few evidence-based interventions directly address trauma survivors' experience of traumatic dreams. The challenge appears to be how best to measure disturbing experiences, such as those of traumatic nightmares. Nightmare therapy outcomes are often not quantifiable, nor are counseling or psychotherapy sessions measured in any systematic fashion. Therefore, it has been observed by the author that interventions that focus on the recurrent, war-related, content referenced within nightmares are often not addressed or prioritized by PTSD therapists, in spite of nightmares being a frequently reported symptom by veterans diagnosed with PTSD (Mellman, et al., 1995b, 2001). In contrast to the evidence-based PTSD interventions, nightmare therapy facilitates a dialogue about war-related memories—which intensely focuses on a client's traumatic nightmare story more than any other psychotherapy intervention (Brockway, 1987; Coalson, 1994; Daniels & McGuire, 1998).

The prevalence of nightmares as a major component of a PTSD diagnosis among combat veterans (and non-combat trauma survivors) suggests the relevance and importance of addressing PTSD nightmares in psychotherapy (i.e., Hartmann, 1996; Krakow, et al., 2002; Mellman, et al., 1995a, 1995b, 2001; Picchioni, et al., 2010; Pillar, Malhotra, & Lavie, 2000; Woodward, et al., 2000). Existing treatment interventions vary greatly and some publications detail the prevalence of trauma-based nightmares among trauma survivors (King, Buckeley, & Welt, 2011; Mellman, et al., 1995a); while a smaller number of publications suggest techniques that may be used by mental health providers to assist in the process of alleviating traumatic dreams. The latter includes interventions geared specifically to combat-related traumatic dreams (i.e., Brende & Benedict, 1980; Brockway, 1987; Coalson, 1994; Daniels & McGuire, 1998; Groesbeck, 1982; Lu, et al., 2009; Thompson, Hamilton, & West, 1995; Wilmer, 1996), and "civilian" or non-war-related traumatic dreams (such as sexual assault, murder, intimate partner violence, i.e., Cellucci & Lawrence, 1978; Geer & Silverman, 1967; Glaubman, et al., 1990; Halliday, 1982, 1987; Hartmann, 1996; Kales, 1982; Kingsbury, 1993; Krakow, et al., 2001; Lansky & Bley, 1995; Miller & DiPilato, 1983; Schindler, 1980; Shorkey & Himle, 1974; Silverman & Geer, 1968).

Nightmare therapy also differs from quantitatively researched interventions in that emotional aspects of traumatic memories are allowed to be the focus of the recovery process. This approach has better "goodness of fit" with the war survivor's healing process for two reasons: first, emotionally focusing on memories emerging through a nightmare allows the mental health provider to "begin where the client is"—addressing a nightmare at the same "level" as the nightmare is experienced by the survivor (more emotional, less cognitive); and, second, permitting catharsis during therapy allows a trauma survivor to purge emotions which are typically resisted by many clients diagnosed with PTSD.

The nightmare therapy/dreamwork process interweaves several opportunities for traumatic stress recovery work, beyond disclosure of a trauma-based nightmare. The process directly addresses two of the three major PTSD symptom clusters: re-experiencing (trauma-based nightmares) and avoidance (detaching from trauma memories). A third major symptom, hyperarousal, is addressed more indirectly; reduced vigilance appears to be a side-effect of nightmare resolution.

Like many other therapies provided for those suffering from PTSD, follow-up with information gleaned from a nightmare therapy session is essential. The outcome of a dreamwork session is influenced by both the disclosure and detailed description of a nightmare, and by the Action Plan established after a dream/nightmare has been discussed thoroughly (Brockway, 1987).

Dreamwork/Nightmare Therapy

Five objectives are accomplished by proactively working with nightmares:

1. Psycho-education about problematic sleep patterns can initiate a dialogue between therapist and client about various sleep issues (including nightmares), which can segue eventually into more in-depth conversation about recurrent trauma-based nightmares. Given many clients' initial uneasiness with mental health interventions, a transitional

(and safer) topic of sleep problems (versus actual traumatic events) may ease veterans or service members into the process, as well as provide helpful information.

2. Open dialogue about recurrent nightmares normalizes this particular symptom and begins the process of disempowering the nightmare's impact in someone's life. Often, war veterans/soldiers appear relieved to realize that they are not alone in their struggles with nightmares and sleep problems.

3. Use of a format to discuss traumatic nightmares appears to break apart existing PTSD symptom patterns by methodically unraveling the disclosure of a distressing re-experiencing symptom (nightmares). In turn, discussion about a traumatic nightmare is metaphorically taking a "back door route" to traumatic event disclosure, and encourages open discussion of painful memories and feelings (Brockway, 1987).

4. The intermediary step of describing to a client the structure of a nightmare therapy session, and showing the format of such a discussion, appears to alleviate client anxiety about what is going to happen next. In a group setting of war veterans, explanation about the procedure helps contribute to other veterans becoming knowledgeable with regard to the nightmare therapy procedure. The "plan of attack" against continued nightmare problems is clear and visible; therefore, veterans may be more willing to work through accessible traumatic content.

5. Lastly, dreamwork dialogue allows an examination of whether nightmares which include images of people/places from present day "civilian life" (versus traumatic images from the military) also contain traumatic event memories represented in hidden form. A trauma-based nightmare "in disguise" also can be identified by noting if the predominant emotions within a nightmare include fear, guilt, and helplessness.

A Traumatic Dreamwork Vignette

Dreamwork avails a process that helps to reveal the memories underneath the dream's "disguise." A Vietnam veteran shared a nightmare which started out with him attending a football game at his son's high-school, and noting that the son was wearing the same numbered jersey as the veteran wore while in high school. The nightmare story included the veteran watching his son catch a football, then fall down a cliff which suddenly appeared in the dream. The veteran then could hear calls for "Medic! Medic!" as he scurried toward the bottom of the cliff and searched for his son.

Numerous questions were asked of the veteran and emotions identified within the dreamwork session included his intense feelings of guilt and helplessness. When asked about *falling over a cliff* and *hearing someone screaming "Medic!"*, the veteran shared recollections of an incident that occurred during the Vietnam War. He had driven a large vehicle and, by avoiding an obstacle in the road, the truck (and all passengers) tumbled down a cliff. Upon awakening at the bottom, he could hear calls from other injured soldiers: "Medic! Medic!" Further work on this war memory provided additional information, namely that the day before having this dream he had engaged in a phone conversation with his wife about one of their sons who had been struggling emotionally. The veteran admitted that the phone conversation prompted feelings of guilt about his own PTSD, his need for treatment, and his perceptions of being less than an ideal paternal role model. The nightmare story paralleled these feelings of helplessness, guilt, and responsibility for the negative occurrences in his son's life. The "disguised" parts of this nightmare included a trigger for his guilt (prompted by the phone conversation), which connected with his war memory of the truck falling down the cliff. Follow-up from this case (the dream's "call to action") focused on the veteran's guilt embedded within his relationship with his son, as well a trauma-processing of the vehicular accident in Vietnam. Action Plan suggestions for nightmares which include feelings of guilt are detailed later.

Trauma Triggers

Another major goal of traumatic dream work is to learn about the experiential and/or environmental triggers that precede one's experiences of a nightmare. In group and individual therapy, a discussion of traumatic symptom triggers can provide a wealth of information for both the psychotherapist and trauma survivors. Trauma triggers are sometimes obvious but, often, are very subtle. Categories of more obvious environmental trauma triggers may include sights, sounds, and smells/scents. Subtle triggers can be categorized as anniversary events, bodily sensations (including pain), and emotions/feelings. The process of openly discussing nightmares provides opportunities to better identify what obvious or subtle triggers contribute to clients experiencing particular nightmares at particular times.

A practitioner must be tenacious in this process and probe with numerous questions about possible trigger sources. It is not uncommon for a few of the more subtle triggers in one's current life situation to be revealed for the first time through this process. One method of assessing triggers is to merely have the PTSD-suffering client describe, in full detail, the 24–48 hours before they experienced the nightmare (i.e., asking them about television programs they viewed, conversations with others, songs they heard, and/or any outings or other activities). It also is imperative that the questions focus upon emotions experienced and whether the nightmare occurred during significant times of year for any personal and/or significant life events. A detailed description of activities may not reveal an obvious connection between recalled activities and the experience of a nightmare later that night. However, possible triggers are often embedded in those activities, which may increase the likelihood that a war veteran survivor may experience a nightmare on that particular night (versus any other night of the week).

Using the previous example, a veteran client was asked about conversations he had 24–48 hours prior to having the nightmare, along with other questions trawling for possible triggers, and it was through this level of rigorous questioning that hidden triggers were revealed.

Questions to Initiate Dialogue About Traumatic Dreams

The following are suggested questions that treatment providers may use to initiate a dialogue with war veterans or service members about their traumatic dreams. Questions directed at "assessing a nightmare" may help normalize the experience of traumatic dreams for survivors, and build rapport between the interviewer and client, as well as provide a means of understanding the impact of traumatic events on sleep (Brockway, 1987; Daniels and McGuire, 1998).

1. What was your sleep pattern like before the military? What was your sleep cycle like before your deployment to a war zone?
2. When did you first notice a change in your sleep pattern? (Describe the changes.)
3. What was your sleep pattern like after returning from deployment?
4. Did you have sleep problems when you were a child? If so, describe these problems.
5. Do you have nightmares currently? If so, approximately how often do you have nightmares?
6. Have you ever had the same nightmare more than once?
7. Are your nightmares referencing, in any way, an actual event that has occurred in your personal history? If so, are any of these also referencing your military life in some way (e.g., are you or others in uniform in the dream)?
8. If the nightmare is of an actual event, is there any distortion from the actual event in your life, or is the nightmare completely accurate with respect to the real-life event without distortions? (Describe the changes/distortions in the dream that are different from the actual event.)
9. When was the first time you recall having this nightmare/traumatic dream?
10. When was the last time you had this nightmare/traumatic dream? (Be as specific as to date as possible.)
11. If you have had this nightmare more than once, how often do you experience this particular recurring nightmare/traumatic dream? (How many times per month, per week, or per year?)
12. What are your very first thoughts upon awakening from this nightmare/traumatic dream?
13. What are you feeling emotionally when you awaken from this nightmare/traumatic dream?
14. Have you ever discussed your nightmares/traumatic dreams with anyone before?
15. Do you have more than one recurring nightmare/traumatic dream?
16. If so, are any of these other nightmares referencing or replicating an actual event from your personal history?

In addition, there is a psychometrically-validated sleep assessment and nightmare questionnaire (originally developed through clinical experiences with combat veterans) that therapists may access as a more comprehensive instrument (Donovan, et al., 2004).

Nightmare Therapy in Three Parts

The nightmare therapy process has three primary components: psychoeducation, disclosure and emotional processing of a traumatic nightmare, and the Action Plan.

Part 1: Psychoeducation

A helpful segue toward preparing a client for traumatic nightmare work is to provide basic psychoeducation about dysfunctional sleep, traumatic nightmares, and goals for resolving nightmares, as well as educating clients regarding their own unique traumatically-based nightmares. Examples of educational material about sleep should include graphs about sleep cycles and electroencephalogram (EEG) patterns showing different levels of sleep and rapid-eye movement (REM) sleep occurrences; guidelines for healthy sleep habits; information about the specific categories of nightmare information—originally identified based on war veterans' nightmares (Wilmer, 1996)); and basic information about the relationship of traumatic nightmares and PTSD symptoms. The model in Figure 9.1 provides a visual demonstration of the goals of nightmare therapy (Daniels, unpublished manuscript).

Part 2: Sharing a Nightmare Story and Emotional Processing

The following is a brief summary of a much more comprehensive process of nightmare disclosure and subsequent emotional processing. Since the emphasis of this chapter is on Part 3, the Action Plan, the reader is referred to other sources for a more detailed description of the nuances of dreamwork/nightmare therapy disclosure (Brockway, 1987; Coalson, 1994; Daniels & McGuire, 1998). However, in order to provide a larger context for the Action Plan, it is important to summarize the structure of nightmare therapy.

Immediately following the client's description of their nightmare, and prior to any "processing" of a nightmare story, it is useful to assess the *thoughts* experienced by the dreamer during the nightmare and immediately upon awakening. The client is then asked about their *feelings* or *emotions* upon awakening, and throughout the nightmare. If a nightmare is written down during their disclosure, a therapist can underline and focus upon specific words or phrases contained therein. This provides a segue between dream content and unresolved issues (Brockway, 1987). For each of the underlined words or phrases, three questions can be posed by a therapist to assist this part of the uncovering procedure (Daniels, unpublished manuscript):

Figure 9.1 The ultimate goal for nightmare therapy is to break the cycle of traumatic nightmares. A possible secondary benefit is the lessening of symptoms related to traumatic stress responses and dysfunctional sleep patterns.

1. *Describe it—in detail.* (This provides the dreamer with the opportunity to describe an object, a person, or a sensation, thereby allowing the provider to clearly visualize what the dreamer is experiencing within a nightmare.)
2. *Have you seen this before? If so, where or when?* or *Has this ever happened to you before?* (Depending on the underlined phrase, this can be a memory and/or include physical sensations, e.g., falling or flipping over. Hint: if there is a sudden shift in movement or emotion in the dream content, it may be important to prompt the dreamer to provide personal history information associated with these shifts—even if it may initially not appear important or relevant.)
3. *How do you feel (emotionally) about it?* (As much as possible, have the dreamer discuss each underlined word or phrase, using words conveying emotion.)

Responses to these three questions, for each underlined word/phrase, can reveal underlying representations, associations, or unresolved conflicts within the nightmare. A client is more likely to identify a traumatic memory once these are more apparent, and this allows the therapist to discuss the emotional impact of a traumatic event more openly.

Part 3: The Action Plan

Although left for the very end of a session, the Action Plan component is an essential step of the process, because it provides real-life application of insights and revelations emerging from nightmare therapy discussion (Brockway, 1987). Specifically, an Action Plan may include suggestions for future therapy, writing assignments, performing grief rituals, or other ideas which target unresolved issues identified in the dreamwork session. Suggested Action Plan ideas are generated from the knowledge gained through nightmare therapy sessions, and are written in the Action Plan section of a dreamwork form (Brockway, 1987; Daniels & McGuire, 1998; Daniels, unpublished manuscript). A dreamwork form provides sections to be completed (e.g., content of nightmare story, thoughts/feelings, triggers, key phrases/meanings, and Action Plan), the culmination of which are guidelines to identifying underlying emotional "stuck points" manifested within a nightmare, and the needs of a trauma survivor's healing process (Brockway, 1987).

An individual's traumatic experience, and the manifestation of that experience woven into a nightmare story, varies from person to person. Therefore, it is difficult to describe a typical action plan. However, there are *some helpful categories* which a provider may be able to use to guide this next step.

Grief

Clients often fail to identify nightmares (including those in which they see deceased people they have known) as indicative of unfinished or unresolved relationships. A transition between disclosure of an "unresolved relationship nightmare" (that features deceased people) and the development of an action plan may occur through what is *not* stated in the discussion of a nightmare story line and what *didn't* happen in the relationship between the survivor and the deceased. Examples typically include thoughts of, "I should have told her/him__, but I never did," or "We made this plan together, then s/he was killed and we never got to fulfill the plan." Therapists attune themselves to the story's gaps or emotional challenges, stemming from what failed to occur in the relationship, as these may provide clues for future direction and information in order to achieve relationship closure.

Depending on the traumatic situation, and the types of losses experienced, the grieving process can vary greatly. A provider can assess what losses have been incurred during a traumatic event, such as loss of a sense of immortality, spiritual connection, plans being fulfilled, or loss of life. Nightmare stories which include the appearance of deceased individuals may help determine what aspects of this relationship were not addressed. Often, this is evidenced by how the client feels after having a dream that includes the deceased. For example, if the client reports feeling happy after having "seen" the deceased again, and has an opportunity to establish a connection, then an Action Plan focused on real-life ways of acknowledging that connection may be appropriate. However, if the client struggles with the loss of life, and an inability to grieve his or her loss, a possible Action Plan recommendation may include some sort of activity that focuses on communicating that loss: for example, writing a letter to the deceased. Such a letter might communicate emotions and attachments to that individual, including how stuck the client has been after the loss, how s/he emotionally feels about the deceased individual, and include any other specific information appropriate to the lost relationship. The act of writing such a letter can be very emotionally cathartic, and a possible outlet for emotions that have been repressed for many years. The most important aspect of this is to allow a method by which the client is able to express his or her feeling/emotions, and communicate these concerns verbally. "Saying it out loud" (via writing and speaking) appears to validate the legitimacy and reality of the loss, and the impact that such losses have had on the survivor.

One stuck point for both therapists and clients has been what to do with the letter once it has been written. However, with some creative thought and input from the survivor, these letters can be delivered to the intended recipient in such a way that emotional movement can result. Methods from other cultures that have established rituals for remaining connected to deceased individuals can be modified in order to facilitate the "mailing" of a letter by a trauma survivor. One possible delivery method is a modification of a Chinese Taoist ritual which delivers "money" to ancestors who have passed on. This ritual was witnessed by the author, as a child, when her grandmother burned Joss paper (thin, square, special Chinese red paper) at the headstones of great-grandparents. The Taoist belief is that the "money" will burn and the smoke ascend into the atmosphere as a form of delivery (the ancestors would receive the money intact). A variation of this burning of Joss paper would use this same type of delivery system to "mail" a grief letter written by a war trauma survivor.

After a client writes and reads his or her letter to the deceased, a therapist can assist with where to "mail" the letter by asking the client about locations at which they would wish to have a conversation with the deceased, if the deceased were still alive. A trauma survivor is also encouraged to invite those people in his or her life who are supportive of the recovery process, to be a part of the "mailing" ceremony. By watching the letter burn, with smoke and ashes floating up into the atmosphere, clients often feel as if the communication has been sent to those who have passed on. Other methods of "mailing" a letter to the deceased include leaving a letter at a cemetery or floating it into the ocean or down a river.

Providers can help identify cultural rituals which focus on connecting to ancestors and/or other deceased individuals, or formal or informal rituals stemming from a veteran's military culture or the client's own native/ethnic culture. Whichever grieving and closure rituals appear to fit for a client, consistent with the relationship for which they are grieving, will guide the appropriate method of sending a client's sentiments forward.

Action Plan with a World War II Veteran

An example of an Action Plan that suggested a letter mailing (burning) ritual is that of a WWII veteran. Nightmare therapy determined that his terrifying nightmare of the war zone also incorporated his unresolved sadness about his deceased mother. When the veteran was a boy, and thus prior to his military service, the veteran's mother had been killed in an accident. Being ill with chicken pox, he was unable to attend her funeral. Many years later, while the veteran was in Europe, during a fire-fight he heard injured German soldiers cry out for their mothers. The soldiers wore white snowsuits at the time and, decades later, the veteran complained of having a recurrent nightmare of large white figures. He did not identify them as the German soldiers until work was undertaken to focus on these entities (e.g., asking the question, "Have you ever seen large white figures, such as these, ever in your life before?"). The realization that the large white figures were the German soldiers crying out for their mothers was the "tipping point" of the nightmare therapy session. As he disclosed more about hearing the Germans call for their mothers, for the first time in therapy, the veteran shared his inability to grieve the loss of his own mother. His unresolved emotional grieving was identified as a similar voice within himself, crying out for his own mother. The Action Plan emerging from this therapy session resulted in the veteran and his therapist (the author) going to a chosen beach park (where he imagined he would want to spend time with his parents). The veteran read from a card, expressing his heart-felt sadness at never getting to say goodbye to his mother, and his continued grief for the loss of this relationship. He then lit a small burner (which he also brought with him), carefully burned the card and watched the ashes float into the sky. Immediately following this, the veteran tearfully stated that he felt certain that his mother received his card.

Guilt

Guilt embedded within a traumatic memory is frequently a predominant emotion that maintains PTSD symptomatology, much of which may be based on a survivor's frustration about not having more power/control in order to change the outcome of a traumatic event (Kubany & Watson, 2003). In spite of this, few clinicians are willing to spend a significant time discussing a client's guilt and the consequential self-punitive thoughts and behaviors which accompany self-blame. Techniques addressing a client's guilt (especially those which focus on highly detailed descriptions of a traumatic incident and various decision points) may provide an opportunity for the client to hear an objective perspective and insights regarding one's realistic level of control, power, and responsibility, during a crisis. This, in turn, may be very helpful when processing unresolved memories. Using a "percentages of responsibility" technique (Scurfield, 1994; Scurfield & Platoni, this volume) or "hindsight bias" perspective (Kubany & Watson, 2003) may be very helpful when dealing with guilt feelings underlying one's traumatic memories. Once an individual has identified more accurate (and realistic) levels of "responsibility" regarding the traumatic event, an Action Plan can include recommendations which allow a survivor to move toward healing—versus maintaining their self-destructive patterns based upon guilt. Should the guilt experienced by trauma survivor be about their contribution to a loss of life, one suggested action activity would be for them to contribute to life in some capacity. More so, a survivor may be tasked to honor the loss of life in a trauma by "giving back"—working to improve the quality of life for those who are similar to the deceased. Suggestions consistent with this option include planting and nurturing a tree, or volunteering time toward the enhancement of life of those less fortunate. There are many options for "giving back in a healthy way," and the more personally involved a client is with the action activity (i.e., in person, active, contribution of energy), the more impact the intervention may have in resolving the conflict.

Case Example with a Vietnam Veteran

One example of addressing guilt is illustrated in the case of a Vietnam veteran who, during a group therapy session, reported feeling distressed about problematic sleep. He shared a nightmare story that centered around him being tied to a chair and watching a line of severely wounded soldiers walking by him. He stated that he knew that each one of these soldiers represented dead soldiers, and each one would walk toward his chair and, afterward, with disgusted looks on their faces, walk away. Through the nightmare therapy process, the veteran was able to better understand his tremendous guilt about being assigned from the battlefield to a rear-area desk job ("tied to a chair") for the last few months of his deployment to Vietnam. His duty at the desk job was to monitor the radio transmissions of those still fighting in the combat areas, including medevacs being called in to assist with the wounded. The Action Plan emerging from his dreamwork addressed his guilt and helplessness in not being able to be more involved in direct fighting (which he had been doing prior to his reassignment). The nightmare therapy session assisted in better identifying his survival guilt, while the subsequent Action Plan suggestions included his eliciting written comments from his veteran group members, all of which stated that he was a legitimate contributor throughout his tour in Vietnam and that he did not abandon his colleagues during the war.

Guilt Coupled with Grief and Use of Sandplay Vignette

Another example of an Action Plan based upon a "guilt coupled with grief" nightmare is illustrated in a case of a Vietnam War veteran of Pacific Islander ethnicity. While in-country, the veteran had endured several weeks of harassment and threats by others in his unit (due to his resemblance to the enemy), which resulted in his increasing fear and isolation. In one situation, the veteran was ordered to shoot and kill an enemy soldier after an interrogation, in order to prove his allegiance to the American military. Decades later, in therapy, the veteran shared his belief that refusing the order would have resulted in him either not being protected by his unit colleagues in future battles or eventually being killed by them (because he wasn't a "true American"). The outcome of this particular situation haunted him as a recurrent nightmare with no distortions from the actual event.

Using sandplay (Daniels & McGuire, 1998), the client demonstrated the specifics of the actual event and also expressed sorrow and grief for his decision to obey the command. His nightmare version, however, omitted most of the other people involved in the actual event—and reduced the scene to only him and the captured man. *What did not happen* during the traumatic incident was the veteran being able to communicate to the captive how horrible he was feeling about taking a life and his fear of not following orders (and being watched by those who had made racist comments to him). In order to process the losses he experienced, of which he was reminded by this nightmare, the Action Plan included the veteran communicating his sincere feelings of remorse and sorrow (via moving the sandplay figures and directing his comments to the figures). The veteran also requested that he be able to bury the captive man figurine with honor and dignity (none of which was possible in the war zone). Once he buried the figure in the sandbox, the final image of the burial (with flowers added) was photographed for him, so that he could place the photo in a spot where he would view this daily. The veteran reported, many weeks after the dreamwork session, that his nightmare never occurred again. This particular example demonstrates both the addressing of guilt and grief in therapy, and the implementation of an Action Plan that moved the healing process forward while in the midst of a therapy session.

If guilt experienced by a trauma survivor does not involve loss of life, an assessment or full understanding of the underlying "message of guilt" (e.g., "I didn't do anything" or "I should have done something differently") will be the guiding premise for the Action Plan.

Action Plan Activities

Action Plan activities might include:

- War Memorial visits with a small ceremony (e.g., candles, flowers, notes).
- Participation in activities that the deceased would have enjoyed (honoring the relationship in healthy way); these may include attendance at veteran-focused parades, ceremonies, or gatherings.
- Art therapy projects.
- Donations to charities that serve similar victims, as a form of giving back (to rebalance what was taken away).
- Volunteering time in which to provide personal experiences (which also helps the client identify him or herself as a helper, rather than one who is helpless). This also may include donating time to military family members or family service entities in such a way that it attempts to accomplish a rebalancing from the loss—or even to provide a "gain."

Closing

Using nightmare stories in therapy can produce rich outcomes once avoidance is overcome and combat veterans are encouraged to converse about their military-related nightmares (whether recurrent or one-time only). Dreamwork/nightmare therapy provides a structure with which to communicate with a trauma survivor about his or her nightmare(s), and which affords emotional processing opportunities as well as development of an Action Plan to move recovery efforts in a positive direction. The ultimate goals are to address problematic sleep, work with "stuck" emotions, teach war veterans about their abilities to address their own suffering, and attend to their traumatic memories as a means of reducing distress and anguish. Therapists can proactively assist their war veteran clients by facilitating and supporting them through yet another courageous decision: to reconcile issues underlying trauma-based nightmares and employ their nightmare stories as a Call to Action.

References

Alvarez, J., McLean, C., Harris, A. H. S., Rosen, C. S., Ruzek, J. I., & Kimerling, R. E. (2011). "The Comparative Effectiveness of Cognitive Processing Therapy for Male Veterans Treated in a VHA Post-Traumatic Stress Disorder Residential Rehabilitation Program." *Journal of Consulting and Clinical Psychology*, Published online 11 July 2011.

American Psychiatric Association (2000). *Diagnostic and Statistical Manual of Mental Disorders—TR*. Washington, DC: American Psychiatric Association.

Brende, J. O., and Benedict, B. D. (1980). "The Vietnam Combat Delayed Stress Response Syndrome: Hypnotherapy of 'Dissociative Symptoms.'" *American Journal of Clinical Hypnosis*, *23*(1): 34–40.

Brockway, S. S. (1987). "Group Treatment of Combat Nightmares in Post-Traumatic Stress Disorder." *Journal of Contemporary Psychotherapy*, *17*(4): 270–284.

Cellucci, A. J., & Lawrence, P. S. (1978). "The Efficacy of Systematic Desensitization in Reducing Nightmares." *Journal of Behavioral Therapy and Experimental Psychiatry*, *9*: 109–114.

Coalson, B. (1994). "Nightmare Help: Treatment of Trauma Survivors with PTSD." *Psychotherapy*, *32*(3): 381–388.

Daniels, L. R., & McGuire, T. L. (1998). "Dreamcatchers: Healing Traumatic Nightmares using group Dreamwork, Sandplay and other Techniques of Intervention." *Group: Journal of the Eastern Group Psychotherapy Society*, *22*(4): 205–227.

Daniels, L. R. (unpublished manuscript). *A Missing "Peace" of PTSD Recovery: The Science and Art of Intervening with Traumatic Nightmares: Treatment Intervention Manual*.

Donovan, B., Padin-Rivera, E., Chapman, H., Strauss, M., & Murray, M. G. (2004). "Development of the Nightmare Intervention and Treatment Evaluation (NITE) Scale." *Journal of Trauma Practice*, *3*(3): 47–68.

Freud, S. (1900). *The Interpretation of Dreams*. New York, NY: Basic Books.

Geer, J. H., & Silverman, I. (1967). "Treatment of a Recurrent Nightmare by Behavior Modification Procedures: A Case Study." *Journal of Abnormal Psychology*, *72*(2): 188–190.

Glaubman, H., Mikulincer, M., Porat, A., Wasserman, O., & Birger, M. (1990). "Sleep of Chronic Post-Traumatic Patients." *Journal of Traumatic Stress*, *3*(2): 255–263.

Groesbeck, C. J. (1982). "Dreams of a Vietnam Veteran: A Jungian Analytic Perspective." *Psychiatric Annals*, *12*(11): 1007–1010.

Halliday, G. (1982). "Direct Alteration of a Traumatic Nightmare." *Perception Motor Skills*, *54*(2): 413–414.

Halliday, G. (1987). "Direct Psychological Therapies for Nightmares: A Review." *Clinical Psychology Review, 7*: 501–523.

Hartmann, E. (1996). "Who Develops PTSD Nightmares and Who Doesn't." In D. Barrett (Ed.), *Trauma and Dreams*, Cambridge, MA: Oxford University Press: 100–113.

Hoge, C. W. (2011). "Interventions for War-Related Post-Traumatic Stress Disorder: Meeting Veterans Where They Are." Editorial. *Journal of the American Medical Association, 306*(5): 549–551.

Kales, J. D. (1982). "Psychotherapy with Night-Terror Patients." *American Journal of Psychotherapy, 36*(3): 399–407.

King, P., Buckeley, K., & Welt, B. (2011). "Dreaming and Psychotherapy." In *Dreaming in the Classroom: Practices, Methods, and Resources in Dream Education*. Albany, NY: SUNY Press: 145–148.

Kingsbury, S. J. (1993). "Brief Hypnotic Treatment of Repetitive Nightmares." *American Journal of Clinical Hypnosis, 35*(3): 161–169.

Krakow, B., Schrader, R., Tandberg, D., Hollifield, M., Koss, M., Yau, C. L., & Cheng, D. (2002). "Nightmare Frequency in Sexual Assault Survivors with PTSD." *Journal of Anxiety Disorders, 16*(2): 175–190.

Krakow, B., Hollifield, M., Johnston, L., Koss, M. P., Schrader, R., Warner, T. D., Tandberg, D., Lauriello, J., McBride, L., Cutchen, L., Cheng, D. T., Emmons, S., Germain, A., Melendrez, D., Sandoval, D., & Prince, H. (2001). "Imagery Rehearsal Therapy for Chronic Nightmares in Sexual Assault Survivors with Post-Traumatic Stress Disorder: A Randomized Controlled Trial." *Journal of the American Medical Association, 286*(5): 537–545.

Kubany, E., & Watson, S. (2003). "Guilt: Elaboration of a Multidimensional Model." *Psychological Record, 53*(1): 51–90.

Lansky, M. R., & Bley, C. R. (1995). *Post-Traumatic Nightmares: Psychodynamic Explorations*. Hillsdale, NJ: Analytic Press.

Lu, M., Wagner, A., Van Male, L., Whitehead, A., & Boehnlein, J. (2009). "Imagery Rehearsal Therapy for Post-Traumatic Nightmares in US Veterans." *Journal of Traumatic Stress, 22*(3): 236–239.

Mellman, T. A., David, D., Bustamante, V., Torres, J., & Fins, A. (2001). "Dreams in the Acute Aftermath of Trauma and their Relationship to PTSD." *Journal of Traumatic Stress, 14*(1): 241–247.

Mellman, T. A., David, D., Kulick-Bell, R., Hebding, J., & Nolan, B. (1995a). Sleep Disturbance and its Relationship to Psychiatric Morbidity after Hurricane Andrew. *American Journal of Psychiatry, 152*(11): 1659–1663.

Mellman, T. A., Kulick-Bell, R., Ashlock, L. E., & Nolan, B. (1995b). "Sleep Events among Veterans with Combat-Related Post-Traumatic Stress Disorder." *American Journal of Psychiatry, 152*(1): 110–115.

Miller, W. R., & diPilato, M. (1983). "Treatment of Nightmares via Relaxation and Desensitization: A Controlled Evaluation." *Journal of Consulting and Clinical Psychology, 51*(6): 870–877.

Perls, F. S. (1969). "Dreamwork Seminars." In *Gestalt Therapy Verbatim*, Moab, UT: Real People Press.

Picchioni, D., Cabrera, O. A., McGurk, D. M., Thomas, J. L., Castro, C. A., Balkin, T. J., Bliese, P. D., & Hoge, C. W. (2010). "Sleep symptoms as a Partial Mediator Between Combat Stressors and Other mental Health Symptoms in Iraq War Veterans." *Military Psychology, 22*(3): 340–355.

Pillar, G., Malhotra, A., & Lavie, P. (2000). "Post-Traumatic Stress Disorder and Sleep: What a Nightmare!" *Sleep Medicine Reviews, 4*(2): 183–200.

Schindler, F. E. (1980). "Treatment by Systematic Desensitization of a Recurring Nightmare of a Real Life Trauma." *Journal of Behavioral Therapy and Experimental Psychiatry, 11*: 53–54.

Scurfield, R. M. (1994). "War-Related Trauma: An Integrative Experiential, Cognitive, and Spiritual Approach." In M. B. Williams & J. F. Sommer (Eds.), *Handbook of Post-Traumatic Therapy*, Westport, Connecticut: Greenwood Press: 179–204.

Shorkey, C., & Himle, D. P. (1974). "Systematic Desensitization Treatment of a Recurring Nightmare and Related Insomnia." *Journal of Behavioral Therapy and Experimental Psychiatry*, 5: 97–98.

Silverman, I., & Geer, J. H. (1968). "The Elimination of a Recurrent Nightmare by Desensitization of a Related Phobia." *Behavioral Research and Therapy*, 6: 109–111.

Thompson, K. E., Hamilton, M., & West, J. A. (1995). "Group Treatment for PTSD-Related Nightmares." *National Center for PTSD Clinical Quarterly*, 5(4): 13–17.

Wilmer, H. (1996). "The Healing Nightmare: War Dreams of Vietnam Veterans." In Barrett, D. (Ed.), *Trauma and Dreams*, Cambridge, MA: Oxford University Press: 85–99.

Woodward, S. H., Arsenault, N. J., Murray, C., & Bliwise, D. L. (2000). "Laboratory Sleep Correlates of Nightmare Complaint in PTSD Inpatients." *Biological Psychiatry*, 48(11): 1081–1087.

Part IV

Mind–Body Approaches

10 Mindful-Awareness Practice to Foster Physical, Emotional, and Mental Healing with Service Members and Veterans

Colleen Mizuki

The men and women who have served in Iraq with Operation Iraqi Freedom (OIF) or, currently, with Operation New Dawn (OND), and in Afghanistan with Operation Enduring Freedom (OEF), deal—like any combat veteran—with a wide range of complicated issues. All wars leave scars—some visible, some not—but the current conflicts appear to have particular characteristics that set them apart from previous engagements. These differences, on top of painful lessons learned from the lack of support for our Vietnam veterans, have resulted in a call to widen the scope of approaches to assist our OIF/OEF/OND service members. This chapter responds to an aspect of that call by proposing the addition of mindfulness practice to programs that foster physical and mental healing. This chapter will discuss some of the particular challenges faced by our service members in Iraq and Afghanistan; provide an overview of mindfulness practices; mention research showing how such practices contribute to positive change, healing, and growth; and briefly discuss their integration into the psychotherapeutic context. Resources to further explore mindfulness practices and associated research are provided at the end of the chapter.

Mindfulness Basics

Mindfulness is a term bandied around quite a lot these days. While based in principles of Buddhism, there is growing recognition that it can be very beneficial for day-to-day living or as a means of improving mental and physical health and well-being—all without the need to engage in the study or practice of Buddhism. There are variations in current Western definitions of mindfulness but, basically, it refers to the skill of *attending fully to an experience (e.g., thought, emotion, action, sensation), in the moment (as it is happening) in an open and accepting manner.* There are myriad forms of mindfulness practice, all of which are intended to increase the practitioner's awareness of an experience as it is occurring and without judgment. When we are in a mindful state, we notice a thought, an emotion, an action/reaction, or physical experience as it occurs, and without attaching a judgment to the experience as being, for example, positive versus negative, beneficial versus detrimental, or healthy versus unhealthy.

Mindfulness practices develop our ability to be aware of an experience without emotionally engaging with it, enabling us to become a curious observer. It allows us to realize that these thoughts, sensations, emotions, pain, etc., are transient—they come and they go. With practice, this observer stance facilitates a shift in our relationship with the experience, helping us see it as outside of ourselves, rather than identifying with it, or trying to ignore it, or eliminate it. The benefits extend to improving our emotional regulation and increasing our mental flexibility, which are relevant to the stressors that veterans face, both in the war zone and when transitioning home. (Note that, because a core element of mindfulness is awareness of an experience, the term "mindful awareness" is used interchangeably with "mindfulness" in this chapter, and also reflects the usage of the terms in current literature and practice. Therefore, the reader will see "mindfulness," "mindful awareness practice(s)" and "mindfulness practice(s)" used.) Before launching into a discussion of issues faced by our combat veterans, it is helpful to engage in a short mindfulness practice in order to develop an introductory sense of the experience. There are many ways to practice mindfulness, ranging from more the traditional to the informal (ordinary activities conducted with focused attention). Traditional practices include mindful breathing, walking, eating, or sitting meditations; yoga; and body scans (moving from one part of the body to the next, focusing attention on sensations in each region). Informal practices can be as simple as paying full attention to movements making up a larger activity, such as attending to steps when going from the car to the house, or walking the dog; washing dishes; gardening; or brushing teeth. For example, when washing dishes, we may notice how the water flows over our hands, and then shift our attention to the feel of the sponge against our skin or the pressure involved in grasping a cup. In the garden, we could become acutely aware of scents or sensations when holding a plant or touching the soil. Full attention to the toothbrush as it moves from tooth to tooth is another opportunity to practice mindfulness, as is any daily activity. This chapter will limit the description of mindfulness practices to breathing and listening exercises, primarily because focusing attention on the breath or a sound can be done almost anywhere, anytime, for varying durations, and is a fundamental building block of mindful awareness.

Mindful Breathing Practice

Before proceeding through the chapter, it is helpful to have your own experience of mindful breathing. Taking a few minutes to do this exercise will give you an idea of a fundamental mindfulness practice and the calming effect this can have on the body and mind even after only a few minutes.

Start by sitting in a comfortable position on a chair or a cushion. It is best if your back is not leaning against anything, but is upright without being "ramrod" straight. If you feel comfortable closing your eyes, this helps reduce external distractions. If you prefer to keep your eyes open, focus them in front of you at approximately a 45-degree angle off the floor. Now, simply breathe normally and notice your body just as you are sitting: notice your posture, how your body feels in that position, and where you sense pressure or weight. Then, shift your attention to your breath. Do not do anything deliberate with your breath; let it flow in and out of your body and notice the sensation. Perhaps you feel the breath most prominently in your abdomen as it expands and contracts when air flows in and out. You might notice it in your chest as the air moves down toward your abdomen, or you may be more aware of the flow of air in your nostrils as it enters and exits. Try to be a very curious observer of your experience of breathing.

As you do this, your mind will very likely wander to a thought, a physical sensation, a sound, etc. As soon as you become aware that your mind has wandered away from the breath (and it will!), you are being mindful. When this happens, gently (without internal commentary or judgment of yourself and the experience) guide your attention back to your breath. Continue focusing on your breath for about five minutes, noting when your mind wanders off, and gently bringing it back. Then, gradually open or lift your eyes, notice your body (has anything changed?) and return to awareness of your environment. Take a moment to reflect on the experience: what happened when you tried to focus on your breath; what it was like to notice that your mind had wandered to a sensation or thought; and how you responded.

Relevance of Mindfulness Practice to Current Conflict Environments

How, then, can mindfulness practices be useful to our service members? At first glance, they may seem too simplistic to be of value to those who have deployed to the wartime theater. The following section will discuss how many of the challenges of our current conflicts demand mental flexibility (which mindfulness can build) in highly stressful and complex situations. It will also look at how, after combat, mindfulness can be helpful in managing emotions and rebuilding cognitive abilities that are degraded from continued exposure to chronic, high, stress. Practices, such as this mindful breathing exercise, if done consistently over a period of time, increase the ability to shift attention at will and to develop mental and physical resilience overall, as well as increase mental flexibility. This is something to be called upon, particularly during times of stress and complex mental and emotional situations, such as those required of our servicemen and women in the war zone, as well as for redeployment and post-deployment reintegration. The following sections will highlight the particular challenges of today's conflicts.

Counter-Insurgency Warfare

An overarching theme of the complexity of our current conflicts is the counter-insurgency warfare in which our service members are engaged. Fighting insurgents means fighting for human capital (i.e., the resource and investment in each human, from skill and education, to loyalty and service, to group or community) as well as territory, which is particularly difficult in regions that present significant cultural, tribal, historical, religious, and values differences. In this situation, a level of cultural, emotional, and situational awareness is needed that extends far beyond standard combat readiness. Winning hearts and minds demands that the deployed service member has to frequently shift between combat and other operational modes (humanitarian, tribal-dispute resolution, peacebuilding, stabilization, etc.). We saw the impacts of this type of mental shift during the Vietnam War, when "winning the hearts and minds of the Vietnamese" was a motto that reflected the military's realization that a guerilla war could not be won just by military prowess, but also required "winning over" the Vietnamese people (Scurfield, 2004). It places high demands on our troops for greater moment-to-moment awareness and mental flexibility, which mindfulness practices can help develop.

While managing the dual mission of defeating the enemy and winning hearts and minds, many service members may also be struggling with hatred for the Afghans and the Iraqis. There are several potential sources of the hatred, as suggested by an Army Ranger who served as infantry in Iraq and now works in the area of psychological health for soldiers. He recently pointed out that Iraqis and Afghanis, while not directly responsible for the Twin Tower tragedies, represent—to many service members—those who committed the acts. Secondly, even without preconceived biases, merely being pulled from home, away from their comfort zone, and placed in harsh living conditions in an unfamiliar country can push soldiers and Marines toward hatred. The Iraqis and Afghanis could be blamed for the hardships faced on the ground. Thirdly, this Ranger describes that the minute a firefight is over, and a soldier or Marine has survived (but maybe a buddy has not), hatred can naturally develop as an emotional artifact of the experience. In addition to the intense stress of a firefight, the soldier or Marine often does not know who will, at any time, walk over and blow himself or herself up. The huge uncertainty about who, and where, the enemy is adds to the mental challenges (personal communication, October 31, 2011). Another distinctive characteristic of these conflicts is the possibility that, no matter the rank, the soldier or Marine may, in moments, have to make strategic decisions that could impact American policy in the region. Whether at a checkpoint in Iraq or a remote forward operating base (FOB) in the mountainous regions throughout Afghanistan, mission success may be very dependent upon small-unit leadership; "strategic corporal" has become the current terminology to describe such situations. In our current conflicts, this "strategic corporal" refers to the NCO (non-commissioned officer) who may be one of the most visible representatives of the U.S. government, thereby adding significant importance (and an even higher degree of stress) to each split-second decision that must be made. Service member readiness now requires greater mental agility in order to carry out the expanded military mission.

Training in mindfulness practices prior to deployment would provide service members with basic tools for better managing the multiple operational stressors mentioned above. This training could take place over eight weeks, with a two-hour class per week, a short workshop, and time built into the schedule for daily individual practice to support the exercises taught in class (breathing, movement, listening, etc.). Pre-deployment training should provide examples of how to integrate mindfulness into war zone activities, such as cleaning weapons, waiting in the chow line, walking, working out, and so on. Ideally, once in theater, service members would be supported in their practice with recorded guided meditations and/or access to someone reasonably well trained in mindfulness who can answer questions and encourage continued efforts. The key is for service members to have an opportunity to practice without feeling weird. This will come with fuller acceptance in the military of the benefits of the practice for managing operational stress and the effects of injuries. It is also important for service members to know that mindful awareness practices do not shut them off from ambient activities or diminish preparedness. Therefore, focusing on the breath or walking mindfully does not preclude a warrior, for example, from being ready to put on his or her battle gear to go "outside the wire" (leave the base), return fire, or head to the bunker when the situation calls for it.

Multiple Stakeholders

An added challenge in our current conflicts is the requirement for our military to work in close cooperation with international and joint military forces and numerous non-military stakeholders, such as the U.S. State Department and Development and

Reconstruction Teams (called Provincial Reconstruction Teams, or PRTs, in Afghanistan) populated by civilians and members of local organizations. This adds enormous complexity to a military mission and requires continually shifting mindsets and perspectives, all of which taxes an already stressed brain trained for combat. At the "Transitions, Issues, Challenges, and Solutions" conference in November 2010, hosted by the Peacekeeping and Stability Operations Institute (PKSOI) of the Army War College in Carlisle Barracks, PA, the author participated in discussions regarding how to best prepare our military for future conflicts. The outcome of the small group discussions was consistent with a U.S. Joint Forces Command study about the future of warfare, indicating that: "the next quarter century will challenge the U.S. joint forces with threats and opportunities ranging from regular and irregular wars in remote lands, to relief and reconstruction in crisis zones, to sustained engagement in the global commons" (Joint Operating Environment, 2008). Therefore, the assumption is that these types of conflicts involving multiple stakeholders, culturally complex situations, and shifting missions, will likely be the nature of future U.S. military engagements around the world. This provides even greater impetus to determine the most effective means of assisting our service members to be more mentally flexible as part of maintaining the highest standard of combat readiness. Again, mental flexibility (ability to shift perspectives) is increased with consistent mindfulness practice.

The Nature of Wounds, Injuries, and Impairments

In addition to a highly complex working environment, there are particular issues emerging from these conflicts which veterans, care providers, and society at large will be addressing for many years to come. Due to the type of body armor available and advanced battlefield-injury treatment, we have more servicemen and women surviving devastating combat wounds and traumatic amputations than in past wars. While no one would have it otherwise, the type of injuries and sheer number of badly wounded pose a new challenge for veterans, the mental and physical healthcare systems, and our society that must be readied to receive them. The improvised explosive device (IED)—the roadside bomb—is the preferred weapon of the enemy in Iraq and Afghanistan and one of the resulting signature wounds of these weapons is traumatic brain injury (TBI). The Armed Forces Health Surveillance Center estimates that, from 2001 to 2011, 212,742 service members have been diagnosed with a form of TBI, ranging from mild to severe. In fact, there was a marked increase in TBI-related visits to emergency centers from 2008 to 2010 (Armed Forces Health Surveillance Center, 2011). This trend can be expected to correlate with the number of troops serving in the wartime theater, and it is possible that mindfulness practices may offer valuable benefits to emerging TBI treatment protocols.

Brain dysfunction, often showing up as neuropsychological impairment, is a concern for our returning veterans, and not just in those suffering from a TBI. As highlighted in the August 2, 2006, issue of *JAMA*, while neuropsychological (such as cognitive and emotional) impairment was the fourth highest complaint among Gulf War veterans, the related effects of deployment to a war zone are not well understood. In an effort to better understand the consequences of these deployments, a study of male and female soldiers who served in Iraq between April 2003 and June 2005 was conducted for the

Neurocognition Deployment Health Study. Findings indicate that soldiers returned from Iraq with an increased risk of mildly compromised neuropsychological functioning, including impacts on sustained attention, verbal learning, visual-spatial memory, and tension. This will likely impact the psychosocial and occupational success for this population of impaired veterans (Vasterling, et al., 2006). While the *JAMA* study specifically looked at a cohort that deployed to Iraq, it is not a stretch to imagine that the same consequences result from serving in Afghanistan. Furthermore, given the young age of the majority of our service members, we can expect these issues to have very long-term psychological and social implications.

The author wonders if the complexity of the operating environments in Iraq and Afghanistan—counter-insurgency warfare, complex cultural factors, shifting missions, multiple stakeholders, the mental demands placed on the "the strategic corporal," and, of course, TBIs—might be creating even greater issues of cognitive impairment than might have been the case in previous wars. Of particular concern is working memory capacity (WMC)—basically, the ability to stay on task and remain goal-oriented without becoming distracted by separate tasks or by irrelevant information—a vital aspect of cognitive function and emotional self-regulation. Research demonstrates that people with higher WMC are better at managing their emotions (Schmeichel, Volokhov, & Demaree, 2008; Schmeichel & Demaree, 2010). A key concern for our veterans is that WMC is degraded when humans are exposed to persistent high-stress environments—the state of affairs in the current and, indeed, in almost any, wartime theaters of operation.

Issues and Challegnes: Transition from Deployment to Home

Reintegration is another significant challenge for our military men and women. Coming *back* after being in a combat zone is not the same as coming *home*. A successful reintegration into the *home*—wherever that is, or however that is defined—may take a month or may take years and the path is often riddled with difficulty. Not only does the service member face reintegration challenges, but so do family members and even close civilian friends or co-workers (this is of particular concern for National Guard and Reserve members who are quickly thrust back into civilian lives after returning). They, too, have changed during the veteran's absence, often without realizing it. In spite of everyone changing, the expectation, often, is for the veteran to *be home* soon after coming back and for everyone to settle back into the way it was. Even those who recognize that changes have occurred may not know how to create a *new normal*—a way of being together that incorporates the time spent apart, the experiences everyone has had, the shifts in behavior and thinking, and any psychological or physical challenges resulting from the deployment. The potential for disconnect during the reintegration phase is significant and severely impacted by the perspectives that stem from different experiences, needs, and expectations. There is insufficient space here to address this important topic more than superficially. However, reintegration deserves a great deal of attention, as this is an absolutely crucial phase that, if not traversed successfully, may have a long-term detrimental impact on the soldier and loved ones. Reintegration is a challenge for National Guard (see Courage, 2012), Reserve (see Rabb & Rasmussen, 2012) and Active Duty service members alike. This is made all the more difficult due to the fact that we rely upon an all-volunteer force comprising only about 1 percent of the general population, which results in repetitive deployments for many. Returning to the war zone multiple times has a tremendous impact on the physical, mental, and emotional well-being of our veterans. This is exacerbated by the fact that those returning from deployment often feel misunderstood and disregarded by much of the remaining 99 percent of the American populace. The rest of the population often seems completely disconnected from the conflicts, and ambivalent, if not uncaring, toward veterans' experiences and issues. While, if asked, the average civilian might argue that this assessment of their attitude is not accurate, it is a reality that many of our service members and veterans perceive (and experience) to be true. This has a potentially degrading effect on their reintegration due to feeling undervalued and misunderstood. Reintegration after experiencing war is hard enough without a cultural divide between our military and the rest of society. This is not a good formula for any of us, but particularly not for our service members and their families, who feel they have sacrificed so much for the country, yet are underappreciated.

Evidence-Based Findings Relevant to the Practice of Mindfulness for Service Members

The author believes that mindfulness practices would be beneficial to our veterans in theater as well as during their transitions to post-combat life. Research has shown that a mindfulness practice can help improve WMC in service members (Jha, Stanley, Kiyonaga, Wong & Gelfand, 2010). (Recall that WMC, working memory capacity, is the ability to remain on task without becoming distracted by irrelevant information, and is an important aspect of cognitive function and emotional self-regulation.) Drs. Elizabeth Stanley and Amishi Jha have been taking a close look at the impact of the particular issues related to OIF and OEF deployments, and how mindfulness training might improve combat readiness and reduce potential emotional and cognitive degradation stemming from continuous exposure to the relentless stressors inherent in the wartime theater. Published research is based on findings from an eight-week course in mindfulness-based practice that incorporated a target of 30 minutes of practice outside class time, which comprised 24 hours of instruction to Marine reservists, including how to integrate these practices into standard pre-deployment training and apply them to a counter-insurgency context. Exercises were designed to increase the capacity for concentration, either by focusing on a sensation in the body; the breath; external stimuli; or regulation of psychological or physiological reactions to symptoms from stress and/or trauma. A positive correlation was seen between the amount of time practicing mindfulness during the course and an increase in WMC among the military cohort, as well as lower negative affect (experience of an emotion or a feeling) compared to a military control group that did not engage in the practices (Stanley & Jha, 2009). Dr. Stanley has continued her research with Marines and soldiers, and new findings are expected to be published in 2013. Mindfulness practices enable us to step back and observe our thoughts, emotions, and reactions in a more detached (as in *separate from*) and non-judgmental manner. As a result, we are better able to experience these thoughts and emotions without being overwhelmed and controlled by them. This stated benefit, however, is not quickly accepted by our service members in general. It is not uncommon for an individual to come into the military with some past trauma and to experience additional trauma in the combat zone.

Allowing thoughts, memories, and emotions to come up for observation is of concern to our service members and, quite frankly, makes many, to whom this author has spoken, feel uneasy. Discomfort often relates to not knowing the impact of these emerging emotions, as well as to fears of projecting any vulnerability or weakness as they learn to mindfully observe what comes up. The person drawn to the military is usually one who values mental (and physical) toughness and, understandably, the culture encourages that toughness. Therefore, to ask our warriors to allow thoughts and memories to emerge, in order to practice observing without engaging with them, is not something they are particularly eager to do. Soldiers have told the author that they work hard to *keep* certain thoughts and memories buried, and worry that allowing them out for observation is unsettling at the very least. It takes trust on his or her part to be willing to try mindfulness practices, as it tends to go against much military training and experience. While service members may acknowledge the challenges of being in a war zone, and of having difficulty readjusting after deployment, accepting a practice that requires greater awareness of self and experiences does not naturally follow.

One approach by the U.S. Army toward helping warriors become aware of learned behaviors and reactions that are crucial down range, but that are often not helpful after returning, is the Resilience Training program. It is designed to assist soldiers, leaders, and families in handling the rigors of the deployment cycle and, upon returning from the combat zone, incorporates information previously called "Battlemind" to raise awareness of the risks of applying battlefield survival strategies to the home front. One aspect of this Battlemind awareness is that tactical awareness in country can easily translate (and often does) into hypervigilance back in the States. In virtually every discussion that this author has had with service members about their reintegration after combat— whether instructing in a classroom, co-facilitating Women Warrior group sessions, or having one-on-one conversations—hypervigilance comes up as a challenge. This may manifest as discomfort in, and avoidance of, crowds; exaggerated responses to noises; needing to sit with the back to a wall in a restaurant and constantly scanning the room; flashes of anger when personal space is invaded; highly defensive driving and suspicion of items (e.g., paper bags) on the side of the road; a knee-jerk reaction to a loved one reaching up to touch the service member's face; and myriad other strong responses to a perceived lack of safety in one's surroundings. It is important to note that these are normal reactions to combat experiences, but often create problems during reintegration.

While the service member may wish to reduce post-deployment hyper-vigilance and cease other thought patterns and behaviors that stem from life-saving strategies reinforced in the combat theater (and military training in general), many do not know how to go about it. The first step to any behavioral or cognitive change is awareness of that behavior, thought, or mindset. It is quite difficult, however, to catch ourselves *in the moment*—at the cusp of having the behavior or thought. Mindfulness practices, by definition and nature, offer building blocks to precisely that type and level of awareness. They enable us to observe internal and external experiences in a more non-reactive manner, which fosters greater awareness of the influence of these experiences. Through this practice, we are better able to stand back and watch our thoughts and reactions, allowing us to check our assumptions, question our interpretations, and eventually to choose a response that is more in line with a fulfilling lifestyle (relational, psychological, and physical). Ideally, mindfulness practices would start before, and continue during, deployment. A soldier currently deployed with a Combat Stress control unit in Afghanistan, and who provides basic mindfulness training in theater, shows soldiers how this practice can help to "decrease stress arousal and develop a positive way to cope with traumatic events and operational demands." He helps his soldiers understand that mindfulness can be part of their downtime, when they are not out on a mission (and, therefore, forced to focus on multiple variables). He emphasizes that this does not have to be traditional meditation by any means. As he tells them, it can be incorporated into cleaning their weapon, for example, by focusing attention very intently on each discrete task. This leader has observed the benefit of these mindfulness practices in that ". . . soldiers learn about focusing on one task at a time and ground themselves in the moment they are in" (personal communication, November 5, 2011).

There are myriad benefits to mindfulness training, including addressing physical health challenges. Extensive research in the mindfulness-based stress reduction (MBSR) approach illustrates the effectiveness of meditation (a form of mindfulness practice) in improving physical health, managing pain, and promoting wellness overall. The MBSR program incorporates information about the relationship between stress and health with mindfulness practices including breathing, body scan (focusing on specific body regions and sensations in those regions), walking, yoga, and martial arts such as qigong. Participants meet for two hours, every week, for eight weeks. They are highly encouraged to practice outside of class and to attend a full-day silent meditation retreat at the end of the course.

There is such an abundance of research linking the benefits of mindfulness practices, such as those taught in the MBSR course, to physical health, that it is impossible to provide a complete listing of supporting publications. For an excellent overview of this work, refer to the University of Massachusetts Medical School Center for Mindfulness in Medicine, Healthcare and Society website. This site offers a selected bibliography, resources, and access to MBSR programs around the U.S. (http://www.umassmed.edu/content.aspx?id=41252). In addition, the founder of the Center for Mindfulness, Dr. Jon Kabat-Zinn, is the author of a highly informative text about mindfulness for managing stress, chronic pain, and illness: *Full Catastrophe Living: Using the Wisdom of Your Body and Mind to Face Stress, Pain, and Illness* (Kabat-Zinn, 1990).

Integration of Mindfulness into Psychotherapeutic Approaches

While meditation-based mindfulness practices have existed for thousands of years in various cultures, and Western research into the benefits of this practice for physical health abounds, it is more recent that this approach has been integrated into psychotherapy. Currently, mindfulness practices are part and parcel of a few psychotherapeutic practices: mindfulness-based cognitive therapy, DBT (Dialectical Behavior Therapy), and ACT (Acceptance and Commitment Therapy).

Mindfulness is certainly not yet a standard part of all forms of psychotherapy, but the research base demonstrating it to be an effective adjunct has expanded to include treatment for a variety of psychosocial dysfunctions, such as depression and anxiety (Williams, et al., 2007); obsessive-compulsive disorder (Schwartz & Begley, 2002); and, quite possibly, PTSD (Bernstein, Tanay, & Vujanovic, 2011; Vujanovic, et al., 2009; Walser & Westrup, 2007). Research has shown that the MBSR program developed by

Dr. Kabat-Zinn reduces the tendency for rumination about, and emotional reactivity to, thoughts and physical sensations (Ramel, et al., 2004). In fact, due to the impressive literature on the positive benefits of mindfulness practices for various aspects of emotional dysregulation, the VA encourages mindfulness practices as an addition to its repertoire of evidence-based treatments, such as prolonged exposure therapy and cognitive processing therapy (http://www.ptsd.va.gov/professional/pages/mindful-PTSD.asp).

The author sees no reason why mindfulness cannot be practiced in conjunction with any theoretical orientation, whether individualistic (such as psychodynamic, experiential, existential, e.g.), systems (family, feminist, e.g.), or postmodern (solution-focused, narrative, e.g.). Each approach relies upon some aspect of insight, self-awareness, and emotional regulation, all of which have the potential to be greatly enhanced, in terms of therapeutic benefits, by consistent mindfulness practice (Schmeichel & Demaree, 2010). After all, helping our combat veterans really comes down to helping them change thought patterns, reactions to stimuli, behaviors, and relationships with others, as well as with themselves—who they are, physically, emotionally, and mentally after returning from war. Awareness of self is crucial for those changes, and mindfulness practices fundamentally increase our awareness of experiences and, thus, self.

Strengthening our awareness of experience *as it occurs* can improve emotional regulation and cognitive abilities (Moore & Malinowski, 2009). Studies have shown that regular mindfulness practice increases grey matter in regions of the brain associated with memory, emotional regulation, self-appraisal and introspection (Hölzel, 2009; Jha, et al., 2010).

Mindfulness, Neuroplasticity, and Change

For this author, one of the most exciting and encouraging areas of neuroscience is around *neuroplasticity*—basically, the brain's ability to create new connections between cells (pathways) and new functions as the result of experiences. In essence, it is the capacity for the brain to rewire itself (Schwartz & Begley, 2002, p. 15). When we have a thought, call up an image, or practice a motor skill, for example, and do this repeatedly, the connections involved in that thought, image, or skill become stronger, making it easier to do as time goes on.

Neuroplasticity is at play during a mindfulness practice, when we work to keep our minds focused on one thing (the breath, each step when walking, a word, etc.). We strengthen the brain's capacity for focused attention each time we become aware that our mind has wandered and bring attention back to the object of focus. This ability to intentionally harness our attentive energy toward, say, one thought over another, literally changes the brain. As Dr. Jeffrey Schwartz of UCLA states, "The power of the mind's questioning ('Shall I pay attention to this idea?') to strengthen one idea rather than another . . . silences all the others and emerges as the one we focus on" (Schwartz & Begley, 2002, p. 353). The ability to be aware of thoughts (and their impact), and to redirect them, is particularly important for those returning from the war zone.

The issue is that, without awareness of momentary experiences (thoughts, memories, pain, reactions, etc.), we cannot very easily determine when helpful thoughts, behaviors, and mindsets turn harmful. As Dr. Daniel Siegel, Professor of Psychiatry at the UCLA School of Medicine tells us, "our mind uses the brain to defend us from pain" (Siegel,

2010, p. 124). When down range, for example, the ability to shield the brain from detecting pain (physical or emotional) is crucial, enabling mission focus and lives to be saved. Once back to the States, however, blocking pain may disconnect the service member from loved ones. This author frequently hears from soldiers that one of the greatest issues after deployment to Iraq or Afghanistan is the inability to feel any emotion besides anger.

The tendency to obstruct the perception of pain in the wartime theater may make reintegration more difficult, as it reduces opportunities for emotional connection and healing. Dr. Daniel Siegel reminds us that if we try to remove pain from our conscious experience, we may avoid the pain for the moment, but it does not disappear. It simply manifests in some other way. Blocking negative feelings or pain also blocks positive feelings and emotions, thus inhibiting access to the full range of experiences. The result, states Dr. Siegel, can be that we end up with "a deadened emotional life and a cut off from the wisdom of the body" (Siegel, 2010, p. 126). Mindfulness practices build a resilience and capacity for allowing a full range of mental, physical, and emotional experiences without being controlled by them. As mentioned previously, improving our mindfulness does not require hours every day. Rather, benefits can be achieved through simple exercises integrated into daily life, such as that outlined in the following section.

Mindful Listening Exercise

Find a comfortable place where you can sit quietly without concern that others will interrupt you, and where you can allow yourself to close your eyes and feel safe. This may be your office, your backyard, a favorite spot in the forest, or even in the car parked in front of your home. Once you are settled, and your eyes are closed, take a moment to be aware of your body. Notice how you are sitting. Be aware of any tension in your shoulders, hands, face, etc. If you do notice tightness, as you inhale focus your attention right there, and when you exhale try to release the tension in those muscles. That may mean dropping your shoulders, relaxing your jaw muscles, unclenching your hands, and so on. Breathe slowly for a minute, continuing to release any tightness that you find. Tension has a way of coming right back into our muscles, so allow yourself enough time to catch it and let it go until you truly feel more relaxed.

Now . . . just listen. What do you hear? What sounds come in and out? Which rise and fall? Be acutely aware of the various sounds you hear. Next, choose one sound to focus on: birds, cars, wind, air conditioner, dogs barking—any discrete sound—and try to listen without judging it as pleasant or unpleasant. Once you have selected the sound that will be the object of your attention, become very curious about it: listen for every aspect of it that you can detect. Does it get louder and then softer? Is it sharp or flat? Let it enter your hearing realm and then notice that it leaves; the sound waves come and they go. Try to keep your attention on this chosen sound for several minutes. Your mind will likely wander to a thought, to a physical sensation, or perhaps to another sound. As soon as you notice that your attention has moved away from the intended target, gently (and without judgment of your ability to focus) bring it back.

Continue to focus your attention on this one sound, or choose another one to attend to and go through the same process of investigating the sound. Practice this exercise for 3 minutes and work your way up to 10 or 15 over time. At the end of each practice, before bringing your awareness back to all of the hustle and bustle of life, take a minute to pause and notice your body in space and, then, gently return to all that is going on around you.

The Value of Mindfulness for Care Providers

The mind is a wanderer, and building the strength to keep it focused, even for short periods, can be challenging for any of us. The beauty of mindfulness practices, however, is that we can stop at any moment and be mindful: of our breath, of sounds, of movement, of what is in our visual field, etc. Each minute that we are able to focus our attention on one experience we benefit ourselves and those around us. As care providers, we often do not take time to nurture ourselves sufficiently to ensure our own practice of self care. We seem to think that any time taken away from those we serve is self-serving. Yes, it is just that! It is *self-serving* to regenerate, but it is not *selfish*.

Building our own mindfulness practice gives us greater energy and helps ground us in our intentions. It can provide necessary internal resources that enable us to offer quality assistance to others. The best way to be present for our clients is to be present for, and to, ourselves; mindful awareness is one way to achieve that sense of presence. If mindfulness approaches appeal to you, there are many resources and groups to help you get started and to assist you as you deepen your practice. There are, in fact, books and resources too numerous to list here. While the author has her favorite techniques, books, retreats, and orientations, part of the path is choosing those that fit for you. If you find that the idea of incorporating mindfulness work into your clinical practice is of interest and importance, the most effective steps are to develop your own practice at whatever level you can and to continue exploring and strengthening it. This author, for example, typically has one long sitting meditation (or several short breathing exercises) during the day; a body scan; and/or frequent walking, eating, or listening meditations. While a longer meditation (30 minutes to an hour or more) yields deeper benefits than a 10 minute breathing exercise, it is important to start where you are, and know that focusing on breathing, sounds, or walking for 5 or 10 minutes is still progress toward strengthening your mind/brain capacity to focus and be mindful! Remember to leave judgment out of this.

Closing: Mindfulness, Growth, and Healing

OIF/OEF/OND warriors and veterans confront exceptionally challenging situations during their deployments, as well as upon returning to the home front. Asymmetric warfare (unequal military power leading to significantly different strategies, tactics, use of resources, and rules of engagement than conventional warfare) and urban warfare alone demand significant mental resilience. We must add to that multiple deployments, the diverse roles service members are required to play (such as the "Strategic Corporal" and winning hearts and minds while engaging in standard warfare), and the complicated tribal, ethnic, and religious differences they must negotiate. Any of these can create intense mental distress. Moving through the changes that take place physically, emotionally, and mentally from such experiences is no simple task for either the veterans or their loved ones after returning from war. It requires commitment to positive change, growth, and healing, and a willingness to face fears and do the hard work of engaging in heightened awareness. Mindfulness practices, in that they enhance our self-awareness and the ability to observe our experiences without emotionally engaging with them, offer a powerful tool to support physical and mental resilience, growth, and healing.

In the author's work with service members, either preparing to deploy or reintegrating after deployment, it becomes more evident with each encounter that mindfulness practices can be, at the very least, helpful. For some, they may be transformational. This is a simple (yet not necessarily easy) way to increase awareness and capacity for all experiences, pleasant and painful, internal and external, within our minds and bodies. Mindful awareness offers a host of advantages—physical and mental—from an increase in working memory capacity to a more loving and kind approach to oneself and others. A consistent mindfulness practice creates, in a sense, a more flexible mind, something that this author believes is crucial to successfully overcoming the many risk factors associated with serving in conflicts such as OIF, OEF, and OND, ranging from integrating combat experiences to reintegrating into post-combat life.

For mental and physical healthcare providers, mindfulness practices encourage and support our own self care, which enables us to do our best work and stay grounded in our true intentions toward serving our men and women in uniform. It is the wish of this author that we offer the widest possible range of skills and services to our honorable service members and that mindfulness practices be considered a potential building block to the physical, emotional, and mental healing they so deserve. Mindfulness expert Jon Kabat-Zinn aptly titled one of his meditation books *Wherever You Go, There You Are* (Kabat-Zinn, 1994). Our thoughts, reactions, and challenges are with us everywhere and impact us all of the time; contrary to a common belief, ignoring them does not make them disappear. Mindful awareness is an effective way to change our relationship with challenges and to reduce their power over us. As a Navy medic, Hermes Oliva, who participated in research with Drs. Jha and Stanley (Jha, et al., 2010) said of his experience in Iraq, after completing their mind fitness training, "In the tent at night, all by myself, I started to do those exercises. It would help me recognize the symptoms in my body before they got out of control" (Gregory, 2010, p. 82). There is no better way to say it.

References

Armed Forces Health Surveillance Center. (May 2011). *Medical Surveillance Monthly Report*, *18*(5): 15. Available from: http://www.afhsc.mil/viewMSMR?file=2011/v18_n05.pdf.

Bernstein, A., Tanay, G., & Vujanovic, A. A. (2011). "Concurrent Relations between Mindful Attention and Awareness and Psychopathology among Trauma-Exposed Adults: Preliminary Evidence of Transdiagnostic Resilience." *Journal of Cognitive Psychotherapy*, *25*: 99–113.

Gregory, V. (2010). 'Meditation Fit for a Marine." *Men's Journal*, *19*(9). Retrieved December, 1, 2011, from: http://www.mensjournal.com.

Hölzel, B. K. (2009). *Neurobiological Underpinnings of Mindfulness and Meditation*. Center for Mindfulness, University of Massachusetts Medical School 7th Annual International Scientific Conference. Worchester, MA. March, 2009. Conference presentation recording.

Jha, A. P., Stanley, E. A., Kiyonaga, A., Wong, L., & Gelfand, L. (2010). "Examining the Protective Effects of Mindfulness Training on Working Memory Capacity and Affective Experience." *Emotion*, *10*(1) 54–64. Retrieved November, 14, 2010, from: http://www.mind-fitness training. org/MMFT_Emotion_working_memory.pdf.

Joint Operating Environment. (2008). *Challenges and Implications for the Future Joint Force*. U.S.

Joint Forces Command. Retrieved January 12, 2011, from: http://www.jfcom.mil/newslink/storyarchive/2008/JOE2008.pdf.

Kabat-Zinn, J. (1994). *Wherever You Go, There You Are: Mindfulness Meditation in Everyday Life.* New York, NY: Hyperion.

Kabat-Zinn, J. (1990). *Full Catastrophe Living: Using the Wisdom of Your Body and Mind to Face Stress, Pain, and Illness.* New York, NY: Delta Trade.

Moore, A., & Malinowski, P. (2009). "Meditation, Mindfulness, and Cognitive Flexibility." *Consciousness and Cognition, 18*(1): 176–186. Available at: www.elsevier.com/locate/concog.

Ramel, W., Goldin, P. R., Carmona, P. E., & McQuaid, J. R. (2004). "The Effects of Mindfulness Meditation on Cognitive Processes and Affect in Patients with Past Depression." *Cognitive Therapy and Research, 28:* 433–455.

Schmeichel, B. J., & Demaree, H. A. (2010). "Working Memory Capacity and Spontaneous Emotion Regulation: High Capacity Predicts Self-Enhancement in Response to Negative Feedback." *Emotion, 10*(5): 739–744.

Schmeichel, B. J., Volokhov, R. N., & Demaree, H. A. (2008). "Working Memory Capacity and the Self-Regulation of Emotional Expression and Experience." *Journal of Personality and Social Psychology, 95*(6): 1526–1540.

Schwartz, J. M., & Begley, S. (2002). *The Mind and the Brain: Neuroplasticity and the Power of Mental Force.* New York, NY: Regan.

Scurfield, R. M. (2004). *A Vietnam Trilogy: Veterans and Post-Traumatic Stress, 1968, 1989 & 2000.* New York, NY: Algora.

Siegel, D. (2010). *Mindsight: The New Science of Personal Transformation.* New York, NY: Bantam.

Stanley, E. A., & Jha, A. P. (2009). "Mind Fitness: Improving Operational Effectiveness and Building Warrior Resilience." *Joint Force Quarterly, 55:* 144–151.

Vasterling, J. J., Proctor, S. P, Amoroso, P., Kane, R., Heeren, T., & White, R. F. (August 2, 2006). "Neuropsychological Outcomes of Army Personnel Following Deployment to the Iraq War." *JAMA (Journal of the American Medical Association), 296*(5): 519–529.

Vujanovic, A. A., Youngwirth, N. E., Johnson, K. A., & Zvolensky, M. J. (2009). "Mindfulness-Based Acceptance and Posttraumatic Stress Symptoms among Trauma-Exposed Adults without Axis I Psychopathology." *Journal of Anxiety Disorders, 23:* 297–303.

Walser, R. D., & Westrup, D. (2007). *Acceptance & Commitment Therapy for the Treatment of Post-Traumatic Stress Disorder and Trauma-Related Problems: A Practitioner's Guide to Using Mindfulness and Acceptance Strategies.* Oakland, CA: New Harbinger Publications.

Williams, M., Teasdale, J., Segal, Z., & Kabat-Zinn, J. (2007). *The Mindful Way Through Depression: Freeing Yourself from Chronic Unhappiness.* New York, NY: Guilford.

11 Hypnotherapy in the Wartime Theater

OIF, OEF, and Beyond

COL Katherine Theresa Platoni (ODS and OIF/OEF)

Hypnotherapy has an extensive history as a powerful and effective intervention in the treatment of trauma and, more specifically, in the treatment of PTSD. This treatment approach should only be utilized by appropriately trained, credentialed (as in the case of the military) and experienced clinicians. This chapter will provide a brief history of hypnosis as a treatment strategy, dispel popular myths regarding the nature of hypnosis, and confront issues surrounding the legitimacy of hypnosis as a viable and practical treatment intervention in the wartime theater and beyond. Also included is a comprehensive description of those essential factors required to produce a hypnotic state and an understanding of hypnotizability, the role of hypnotherapy in treating dissociation/complex PTSD and specific hypnotherapeutic treatment strategies utilized by the author. Finally, a case vignette will apply trauma-focused hypnotherapy with a soldier while he was deployed to Afghanistan.

Hypnosis as a Viable Therapeutic Strategy

The very image conjured up by the word hypnosis is typically one of swinging pendulums and powerless patients falling under the spell of "Svengali-like" figures in dimly lit rooms, "mesmerized" by the forces of animal magnetism to promote cures for any number of ills, real or imagined. The first references to the use of hypnosis, mystical though it may seem to the untrained eye, have been found in Biblical texts (when "God caused Adam to fall into a deep sleep while He removed Adam's rib for the creation of Eve" (Craig, 1990)) the Talmud, and both the Old and New Testaments (Platoni, 2000). Over the course of centuries, and as old as the study of medicine itself, hypnosis has been used to treat pain, suffering, and illness, long before the advent of chemical anesthesia. Hypnosis is considered "the art of securing the patient's attention by effective communication of ideas that promote and enhance the motivation to alter perceptions" (Hammond, 1990) and sensations. Hypnosis enlists the subject or patient's participation in the joint endeavor of promoting desired change but, in and of itself, does not provide the treatment or the cure. Trust and rapport with the therapist, however, are indispensable. The patient's motivation, hypnotic abilities, and the quality of the therapeutic relationship, dictate the success or failure of any hypnotic endeavor.

The term hypnosis, first coined by British physician James Braid in 1841, is derived from the Greek word *hypnos*, meaning sleep (Wester, 1987). Contrary to popularly-held beliefs, hypnosis is not sleep but, instead, is defined as the uncritical acceptance of suggestions; a misdirection of attention away from extraneous stimuli; a reduction in peripheral awareness, a roused and attentive state of focused concentration, a state of intensified attention, and receptiveness to an idea or set of ideas (Crasilneck & Hall, 1975; Platoni, 2000) and a form of naturally occurring selective attention (Wester, 1987).

Throughout the course of our everyday lives, we ordinarily become absorbed in thoughts, images, memories, and fantasies, as in being deeply engrossed in a book or movie, to the exclusion of any other transpiring in our midst. Neither is it unusual to become so deeply preoccupied that we experience what is commonly referred to as "highway hypnosis," whereby one drives without conscious awareness and is yet guided by subconscious processes that allow the driver to remain safely on the road (ibid.).

Hypnotherapy is not considered a form of psychotherapy but, rather, a technique or strategy used to facilitate changes in thoughts, feelings, and behaviors, to reduce or eliminate distressing physical sensations such as chronic or acute pain, and to change or modify unhealthy lifestyle habits, such as overeating, nail biting, habitually working excessively long hours, and smoking. There are countless and legitimate uses of hypnosis and a vast array of research studies and clinical data to support and substantiate evidence-based practice of hypnosis. These may include, but are not limited to, treatment of acute and chronic pain, any number of invasive dental and medical procedures, pre- and post-surgical interventions, childbirth, gastrointestinal disorders, treatment of anxiety disorders, such as phobias and post-traumatic stress disorder, and interventions for treatment of depressive disorders, sleep disorders, dissociative disorders, stress management, and the like. The author has undergone 58 major and minor surgical procedures since 1983, primarily maxillofacial reconstructive and plastic surgery procedures, the great majority of them performed with hypnosis as the sole anesthetic due to a severe intolerance to chemical anesthesia and long-standing side effects (principally, immediate and short-term memory impairments). This illustrates the immeasurable value and effectiveness of hypnotic techniques in the hands of credentialed and trained clinicians and in situations that would otherwise involve enormous pain and suffering. According to Barretta and Barretta (2006) and affirmed by the author's experiences with hypnosis, both as patient and as clinician, therapeutic outcomes are *generated in more rapid succession with the use of hypnotherapy than with more traditional therapies, as this technique rapidly taps into the patient's creative resources.*

Dispelling Myths, Hypnosis Training, and Public Education

It is vital to dispel the many unsavory connotations, myths, and misconceptions that are the substance of popularly-held belief systems, even within the realm of mental health professionals. Hypnosis is not a form of mind control or submission, and no one can be hypnotized against their will. Hypnosis is a futile endeavor with unmotivated or resistant patients. Regardless of the skill level or expertise of the clinician, the patient will not lose consciousness or control, be controlled against their will, or violate their basic principles, morals, ethics, values, or belief systems. One must only consider the limited success of hypnotic interventions in weight loss/management or smoking cessation to be reassured that this is the case. Patients will never fail to re-enter a natural state of consciousness and complete awareness—or, in other words, to be de-hypnotized (Barretta & Barretta, 2006; Platoni, 2000). To an uninformed public, the semantically-loaded concept underlying hypnosis is perceived as an entity to be feared . . . as is fire, electricity, operating machinery, or driving (Barretta & Barretta, 2006).

There is certainly no shortage of unscrupulous practitioners of hypnosis, as is the case within any healthcare discipline. There is no legitimacy whatsoever to the multitude of weekend seminars and diploma mills that disseminate convincing-looking diplomas demonstrating one's hypnotherapeutic expertise and offering nonexistent credentials. The answer to the dilemma of bringing harm to an unsuspecting public, regardless of the type of therapeutic intervention, lies in public education, as anything less would be considered a disservice to those who may find themselves in our care. Equally as significant is the necessity of selecting reputable and professionally trained and credentialed practitioners of hypnosis (Barretta & Barretta, 2006; Platoni, 2000). Finally, legitimate hypnosis practitioners must possess graduate levels of clinical education in psychology, medicine, social work, or nursing, as well as advanced training in the practice of hypnosis, preferably by training bodies embraced, advocated for, or sponsored by, the American Society of Clinical Hypnosis (www.asch.net) and/or the Society of Clinical or Experimental Hypnosis (www.sceh.net).[1]

The Production of Hypnosis

There are four essential factors to consider in the production of a hypnotic state: the biological gift that resides within every individual, suggestibility, motivation and expectations, and trust/rapport in the therapist/operator. Some theorists also include imaginativeness as an additional vital component to the achievement of behavioral and lifestyle changes, upon which successful goal completion is virtually dependent.

It is not the hypnotic trance itself that promotes change or generates a desired response, but specifically tailored suggestions and imagery. These can result in very positive therapeutic outcomes and profound alterations in behavior, particularly with reinforced practice to emphasize and solidify permanency in these changes. Trance is the state in which subconscious learning and openness to change are more likely to occur, and where patients are able to intuitively understand underlying meanings of dream material, symbols, and other subconscious expressions (Rosen, 1982). This naturally occurring state is most familiar in the context of daydreaming, meditation, and even prayer (ibid.).

The subconscious mind may be considered the storage area for all information not available to the conscious awareness, such as memories, belief systems, and automatically elicited thoughts and feelings in response to demands. It is the use of indirect suggestions—in the form of metaphors or storytelling, such as those used by the distinguished Dr. Milton Erickson—which suggests that hypnotic responsiveness is mediated primarily by the subconscious mind. Hypnosis provides the vehicle by which integration of cortical and subcortical processes are integrated and incorporated (Wester & Smith, 1991).

Hypnotizability

Additionally, there is an issue of intensity or degree, in that some individuals are able to reach a deep state or level, with the associated subjective experiences of age regression, time distortion, both positive and negative hallucinations, and control of blood flow. Others may only be capable of reaching a light level of hypnosis, as evidenced by shallow diaphragmatic breathing, physical relaxation, minimal muscle flaccidity, and time lag (Barbarasz, et al., 2010). Any of these states may be elicited by either formal hypnotic inductions or by self-suggestions (self-hypnosis). Nevertheless, the practitioner only becomes concerned about depth of hypnosis when certain hypnotherapeutic techniques call for a deep levels or states, such as those required for invasive medical procedures or surgery (ibid.).

It is estimated that anywhere from 80 to 95 percent of the general population is hypnotizable to varying degrees; the greater likelihood is that our brain circuitry is genetically wired with hypnotizability, a biological gift possessed by each of us from birth. The capacity to become hypnotized is genetically encoded into the central nervous system, as it has likely been for centuries. Between 10 and 20 percent of the general population is considered highly hypnotizable: exceedingly imaginative, less analytical, and able to experience "disembodiedness" or out-of-body experiences and a complete sense of timelessness while in a deep state of hypnosis.

There are also those who are considered hypnotic virtuosos, who can dissociate from the invasive pain of major surgical procedures, and painful stimuli that others may consider excruciating, without any degree of suffering. Regardless of the level of hypnotizability, motivational factors play the more significant role. Significant medical, or any number of psychological problems, in addition to psychological resistance, will interfere with an individual's ability to attend and focus sufficiently to respond to hypnotic suggestions (Platoni, 2000).

Hypnosis, Dissociative Phenomena, and PTSD

Foa, Keane, and Friedman (2004) describe the most salient and significant dynamics concerning traumatic exposure. The feelings of helplessness and powerlessness frequently generated by traumatic exposure may readily pose challenges to the usual ways of processing perceptual, cognitive, affective or emotional, and information pertaining to interpersonal relationships, traumatic events typically producing a narrowed focus of attention and indifference to peripheral information. Similarly, attentional processes in the production of hypnosis may be associated with alterations in consciousness, to include dissociative phenomena, which are further defined as an experiential detachment or disengagement from the self and/or the environment, and alterations in self-perception, agency or will, memory, affective expression, and self-identity (if maintained more than momentarily) (ibid.). During or following a traumatic event in which the senses are overwhelmed, a large majority of patients will experience dissociative phenomena, involving experiential or passive detachment and alterations in both memory and perception.

There is also evidence that dissociation is a strong predictor of subsequent PTSD, already a distinct diagnostic feature of Acute Stress Disorder (APA, 2000). It is noteworthy that in a number of studies, victims of trauma were found to be more susceptible to the experience of dissociation, whether intentional or not. It may be a well-established fact that those exhibiting post-traumatic symptomatology are highly hypnotizable, and "are significantly more so than most other clinical and non-clinical groups" (Foa, Keane, & Friedman, 2004). Additionally, trauma may activate hypnotic responses spontaneously, and facilitate absorption in the hypnotic encounter by means of the experience of dissociation. Trance-like features may be observed through the reactivation of traumatic material:

captivation of the patient's attention, disorientation regarding time and space, and the processing of experience in a dissociated fashion (see Barabasz, et al., 2010). Certainly, this is fear-provoking in nature, constituting the arousal of memories that are emotionally-laden: all the more reason to invest in the readily accessible hypnotic experience.

The Rationale for the Use of Hypnosis in PTSD Treatment[2]

As many PTSD patients already experience dissociative symptomatology, hypnosis may be readily employed with this patient population, due to their prevailing or pre-existing hypnotizability and the increased probability of its effectiveness with moderately to highly hypnotizable individuals, in addition to those expectancies that may determine outcomes to hypnotic interventions (Foa, Keane, & Friedman, 2004).). Many patients diagnosed with PTSD experience dissociative symptomatology, considered a spontaneous form of self-hypnosis; the very element of hypnosis that may permit the induction/creation of the dissociative experience. Thus, patients may be taught specific strategies to employ hypnosis as a controlled form of dissociation in a structured fashion, in order to assert a greater degree of control over disturbing and troubling symptomatology and to restructure and harness dissociative phenomena for therapeutic purposes. In essence, hypnosis may be considered a controlled form of dissociation and, likewise, dissociation may be a form of spontaneous self-hypnosis (Barabasz, et al., 2010).

The Complex PTSD Diagnosis

Complex PTSD applies to chronic and repetitive interpersonal trauma that is frequently, but not always, associated with childhood onset (as this applies to traumatic exposure in the form of incestuous relationships, torture, abandonment and neglect, physical and/or emotional abuse, child sexual abuse, child enslavement and exploitation, domestic violence, and prisoner of war or concentration camp status). Complex PTSD may be diagnosed in such cases, leading to more wide-ranging symptomatology (APA, 2000; Barabasz, et al., 2010; Whealin & Sloane, 2007). Symptoms of Complex PTSD may be expanded to include profound and intense feelings of guilt and self-blame for having survived when others may not have, resulting in repressed and stifled emotions. According to Barabasz, et al. (2010), this conflict may be manifested, more acutely, in the form of an agitated depression, associated with frequent or recurrent dreams of friends and buddies dying in combat, for instance, and in the escape and evasion of interpersonal intimacy for fear of abandonment and/or death (sometimes one in the same).

Treating Trauma and PTSD with Hypnosis

In conjunction with cognitive behavioral therapies, hypnotic interventions for trauma and PTSD symptomatology may offer numerous benefits, particularly as the dissociative aspects of trauma precede the formality of the hypnotic intervention and may add to the vigor and effectiveness of the combined therapeutic interventions overall. Flash-backs, or the formidable reliving of traumatic events, alone provide abundant reason for the practitioner to consider hypnosis as a practical and worthwhile intervention. Positive results may be generated more rapidly than with traditional therapies, allowing the patient to access his or her subconscious and creative resources more readily (Barretta & Barretta, 2006). Also, hypnosis is the preferred form of treatment for a number of conditions, including what was previously referred to as "war neurosis" (Kingsbury, 1988) as opposed to PTSD. The field of neuroimaging has elucidated the recovery and retrieval features of traumatic memories. By studying neurological and neuropsychological functioning during the process of traumatic recall, emotions inextricably linked to trauma have been pinpointed (Barabasz, et al., 2010).[3] In the case of PTSD, disturbing or distressing cues frequently unleash a "cascade" of anxiety and fear-related symptomatology, with all the sights and sounds and smells reminiscent of the original traumatic event, even without conscious awareness of these events. These traumatic stimuli are not always readily identifiable, but their resurgence may also be triggered by events that are either obvious or metaphorical in nature (ibid.). Regardless, traumatic memories are unforgettable, enduring and, most likely, will never be eradicated. Hypnotic techniques have been utilized for over a century in the treatment of trauma and, in more recent years, of PTSD. These primarily involve suggestions involving emotional support, uncovering techniques, integration or abreaction of traumatic memories, and reconstruction of past events.[4] Hypnotic trauma treatment may be divided into stages or phases, and each has its own objective goals and objectives, all of which involve 1) the establishment of trust and rapport in the therapist and the provision of short-term symptomatic relief and stabilization through symptom management and the development of coping skills; abreaction and integration of traumatic events and associated memories; and the promotion of further integration of traumatic events, and the development of beneficial relationships with the self and others (Foa, Keane, & Friedman, 2004).[5]

The duration of hypnotic interventions with this model is dependent upon several factors:

1. The nature of the traumatic event(s) (natural disasters or human-induced events) and whether or not these were single or multiple events.
2. The length of time passage between event and initiation of treatment.
3. The presence of comorbid disorders and organized thoughts and patterns of behavior as they relate to self and interpersonal relationships (ibid.).

Patients who have experienced solitary traumatic events typically respond to hypnotic treatment within a few sessions. In the case of more chronic and severe cases of PTSD, months or years of treatment may be necessary (ibid.).

Phase I: Symptom Stabilization and Reduction

In this initial stage, hypnosis may be utilized to stabilize patients with the use of techniques designed to produce feelings of calm and relaxation that endure outside of the therapeutic context and the therapy session itself. These also serve to promote trust and rapport within the patient–therapist relationship. Ego strengthening techniques are also recommended as a means of generating a sense of safety and security, to contain (restrain) and suppress the intrusion of traumatic memories with specific hypnotic suggestions, and to reduce and establish a greater degree of control over symptoms related to subjective feelings of anxiety and agitation, anger, hyperarousal, and hypervigilance

(Foa, Keane, & Friedman, 2004).[6] Hypnotically-produced progressive muscle relaxation, and other relaxation and guided imagery strategies, have been extensively used by the author to encourage more durable feelings of "calm," "peacefulness," "tranquility," and "serenity." These are ordinarily recorded for patients, in order to encourage practice of these techniques outside of the therapy session, where the real work of therapy occurs for the more motivated of patients.

Phase II: Treatment of Traumatic Memories

Following the establishment of a working therapeutic alliance and the development of sufficient coping abilities and resources to withstand and diminish traumatic memories and the host of associated distressing symptoms, a variety of hypnotic strategies may be employed to integrate the various components of traumatic memories into a "structured whole." This includes bringing forgotten aspects of the traumatic event into conscious awareness. Frequently, there will be a spontaneous and unexpected appearance of additional details surrounding traumatic events and of new, relevant, memories as well (ibid.). It is the author's experience that timing is of the essence in unearthing traumatic material. It is only when patients have been able to create their own safe haven, both in the hypnotic and awake states, and to assert a sufficient level of control over disquieting symptoms with the use of relaxation therapies or routine/reinforced practice of self-hypnosis, that it is prudent to proceed with this phase of hypnotic treatment. This is where ego strengthening hypnotic strategies may be most effective and beneficial, both in terms of a sufficient degree of personal and interpersonal safety and security, and in promoting the belief that the self will not disintegrate upon exposure to what is often overwhelming and emotionally-laden traumatic material.

Phase III: Personality Reintegration and Rehabilitation

The primary goal of the third and final phase serves to achieve the most adaptive means of integrating all aspects of the traumatic experience(s) into the life of the patient, while also preserving and stabilizing those gains and improvements accomplished within the first two phases of treatment (ibid.). Furthermore, the development of the self as separate from the victimized version of a trauma survivor, fostering of mutually beneficial interpersonal relationships, reducing or alleviating the physiological correlates of PSTD and the traumatic experience itself, regulating distressing impulses and emotions, and encouraging a sense of success and mastery—as opposed to the resolute sense of helplessness that arises in the face of an unrestricted flood of emotions—are vital to trauma recovery and reintegration of the self (ibid.). It is also key for the patient to retain those coping skills and abilities that enables him or her to focus and attend to sensations and emotions that are in direct contrast to those elicited by traumatic events, and to be granted full permission to call these forth.

What is so invaluable about the use of hypnosis is that this technique can be considered a "catalyst for emotional catharsis as a form of release therapy," permitting the discharge of painful affect connected to traumatic events and, thus, making this the treatment of choice in the hands of clinicians experienced in the use of hypnotic interventions (e.g. Barabasz, et al., 2010). The unwelcome and alarming aspects of unresolved trauma associated with PTSD may only come to the point of resolution with the development of those requisite skills that allow one to revivify and then to release the painful affect connected to these experiences (ibid.). Many clinicians would agree that treatment duration may also be reduced with the use of hypnotic techniques, though this hypothesis has not yet been tested (Foa, Keane, & Friedman, 2004).[7]

Hypnotic Strategies in the Treatment of PTSD

In both civilian and military settings, the author has encountered any number of patients exposed to catastrophic life events, such as service members ambushed on the battlefield or in urban combat, law enforcement officers exposed to fatal accidents and shooting incidents, survivors of both civilian and military motor vehicle accidents, individuals who have awakened during major surgical procedures, victims of workplace violence and exceedingly destructive work environments, and the like. In any of these cases, there is no one standard or characteristic presentation of PTSD symptomatology. Creativity upon demand has become the order of the day in developing tailored approaches to confronting any number of these traumatic life events. There is no one collection of hypnotic strategies that is more successful or effective for any one person. One must, most importantly, know thy patient and be willing to attempt any number of approaches in order to achieve desired outcomes and to bring about the necessary conditions that allow for this. All of this author's approaches typically adhere to the following protocol.

Hypnotic Relaxation Induction

The hypnotic induction is the actual process of creating the conditions necessary for increased suggestibility and, thus, for hypnosis to occur and for patients to enter a trance state. Trance, very simply, is defined as a "trait of hypnotic responsiveness or the hypnotic state" (Kroger, 1977) and may be considered as the level or depth of hypnosis achieved by the subject. Hypnotic induction is designed to create some degree of internal quiet and to "lower the volume" (Gucciardi, 1998) or the intensity of arousal symptoms and trauma-induced distress. Eye closure is encouraged, though many patients find this difficult until a sufficient level of trust in the process is achieved. This may include progressive muscle relaxation, relaxation or diaphragmatic breathing and in some cases even prayer, if this is the patient's desire. The goals of each induction strategy involves the creation of states of calm, peacefulness, tranquility, and mental alertness, as well as reinforcement of the knowledge that the patient retains full control of the entire process at all times. In fact, patients are reminded continuously to reinforce the belief in their own success and mastery. Several treatment sessions may be required in order for the patient to successfully accomplish some degree of relaxation, calm, and a reduction in arousal symptoms. Although introduced in this first phase, deepening techniques are interspersed throughout each phase of the hypnotic experience, as induction is a continuing process that gradually evolves into an "increasingly profound involvement in the hypnotic modality" (Barabasz & Watkins, 2005). Moreover, each hypnotic suggestion is thought to increase the patient's involvement in the entire process of enhancing depth of trance (ibid.).

Hypnotic Guided Imagery or Visualizations

Utilizing directed guided imagery strategies, the patient is encouraged to connect with a safe place or peaceful sanctuary. Oftentimes, this author imaginatively "constructs" a protective bubble or guardian shield in which patients can surround or blanket themselves in feelings of safety and security, "which grows and deepens and intensifies with each and every breath." Specific suggestions are offered to permit patients to return to this safe haven when emotions, thoughts, and memories become overwhelming. This stage also involves a reduction of the physiological correlates indicative of autonomic hyperarousal and excessive stress reactivity. At this stage, usually several hypnotically-generated imagery strategies are created for each patient, dependent upon goodness of fit and what is—often through trial and error—deemed pleasant by them. In many instances, this stage requires a large number of sessions, spanning the course of several months or more, until the goal of creating a safe haven is reached and the patient can generate this independently.

Re-Entering the Scene of the Traumatic Event

In this phase of hypnotic treatment, it is essential to ease the patient into the process to avoid re-traumatization, although, in the wartime theater, the prolonged and repetitive exposure to trauma is virtually inevitable. Triggers for these events are pervasive and ever present. For service members who have acquired a long-standing history of exposure to multiple traumatic events, it may be necessary to hypnotically process each of them separately. In other instances, there is frequently a blending of events that cannot be separated and yet, as a combined entity, they remain unforgettable on their own merits. It is judicious to discuss the time and place to initiate this aspect of the treatment plan and to assure oneself, as a clinician, that the patient feels safe in confronting the very essence of his or her traumatic exposure(s). It is also imperative to proceed with caution by easing the patient into the task of confronting these seminal events in what may be experienced as a "head on," with all their associated senses blaring and coming to the fore. Abreaction may be permitted to the degree that the patient feels that he or she remains in safe hands. Patients are then further encouraged to relate the full accounting of the chronology of events as they occurred, while permitting the continued release of powerful emotions if they are present. The practitioner should provide supportive statements to further encourage this process, while interspersing deepening techniques (usually relaxation breathing suggestions) and re-emphasizing the notion of safety and security (and remaining out of harm's way). The ultimate goals are to diminish the impact of the traumatic events and to restore a sense of control (as opposed to an overwhelming sense of helplessness). This technique tends to have excellent utility, regardless of the venue. It is in this manner that the patient comes to re-experience the trauma "in a safe way" (Gucciardi, 1998).

Reintegration, Restructuring, and Coming All the Way Home

As a variation of Spiegel and Spiegel's Split Screen Technique[8] (Barabasz, et al., 2010), the author has devised a number of strategies that allow the patient to perceive him or herself no longer as a helpless victim of circumstance but, instead, as an individual with unsurpassed survivorship skills and full capabilities for detaching facts and memories from those emotionally-encumbered elements that have posed enormous obstacles to healing and recovery. Two examples of such strategies:

- In order to powerfully bolster and strengthen the notion of self-efficacy, patients are often encouraged to select an object to be carried with them (such as a coin or small item that generates additional feelings of safety and calm), so that they may infuse any remaining disturbing or uncomfortable emotional underpinnings directly into this object, validating their excellence at adapting to and overcoming often enormous levels of trauma and extreme emotional discomfort.
- Another modification of this technique is to suggest that the patient project distressing emotions, sensations, and memories behind an imaginary dark velvet curtain—such as those found in movie theaters of times past—and then to close the curtain when the task is completed, leaving behind all the painful elements of traumatic events, while retaining the memories themselves, now devoid of any harmful effects.

Sean's Story[9]

Afghanistan

The bottomless pain and anguish that encompass the whole of Sean's life began in the winter of 2010, in a Stone Age village along the banks of a small river in a Taliban stronghold of southern Afghanistan. It was three enormous IED explosions, followed by a barrage of small arms fire, that took the lives of four members of his platoon in rapid succession, including his very best friend. As he came upon what was left of Josh—no legs, no left arm, no back to his head—he leaned down, patted him on the shoulder, and assured the deceased, "Hey, buddy, we're going to get you out of here." He carried Josh's remains to the Casualty Collection Point (CCP) and handed them off to two other members of his platoon to make their way back across the river. "That's when the third IED went off," taking the lives of the two soldiers who had come to his aid.

Aftermath and Interventions

Even the Bronze Star with Valor awarded to this young hero is insufficient to assuage the terrible survivor guilt that sears his soul. Upon release from a military hospital, Sean and the entirety of his platoon were referred to our combat stress control team for traumatic event management and supportive treatment services. The severity of Sean's psychological injuries pitched him directly to the flashpoint of crisis, often fueled by guilt and self-blame of infinite proportions. His autonomic hyperactivity had become so extreme that this would likely compromise his mission performance. It was determined that Sean was an excellent candidate for hypnosis, his high level of hypnotizability made evident early on in his treatment.

His initial hypnotherapeutic goal was to reduce uncontrolled and frenzied hyperarousal symptoms and severe sleep disturbances, both of which were exacerbated by continuous and devastating survivor guilt. We began with basic relaxation and diaphragmatic breathing inductions and intricate progressive muscle relaxation exercises, followed by deepening techniques and the offering of permission to let go and release "any and all uncomfortable or unpleasant sensations, thoughts, and feelings, as you enter deeper and deeper states of relaxation, sinking and floating, drifting and dreaming, and giving yourself full permission to release all negativity and to replace it with the deepest and most peaceful state of tranquility, serenity, and calm ever before experienced."

A variety of hypnotic strategies were presented to Sean, drawing upon those images that he proposed as pleasant and comforting. Some of the hypnotically-induced images employed in our treatment sessions involved (a) the creation of a protective armor or shield to safeguard him and to filter out all negative sensations, emotions, and perceived threats to his safety and security, both physically and psychologically, (b) the representation of a dry erase board that he could "wipe clean" of all torment and self-blame, and (c) the fostering, "in his mind's eye," of an image of a body of water on which he could load small cargo boats with each of his burdens and send them down river until they disappeared, never to return. Any number of elaborate strategies were created for Sean, cues derived from his own imaginative preferences. When technology permitted, these were recorded for him with instructions for practice, enabling him to utilize them to facilitate the sleep which remained completely elusive for him for the remainder of his deployment.

Regardless, over the course of Sean's treatment and until his redeployment back to the home front, he invested an immense amount of effort into promoting his own healing from the holocaust of massive death in which all of his waking and sleeping hours had been immersed. In time, the agonizing details of events returned to him in piecemeal fashion, until a coherent picture of events emerged when he felt sufficiently safe to reveal it. He was then given permission to repress those aspects of this harrowing series of occurrences behind the black velvet curtain of his subconscious mind . . . or to return to the scene imaginatively in order to process his own perpetual grief and to begin the even more difficult process of self-forgiveness for tragedies for which he was blameless.

Closing

The success and mastery generated by the hypnotic interventions described in this chapter have exceptional value in the wartime theater and in working with service member veteran populations, particularly as hypnosis may provide the framework for a more rapid reduction in symptoms than those of more traditional psychological interventions. The essence of hypnosis is that it draws upon the patient's resources and imaginative gifts to provide rapid relief from a wide constellation of distressing symptoms. Finally, the provision of hypnosis must be administered in the trained and experienced hands of graduate level mental health professionals with advanced training in this specialized treatment arena.

Notes

1. The most recent research in the arena of hypnosis, advances and innovations in treatment, and clinical breakthroughs and discoveries, may be found in two primary journals in the field of hypnosis: the *International Journal of Clinical and Experimental Hypnosis* and the *American Journal of Clinical Hypnosis* (Barabasz, et al., 2010). As with any therapeutic skill or endeavor, subsequent to basic training workshops taught by recognized professionals in the field of hypnosis or hypnotherapy, advanced training and ongoing peer supervision and mentorship should be undertaken and are essential (ibid.).

2. Much of the information in this paragraph is derived from Foa, Keane, and Friedman (2004), whose work also references the research contributions of Levitt (1994), Spiegel, Detrick, and Frischholz (1982), Cardeña (1996), and many other contributors.
3. Neuroimaging studies have been referenced by Vermetten and Bremner (2004) and Vermetten and Spiegel (2007).
4. Abreaction, a psychoanalytic term, is described as the reliving and releasing of repressed traumatic memories and experiences to relieve and release the painful emotions that surround them. This is also considered a form of catharsis, bringing repressed memories into conscious awareness in a controlled, safe, environment. See also "Abreaction" (2011) at http://en.wikipedia.org/wiki/Abreaction.
5. See Foa, Keane, and Friedman (2004) and their referencing of the many authors who have contributed to the phase-oriented model of treatment: Kardiner and Spiegel, 1947; Brown, Scheflin, and Hammond, 1998; van der Hart, Brown, and van der Kolk (1989). Van der Hart, Brown and van der Kolk also describe the seminal work of Pierre Janet (1859–1947).
6. This treatment model stems from the original extensive work of Cardeña (2000), referenced in Foa, Keane, and Friedman (2004). The author has used this model extensively in PTSD treatment, both in the civilian and wartime theaters, with many variations including the creation of many "safe places" and "peaceful sanctuaries."
7. This stems from the original psychoanalytically-based work of Fromm and Nash (1997).
8. This landmark projective technique, developed by Spiegel and Spiegel (1987), involves the projection of the patient's sensations, thoughts, and emotions onto an imaginary screen chosen by the patient (whether a movie screen, computer screen, a blue skies, etc.) in order to separate out painful emotions from traumatic events themselves, thereby "attenuating" abreaction in the process of reconstructing traumatic memories. The patient is then asked to divide the screen, projecting the trauma onto the "sinister" side, while projecting self-protective measures and adaptive means of managing/resolving the traumatic event(s) onto the right side. Watkins and Barabasz (2008) further developed this technique by instructing patients to control the "intensity" of the content of traumatic memories by means of adjusting the color, size, and proximity to the screen of their perceived sensations, thoughts, and emotions. Patients are also permitted to turn the screen off if the image becomes intolerable or unbearable.
9. This soldier provided full permission to use his name and to tell his complete story.

References

American Psychiatric Association. (2000). *Diagnostic and Statistical Manual of Mental Disorders IV—TR* (4th Edn). Washington, DC: American Psychiatric Association.

Barabasz, A., Olness, K., Boland, R., & Kahn, S. (Eds.). (2010). *Medical Hypnosis Primer: Clinical and Research Evidence.* New York: Routledge Publishers.

Barabasz, A., & Watkins, J. G. (2005). *Hypnotherapeutic Techniques 2E.* New York: Bruner-Routledge Publishers.

Barretta, N., & Barretta, P. (2006). "Hypnosis? 'Stuck' in Trance? Can't Be Hypnotized? Isn't It Dangerous? Couldn't It Be Harmful?" Published in the *Clinical Corner*, a newsletter of the American Society of Clinical Hypnosis (out of print).

Brown, D., Scheflin, A., & Hammond, C. (1998). *Memory, Trauma Treatment, and the Law.* New York, NY: Norton.

Cardeña, E. (1996). "Dissociativity in Gulf War PTSD Patients."*International Journal of Clinical and Experimental Hypnosis, 44*: 394.

Cardeña, E. (2000). "Hypnosis for the Treatment of Trauma: A Probable but Not Yet Supported Efficacious Intervention." *International Journal of Clinical and Experimental Hypnosis, 48(2)*: 225–238.

Craig, J. L. (1990). "Hypnosis: Trick or Treatment." *Menninger Perspective, 1*: 17–20.

Crasilneck, H. B., & Hall, J. A. (1975). *Clinical Hypnosis: Principles and Applications.* New York: Grune and Stratton, Inc.

Foa, E. B., Keane, T. M., & Friedman, M. J. (Eds). (2004). *Effective Treatments for PTSD.* New York: The Guilford Press.

Fromm, E. & Nash, M. R. (1997). *Psychoanalysis and Hypnosis.* Madison, CT: International Universities Press.

Gucciardi, I. (1998). *Hypnotherapy and Post Traumatic Stress Disorder.* Accessed from: http://www.health-concern.com/Articles/hypnotherapy_&_ptsd.htm.

Hammond, D. C. (1990) *Hypnotic Suggestions and Metaphors.* Des Plaines, IL: American Society of Clinical Hypnosis.

Kardiner, A., & Spiegel, H. (1947). *War Stress and Neurotic Illness.* New York: Hoeber. Kingsbury, S. J. (1988, October). "Hypnosis in the Treatment of Posttraumatic Stress Disorder: An Isomorphic Intervention." *The American Journal of Clinical Hypnosis, 31*(2): 81–90.

Kroger, W. S. (1977). *Clinical and Experimental Hypnosis in Medicine, Dentistry, and Psychology.* Philadelphia: J. B. Lippincott Company.

Levitt, E. E. (1994). "Hypnosis in the Treatment of Obesity." In S. J. Lynn, J. W. Rhue, & I. Kirsch (Eds.), *Handbook of Clinical Hypnosis* (pp. 533–553). Washington, DC: American Psychological Association.

Platoni, K. (2000). "Hypnosis: Myth, Mysticism, or Good Medicine." *Lifeline: The Newsletter of the National Chronic Pain Outreach Association, Inc,* 1–4.

Rosen, S. (Ed.). (1982). *My Voice Will Go With You: The Teaching Tales of Milton H. Erickson.* New York, NY: W. W. Norton Company, Inc.: 26–27.

Spiegel, H., & Spiegel, D. (1987). *Trance and Treatment: Clinical Uses of Hypnosis.* Washington, DC: American Psychiatric Press.

Spiegel, D., Detrick, D., & Frischholz, E. (1982). "Hypnotizability and Psychopathology." *American Journal of Psychiatry, 139*: 431–437.

Van der Hart, O., Brown, P., & van der Kolk, B. A. (1989). "Pierre Janet's Treatment of Post-Traumatic Stress." *Journal of Traumatic Stress, 2*: 379–396.

Vermetten, E., & Bremner, D. J. (2004). "Functional Brain Imaging and the Induction of Traumatic Recall: A Cross-Cultural Review Between Neuroimaging and Hypnosis." *International Journal of Clinical and Experimental Hypnosis, 52*: 280–312.

Vermetten, E., & Spiegel, D. (2007). "Perceptual Processing and Traumatic Stress: Contributions from Hypnosis". In E. Vermetten, M. Dorahy, & D. Spiegel (Eds.), *Traumatic Dissociation: Neurobiology and Treatment* (pp. 239–259). Washington, DC: American Psychiatric Press.

Watkins, J. G., & Barabasz, A. (2008). *Hypnoanalytic Techniques* (2nd Edn). New York: Brunner-Routledge.

Wester II, W. C. (1987). *Clinical Hypnosis. A Case Management Approach.* Cincinnati, OH: Behavioral Science Center Publications, Inc.

Wester II, W. C., & Smith, A. H, (1991). *Clinical Hypnosis. A Multidisciplinary Approach.* Cincinnati, OH: Science Center Publications, Inc.

Whealin, J. M., & Slone, L. (2007) "How Does Short Term Trauma Differ from Chronic Trauma?" National Center for PTSD, U.S. Department of Veterans Affairs Professional Section. Accessed at: www.ptsd.va.gov/professional/pages/complex-ptsd.asp.

12 Cranial Electrotherapy Stimulation (CES) with Alpha-Stim

Mild Electrical Triage of the Brain with War Veterans

Daniel L. Kirsch

What would you do if there was a technological treatment for pain that was portable, about the size of a deck of cards, indefinitely reusable, and had no serious side effects? What if it had a side benefit of helping anxiety, insomnia, and depression? Would you want to try it? These were the opening questions by psychologist Patricia N. Lyle, PhD, SMSgt (RET) USAF (Lyle, 2011), an Alabama licensed psychologist, to the 2011 VA Employee Innovation Competition. Her report was titled *Using Technology to Assist with Pain Management.*

Dr. Lyle continued:

> We have this technology available right now! However, we need education for the medical community within the VA about the risk/benefit ratio of using this technology on a widespread basis. This one device could improve the quality of life and access to care for patients with pain. It could reduce long-term cost of treating chronic pain. It could empower veterans in managing their own symptoms. There are no serious side effects, and it works to a significant degree for over 90 percent of those who have used the device to control pain. Let's set up CES clinics in every major VA and start providing this technology to our veterans.

The cranial electrotherapy stimulation that Dr. Lyle was suggesting should be in more widespread use is called Alpha-Stim, and is manufactured by Electromedical Products International, Inc., a 31-year-old medical device company located in Mineral Wells, Texas. It is a prescriptive electromedical device about the size of a smart-phone. It uses two electrodes that clip onto the ear lobes, sending a mild electrical current through the brain to induce a calm, relaxed, yet alert state of mind in a 20 minute treatment. It is already in use in many programs throughout the DOD for PTSD, anxiety, insomnia, depression, substance abuse, and pain management. Alpha-Stim CES devices have also been ordered by over 70 VA medical centers over the past decade, and prescribed by more than 200 DOD practitioners. The Army and other government agencies, such as the National Institutes of Health and the National Cancer Institute, have invested millions of dollars to study Alpha-Stim CES.

Introduction

The stress of multiple deployments into the wartime theater, continued exposure to combat, endless family separations, and returning to the home front to face economic hardships, have resulted in an unprecedented need for mental health and pain management services for our men and women in uniform. For the first time in history, hospitalization for mental health disorders has surpassed the numbers of cases of combat-related physical injuries from wartime service (Casey, Macri, & Davidson, 2010). Who could come home without significant risk, after witnessing the brutalities of the fractured society that we have been battling since 1991, while the rules of engagement hamstring our abilities to fight back and even defend ourselves? An Army psychologist at Brooke Army Medical Center informed me that she has 400 service members waiting to see her. I enquired of a civilian psychologist about the size of her caseload and her reply was 27. In my nearly four decades as a scientist and healthcare clinician and educator with a specialty in pain and stress management, I have come to realize that there has never been a more deserving patient population than our service members, who deserve nothing short of our best efforts to help them prepare for war, assist them at war, and facilitate their recovery and reintegration back into American culture following their return from war. In considering this and the debt owed the word "triage" came to mind. The aforementioned Army psychologist had already used various technologies with this population, such as Alpha-Stim CES and neurotherapy (EEG biofeedback). I suggested that she establish a treatment lounge, administered by one person with ten CES devices and ten chairs, and a television displaying a fish tank on DVD so the service members would be able to view something noted for its relaxation potential during a 20 minute CES treatment session designed to "de-stress" them. In this manner, 30 service members would be able to undergo 20 minute treatment sessions every hour. Indeed, with this approach, one person could treat more than 1,000 service members in a week, in a single room and at very little expense.

Since the Department of Defense never closes, if this plan could be undertaken for 10 hours a day, 7 days a week, 2,100 treatments could be provided each week for less expense than the DOD pays now for a single psychologist. The result of a single 20 minute treatment is an immediate relaxed-yet-alert state, where worries are diminished in conjunction with reduced physical symptomatology such as pain. For some, this is sufficient. For others, this approach could be complementary to other forms of treatment, such as EMDR, CBT, relaxation therapies, biofeedback, acupuncture, hypnotherapy, and reimmersion therapy with virtual reality. All of these non-pharmaceutical interventions could be combined as resources permit. This simple conceptualization is revolutionary in terms of maximizing benefits with minimal resources.

The Cranial Electrotherapy Stimulation Experience

When author Michael Hutchinson (1986) first heard about CES, he decided to try it for himself. Visiting a busy biofeedback company in New York City, he wrote in his book *Megabrain*:

> CES sounded like something both interesting and desirable to me, which is why I was sitting there beside the Alpha-Stim with those electrodes clamped to my earlobes. The machine was turned on, and I felt a tingling sensation of tiny pinpricks in my earlobes, as a few microamperes of 0.5 Hz passed into my brain . . . the shift in consciousness was quick and unmistakable. My body immediately felt heavier, as

if I was sinking down into myself. I realized I was becoming extremely relaxed, and all of a sudden, there I was. It was that feeling you get when all at once you blink your eyes and realize that you're awake. Not that you had literally been sleeping, but you hadn't been paying attention to things as carefully as you might, you had been sleepwalking through your day, and now you're awake and things are very, very clear. It was not a feeling of being in some strange stoned or otherworldly state, but rather a feeling of being exactly as you should be, at home in yourself and feeling that your brain was operating correctly, efficiently, clearly . . . My body was no longer heavy, but very light, full of energy. The feeling was one of openness, clarity, as though I had been wearing sunglasses for weeks and had suddenly taken them off. It was no big thing. Nothing special, really, except I couldn't help but feel that this is the way we are supposed to be all the time.

Methodology

Cranial electrotherapy stimulation is a simple treatment that can easily be administered at any time. The current is applied by ear clip electrodes. Felt pads are attached to the clips. These are first moistened by a conducting mineral solution, then clipped onto the ear lobes. The current is turned up slowly until a dizzy feeling—rather like rocking gently on a boat—is experienced, then immediately reduced below the level that causes that "rocking" sensation or mild, lightheaded, feeling. A mild tingling sensation at the electrode sites may be experienced during treatment, but the current should never be raised to a level that is uncomfortable for any patient.

A recommended CES protocol for the treatment of PTSD is to apply CES for 20 minutes to an hour each day, or every other day, for three weeks, with the patient determining their own comfortable level of current between 100 and 500 microamperes. Electrical current is measured in amperes and one microampere is equal to one millionth of an ampere. To put that into perspective, another electrical modality that is commonly used for back and joint pain known as transcutaneous electrical nerve stimulation or TENS, uses 60 to 100 milliamperes. One milliampere is a thousandth of an ampere. CES uses up to one-half of one milliampere of current, delivered very slowly. One CES pulse of electricity can take up to 2,500 times longer than a pulse of TENS current. Dosage is current indirectly proportional to time with the use of this medical device. This means that the higher the current level is turned up, the less time is required for the treatment. As a rule of thumb, a person who is comfortable at a current of 200 microamperes or more can be treated in 20 minutes. Those who experience side effects, such as vertigo, nausea, or headaches, at currents over 200 microamperes should conduct one hour treatment sessions at 100 microamperes to avoid any unpleasant feelings during the treatment. If the patient feels heavy and disoriented at the end of the allotted time, the treatment must be continued until at least two minutes after the heaviness lifts and a light feeling ensues.

Preliminary studies show that the symptoms of PTSD are reduced with each treatment and that, over time, the improvement becomes more stable so the service member is not as affected by the multitude of minor stressors to which one might be exposed in the course of daily living. Once the PTSD symptoms subside, the treatment may be continued on a once or twice weekly schedule, or whenever needed, and for as long as necessary.

Stress Resiliency

A U.S. Navy lieutenant commander (Reese, 2006) wrote:

> I'd like to report that I am delighted with the Alpha-Stim! There has been a noticeable difference in my sleep and well-being since I started using it. I don't get reactive over stupid drivers any longer—a big plus. I have taken control of my anxiety levels over many things, and I believe it is a result of using this device. And this is while I am retiring from the military in two months, and have been undergoing a prolonged divorce that includes separation from my kids. I don't have a job as of now.

Some CES users find that they must continue to use the device for an extended period of time to maintain adequate results. One soldier (Grilliot, 2009) realized how well the device was working once his device was no longer available to him, stating:

> I am in the US Army and I have had the Alpha-Stim for post-traumatic stress disorder, anxiety, and depression. During the trial period it was very effective. I started to feel better about myself and started doing things at home that I have had a hard time doing. One day my truck burned up and the Alpha-Stim went with it. At that time I realized how much it helped me, because now I do not have it and I regressed into a state of exclusion where I stay in my house not wanting to leave. My depression and anxiety returned. My insurance would not cover the cost, so the military did. When I got my new Alpha-Stim, I felt a lot better again and I was able to go outside again.

Cranial electrotherapy stimulation is ideal for military personnel: it leaves the user alert while inducing a relaxed state of body and mind, often referred to as the Alpha State. The effect differs from pharmaceutical treatment, in that there are no untoward side effects that would impair performance. Most people report the experience of feeling that their bodies are lighter, while thinking is clearer and more creative. CES may also be used as an adjunct to anxiolytic or anti-depressive medication. When undergoing CES treatment, the dosage of the medication should be reduced by approximately one-third (Stinus, et al., 1990). CES is also proven to be an effective complementary treatment as an adjunct to all forms of psychotherapy, biofeedback training, and even surgical anesthesia (Kirsch, 2002). For people who have difficulty falling asleep, CES should be used in the morning, or at least three or more hours prior to going to sleep, in order to avoid the possibility of increased alertness that may interfere with sleep.

Following a CES treatment, most people report just feeling better overall. They are less distressed and more focused on mental tasks (Madden & Kirsch, 1987). They generally report sleeping more productively, having improved concentration, and also having increased learning capabilities. Cranial electrotherapy stimulation users are more resilient to stressful situations by virtue of the confidence that comes from knowing there is always help at hand.

The effects of CES are often subtle. Most people can resume normal activities immediately after treatment. Some people may experience a euphoric feeling, or a state of deep relaxation that may temporarily impair their mental and/or physical abilities for the performance of potentially hazardous tasks, such as operating a motor vehicle or heavy machinery. Such a feeling may last for up to several hours after treatment. These are rare occurrences, however.

Nothing works for everyone, and Alpha-Stim is no exception. Doctor and patient surveys conducted in the 1990s show a consistently robust effect in nine out of ten people who use it (Kirsch, 2002). Since then, the Department of Defense, the Veterans Affairs medical centers, and Tricare have become the biggest users of this technology. A 2011 survey (Price, 2011), including many service members and veterans along with civilian users, surprised everyone when it revealed that 99.9 percent of 1,745 people who used Alpha-Stim CES answered "yes" when asked if they considered Alpha-Stim to be effective for the specific reason it was prescribed for them.

How Alpha-Stim Actually Works

Alpha-Stim cranial electrotherapy technologies (CES) are a group of prescription medical devices. They are used by civilian physicians and therapists in many military medical centers, and in more than 70 VA medical centers, for the treatment of anxiety, insomnia, depression, and pain management. They utilize a very low level current, previously discussed, of less than one milliampere, delivered directly into the brain via ear clip electrodes for 20 to 60 minute sessions. Alpha-Stim is supported by more clinical studies than any therapeutic medical device in its class in the world (Kirsch, 2002). The Food and Drug Administration mandated that all CES manufacturers submit all safety and effectiveness data to them in 2009. At that time, there were 144 completed scientific studies of CES (Kirsch, 2009).

We all know that the brain functions electrically, so it is only logical that it can also be affected by electrical therapies. Alpha-Stim technology is thought to normalize the emotional centers of the brain, along with autonomic functions such as breathing, heart rate, and muscle tension. Kennerly (2006) measured changes in brain waves by electroencephalogram (EEG) from a single 20 minute Alpha-Stim treatment session in 30 students at the University of North Texas. Significant increases were found in alpha waves (8–12 Hz), signifying increased relaxation. Significant decreases in the delta waves (0–3.5 Hz) correlate with mental alertness or clarity and reduced drowsiness. Decreases were also found in beta wave frequencies (12.5–30 Hz), primarily between 20–30 Hz, that correlate with reductions in anxiety, ruminative thoughts, and obsessive/compulsive-like behaviors. Low resolution electromagnetic tomography (LORETA) performed at the University of North Texas, and functional magnetic resonance imaging (fMRI) studies from the University of California at Los Angeles (Feusner, et al., 2012), showed that the Alpha-Stim waveform reached all cortical and subcortical areas of the brain, producing changes consistent with significant reductions in anxiety.

It is effective for both situational (acute) anxiety, such as in the theatre of war, and trait (chronic) anxiety, such as that which may occur three to six months (or more) following traumatic events. When CES becomes widely recognized as the valuable modality that it is, it will emerge as an effective means of reducing, and in many cases eliminating, the need for medications. Cranial electrotherapy stimulation is changing the nature of healthcare as a disruptive technology to drugs, in much the same way that the internet is disruptive to the post office.

After the great earthquake in Wenchuan, Sichuan, in 2008, I donated CES devices to the Jiangsu Support Sichuan Disaster Psychological Rescue Team, and taught 400 mental healthcare workers about its use at the medical school located in Nanjing (*Yangtze Evening Post*, 2008). The Chinese were quite receptive to this modern, drug-free, method of managing the traumatic stress found in hundreds of thousands of affected survivors. I also explained to the Chinese media that it is important to retain some of the survivors on site to assist others. As we well know in the military, someone who has shared the trauma can be particularly effective at helping, even when compared with the most credentialed and experienced mental health professional. CES was found to be quite helpful, and sometimes the only therapy needed (Chen, 2011). As a result, cranial electrotherapy stimulation is now in rapidly growing use in China. At a subsequent visit in 2011, I was informed by senior People's Liberation Army Officers that they were convinced of the effectiveness of CES, having observed it "cure" depression. They then went on to ask several essential questions about how to best utilize this American technology in the best interest of their soldiers.

A Study of Veterans' Treatment Preferences Among Five Complementary and Alternative Modalities

For some disorders, such as high blood pressure, elevated blood sugar/diabetes, and high cholesterol, clinicians require specific tools in order to assess the nature and the extent of these problems. However, no healthcare professional can precisely assess the level of mood disorders or sleep problems, or the nature and severity of acute or chronic pain that any individual might be experiencing at a given time. Subjectively speaking, most people generally know when they feel bad and what makes them feel better.

Taking this logic into account, psychologist and researcher Gabriel Tan, PhD (Tan, et al., 2010), of the Michael E. DeBakey Veterans Affairs Medical Center in Houston, studied 32 veterans undergoing 197 group visits at a complementary and alternative medicine (CAM) clinic. These veterans were taught how to use five treatment modalities, and then were able to select their preferred form of treatment or to switch forms of treatments as often as they liked. For convenience, the clinics were set up on a drop-in basis, without the need to schedule appointments. One of the choices offered was CES using the Alpha-Stim medical device. Two biofeedback devices offered were Stress Eraser and EmWave, both of which measure heart rate, and signal the user to breathe at the appropriate times to regulate cardiovascular activity and produce a calmer state of mind and body. The fourth choice was also a biofeedback device called Respirate, which aids in lowering blood pressure through breathing exercises. A fifth device, an audio-visual entrainment device called the David Pal, uses sound and lights delivered through special glasses that the manufacturer claims are effective in producing a calming response. Of these choices, only CES is an FDA-regulated medical device.

Three out of four times (73 percent of the time), veterans chose CES as their preferred treatment modality. 11 percent of the veterans in the study selected the Stress Eraser, 6 percent chose the EmWave, another 6 percent chose the Respirate, and 4 percent chose the David Pal. The study used each veteran as his or her own control by comparing approximately three months of pre-treatment data with three months of post-treatment data. The benefits observed following the introduction of these therapies included improved attendance and involvement in group-based therapies. There were also significant reductions in pain levels. Veterans who participated in the CAM therapies also reported improvements in a number of quality of life measures. Specifically, these veterans reported an average improvement at the end of each session as 83 percent for "relaxation," 77 percent for "mood," and 80 percent for "well-being."[1] When asked to rate "improvement since last session" of treatment across a variety of symptoms, a sizable portion of the participants answered "yes," especially with respect to their pain (73 percent) and an improved overall sense of well-being (74 percent). Well-being is always a good measure to assess for veterans, in particular, as it denotes a contented state of happiness, good physical health, and prosperity. These are the conditions people strive to achieve and, when successful, indicate a strong chance for successful reintegration into society and a productive life.

The authors added that perhaps the greatest potential benefits of these therapies lies in the fact that the Alpha-Stim and the Stress Eraser could potentially be used as forms of self-management, empowering the veteran to treat him or herself whenever needed. Having an effective form of treatment always available may provide the confidence necessary for success and mastering self-regulation of any number of symptoms. These therapies can also be combined with other interventions, such as cognitive behavioral therapies or hypnotherapy, to produce even better treatment benefits. The cost for acquisition of these devices is relatively inexpensive, especially when compared to the costs of other medical interventions. For example, a single nerve block injection for low back pain typically costs approximately $600.00, including facility or clinic fees and professional charges for services rendered. The authors concluded that veterans require very minimal instruction for the appropriate utilization of these devices. As these devices are also designed for home use, this permits far greater accessibility of effective treatment to those residing in rural settings, or where the cost of frequent traveling to their local VAMC becomes an obstacle. Finally, unlike other psychological treatments, these modalities appear to be the least stigmatizing with veterans. This is particularly notable for those OEF/OIF veterans who have shown a tendency to avoid mental health treatment, even when referred by medical providers for psychological services. The authors also observed that portable devices such as Alpha-Stim and Stress Eraser are more appealing to many OEF/OIF veterans, because they are typically more technologically savvy than veterans of previous wars.

Lieutenant Colonel Mark Kinder, PhD (2009), of Saint Francis Medical Center in Cape Girardeau, Missouri, who completed a tour of duty in the Middle East as an Army psychologist, and his colleague, Stephen Jordan, PhD, specialize in treating soldiers diagnosed with post-traumatic stress disorder. They have reported similar results to that of the Tan (2010) study. After providing three or four CES treatments in their clinic, the Alpha-Stim CES device is prescribed for those who respond favorably. They have found that 70 to 80 percent of their patients diagnosed with anxiety, insomnia, depression, and/or chronic pain have demonstrated at least a 50 percent improvement in their symptoms. Kinder and Jordan (2009) consider CES to be a revolutionary addition to their spectrum of treatment modalities, particularly because many of their patients obtained significant relief far more rapidly when compared with other psychological interventions.

Anxiety, War, and Post-Traumatic Stress

Occupational therapy is becoming an increasingly necessary treatment intervention, as improvised explosive devices (IEDs) continue to claim limbs from service members by traumatic amputation. A small study of two veterans was undertaken by Alfred G. Bracciano, Ed.D., OTR/L, FAOTA, Associate Professor of Occupational Therapy at Creighton University and Chair of the Occupational Therapy Standards Committee of the International Commission on Healthcare Professions. He studied (Bracciano, et al., 2012) the effects of CES on the prevalence and intensity of PTSD and efficacy of occupational performance in war veterans. The Canadian Occupational Performance Measure and the PTSD Symptom Scale Interview (PSS-I) were administered before and after four weeks of CES treatment. PTSD symptoms decreased for both participants. Self-perceived improvements of occupational performance was also observed, meaning that participants felt more positive about their ability to carry out their job tasks and to return to work. Overall, the severity of the participants' daily symptom ratings, measuring impaired concentration, anxiety, irritability, and insomnia, decreased over the course of the study. Scores on the PSS-I are rated within a range of 0 to 51. This was reduced in Participant One from 34 to 13, and from 29 to 10 for Participant Two. Re-experiencing symptoms (flashbacks, nightmares, and intrusive recollections), with a range of 0 to 15, decreased from 7 to 2 and 9 to 2 respectively in the two participants. Avoidance symptomatology (efforts to avoid thoughts, feelings, or conversations about the trauma, or activities, places, or people that arouse recollections of the trauma; an inability to recall an important aspect of the trauma; markedly diminished interest or participation in significant activities; feelings of detachment or estrangement from others; restricted range of affect; sense of a foreshortened future) dropped from 15 to 7 and 9 to 5 on a 0 to 21 scale, and increased arousal decreased from 12 to 4 and 11 to 3 on a 0 to 15 scale.

These results are consistent with prior research studies and surveys that demonstrate the effectiveness of CES on symptoms of anxiety, hyperarousal, irritability, sleep disturbances, and impaired concentration, all of which are core symptoms of PTSD (Kirsch, 2002; Bracciano, et al., 2012). The author concluded that this preliminary study indicated that CES can provide therapists with a safe and effective way to reduce the symptom burden of PTSD, thus decreasing the duration of therapy while increasing the therapeutic effectiveness for a rapidly escalating population of war veterans in critical need of psychological services.

Cranial electrotherapy stimulation has also been used directly in the wartime theatre. While finishing his deployment in Iraq, Major Brian S. Earthman, M.D., a psychiatrist, wrote (2009) that the results from treatment with CES in his private psychiatric practice in Austin, Texas, far exceeded his expectations. He stated that:

> I went in thinking that it might be useful for a handful of patients that had mild symptoms and were adamant about not taking medications. After seeing some initial results, I decided to offer it as a treatment option to all of my patients with depression, anxiety, insomnia, or migraines. I was taken by surprise at how many patients were thrilled to have an alternative to medication. Not every patient responds to CES treatment, but my observation is that Alpha-Stim is as robust as medication treatment. The amazing thing is that there really are no side effects. I do occasionally get a patient

who gets dizzy, but that stops after the treatment is done. The lack of side effects has been particularly important here in Iraq. The soldiers need to be alert and ready to go at a moment's notice. This presents some obvious problems for prescribing anxiolytics and hypnotics that can impact cognitive function for over 12 hours after taking them. With Alpha-Stim, they get 20 minutes of treatment and are more alert than before treatment started, a tremendous advantage. Many of the soldiers I have treated have had remission of their symptoms without ever starting medication.

A study (Bystritsky, Kerwin, & Feusner, 2008) of CES for generalized anxiety disorder was conducted by Alexander Bystritsky, MD, PhD, at the Anxiety Disorders Program of the Semel Institute for Neuroscience and Human Behavior, University of California, Los Angeles. Nine patients who were diagnosed with anxiety disorders completed the trial. They had been prescribed SSRI or SNRI medications for at least three months, and had remained symptomatic, or were prescribed benzodiazepines to take as needed, but not more than two dosages per week. Five patients (41.7 percent) had been taking psychotropic medications (Venlaflaxine, N = 2; Alprazolam, N = 2; and Lorazepam, N = 1). Two had failed two previous adequate (>six week) trials of SSRIs.

Alpha-Stim CES was administered for six weeks, on a home use basis, for 60 consecutive minutes daily. Cranial electrotherapy stimulation caused a significant decrease in the Hamilton Anxiety Scale (HAM-A), the same tool utilized in drug research to measure improvement in anxiety levels as the result of prescribed anxiolytic medications. These results were confirmed by administration of a second anxiety measure, the Clinical Global Impressions-Improvement Scale (CGI-I) and the Hamilton Rating Scale for Depression (HAM-D-17) showed significant improvement as well.

Adverse effects reported in this study consisted of headaches and nausea, which the authors reported as most likely due to the fixed level of current being set too high for some of the participants. They suggested that these effects clearly indicated the presence of a central nervous system effect, providing further proof that CES treatment has a direct effect on the brain. The current can be reduced for each individual, in order to avoid such effects. The authors concluded that the results of their study indicate that CES may reduce symptoms of generalized anxiety disorder. They added that the efficacy and overall tolerability of CES suggest that the clinical use of CES and its theoretical mechanisms of action clearly warrant investigation in further studies.

While many anxiety patients experience partial to complete symptomatic relief in one treatment (Heffernan, 1995; Winick, 1999; Voris, 1995; and Eidelman, 2009), for most patients a series of treatments is necessary over a period of three weeks or more. Typically, anxiety symptoms have subsided significantly by the end of the first or second week of treatment, bringing the patient back within, or even below, established norms on psychometric measures of anxiety. However, severe depression requires a much longer treatment regimen to achieve a measurable effect. Depressed patients often require approximately three weeks of daily treatment before significant results are observed.

Effective Pain Management

In many cases, effective pain management for our veterans is vital and life sustaining. For several years, the VA has incorporated multiple disciplines and modalities to treat chronic pain. Treatments have been identified such as psychotherapy, physical therapy, occupational therapy, NSAIDS/analgesics, non-narcotic medications, electrotherapy (TENS), acupuncture, trigger-point injections, relaxation training, meditation, yoga, and more, to help veterans with chronic pain. Veterans with chronic pain face numerous challenges in finding adequate relief from pain. According to a VAHCS Memorandum (Department of Veterans Affairs, 2010), treatment compliance, fear of addiction, tolerance to pain medications, fear of worsening disease, and side effects of drug-related treatments, can adversely impact the effectiveness of certain pain management strategies.

According to research from the journal *Psychological Services*, by Gabriel Tan's team (Tan, et al., 2010), 56 million Americans experience chronic pain, including low back, arthritic, migraine, jaw, facial pain, and neuropathic pain. Around 80 percent of all physician visits are pain-related, with a cost of about $70 billion annually. Among OEF/OIF veterans, approximately 43 percent report some degree of pain and 63 percent experience moderate to severe pain; 20 percent of those experiencing pain report a pain duration greater than three months. The most common treatments for chronic pain include analgesics for pain management (e.g., aspirin, opioids, NSAIDS) antiepileptic drugs, tricyclic antidepressants, and SNRIs (e.g., Serotonin-Norepinephrine Re-uptake Inhibitors) targeting the inhibition of norepinephrine re-uptake.

The VA has been involved in research using Alpha-Stim microcurrent technology for pain management, and has a contract for the purchase of Alpha-Stim microcurrent devices. Microcurrent electrical therapy (MET) delivers the same electrical waveform as CES through hand-held probes or adhesive patches. The device generates a modified square bipolar waveform of 0.5, 1.5, or 100 pulses per second (Hz), 10 to 600 millionths of an ampere (μA), using a battery to supply its current (EPI, 2006). It is designed for use in a practitioner's office or for home use with patients.

Cranial electrotherapy stimulation (CES) delivers the microcurrent through the use of ear clips, to direct the current across the brain stem where it is believed to cause the effects seen, and has the benefit of general pain management in addition to well-documented effects involving the reduction of anxiety, depression, and insomnia. Existing research shows that there are no known side effects except possible mild vertigo (while in use) and occasional irritation of the earlobes. Both effects are self-limiting. Use of Alpha-Stim technology is contraindicated for those with electronic pacemakers. The manufacturer cites research demonstrating that 65 percent of pain patients reported moderate to marked (50 to 99 percent) relief from pain, and 91 percent of all patients reported significant benefits (greater than 25 percent relief).

Service members in the wartime theater of operations have utilized Alpha-Stim technology for several years in both OIF and OEF, and the use of CES and MET has become increasingly familiar within medical and mental health practice in deployment settings. There are a number of VAMC pain clinics employing this technology to augment pain management, particularly when patients experience adverse reaction to certain medications or have difficulties with compliance or tolerance. Unfortunately, there is a great deal of misinformation and resistance to using this technology among certain medical professionals, due to inexperience and adherence to traditional pharmacotherapies even when these are not in the best interests of their patients. Ideally, any veteran should have access to a personal CES or CES/MET device that he or she can use indefinitely and on demand to help control pain as well as associated anxiety, insomnia, and depression.

If this technology is utilized to its fullest, and offered to every veteran suffering with chronic pain, the overall cost savings could be phenomenal. Furthermore, clinical experience and research indicates that these adjunctive/alternative medical interventions would reduce service members' and veterans' dependence upon opioid medications, increase movement/mobility, improve quality of sleep, perhaps reduce the number of medical visits, and empower each pain patient to have a far greater degree of personal control over his or her pain symptoms and magnitude of suffering. A viable triage would be to create an Alpha-Stim treatment room, or lounge where service members or veterans would, on a walk-in basis, first be able to receive CES treatment. If they achieved relief, then the device could be ordered for personal use.

More Research and the First Staff Standard Operating Procedure for CES

At present, there are more than 144 completed research studies using CES in humans, and 20 experimental animal studies (Kirsch, 2009). No significant lasting side effects have ever been reported. Occasional self-limiting headaches (1 out of 977 people), discomfort or skin irritation underneath the electrodes (1 out of 1,465 people), or light-headedness may occur. An atypical patient with a history of vertigo may experience dizziness for hours or days after treatment, but this is quite rare.

Aside from specific pathological disorders, a growing number of studies being conducted demonstrate increases in cognitive functions with the use of CES. Michael Hutchison (1986) discussed several mind enhancement techniques in his book, *Megabrain*, devoting chapter 9 to CES as a tool for attaining higher levels of consciousness. Sparked by Hutchison, Madden and Kirsch (1987) completed a study that demonstrated CES to be a useful tool for improving psychomotor abilities, such as typing. Smith (1999) demonstrated that CES significantly improved attention deficit hyperactivity disorder after only three weeks of treatment. This effect was maintained through an 18 month follow-up assessment. A subsequent doctoral dissertation (Shultz, 2010) found that CES improved auditory, but not visual, attentional focus.

The U.S. Army has successfully utilized CES for the management of compassion fatigue at the U.S. Army Institute for Surgical Research (USAISR), the Army's Burn and Amputation Center located within San Antonio Military Medical Center (SAMMC). Compassion fatigue occurs when practitioners' capacity for compassion becomes overwhelmed over time, usually due to experiencing or witnessing the effects of extreme war trauma or an excessive degree of human suffering. Cranial electrotherapy stimulation has assisted the professional staff at this burn unit to relax more fully, so they can recover faster from the tremendous stressors to which they are continuously exposed, in order to be able to focus on the most exceedingly difficult tasks of keeping these service members alive and to rehabilitate their minds and bodies. To supersede the prescription requirement for CES required by the Food and Drug Administration for treatment of mood and sleep disorders, and thus avoiding having to diagnose the staff and to record progress notes, the Army has issued SOP 09-207, a standard operating procedure for CES, authorized in 2009. This enables medical staff at USAISR to employ CES for the promotion of an increased state of relaxation among burn unit staff, without a prescription.

How Safe is CES?

Readers might ask how safe it is to use CES. Extensive clinical experience, and the large number of research studies conducted and cited in this chapter, reveal *no significant lasting harmful side effects* from any microcurrent level treatment of the body or brain. As with all electrical devices, caution is advised during pregnancy, although the risk/reward ratio favors CES over pharmaceuticals when necessary. In addition, it is recommended that people who have a very strong relaxation effect from CES should not operate complex machinery or drive during, and shortly after, a CES treatment. With these caveats, the evidence is compelling that there is a paucity of risks.

Closing

Cranial electrotherapy stimulation induces a relaxed-yet-alert state of mind, and has been well researched and clearly proven to be a safe and effective method of treatment for anxiety and anxiety-related disorders, including PTSD and the generalized stress ubiquitous in service members. It is also highly effective for depression and insomnia, muscle tension, fibromyalgia, and headaches. In addition, there is mounting evidence that CES can enhance cognitive functions, sharpening mental focus. Because of its proven record of safety and effectiveness, CES should be the first line defense for a broad range of service-related disorders. It is easy enough to offer CES in a clinical setting, and over time it is cost effective for service members and veterans to own their own CES devices.

Many letters attest to the effectiveness of this non drug treatment, such as this one from Barbara Rhodes (2008):

> I am a 100% disabled Gulf War veteran with extreme anxiety, depression, and PTSD with panic attacks. Nothing has ever helped my condition, only masked it. [It is] like a big band aid covering up the problem, which took years of lacking continuity of care to only worsen with misdiagnosis and way too many narcotics. Alpha-Stim has actually worked and changed my life. I no longer hide in the closet when the doorbell rings, and I react to situations with some control and coping skills for the first time in such a long time. I can cut back on anxiety medications; [this] now allows me to think again, as all the side effects of the meds steal your life and who you are and you cannot think clearly. I now have hope and have seen real, life-changing, results with the Alpha-Stim and EMDR.

Service members and veterans deserve the very best treatment options available. America's healthcare system is being bankrupted by reliance upon medications that often fail to produce the desired effects. Cranial electrotherapy stimulation is a viable solution to improve both healthcare and the economy. The powerful pharmaceutical lobbies exert great influence over the government, reducing choices in healthcare. This too often results in the overuse and misuse of drugs by those who serve. Unquestionably, CES is not addictive and, hence, there are no withdrawal symptoms from stopping CES. As the word gets out about CES, some veterans are finding it to be the best way to keep themselves functional within society, maintaining employment and relationships. It is incumbent upon us, as clinicians, to utilize those technologies that are proven to help service members and veterans reintegrate into society and that, in addition, offer a far greater degree of safety and cost effectiveness.

Note

1 Please note that these are "aggregated" findings that have collapsed together responses from *all* participants who used any of the five therapy alternatives, but remember that 73 percent of the participants who reported these improvements in various quality of life measures used CES. Thus, with that caveat, it would seem reasonable to "claim" these results as representing the impact of CES.

References

Bracciano, A. G., Chang, W.-P, Kokesh, S., Martinez, A., Meier, M., & Moore, K. (2012). "Cranial Electrotherapy Stimulation in the Treatment of Posttraumatic Stress Disorder: A Pilot Study of Two Military Veterans." *Journal of Neurotherapy*, *16* (1): 60–69.

Bystritsky, A., Kerwin, L., & Feusner, J. (2008). "A Pilot Study of Cranial Electrotherapy Stimulation for Generalized Anxiety Disorder." *Journal of Clinical Psychiatry*, *69*: 412–417.

Casey, J., Macri, M., & Davidson, T. (2010) "Increasing Rates of Post-Traumatic Stress Disorder Associated with the Iraq and Afghanistan Wars." *Validated Independent News*. http://www.mediafreedominternational.org/2010/12/19/increasing-rates-of-post-traumatic-stress-disorder-associated-with-the-iraq-and-afghanistan-wars. Accessed November 17, 2011.

Chen, L. (2011). Personal Communication. General Manager, Haole, Nanjing, People's Republic of China.

Department of Veterans Affairs. (2010). *VAHCS Memorandum 516-10-11-085.*

Earthman, B. (2009). "Testimonial Submitted to Electromedical Products International, Inc." http://www.alpha-stim.com/endorsements/iraq-brian-s-earthman-md. Accessed September 23, 2011.

Eidelman, W. S. (2009). "Control of Cigarette Cravings with Cranial Electrotherapy Stimulation." *The Townsend Letter for Doctors*, *311*: 81–85.

Feusner, J., Madsen, S., Moody, T., Bohon, C., Hembacher, E., Bookheimer, S., & Bystritsky, A. (2012). "Effects of Cranial Electrotherapy Stimulation on Resting State Brain Activity." *Brain and Behavior, 2012*: 1–10.

Grilliot, K. L. (2009). "Testimonial Submitted to Electromedical Products International, Inc." http://www.alpha-stim.com/testimonials/kansas-keith-l-grilliot. Accessed September 23, 2011.

Heffernan, M. (1995) "The Effect of a Single Cranial Electrotherapy Stimulation on Multiple Stress Measures." *The Townsend Letter for Doctors*, *147*: 60–64.

Hutchison, M. (1986). "We Sing the Mind Electric, Part Two: The Alpha-Stim." In *Megabrain* (pp. 28–159). New York, NY: Ballantine Books.

Kennerly, R. C. (2006). *Changes in Quantitative EEG and Low Resolution Tomography Following Cranial Electrotherapy Stimulation*. PhD Dissertation, the University of North Texas.

Kinder, M., & Jordan, S. (2009). "Alpha-Stim." *Saint Francis Medical Center* [St Louis, MO] *Weekly Health Page, 9*: 5.

Kirsch, D. L. (2002). *The Science Behind Cranial Electrotherapy Stimulation* (2nd Edn). Edmonton, Alberta, Canada: Medical Scope Publishing.

Kirsch, T. B. (2009). "Summary Information in Support of Reclassification of a Medical Device: Alpha-Stim Cranial Electrotherapy Stimulator Intended for the Treatment of Anxiety, Insomnia and Depression." FDA Docket No. FDA-2009-M-0101.

Lyle, P. N. (2011). "Using Technology to Assist with Pain Management." 2011 VA Employee Innovation Competition. https://vha.ideascale.com.

Madden, R. E., & Kirsch, D. L. (1987). "Low Intensity Transcranial Electro stimulation Improves Human Learning of a Psychomotor Task." *American Journal of Electro medicine, 2*: 41–45.

Price, L. R. (2011). "Alpha-Stim Patient Survey 2006–2011." FDA Docket No. FDA-2011-N-0504.

Reese, S. A. (2006). "Testimonial Submitted to Electromedical Products International, Inc." http://www.alpha-stim.com/testimonials/bethesda-md-lcdr-s-a-reese-msc-usn-mph-rehs. Accessed September 21, 2011.

Rhodes, B. (2008). "Testimonial Submitted to Electromedical Products International, Inc." http://www.alpha-stim.com/testimonials/barbara-rhodes. Accessed September 23, 2011.

Shultz, J. C. (2010). *The Effects of Cranial Electrotherapy Stimulation on Attention: A Double-Blinded Placebo Controlled Investigation.* Psy.D. Dissertation. The Chicago School of Professional Psychology.

Smith, R. B. (1999). "Cranial Electrotherapy Stimulation in the Treatment of Stress Related Cognitive Dysfunction with an Eighteen Month Follow-Up." *Journal of Cognitive Rehabilitation, 17*: 14–18.

Stinus, L., Auriacombe, M., Tignol, J., Limoge, A., & Le Moal, M. (1990). "Transcranial Electrical Stimulation with High Frequency Intermittent Current Potentiates Opiate-Induced Analgesia: Blind Studies." *Pain, 42*: 351–363.

Tan, G., Dao, T. K., Smith, D. L., Robinson, A., & Jensen, M. P. (2010). "Incorporating Complementary and Alternative Medicine (CAM) Therapies to Expand Psychological Services to Veterans Suffering from Chronic Pain." *Psychological Services, 7*(3): 148–161.

Voris, M. D. (1995). "An Investigation of the Effectiveness of Cranial Electrotherapy Stimulation in the Treatment of Anxiety Disorders Among Outpatient Psychiatric Patients, Impulse Control Parolees and Pedophiles." *Delos Mind/Body Institute Newsletter*, Dallas, Texas: 1–19.

Winick, R. L. (1999). "Cranial Electrotherapy Stimulation (CES): A Safe and Effective Low Cost Means of Anxiety Control in Dental Practice." *General Dentistry, 47*: 50–55.

Yangtze Evening Post. (2008). Accessed at http://www.alpha-stim.com/media/yangtze_evening_post.html. Accessed September 23, 2011.

Part V

Animal Assisted and Outdoor Approaches

13 Service Dogs and Other Canine Assistance Services for Wounded Warriors

Mary Cortani (Post-Vietnam Era)

When I returned home, I was no longer able to do a lot of things that we all take for granted. I couldn't go to the movies or other crowded spots. At restaurants, I would make sure my back was to the wall and that I was in full view of the door. I was always on full alert, but, soon after I got Rocky, things started to change. The first change I noticed was that Rocky forced me up every morning to take him out. I now had a reason to be up and out of bed. That, in itself, was a huge factor for me because, before, I felt I had no reason to get out of bed and start my day. I now feel motivated in the morning, knowing I get to train my own service dog.

I now can go out in public feeling a little more relaxed because, being able to train my service dog, I learned to read Rocky's body language. I don't have to be so vigilant now, knowing Rocky is watching and sensing everything around us. In public, I can have conversations with strangers, something I couldn't do before. If I start to feel uncomfortable, I give the "block" command, and Rocky will step in front of me and make a barrier between myself and the person I'm talking to. Having a service dog has helped me in so many different ways, from making me feel calm to just being a best friend when I need one.

The content of this chapter is of vital importance to me, and is grounded in real life experiences. I will provide a brief overview of a simple lunch conversation; it brings to light the lack of understanding that our men and women face every day when they come home. Simple things are no longer simple. For too many, the mission is gone, the purpose is gone, but unfinished, as battle buddies are left behind. Self-worth has vanished. Physical injuries only add severity to the mental battle raging inside.

I was talking to a friend over lunch, trying to explain what I do with veterans and others with disabilities and their service dogs, when I realized that my friend had a deer-in-the-headlights look. I realized that I needed to take a step back and explain military life and culture, based on my nine year military career as a 95B (MP K9 Instructor) in the Army. I left active duty in 1984 and then served as a Reservist for a few years, leaving the military in 1986. I explained that the day one signs up and arrives at basic training, all rights and liberties are relinquished. You become government property. Simple things like saying, "Hey, lets have lunch together!" might not be possible. Making comments about the current state of affairs with regards to political events were virtually disallowed; a no-no. Getting sunburned could result in disciplinary action because government property was damaged. From day one, basic trainees are informed and reminded that if Uncle Sam wanted them to have a spouse or a family, they would have issued them one. You are never to forget that your battle buddies have become your family, and you are always to stay focused on them and your mission.

Once I explained this and the fact that the military never teaches service members how to be civilians, only to be soldiers, Marines, airmen or Navy corpsmen, and so on, dedicated and disciplined to complete the mission, my friend then began to understand. We then started discussing PTSD, TBIs (traumatic brain injuries), anxiety, hypervigilance, and so much more about the impact of military service.

This chapter describes the Operation Freedoms Paws Program, and provides an overview of service dogs, service dog requirements, the canine–human bond and its unlimited benefits, and VA obstacles to the full utilization of service dogs. Finally, there is an in-depth case discussion of an OEF veteran and his relationship with his service dog, Murphy, and an OEF/OIF veteran and his wife who both describe his experience and relationship with his service dog, DJ.

The Challenges Facing Military Veterans

To better understand the challenges facing military veterans, all one has to do is to read the following letter received from a veteran participating in the Operation Freedoms Paws Program (http://operationfreedomspaws.org/). His experiences and viewpoint are common among the many veterans I have known who have participated in this invaluable program.

> To whom it may concern,
>
> My name is Soldier, Marine, Sailor, or Airman, and I have Post-Traumatic Stress Disorder, also known as PTSD. Though you may not be able to see them, my wounds run very deep and have literally cracked the foundation of my soul and who I am. Daily, I am haunted by the experiences of combat, and the loss of friends that were my brothers and sisters in arms. I am grateful to have returned to a nation that is proud of my service, yet there is emptiness as big as all the oceans that now fill my heart. The person that I once was, I no longer recognize, and the one I want to be seems as far away as those I mourn and grieve for, to include myself. So, not only am I left feeling the pain of those lost, but I am left with the confusion of not even knowing the very reflection I see in the mirror.
>
> For extended periods of time since returning from war, I have withdrawn from those that care about me most, shutting them out from the pain I feel. I have built a walled fortress around what I feel is left of me, to prevent myself from caring, or being cared for. Often, I will not even leave my house for fear of what lies beyond the only walls of security I feel I have control over. To most, I appear reclusive and quiet, but withdrawal and isolation are the only things that feel safe to me. In truth, I never feel safe. Those I love most and strive hardest to protect feel scared of me and my behaviors, which causes me to withdraw from the world even more. I have nightmares, causing sleep to become a dreaded enemy, versus the comforting rest I once knew it to be. Weapons that most view as instruments of violence are now seen by me as the tools necessary just so I can make it through my day and night with some measure of security. I have seen the horrors men can inflict on one another

and, at the same time, I have seen what is best in them. These conflicting images compete for my subconscious, and I am left to deal with what's left. My attempts to get help are often met by organizations that don't quite understand what has happened to me, or how to treat it. Once I am able to get in and get treatment, I often have found that trying to get consistent appointments by a Veterans Affairs hospital is impossible, due to a system that is already backlogged. This often leads to more frustration and further isolation on my part.

In the end, for most vets in my situation, there are usually only three outcomes. The first being suicide, which, among veterans returning from the current wars, is a number rising by the day. The second being a family member that searches and searches for help for their loved and, with some luck and lot of outside help, gets their veteran into a consistent treatment program that may or may not work depending on the organization's level of understanding. And, finally, the third situation, which is further progression of the PTSD symptoms which include depression, anxiety, panic attacks, all of which usually lead the veteran back to thoughts of suicide.

(Harry, Marine, veteran)

About Operation Freedoms Paws

Harry, and others like Harry, are the reason that Operation Freedoms Paws came into existence. Operation Freedoms Paws (OFP) is a 501(c)(3) non-profit organization; it works to empower veterans and others with disabilities to live a quality life. OFP does this by teaching veterans the skills necessary to train their own dogs, capitalizing on the ability of the canine–human relationship to help them regain their purpose, worth, and value to society and their community. OFP then certifies them together as an Assistance Team in a 32 to 48 week program. OFP provides this unique opportunity, enabling the veteran and others to feel safe and secure in their own environment once again. This facilitates their recovery from the trauma of their wartime service or, at the very least, to learn to cope better with, and better manage, their day-to-day lives. They are then better able to get back out in their communities and begin to see life in a new way—with hope—because of the very special therapeutic canine–human relationship. The OFP program is non-traditional, in that it is provided to the veteran or other disabled person at no cost to participants. OFP utilizes dogs from shelters and rescue groups, whose age, temperament, and personality are suited for the individual. (It is relevant to note that it has been our experience that any breed of dog can be a service dog—from chihuahuas to mixed breeds to German shepherds and everything in between—provided that the dog possesses the ability to recognize changes in the human and modify their natural instinctive behaviors to alert the human to these changes.) OFP will also allow individuals to participate in the program with their own dogs, if the dogs meet the criteria. OFP relies on donations from individuals, businesses, foundations, and grant-making bodies.

This chapter is about the impact a service dog can have, yet it comes from a very different perspective than others within the service dog community. When I started Operation Freedoms Paws, I brought with me my experiences in the Army and my civilian life and work, which included management and leadership training. I had finally found my true purpose and passion; my life's mission.

Background

The most advanced technology capable of transforming the lives of people with disabilities is not a pill; rather, it has a cold nose and a warm heart, gives unconditional love and acceptance, looks out for the individual needs of the person, and is capable of always being by his or her side.

Service dogs for veterans is a serious venture, not to be taken lightly. There is no national accreditation program for service dogs in the U.S., let alone an understanding of the special needs of veterans, including those living with "invisible disabilities" such as PTSD and traumatic brain injuries and the unique benefits a dog can provide to veterans with these disabilities. There are a number of challenges that make it difficult for veterans to be able to fully achieve the benefits of participating in well-run service dog programs:

- Large organizations, such as Puppies Behind Bars (http://www.puppiesbehindbars. com/), Guide Dogs for the Blind (http://www.guidedogs.com/site/PageServer), Canine Companions for Independence (Wounded Veteran Initiative) (http:// www.cci.org/site/c.cdKGIRNqEmG/b.3978475/k.3F1C/Canine_Companions_for_ Independence.htm), and a few others, do a superb job of providing service dogs for many people. They train the dog and then send the individuals to participate in two to four weeks of training with their dog.
- Few organizations allow a client to train their own personal dog, or to do so under the guidance of a professional dog trainer. Most prefer and require that they provide the service dog.
- All these organizations use a "cookie cutter" approach, which leaves out tailoring the approach to best meet the individualized special needs of our veterans.
- In order for individuals to achieve optimal assistance, the dogs must be highly trained, yet there is a lack of highly trained service dogs.
- Organizations that do offer service dogs for veterans have very long waiting lists, which can make acquisition of a dog too far out of reach, and too costly for some people with invisible wounds. For example, the cost of a service dog varies from $10,000 to $50,000 dollars, and does not include the cost of ongoing care and maintenance.
- There are advantages to participating at the very core level of service dog training. Since any service dog requires constant upkeep to support the dog's high level of training (regardless of who trained it), learning how the dog was taught from the very beginning can facilitate the healing process for the veteran. Indeed, for some people with invisible disabilities, especially those who tend to isolate themselves (leading to bouts of increased depression), the activity and responsibility of teaching the dog can promote numerous ongoing therapeutic benefits.

Types of Service Dogs

Emotional Support Dogs

An emotional support animal (ESA) (National Service Animal Registry, 2010) is a legal term in the United States for a pet that provides therapeutic benefits to its owner through companionship and affection. It is important to note that emotional support animals are not specially trained to mitigate a disability. They require only as much training as an ordinary pet requires in order to live peacefully among humans, without being a nuisance or a danger to others. Their owners are afforded privileges through a federal grant which allows them to keep the dog in most types of housing, even when there is a "no pets" policy in place. The Air Carrier Access Act, overseen by the FAA, provides guidelines that permit a person with a disability to travel with a prescribed emotional support animal, as long as they have appropriate documentation on hand and the animal is not a danger to or interferes with others. However, emotional support dogs are *not* protected under the ADA if the dog does not mitigate a recognized disability through the performance of specific trained tasks, and does not have to be permitted into public establishments.

Mobility Assistance Dogs

Mobility assistance dogs assist people who require assistance with balance and other issues associated with getting around (Burke, n.d.).

This includes assisting people with disabilities who have trouble reaching light switches, picking up objects that have been dropped out of reach (e.g., a pencil or keys), opening doors, calling for help, retrieving medication, and so on. Some individuals with mobility service dogs require a facilitator, who is typically a parent, spouse, or caregiver who handles and cares for the assistance dog, encourages a strong bond between the recipient and the dog, and is responsible for the customized training needs of the dog.

Psychiatric Service Dogs

Psychiatric service dogs are individually trained to assist people with disabilities such as cognitive deficits, or mental or psychiatric disabilities, including conditions such as panic disorder or PTSD (see the Psychiatric Service Dog Society (PSDS, n.d.) regarding the PSDS task list for PTSD, and related veterans' resources, articles, etc.). Very often, such dogs can be self-taught with professional guidance and training. For veterans eligible for and enrolled at a U.S. Department of Veterans Affairs healthcare system facility, a VA physician can issue a letter or prescription stating that the veteran requires a psychiatric service dog.

Seizure or Medical Alert Dogs

Medical alert dogs are trained to alert the owner or another person to a medical condition, such as detecting a seizure or knowing when a person needs to take a time-sensitive medication. They have learned to distinguish between medically-related "normal" and "abnormal" behaviors and functioning with regard to their human's physical state. While seizure or medical alert dogs are trained to be alert to a medical condition, there are dogs that already have such abilities. These dogs will simply require specialized service dog training for public access and/or added skills. Such dogs are excellent candidates for being self-taught by their owners.

Guide Dogs

A guide dog (also called a seeing eye dog) is an assistance dog trained to lead blind and visually impaired people around obstacles (Guide Dogs of America, 2012; Guide Dog Foundation for the Blind, Inc., 2012; Guide Dogs of the Desert, 2012).

Hearing Dogs

A hearing dog is a type of assistance dog specifically selected and trained to assist people who are deaf or hearing impaired (Dogs for the Deaf, Inc., 2012). Such dogs are able to alert their handler to important sounds, such as doorbells, smoke alarms, ringing telephones, alarm clocks, sirens and other danger signals, and persons calling the handler's name.

Therapy Dogs

A therapy dog is trained to provide affection and comfort to people; its primary job is to allow unfamiliar people to make physical contact with it and to enjoy that contact. This usually involves family pets that have been certified as therapy dogs for the purpose of visiting hospitals, schools, and nursing homes, as well as those with learning disabilities. However, these are *not* service dogs (Delta Society, 2012; Therapy Dogs International (TDI, n.d.). AKC's Canine Good Citizen Program is a good step in the training process, plus it provides an extra patch for your vest if you pass (American Kennel Club, 2012).

Service Dog Requirements

Age

Service dog programs are open to dogs that are 8 weeks to 3 years old (this can depend on the breed and gender of the dog). Dogs older than this are subject to limitations in the amount of service time. Training time will vary with the age of the dog and is 4 to 18 months in duration. It is important to note that at some point the service member may/will require a replacement service dog. Puppies can be used, with many additional benefits to the veteran, such as more rapid bonding and longer training periods. Length of training for service dog certification may be as long as 2 years, due to developmental and temperament evaluations conducted throughout the training process.

Health

A service dog should be maintained in the very best possible health, which can be significantly costly for participants. Prior to entering into a training program, the dog must be examined by, and be under the competent care of, a licensed veterinarian. At a minimum, the dog should be fully vaccinated against canine diseases (including, but not limited to, rabies, distemper, parvovirus, adenovirus-2, para influenza, hepatitis, corona virus, and bordetella). The dog should be prescribed monthly heartworm, flea and tick preventatives, and should undergo a fecal exam no less than annually. The dog's skin and coat should be in optimal condition, so as to reduce shedding of both hair and dander; this requires exceptional nutrition. Finally, frequent nail trimming is essential for a service dog's foot health, and to reduce any damage caused by overgrown nails on public and private property. These service dogs are working dogs.

Behavior

To be enrolled in a service dog course, the dog should not have or display any serious anti-social behaviors, such as fear-based actions, aggression, or excessive exuberance (total lack of self-restraint). The dog should not have strong prey-drives towards small animals or other dogs.

Public Access Test

The public access test evaluates the dog's obedience and manners and the handler's skills in a variety of situations, regardless of the type of service dog or training received by the dog. What matters is the handler and dog team's performance (public access test examples are accessible at Psychiatric Service Dog Society, 2011, and at Assistance Dogs International, 2012).

Americans with Disabilities Act

Keep in mind that it is the person that has the protection of the law, not the dog. The dog is able to accompany its disabled handler because of the function that the dog performs. This is similar to the fact that a wheelchair has no rights, but the person using the wheelchair can take that wheelchair with them due to the function the chair performs. For more than 80 years, assistance dogs have worked successfully in the public sector and won the public's acceptance by attaining high behavioral and training standards which set them apart from pets and other animals. Their exemplary conduct led to state legislatures granting access rights to blind, deaf, and mobility impaired persons. Those early teams paved the way for the Americans with Disabilities Act (ADA, 2010), which has opened the door to individuals with a wide range of physical and mental impairments having access rights. The ADA changed its definitions in the new ADA Regulation on May 24, 2011, to include PTSD dogs, and defined "service animal" as any dog individually trained to provide assistance to an individual with a disability. Emotional support dogs are not included. If they meet this definition, animals are considered service animals under the ADA, regardless of whether they have been licensed or certified by a state or local government (ibid.). Though not considered service animals, businesses are generally required to accommodate the use of miniature horses under specific conditions.

A number of other important laws that are related to service dogs and other animals include:

- Federal Laws pertaining to housing and service animals (USDA, 2011) covered under the Fair Housing Act.
- U.S. Department of Housing and Urban Development (2012).

- Service Dogs Standards (Assistance Dogs International (ADI), 2012).
- There are also laws (by state) pertaining to Service Animals (Service Dog Central, 2011).

It is important to note that there is a huge debate in the world at large as to what qualifies as a service animal. Also, not without importance are those ethical issues faced when we utilize canines as workers. Animal activists often argue that this is cruel and forced labor. Although I do not examine this issue within this chapter, I strongly state and acknowledge that I have no problem entrusting canines to help with the everyday lives of individuals with disabilities and that there are guidelines that must be followed for the care and well-being of our service animals.

The Canine–Human Bond, and Its Benefits

Dogs can give a sense of connectedness at a level often missing in human relationships. This connectedness is felt on a very internal and personal level. The bonding process of canine to human and human to canine can be instantaneous. Humans have used canines throughout history for many tasks. It is believed that as mankind evolved, so did its relationship with the canine.

Humans have verbal (language) communication skills. Canines use their bodies to communicate. By teaching individuals to read their canine's body language, we also teach them life skills associated with everyday life and communicating with each other. For example, we give them the ability to focus on the here and now, rather than the past or on intrusive and disquieting memories; and we help them realize the value of developing a mutually rewarding relationship (between canine and owner), rather than remaining isolated. Hence, by providing a trained service animal, or teaching individuals to train their own dogs, new and valuable skills are learned to assist with navigating everyday life. For example, it seems to me that if we teach individuals to train their own service dogs, we also are easing the all-consuming anxiety of being part of the community. For a veteran returning home, adjusting to a civilian life is stressful enough. Now compare that with injuries such as TBI or PTSD, which may involve a number of problematic behaviors, including interactions with others and the public at large as part of the readjustment process. Specific benefits of the canine–human bond are identified below.

Specific Benefits of the Canine–Human Bond

The canine can help bring lives back into balance. Here are just a few ways:

- Facilitates sensory impact and contact, which can be very calming (touch nose to hand, jump on chest, lick hand).
- Provides a form of social support and initiation of conversation with others interested in animals.
- Provides skilled assistance (the various medical, disability, and other areas mentioned earlier).
- Reminds the veteran to take medication on time.

- Is warm (to snuggle with) and can calm the veteran during a panic attack or at other anxiety-provoking times.
- Interrupts repetitive behaviors, such as pacing, finger tapping, or shaking fingers, legs or feet.
- Attends to the veteran during times of extreme emotional distress, which can provide a calming diversion or effect.
- Alerts the veteran with a learned behavior (such as nuzzling or licking the veteran) when the veteran is experiencing mania, panic attacks, or dissociation; the dog thus alerts the veteran, as the dog has been taught to be insistent until the veteran focuses on it.
- Reduces veteran hypervigilance, by virtue of the veteran knowing that the dog will detect movements and the presence of anyone else as the veteran sleeps, allowing the dog to become a protective warning companion.
- Provides a safe "grounding" presence (creates a safe barrier around the veteran by blocking the front, back, or side).
- Mitigates paranoia with reality-based reactions. Veterans with hypervigilence constantly scan the environment; instead, the veteran is taught to "read" the dog's body language/reaction to the environment. This allows the veteran to learn about the human–canine relationship. The dog's behavior "tells" the veteran if there is an actual environmental threat. Knowing this, the veteran may learn not to "have to" constantly scan the environment in order to feel safe.
- Accompanies the veteran outside the home, in public, offering a sense of security.
- Opens doors, picks up items, turns on lights.
- Alerts other family members if the veteran requires assistance.
- For veterans with balance issues and disorders, the dog stabilizes the veteran when he or she is losing balance by bracing; helps stabilize and lift when getting out of a chair; lets the owner lean on its front shoulders to rest; and enables the veteran to regain balance through the use of a harness.
- Acts as a medical alert regarding seizures, diabetes, core body temperature changes, etc.
- Provides mobility assistance for veterans who are in wheelchairs, as well as those who have suffered traumatic amputations, etc. The dog is taught to retrieve items for the veteran, open doors, help the veteran with balance, etc.
- Awakens veterans from nightmares when the veteran is making noises, thrashing around, etc., by licking, touching, or jumping on the bed.

How Canines View and React to the World

Let us take a moment to look at how canines view the world. Unlike humans, whose first sense is sight, a dog's first sense is smell. An example I use to explain this in the search and rescue world is as follows: imagine a bucket containing sand and some pepper flakes. We see the bucket filled with sand. We may see some black flakes in it, if we see the pepper flakes at all. The dog, on the other hand, smells the bucket, sand, and pepper flakes, and forms a picture of it based on each unique smell. Each has a unique scent and once all the scents are taken in, the dog forms a "picture" of what the bucket is and what it contains. This is important to understand, because it is one of the tools dogs use to assist humans in the context of search and rescue work, and in the case of physical injuries.

One of the lessons I learned early on in my career of working with canines has proven to be very valuable over the years and even more so when working with service animals. A dog reacts in one of two ways: either out of instinct or learned behavior. Humans, on the other hand, act out of emotion, memories, and learned behavior. This is important to note when dealing with invisible wounds, disabilities, or other medical conditions. For example, as the handler and dog work together to resolve hypervigilance and the handler learns to trust and read his or her dog's behavior, the handler becomes less vigilant and the dog reacts/alerts less frequently.

Canines Respond to Vocal Instruction and Body Language

When I train the individual to train his or her own dog or I give a public class, I always talk about the three tones: command, praise, and correction. This involves not only the dog's body language, but our body language. Here is a simple everyday example of how canines respond to vocal instruction and body language. A person acquires a puppy or a small dog. The first thing that everyone does is to bend over at the waist to pet the puppy. Our body language in this case, without saying a word, communicates "come into my space and jump on me." However, we really want that puppy to come to us— but we do not want it jumping on us. Now we add language: we bend over and say, "come and sit," but our body language still says "come and jump into my space." Thus, we have sent mixed signals. Once the puppy starts moving towards us, we learn to kneel down with our upper bodies straight, while giving the command to come to us. The bottom line is that we have to teach dogs our language, which is made up of both verbal and bodily communications. I mention this because, whether we are using dogs in therapy or as service dogs, an individual with speech and language impediments complicates the receipt of a positive response from the dog. And yet, a special attribute of canines is that they often provide strong motivation for continued attempts at speech and language use, as well as interpersonal interactions.

It is important to emphasize that there is no need to yell at a dog—they have very sensitive hearing. Hence, tones and sounds are very important in communicating effectively with dogs. This can help veterans to learn how tones and sounds can have positive consequences in human-to-human interactions, and can help individuals learn to engage in a similar fashion with others. This can help reduce loud behavior, while providing a calming effect. In addition, individuals can learn better how to become aware that they, themselves, are becoming agitated and need to calm down or remove themselves from the situation.

> Life isn't about waiting for the storm to pass . . . It's about learning to dance in the rain.
>
> (Vivian Greene, cited by Anderson and Gallagher, 2009)

The Priceless 24/7 Benefit

The injured veteran may be involved in medical or mental health treatment or therapy once or several times a week. However, there is an additional, truly priceless, benefit of pet or canine-assistance that will never be provided by any governmental agency and by almost no other resource public or private: the canine is with the veteran 24/7 and in all situations, adding their healing touch all day, all week, all year long. The value and impact of such a presence cannot be overstated.

Science and the Benefits of Service Dogs with Veterans

Science cannot always explain connections that resonate on an emotional or sub-physiological level. There is still much to be discovered and learned from our four-legged companions. We are just now scratching the surface in our understanding of human–canine relationships. Scientific research is not always the answer. Sometimes the act of observation holds the key, and we can learn much by simply observing behavioral changes. When we do this, we step outside the box of conventional thought and open our hearts and minds to the simple healing touch of canines.

There is a lack of scientific data with regards to why canines can make such a difference to what I call the "invisible wounds." A lifetime can be spent trying to research and document the effects of a canine on an individual diagnosed with autism, a traumatic brain injury, post-traumatic stress disorder, depression, high/low blood pressure, diabetes, seizure disorders, and the like. It is important to note that some funded research on the therapeutic value of dogs for veterans with PTSD is in the developmental stage. There is a study being developed at the National Intrepid Center of Excellence in Bethesda, Maryland, and, at the time of writing, the University of California at Davis has just received a grant for such a study.

VA Policies That Are Obstacles

Unfortunately, I have heard and discovered that a number of VA facilities have established official and/or unofficial policies that are obstacles for veterans wanting to obtain a service dog for any number of conditions, including PTSD and other mental health conditions.[1] Impediments include:

- Not allowing a PTSD service dog in VA facilities
- Not permitting or funding professional presentations of other treatment models to their staff (such as on the topic of service dogs for mental health conditions) and/or not financially supporting attendance at continuing education offerings—unless the treatment approaches *already have sufficient evidence-based data to support them.*[2]
- Not providing sufficient relevant guidance, cautions, limitations and/or suggestions about the efficacy of this healing approach and its application.

Case Example: An OEF Veteran and His Golden Retriever, Murphy

I currently have a veteran in my program who suffers from severe TBI and PTSD. He also has injuries to his lower back, which cause extreme pain but do not limit his movement. When I first met this young man (we will refer to him as Matt), he was in an inpatient PTSD program outside the VA system. He was halfway through the program when I noticed that he had begun to "hang around" the areas in which we were holding training sessions with veterans and their service dogs. We would say "hello," but his head was always down and his shoulders were forward, with no eye contact. He appeared to be trying to make himself invisible, just wandering through life—but he was drawn to the dogs. I spoke with the staff at the program in which he was enrolled and asked if he could join our training sessions to handle one of the Operation Freedoms Paws dogs, while he determined if he would benefit from having his own service dog. We typically use this approach to assess the individual and his or her interactions with the dogs, and can tell relatively quickly if the individual has the ability to "team" with a dog and what potential types of skills the dog will need to perform for that individual. Once I have assessed the individual's needs, I begin to search for the right dog to match the individual's unique needs and personality. The staff agreed that the Operation Freedoms Paws program would be a good fit for this particular veteran and our journey together began shortly thereafter. We approached him about the program. He was reserved—yet you could see the excitement in his eyes as he looked away; eye contact was not something that came easily to this veteran. (I have found that men and women with PTSD initially have trouble making or holding direct eye contact with others.) We paired him with a female German shepherd named Hanna on the first day so that we could assess his dog handling skills. Hanna is a certified therapy dog and canine good citizen, and is in training with her handler to become a certified service dog. Hanna gets excited when she senses stress or high anxiety in an individual. This is ideal, as we use the dogs to help pull the individual back into the present moment, causing the focus to shift to the dog and not the memory or situation that initially caused the stress or anxiety.

As he began to handle Hanna and learn basic obedience commands, the changes were readily visible in his demeanor, body language, and ability to communicate with others. He was engaging others and asking questions, wanting to know more, and began opening up and sharing his story with others. The TBI that he suffered while serving in Afghanistan has left him with an invisible injury that manifests itself in his inability to remember things from day to day, primarily affecting his short-term memory.

At the same time that I was working with Matt, I had a twelve week old golden retriever named Murphy that I had recently rescued from a local shelter. I was training Murphy to be a service dog for future placement with a veteran or a disabled person. Each time Matt saw Murphy, his face would light up and his attention was focused on Murphy. After a few weeks of training with Matt, we decided that he should handle Murphy during our training sessions. Our training sessions with adult dogs last from four to six hours in one day. However, with puppies we have to take things slower and train for shorter periods of time, from one to two hours a day, with breaks for naps and playtime. Over the course of several months, it became apparent that Matt and Murphy belonged together and could aid one another as they plotted their life course together.

When we would arrive for training, there was Matt waiting for Murphy. At this time, Murphy was living with me, and Matt would see him twice a week at the training sessions. Matt was training with the others and their dogs several times a week, making the long drive (over two hours each way) to attend training, just so he could see Murphy. We do not usually place puppies with individuals until they are close to a year old. However, since Matt was going to relocate to the area after he completed the inpatient program, we formally placed Murphy with Matt.

We spoke with the staff at the program in which Matt was enrolled. It was a one-of-a-kind program, in that it allowed service dogs or service dogs in training to live with the veterans at the facility and while they attended the program. I will never forget the day we told Matt that Murphy was his service dog and that he could keep Murphy with him from that day forward. The hug that Matt gave me will stay with me always. It says more than words could ever express; his smile could have lit up a dark room. Murphy and Matt were starting their journey together.

Prior to Murphy, Matt would remain in his room unless he had group sessions, one-on-one therapy appointments or went to "chow"; basically, he only left his room when necessary. Now that Matt had to walk and feed and care for Murphy 24 hours a day, 7 days a week, he was outside more frequently, taking Murphy with him everywhere he went. The next thing we knew, Matt was out walking several miles to the local town, talking with strangers about his dog and the program. We have since nicknamed him "Chatty Kathy" because he has become a social butterfly. Murphy has given Matt his voice once again, allowing him to focus on taking care of Murphy—which, in turn, has allowed Matt to step outside of his battle-worn comfort zone. For example, Matt suffers from nightmares from which Murphy awakens him by giving him kisses on his face or nudging him with his nose. Matt no longer wakes up with cold sweats or completes his nightmares; rather, he is able to go back to sleep instead of remaining awake and up for the rest of the night, unable to return to sleep. In Matt's own words:

> I have to take meds, but meds don't do what the dog does. Being responsible for taking care of the dog was a step towards taking care of me. If I had to pay Murphy for taking care of me, I'd be broke. Murphy is my best friend; he made me who I am today. Murphy shaking the bed at 6 a.m. gives me a reason to get up every morning. There are no amounts of words I can say for what I've got laying at my feet.

An OEF/OIF Veteran, His Wife, and His Service Dog, DJ

Andrew, an OIF and OEF Army veteran, said:

> Before DJ, I found it a lot harder to live with my disabilities. I have post-traumatic stress disorder, a traumatic brain injury, a seizure disorder, and severe anxiety. Since there's nothing I can do about having these problems, then I can say there's no better way to live with them than with DJ.
>
> Before DJ, these disabilities left me feeling destroyed and alone. Waking up from a seizure, black-out, hallucination or a bad dream used to make me angry because I knew I have to live my life this way. Granted, I'm not happy about having these things happen to me, but waking up to DJ licking my face or scratching at my arm with his paws, sure makes it a lot more tolerable.
>
> Knowing I have him by my side allows me to be a little more eager to go out in public places. Life before him made it almost impossible for me to walk into a grocery store or anywhere that held more than a few people, without experiencing the overwhelming feeling of panic. If I start to feel tense in public, all I have to do is look into DJ's eyes and almost instantly I feel better about where I am. He grounds me faster than I could do it alone. Even standing in line where no one can really help

getting close to each other, DJ "blocks" them by standing in front or behind me, and pushes himself against my legs to create space between us and them.

In the military, most have what they call a "Battle Buddy." But in life, people lose their Battle Buddies and can be betrayed by those people they trusted the most. Although DJ wasn't in war with me, I still consider him my Battle Buddy, my comrade. I know he feels what I feel and picks up on my emotions, and I know that can't be easy for him either. So, in a sense, he's going through it too, and that's what Battle Buddies do. I know that if DJ is concerned about something, I should be concerned about something. He tells me something is wrong with me before I even feel it. How many people can you say that about? Knowing I have DJ, and knowing he won't leave me or betray me, brings me comfort that I couldn't even begin to explain. Having DJ is like quenching a thirst that has been dehydrated for a long time.

I fear going to bed every night because I know I'm going to be swept away to night terrors. I used to dread falling asleep, knowing what was going to come. Now, I call DJ up on the bed and hold him and, miraculously, I fall asleep faster and more at ease than I ever have without him. I know I'm going to have unpleasant dreams, but he calms my brain enough to be able to bypass that feeling of fear and fall asleep.

I enjoy the simple things in life now, like playing ball with him, giving him a bath, brushing his teeth, etc . . . I've had dogs all my life, but there is something so special about the bond DJ and I share, and I wouldn't trade it for the world.

Andrew's wife Rachel said:

To sit back and think about my husband, Andrew, before DJ and my husband after DJ, is just simply amazing. DJ brings him comfort that he says he's never experienced before. He's given my husband a sense of ease to his restless mind. He's given him hope in recovery and a friend he knows would never betray him. He's even given me enough faith to be able to call him my Partner in Crime, as we both look after Andrew now and I don't have to do it alone anymore, because I know DJ will take care of him even if I'm not there to help. When my husband starts to "drift" into another world, DJ jumps into action. DJ seems to predict something will happen long before it actually does. He seems to know that Andrew needs to sit down and relax, even if my husband claims he feels fine. He's proven time and time again that he knows Andrew is about to have a seizure several minutes before it happens. He will follow him around the house, panting, whining, and begging for his attention. Sometimes, all my husband has to do is just hold him, and it seems like DJ takes the stress away. This kind of thing has prevented multiple seizures from occurring. There's a different level of comfort in my husband's life now. No matter what is happening, just knowing DJ is at his side seems to make living his life a lot easier than it ever was after Iraq.

After DJ came into our lives, I've been able to bring my husband places he vowed he would never go. He still has his hard times in crowds, but he knows that all he has to do is focus on DJ, and look into those loving trustworthy eyes, and he knows he's going to be okay, even if just for a moment, which is a lot more than I could say prior to DJ. My husband has a seizure disorder as a result of his traumatic brain injury. After a seizure, DJ doesn't hesitate to lick his face until he wakes up. Even after he opens his eyes, DJ won't give up until he responds to him enough to where DJ feels he's okay again. With or without my commands, DJ takes care of Andrew, and to see it is something words wouldn't be able to describe fair enough.

My story on how much DJ has done for us does no justice to the reality of the situation. He's done so much for my husband's mental health. The improvement since DJ is so dramatic, so amazing, and so exciting to witness every day. To say we're blessed to have DJ would be an understatement. If there was one thing about this experience that I could change, it would be to have done this a lot sooner.

Giving Veterans a New Mission and a Very Special Companion

The service dog is not a pill: it is a partner, companion, and a life-changing process. This is eminently achievable. Do not give up hope. Four paws, two feet, *one team*; this is what I tell my veterans. As Confucius said, "It does not matter how slowly you go so long as you do not stop" (Riegel, 2006).

All sound, scientific data comes from the lives of real people. This chapter included general information about the various types of service and therapy dogs. It also included stories from the veterans and family members with whom OFP has worked. These testimonials reflect the direct impact of the canine in changing their lives. Operation Freedoms Paws believes that by stepping outside the box, taking a look at the wheel, striving to make it better, but not reinventing it, we can achieve great success. The trauma, wounds, injuries, and experiences that our military members face today are only different in this way: technology has changed, weapons have changed and survivability has increased because of medical advancements. Yet, when it comes to treatment programs once they are back home, have we really moved very far ahead? We need to make the wheel better—or, actually, we might need to look beyond the wheel and consider how to optimize and tailor the benefits of four paws for veterans . . .

One strategy at OFP is to train veterans and others to train their own service dogs. OFP gives them a new mission, a Battle Buddy, a companion. And not just a companion, but a very, very, special companion—*someone who loves them unconditionally for who they are now, does not judge them, is with them 24/7 and forever* and provides the range of incredibly meaningful benefits and positives that have been briefly described in this chapter. The benefits they receive cannot be simply or adequately stated in words and must be observed and experienced to be truly appreciated. Indeed, physically and/or psychiatrically disabled veterans could benefit from—and deserve—such benefits, including, but not limited to, the following:

- The ability to better engage in conversation, especially with a stranger.
- The ability to increase memory functions through repetition and the dog performing reminder tasks.
- The ability to begin caring/feeling again.
- The ability to go out in crowds, to go to a movie, a restaurant, the grocery store, family functions.
- The ability to be proud again—despite the pain. The ability to believe that they are needed.

- The ability to believe in themselves again.
- And, lastly, a sense of accomplishment. One mission complete; now a new mission, called life.

Closing

A service dog is not a cure; it is part of the healing process. It is one of many tools that need to be available to help our men and women who so proudly served us, in order to help them to begin to come home. Operation Freedoms Paws is helping to bring them home, one veteran at a time, with the help of our four legged friends . . . four paws, two feet, *one team.*

Maybe, just maybe, the best medicine is not a pill, but four paws and a canine heart.

Notes

1 It should be noted that at least one VA (Tampa, FL) has begun a two-year study of the impact of service dogs on up to 200 veterans with PTSD (see Tamen, 2012), in collaboration with Guardian Angels Medical Service Dogs (2012). This is a welcome initiative, and should provide important evidence-based data about the impact of service dogs on veterans with PTSD.
2 This restriction is discussed further by Scurfield and Platoni in this volume, at Chapter 1.

References

American Kennel Club. (2012). "AKC's Canine Good Citizen Program." Accessed at: http://www.akc.org/events/cgc/index.

Americans with Disabilities Act (ADA). (2010). Accessed at: http://www.ada.gov/regs2010/titleII_2010/titleII_2010_fr.pdf.

Anderson, M., & Gallagher, B. J. (2009). "Learning to Dance in the Rain." Accessed at: http://vivi-angreene.org/learning-to-dance-in-the-rain/.

Assistance Dogs International. (2012). *Public Access Test Example (Assistance Dog Public Access Certification Test).* Accessed at: http://www.assistancedogsinternational.org/publicaccesstest.php.

Assistance Dogs International (ADI). (2012). Accessed at: http://www.assistancedogsinterna-tional.org/.

Assistance Dogs International (ADI). (2012). "Minimum Standards for Training Service Dogs." Accessed at: http://www.assistancedogsinternational.org/Standards/ServiceDogStandards.php.

Burke, A. (n.d.). "The History of Service Dogs." eHow Contributor. Accessed at: http://www.ehow.com/about_5134784_history-service-dogs.html.

Delta Society. (2012). "Animal-Assisted Activities/Therapy 101." Accessed at: http://www.delta-society.org/Page.aspx?pid=317.

Dogs for the Deaf, Inc. (2012). "Hearing Dogs." Accessed at: http://www.dogsforthedeaf.org/hearing-dogs.

Guardian Angels Medical Service Dogs. (2012). Accessed at: http://medicalservicedogs.com/.

Guide Dogs of America. (2012). Accessed at: http://www.guidedogsofamerica.org/.

Guide Dog Foundation for the Blind, Inc. (2012). Accessed at: http://www.guidedog.org/.

Guide Dogs of the Desert. (2012). Accessed at: http://www.guidedogsofthedesert.com.

National Service Animal Registry (NSAR). (2010). "Emotional Suport Animals (ESA)." Accessed at: http://nsarco.com/emotionalsupportanimals.html.

Psychiatric Service Dog Society (PSDS). (n.d.). Website. Accessed at: http://www.psychdog.org/
Psychiatric Service Dog Society. (n.d.). "Veterans' Services." Accessed at: http://www.psychdog.
org/veterans2.html.
Psychiatric Service Dog Society (PSDS). (n.d.). "PSDS Task List for PTSD." Accessed at: http://
www.psychdog.org/tasks.html.
Psychiatric Service Dog Society (PSDS). (2011). "Service Dog Public Access Test." Accessed at:
http://www.psychdog.org/attach/Public_Access_Standard_Test_Sheet.pdf.
Riegel, J. (2006). "Confucius." *Stanford Encyclopedia of Philosophy*. Accessed at: plato.stanford.
edu/entries/confucius/.
Service Dog Central. (2011). "Important Notice: Definition of Service Animal Changed July 23,
2010 (effective March 15, 2011)." Accessed at: http://servicedogcentral.org.
Tammen, K. (2012, January 2). "German Shepherd Helps Army Vet Battle with PTSD." Accessed at:
http://www.miamiherald.com/2012/01/02/2570063/german-shepherd-helps-army-vet.html.
Therapy Dogs International. (n.d.). Website. Accessed at: http://tdi-dog.org/.
USDA (U.S. Department of Agriculture). (2011). "The Animal Welfare Information Center
(AWIC)." Accessed at: http://www.nal.usda.gov/awic/newsletters/v7n2/7n2hende.htm#FHAA.
U.S. Department of Housing and Urban Development. (2012, January 26). "Service Dogs."
Accessed at: http://search.usa.gov/search?affiliate=housingandurbandevelopment&query=service+
dogs.

14 Back in the Saddle and Scuba Warriors

Innovative Therapies to Healing

Janice E. Buckley and Janet Raulerson

"Heartbeat—Serving Wounded Warriors," a 501(c)(3) non-profit organization, is unique in that it offers two "unconventional" therapy programs for wounded warriors. Each of these programs shows great promise for warriors with physical as well as psychological injuries.

Back in the Saddle Warriors consists of two therapies that involve horses: Hippotherapy and Equine Assisted Psychotherapy (EAP). Hippotherapy involves horseback riding, while EAP utilizes the horse as a tool in a therapeutic setting. The second program, Heartbeat's Scuba Warriors, teaches wounded warriors how to dive.

There is a background description of how each of these programs was developed, their rationale, and the basic procedures and activities. Finally, case examples will illustrate participation in each program by wounded warriors, as well as the typical range of benefits and impact.

Heartbeat is unique, in that it assumes all of the costs involved with each of the therapies, including the use of all equipment, the equine arena, and the dive shop. There is no cost to the warrior, and the program relies solely on donations from individuals, businesses, foundations, and grant-making bodies. Providing these services is part of our way of paying these warriors back for all that they have sacrificed for us and our country.

Background: The Development of Equine Assisted Therapies

Liz Hartel (March 14, 1921–February 12, 2009) was the first woman in equestrian sports to win the silver medal in the summer Olympics (1952 and 1956). Though this is an impressive feat for anyone, it was especially true for Ms. Hartel, who was struck with polio in 1944, and was paralyzed from the knees down. She had been told she would never walk again; however, through her therapeutic riding program, she developed enough strength to walk away from her wheelchair and win the silver medal in dressage.

Her achievements have inspired therapists to utilize horses for special needs children (Sports Reference, 2012). By the 1960s, therapeutic riding was established throughout Europe, Canada, and the United States. Therapists began to view horses as an adjunct to physical therapies. In 1969, the North American Riding for the Handicapped Association (NARHA) was established to promote equine assisted therapies; in 2011, the name changed to the Professional Association of Therapeutic Horsemanship International (PATH International, 2012). PATH International believes that horses have the power to change lives. A Navy officer once blogged the following about her horse:

Every single second with him was time spent with a totally forgiving, non-judgmental, soft, warm, empathetic, loving friend. He was the love of my life and my soul mate. I could bury my face in his mane and cry when I needed to cry and he would turn and lay his head on my shoulder. I could climb on and fly and there were no worries or pain. He asked only for love, his basic needs, and an open heart. He gave me back strength and confidence and faith in myself.

(http://forum.equisearch.com/forums/t/36879.aspx)

Hippotherapy

In the 1980s, therapists throughout the United States and Canada began to standardize the curriculum for a particular therapy known as hippotherapy. Hippotherapy literally means therapy "with the help of a horse." The American Hippotherapy Association (AHA), founded in 1992, defines it as:

> the movement of the horse as a strategy by physical therapists (PT), occupational therapists (OT), and speech-language pathologists (SLP) to address impairments, functional limitations, and disabilities in patients with neuromusculoskeletal dysfunction. This strategy is used as part of an integrated treatment program to achieve functional outcomes.

(Benjamin, 2000)

Clients can be positioned on the horse in a number of ways, depending on their individual goals. These positions include sitting or lying frontward, backward, or sideways, and even standing in the stirrups. The therapist then has the patient perform different maneuvers while on the horse. This requires the patient to perform the maneuver and respond to the horse's movements at the same time. The net effect is improved muscle tone, balance, posture, coordination, strength, and flexibility (Borzo, 2002). While a therapist directs the patient, there is also an equine specialist that directs the movements of the horse to help the therapist accomplish the therapy goals.

Equine Assisted Psychotherapy (EAP)

EAP was developed more recently than hippotherapy. During the 1980s, Greg Kersten worked with at-risk youth and horses in Utah, but it was not until the 1990s that he developed the term "Equine Assisted Psychotherapy" to apply to the work he was doing. In 1995, he published the first training manual, and began to certify professionals in the practice of EAP through his own corporation, Equine Services, Inc. Since then, other organizations have integrated many of his exercises to fit their programs (Kersten, 2012).

Back in the Saddle Warriors

Heartbeat has developed two equine assisted therapies, hippotherapy and EAP, under the overall program name of Back in the Saddle Warriors.

Hippotherapy with Warriors

Heartbeat uses hippotherapy to capture those warriors who do not fit in the "normal box" for treatment. For many warriors, sitting in a room with a therapist does not bring the desired results. Using the horse in hippotherapy allows the warrior to "be outside the box," to enlarge the healing process. This therapy is presently being used for warriors with traumatic brain injury (TBI), post-traumatic stress disorder (PTSD), spinal cord injuries, traumatic amputations, and other injuries due to shrapnel damage.

Horses and humans have something in common: a pelvis that works and moves in the same way. Both have identical hip movements when walking. Sitting on a moving horse allows the warrior's body to move naturally. It strengthens muscle groups. Staying upright on a horse requires balance, coordination, and muscle strength. Injuries from war may have affected those abilities, and these can be helped to improve with this type of therapy.

Warriors are natural protectors. It is their job to take charge and perform brave acts every day. Injuries sometimes make it impossible to contribute in a meaningful way. This dramatically changes the warrior's role within the family, job, and society. The relationship between humans and horses has long been a special one. Horses, gentle and sensitive, have a unique ability to sense human emotions. This special bond helps warriors to work through difficult issues. This can build confidence and change their outlook on life. In short, it can help bring about healing.

At Heartbeat, there is a team approach to our hippotherapy program. Although it is an option to use an OT, SLP, or PT, Heartbeat utilizes OTs to establish the treatments and goals for each warrior. There are two OTs that work with this program. They set the pace, determine the therapy goals and the specific exercises used, and assess the outcome to determine what changes need to occur.

The equine specialist works under the direction of the therapists to help achieve the objectives and goals for the warrior while on the horse. She is constantly scanning the arena for any safety issue that may surface during the treatment. She alone is responsible for choosing the horse to be used in a specific session and for a specific warrior.

The horses themselves must posses certain characteristics, such as a calm, kind, temperament. Since horses are prey animals, they have acute vision to the sides and back of their bodies, which alerts them to predators. If a warrior, while mounted, is moving his arms for a specific exercise, the horse must have the temperament or training necessary to not become alarmed with this posturing. The horse also needs to be comfortable with many people around him, as this is part of the therapy. Other aspects that are looked at include the way the legs are set, the width of the chest, the height of the horse, and how smooth the gait is when trotting. In addition, the horse needs to be physically sound. All of these characteristics are important to the comfort and safety of the rider and, therefore, the effectiveness of the therapy. This is the major role of the equine specialist: to decide which horse matches the needs of a particular warrior.

There are also a number of trained volunteers that assist at the sessions. Posted on each side of the horse are two volunteers called side-walkers. Their role is to walk or trot beside the horse and assist the rider as needed for the entire session. The occupational therapist may give suggestions to the side-walkers on how to assist the warrior, and keep the horse moving. The side-walkers can also help stabilize and secure the rider if needed.

Leading the horse is the horse leader, who is also a trained volunteer. His or her primary goal is to lead the warrior's horse during the session. The horse leader is responsible for the horse and needs to be focused on the horse at all times.

At Heartbeat, we serve only wounded military personnel. This therapy is open to all wounded warriors that have participated in the global war on terror. Service members from all branches of the military can apply. Referrals are made by nurse case managers and physicians. Heartbeat relies on them to assess whether a particular warrior can participate in the program, as they understand the warrior's complete medical history. A medical form must be completed by their primary physician and submitted to the OT for approval. This screening process allows Heartbeat to have the clients that would benefit most from the program.

Because it is so important that the warrior be as close to the horse's body as possible, no saddles are utilized. Instead, a therapeutic pad and a surcingle are used. A surcingle is a strap made of leather, or similar material, which fastens around the horse's girth, and has two handles attached for the warrior to hold onto, if needed.

All volunteers are given a copy of Heartbeat training manual, with specific guidelines not only for each of the job descriptions, but also how they are to welcome and treat these warriors. The manual also explains each type of therapy, the goals of therapy, and how the volunteers work as a team to support the warrior. Each page offers information about barn safety, how to fit riding helmets and boots, haltering and leading a horse, and what to do in an emergency situation. At the end of each section is a small test. This manual and the training that the volunteers receive on-site, help prepare them for the therapy session (Mahoney, 2006).

In addition to the manual, each of the volunteers watches a video on equine therapy, in which the most important safety issues are emphasized. There are four training sessions, each approximately three hours in length, in which they practice their roles and the emergency dismount. The emphasis of the program is healing, safety, and support, which is why Heartbeat uses only volunteers with extensive experience with horses.

Sessions are approximately 45 minutes in length, though actual time on the horse may vary, depending on a warrior's ability and individual goals. Lessons are tailored to the goals of the participants, though a typical session follows this format:

- Welcome and helmet fitting.
- Ground lessons and educational activities prior to mounting: these are activities, performed by the equine specialist, to prepare the horse for riding. They include grooming, lunging, and desensitizing exercises. Desensitization involves exposing the horse to objects, such as a lead rope, repeatedly. The equine specialist may pull a rope across the horse's neck, back, or legs for several minutes, until the horse no longer responds to the object. These exercises help quieten the horse and keep it focused during the session. Lunging is used to exercise the horse prior to the session. The horse moves around the specialist in a circle and is controlled by her voice and body language. This gives the equine specialist a chance to monitor the animal's movements and stride.
- Warm-up exercises with the rider: this allows the warrior to become accustomed to the gait and feel of the horse.
- Exercises on the horse: these are as directed by the OT and can include stretching,

lifting their hands over their heads or out to their sides, extending their legs out, and pointing their toes, to name only a few.

- Cool down and dismount.
- Staff discusses the lesson in terms of how the therapy progressed. The warrior is not present at this time, but can meet with the OT separately to discuss the therapy.

Frequently, during the session, the warrior and the OT communicate about how a particular exercise feels and its effectiveness (Mahoney, 2006).

Case Study: David

One particular warrior, David (not his real name), had been participating in the equine program for about six weeks. He had bonded with one of the horses, named Kramer. David had no previous experience with horses, but developed an instant connection to Kramer and was very attached to him. David had both physical and psychological injuries, and looked forward to the work with his horse. One day, in particular, he arrived very depressed, not interacting with any of the volunteers or therapists. He isolated himself and went out to the field to visit Kramer. When David called for Kramer, the horse lifted up his head and came over to him. After that, the warrior became more uplifted, and shared this story with the therapist.

Unfortunately, Kramer sustained a small injury while out in the pasture, and David was devastated. It was just like in the war when a buddy is lost. Kramer was his buddy, and now he was unable to ride him. The team introduced David to a new horse, named Beauty. He mounted the horse from the block and the therapist decided to let Beauty walk a few laps around the arena. After that, the exercise routines started, things went smoothly, and David was interacting more with the OT. He also mentioned, as he was stretching his left arm up, how much better that arm felt, and that he could move his arms a lot more now and without much pain. For the final exercise, the therapist had David close his eyes and ride Beauty in a figure eight around the arena, using his body to turn the horse. This was a very successful exercise and he mentioned that, with his eyes closed, he felt like he could communicate better with Beauty. Riding with one's eyes closed is an extremely difficult thing to do for the everyday rider, let alone an injured warrior. It is an exercise in balance. The individual has to be very relaxed to maintain stability.

The session continued for a total of 35 minutes. He thanked all of the volunteers, and added that he felt compelled to work even harder to get better, since they were volunteering their time to help with this program. David dismounted and began petting Beauty and hugged his neck. As he was talking to the therapist during the session, he mentioned that he had tried to work on these same exercises in his room, but "I did not have the same effect." "It seems to work better when I'm here and on the horse."

Following the hippotherapy session, David was given the opportunity to work with some of the other horses but, instead, wanted to continue to work with Beauty. Heartbeat has recently incorporated an educational program with the hippotherapy, in which the warriors learn how to groom the horses, clean their feet, listen to their heart rate, and take temperatures. This is referred to as Vetting Out. It is all part of the process of caring for the horse and developing a relationship with the horse. This was actually one of

David's favorite parts of the program. Many of the other warriors enjoy it as well. It is calming and, when asked in particular why they like being around the horses, one warrior stated that it was "because they're not going to shoot me or blow me up." Though this may seem like an extreme statement, many warriors coming home are hypervigilant—always "on." With this program, warriors are able to relax when they are at the ranch. They look forward to the program with a feeling of joy, which is new to most of them. Sometimes the joy is anticipatory, experienced several days before the session itself.

Equine Assisted Psychotherapy

Heartbeat also employs a second type of equine therapy that is very different from the hippotherapy, as it utilizes the horse differently. EAP simply means incorporating a horse into the mental health treatment of people. The therapy takes place on the ground; there is no riding involved. The warriors work as a group: sometimes there are eight or ten, sometimes as few as one or two. They may have a drill involving only one horse, or there may be several horses in the arena. All combinations are used. With the horse or horses present in the arena, the warriors complete previously established drills. The drills may be as simple as putting a halter on a single horse, as a team, or as complex as trying to corral a horse into a particular area of the arena, as a group, without speaking or touching the horse. Though the therapists set the scenario, the warriors are encouraged to experiment, take risks, and employ creativity to find solutions that work best for them. One of the core beliefs in EAP is that there is more than one way to accomplish a goal.

If there are limitations, such as no talking or moving, these are established at the beginning of the activity. Limitations force the warriors to "think outside the box" and to create new approaches to problem solving. The drills are a representation of what is happening in their lives now. They have a chance, through the drill, to find new ways that will work more effectively for their lives. As one warrior stated, "This isn't really about the horse; it's about me."

Research has shown that humans remember only 20 percent of what we hear, 50 percent of what we see, and 80 percent of what we do (Mandrell, 2006). This explains the success of EAP, because it gives the warrior a visible metaphor to apply to his or her own life.

Though the horse is used as a tool in the drill, a strong bond between the horse and the warrior usually develops. In general, horses are gentle and sensitive, and have a unique ability to sense human emotions. This special bond helps warriors to work through difficult issues. As Winston Churchill once stated, "There is something about the outside of a horse that is good for the inside of a man" (Cabell, 1946).

The EAP program at Heartbeat utilizes the Equine Assisted Growth and Learning Association (EAGALA) Model, which is a team approach utilizing an equine specialist, a mental health professional, and a horse. The focus is on the ground. EAGALA is a nonprofit organization that was founded in 1999, by Greg Kersten, with a goal of improving the mental health of individuals, families, and groups around the world, by setting standards for EAP (www.EAGALA.org).

During the EAP session, the equine specialist is responsible for choosing the horse that is used in the session. She watches the horse's behaviors and is always alert for any safety issues. Our mental health specialist is a practicing psychologist and is also EAGALA certified. He is responsible for developing the drills and treatment plan, and for observation and documentation of the warrior in the scenario. Because he works with these warriors outside the therapy sessions, he decides who would benefit from this program the most, screens all applicants, and follows up with the warrior to help integrate the equine sessions into his or her overall healthcare program. As with the hippotherapy, referrals can also come from nurse case managers and physicians.

Although other animals can be used, the horse is the perfect team member. Their large size can be intimidating; this offers an opportunity for the warrior to overcome fears, which helps build self-confidence. Also, horses mirror back their direct experiences. Whatever they feel on the inside is what they manifest on the outside. If a person wants a horse to respond differently, he or she must first change how he or she acts towards the horse. In other words, to teach a horse to be calm, trusting, and responsive to an individual, that individual must first acquire those qualities himself (Mandrell, 2006). During some of the timed drills, if a warrior appears to be frustrated, trying too hard to get the exercise done, or is even angry, the horse will pull back, also showing signs of frustration. It may even leave the area and refuse to work with the warrior. This, in turn, causes the warrior to rethink his approach and to try a new tactic. If the horse does not cooperate, a single warrior, no matter how strong, will not be able to force the animal to perform. The psychologist for Heartbeat allows the warriors time to try to figure this out.

During one particular drill, a warrior was leading a single horse across the length of the arena. Outside the arena were several horses running free. How the warrior would lead the horse would determine the horse's reaction. If the warrior was fearful or nervous about the experience, the horse would bolt and run away. But, instead, he held onto the lead rope and walked firmly and deliberately, in a steady gait, across the arena, with the horse right behind him. The horse was not affected by any of the activity around him, and remained calm the entire time.

Sometimes the warrior gives mixed signals to the horse. There was one such warrior who was pulling the rope towards himself, while actually wanting the horse to walk around the perimeter. This frustrated the horse, as well as the warrior, but it did give this warrior a very concrete example of how he was communicating to the horse and, possibly, to other people in his life, as well. These are all feelings and behaviors discussed during processing.

Horses are considered herd animals because they rely on each other for safety and survival. So are humans, whether we act like it all the time or not. Utilizing horses in EAP allows the warriors to work on issues of trust, relationships, patience, and boundaries, in a setting that is very different from the inside of a therapist's office.

Following the session, the mental health specialist meets with the warrior to discuss the activity. This is referred to as processing. Though processing can occur before, during, or after the experience, it commonly occurs at the end of the session. In some instances, it may not occur for several days if the warrior is not ready to discuss with the psychologist what happened and how that affected him or her.

Case Study: Lisa

One particular warrior, Lisa (not her real name), worked alone in an EAP session. The mental health and equine specialists set up the task for Lisa to complete. She was to stand in the center of the arena and to encourage the horse, a gentle mare, to walk around the perimeter. Lisa was not allowed to touch the horse and she, herself, was not allowed to move from her center position. Attached to the horse was a lunge line for Lisa to hold.

As the drill progressed, it became apparent that the horse was not moving. To compensate for this, Lisa moved instead. After several more minutes, the psychologist ended the drill and then asked Lisa what she thought happened. She stated that he did not want to move. At this point, the psychologist clued into the fact that Lisa referred to this mare as a "he." Continuing to press her, the psychologist asked if there was some event in her life that paralleled this. Lisa began to cry, and stated that she did not want to impose her wants and desires on the horse. Crying, or any other strong emotion, can actually release feelings which, in turn, lead to understanding. As she continued, more information was revealed. Lisa did not want to assert herself in this relationship, or any other relationship. Lisa was able to understand the results of the drill as the psychologist continued to peel the layers of confusion away. Even though Lisa was a soldier and put her life on the line every day at work, she was too timid and too afraid to impose her needs on anyone. Though Lisa continued to cry, she obtained support from the psychologist and the equine specialist and began to realize the impact of the drill and its results.

According to our psychologist, one way to categorize people is whether they are more abstract or concrete in their orientation. Concrete people perceive the horse as a horse, not as a metaphor for events or people in their lives. Abstract people can associate the event and the horse with their feelings. For EAP, abstract people tend to understand and connect the drill with their lives in a relatively short period of time; concrete people take a little more time. Lisa was able to see the connection of the drill and the horse to herself and her feelings that afternoon, after a single session; this is unusual. Generally, it takes numerous sessions for the connection to reveal itself.

Since there is so much actually occurring during an EAP session, it is frequently divided into four components. The first component is the activity or task to be completed. Questions to be considered are: How did the warrior feel he or she performed? Was the task completed successfully? If so, how was he or she able to accomplish this? Though the team may, at times, help a warrior sort out what has occurred, it is critical that the warrior able to tell his or her own story as to what he or she believed happened.

The second component refers to the horse itself. This is an essential component, upon which the equine specialist focuses. Questions to be considered include: How did the horse respond? Did the client change how he or she approached the horse? If so, did the horse change, as well, in response to this new approach?

The third component is the client's response to the horse. How did he or she interact with the horse? If multiple horses were available, why did he or she choose this particular one? Finally, if there is more than one client, the dynamics within the group are considered: How did the individuals communicate; how did they plan the activity; was there a hierarchy within the group? These are sample questions that are considered. What is most important is that the client has the freedom, and feels supported enough, to explore many options, including those that lie "outside the box."

Many of these warriors have never been around horses, and are apprehensive at first. But, after a few times, they begin to relax both their minds and bodies. One warrior stated that he felt "real" when he was with the horses. During the war, experiences can be surreal. At the ranch, however, with the horses, they can be who they really are, and not how they are supposed to be. As one warrior put it, "It's about finding yourself."

Scuba Warriors

According to Ken Yates, a combat veteran and master scuba diver certified by the Professional Association of Diving Instructors (PADI), "There is no greater feeling than going diving with combat-wounded warriors" (personal communication, January 14, 2011). He should know. Yates is the creator and original project manager for Heartbeat's Scuba Warriors, a program that teaches wounded warriors how to dive. At the completion of the 3½ week course, each student receives an open water scuba certification card. Though the certification is the end result, the process incorporates therapy into each activity.

Scuba diving has some similarities to being "down range" or deployed. These similarities are what draw the warriors to this type of therapy. They have the opportunity to be a part of a team; they work as a unit, watching out for each other. A combat warrior may have lost all of his team in the war. Now he or she has a chance to be a part of a new team. There is also the physical exertion associated with scuba diving, and the adrenalin rush with each dive. It is exciting, filled with danger, and no two experiences are the same.

However, that's where the similarities end. Jacques Cousteau, a pioneer in marine conservation, explorer of the sea, researcher of all aquatic life forms, and innovator of modern underwater diving, stated once that, "Man has only to sink below the surface of the water and he is free . . . he can fly in any direction—up, down, sideways—by just turning his hand. Underwater, man can fly like an angel" (Atwater, 1960). Scuba diving allows the warrior to move limbs previously injured during the war, which may be too painful to move on land. The water greatly reduces the force of gravity, which is hard on the body, and, instead, offers a weightless and cushioning environment that gently supports muscles and limbs that have been ravaged by combat. The ability to move in a way that is, for the first time, relatively pain-free, can contribute to positive changes in attitudes. Also, with the increase in movement, blood flow and cardiovascular strength are improved. For warriors struggling with PTSD and TBI, the water offers them a quiet place, free from the constant storms in their heads.

Wounded warriors describe the experience of being down range, and how they need to remain hypervigilant to possible danger. They learn not to show fear; to do whatever it takes to keep fear buried deeply. They also learn to keep other things buried; to be more secretive, and to speak less as a matter of their own survival. When they return home, it is a confusing and sometimes painful time. The water is a peaceful place to be, with just the sound of their own breathing. Yates talks about this sense of peace: "I hear the bubbles. I hear the air moving through the system and it is calming. I find I have more energy after diving, as it calms my thoughts."

The pace of the course is flexible, based on the capabilities of each student. The participants are screened by the nurse case manager and physicians first. The OT makes the final decision as to the effectiveness of the program for the individual. According to Yates, diving is taught in steps—crawl, walk, and run. Each student brings his or her uniqueness to the course, and the challenges are physical as well as mental.

The core team consists of Scott Frazier, who was a senior medic in Iraq, Mike Garman, who has thirty years of diving experience, and John Beavers. All are certified divers, either with PADI or the National Association of Underwater Instructors (NAUI). This group of divers manages the course and works with a variety of dive instructors from dive shops in the Puget Sound area. They meet each month to assess the progress of the program and to plan the orientation meetings with the warriors, which explain, step by step, what the program is about, and what is expected of each participant.

The course enrolls only 6 students at a time, and is divided into three main parts, classroom time, indoor pool, and open water. There are approximately 10 hours of classroom instruction. During this time, the students become familiar with the scuba equipment, how to use it, and, more importantly, what to do if something goes wrong with the equipment. They also learn how to communicate with each other underwater. There are approximately 12 hand signals used. This is part of the safety mandate of the program.

Other subjects covered in the class include the science of diving, safety rules and regulations, physics, how the human body reacts underwater, conservation and the importance of the marine environment, dive planning, and a study of the marine life that will be visualized during the open water dive. Woven into the academics of diving is team building—lots of team building. Each student receives a work book, dive logs and tables, and an instruction book. There are discussions, videos, and interactive play with the equipment. The students take the equipment apart and put it together over and over again. Since it is important that they learn to work as a team, the buddy system is critical to dive safety. The warriors, while underwater, work in small groups as a support to each other, and as part of the safety mandate.

Then, the class moves to a swimming pool for 12 to 15 hours of instruction and practice in the water. Because scuba diving is not without risk, and some of the students have never been exposed to it, there are two to four safety divers in the water with the class: one diver for each pair of students, and one floater. The role of the safety diver is to be a secondary resource, next to the instructor, for emergencies. He will position himself behind the students and watch for signs of panic or any other safety issues. All the skills required for open water diving are learned and practiced here. The students become accustomed to the gear, and learn how to communicate with each other underwater. Some of the specific skills include regulator recovery, mask flood, sharing air, emergency ascent, and buoyancy. Safety is always a primary concern. The core team and the other safety divers in the program are able to detect, through the mask and equipment, if a warrior is too anxious to dive at this time. Besides the core team, the instructor, and safety divers, an occupational therapist accompanies the team and remains on land with all the phone numbers close at hand, in case an emergency was to occur.

In the beginning, the instructor remains with the students constantly, while in the water—usually within inches—and is able to read their level of anxiety, even through all of the equipment. If a student is too anxious, the instructor or the core team spends extra one-on-one time with them, until they feel comfortable again. One particular student was struggling with anxiety and ready to give up, but he was isolated from the group for two hours with the instructor, until he was able to develop the skill and move on to the next step. The students begin in the shallow end, and work on the skills they will need for the open water dives. As they progress, the class moves to the deep end of the pool. There is a continuous review of all the skills learned in the classroom.

According to Dr. Wexler, a previous instructor for Heartbeat's program, the students develop muscle memory by continuing to practice the same maneuvers over and over again. This allows specific tasks to be performed without conscious effort, thus allowing the maximum efficiency for the physical responses in diving. Each success builds on the previous success.

The goals of the Scuba Warrior program are two-fold: first, to acquire the physical skills and knowledge that result in being able to dive successfully and safely; and, second, to integrate other real life issues—such as talking about what happened to the warriors during combat—and work on issues of fear, anger, and anxiety, as a result. For example, as the warriors practice breathing exercises for the dive, they learn how to apply this skill as a calming technique for their everyday lives. According to one of the occupational therapists, scuba diving helps with cognitive skills such as problem-solving, memory function, and interpersonal communication.

The pool practice continues until each student is proficient in the skills required for the open water dive. The class spends 10 to 12 hours in the Puget Sound. The various dive shops supply all the gear. The specific training guidelines used for the course are established by the core team. The same skills that were previously learned are practiced again in the open water. The student needs to be able to demonstrate the skills without help. As each one masters the skills, his or her level of confidence builds. The dives are initially limited to 10 to 15 feet, but gradually increase to a maximum of 60 feet.

After all the hours spent diving and in the classroom, the students have to pass a written exam before they receive their certification. Heartbeat's Scuba Program is adaptive, which means that the instructor can certify divers with restrictions. He is able to spell out on the certification whether the diver requires the presence of a safety diver or even a master dive instructor with him when he dives.

Scuba Warriors is offered approximately every other month and, at this time, there is a waiting list of more than 40 warriors. As stated earlier, referrals are generated by physicians, nurse case managers, and occupational therapists. It is a popular therapy because the warriors can apply much of what they learned to their lives. It reinforces the fact that there are still things they can successfully accomplish.

Dr. Wexler remembers one decorated veteran with a family. The warrior had no self-confidence. He did not believe that he could find peace, as he was too broken. After the course, he realized that he could undertake this, and went on to enroll in college.

One of Yates's fondest memories is about Frazier. Yates met Frazier in 2009, when he was medevaced from Iraq, and found they shared a common love for diving. Yates told Frazier about the program he was developing with Heartbeat, and convinced him to go out diving, even though it had been almost 15 years since Frazier's last dive. They both met at Les Davis Pier and practiced the skills necessary for the dive. Frazier mastered these easily, and they both started swimming around, working on buoyancy. Yates could see, through the mask, the biggest smile he had ever seen on Frazier's face.

When Frazier returned home from Iraq after serving 21 months, Yates remembers that:

> He would go from formations and appointments directly back to his room. He didn't talk much to people, was very secretive, and just didn't care about much of anything. But, once he got back in the water, Frazier became one of my best friends. He's outgoing now, and even took my place at the Scuba Expo in Tacoma, talking about the program to total strangers.

Frazier now helps with the program his buddy started, as a safety diver, and is part of the core team for the Scuba Warriors Program. The program changed his life. According to Frazier, "As a wounded warrior, you always have a dark place but, with Scuba Warriors, it doesn't control you any more." Frazier remembers his first dive with Yates. "When I got in the water, I could move freely. There were no aches or pains, and I came out of the water with such a high." As a safety diver, Frazier is doing what he used to do in Iraq, which is a comfort to him. "As a medic, you patch kids up and move them out. I'm still patching kids up and helping them return to their families as a provider and loving father."

Another wounded warrior, Rick (not his real name), returned home from his tour with severe TBI. He wanted to enroll in the course, but was very nervous about it because of his injuries. However, he did enroll, and persevered through the program with extra help from the instructor and his teammates. This was life changing for Rick. Now, he is purchasing his own diving equipment, and taking a course on commercial diving.

One female warrior, Julie (not her real name), was very withdrawn and suicidal. Because of the program, her self-esteem improved, and she became more outgoing. She came up to one of the Heartbeat leaders after the session and gave her a hug. For Julie, the benefit came because she was able to complete something, and complete it well.

One aspect of diving that the Army is interested in researching is the effect, while diving, of pressure and nitrogen and oxygen levels on the brain. According to Dr. Wexler, there is empirical evidence that these changes in levels can help heal damaged tissue and neurons in the brain. A young autistic adult from a previous scuba program was particularly withdrawn and non-communicative. She took twice as long to complete the course as is usual, even with her mother as her dive partner. But the program had a profound effect. After diving, this young woman's verbal ability increased, and she was able to communicate. As her mother stated, when they go diving, for 20 to 24 hours afterwards, she gets her daughter back.

That is the ultimate purpose of Scuba Warriors—to allow these heroes to get their lives back, and to move onto fulfilling their potential instead of being held captive by their past.

Other Equine and Scuba Diving Programs

There are a number of scuba diving programs across the country. Most are offered to healthy individuals interested in a new sport and lifestyle change. Some are for handicapped adults that have sustained their injuries from a variety of sources. Almost all of these businesses charge for the course and offer many different levels of diving and certifications for the client.

But, for wounded warriors, the choices are few. For illustrative purposes, and to acquaint readers with some of the programs that exist elsewhere, the following are selected programs about which the authors have knowledge.

In Virginia, a 501(c)(3) organization called Soldiers Undertaking Disabled Scuba (SUDS) offers scuba certification for Operation Iraqi Freedom (OIF) and Operation Enduring Freedom (OEF) service members who are under the care of a physical therapist or occupational therapist. SUDS is also associated with the Walter Reed Army Medical Center, and is a chapter of the Wounded Warriors/Disabled Sports Project.

Dive Pirates Foundation is also a 501(c)(3) non-profit organization, and provides certification for wounded warriors. It is managed under the auspices of Scuba Schools International (SSI). There are several chapters across the United States, but their main headquarters are in Texas. Dive Pirates Foundation offers adaptive scuba classes for any individual with a physical disability or an inability to pay, as well as for wounded warriors.

For our equine assisted therapies, Heartbeat is one of the few that offers two types of equine therapy for wounded warriors only. Although there are numerous riding programs, there is a distinction between equine assisted therapies (EAT) and therapeutic riding. Many organizations offer therapeutic riding, but relatively few offer equine assisted therapy. Generally, EAT is a medical treatment strategy, while therapeutic riding is considered a sport or recreational/educational activity. EAT's goals are developed and implemented by a medical professional, either an OT, PT, SLP, or psychologist. The established outcomes are used during the evaluation process, and these goals are rehabilitation-related and not horse-related.

Therapeutic riding is to improve social skills, quality of life, and mobility. The goals are horse-related, such as improved riding ability, self-accomplishment, and acquisition of a sports skill. Though therapists may be used as consultants in therapeutic riding, they are not mandatory (Horse Talk Therapeutic Services, n.d.). In Washington state, there are two organizations that offer equine programs. Little Bit in Woodinville is a 501(c)(3) that provides therapeutic riding for handicapped children. Rainier Therapeutic Riding in Yelm has developed a new program, "Horses for Heroes." Rainier Therapeutic Riding is also a 501(c)(3) that provides therapeutic riding for all levels of handicapped individuals. The Horses for Heroes program caters exclusively to wounded warriors from the Joint Base Lewis-McChord area.

The choices for wounded warriors to receive help with innovative therapies involving horses or scuba diving are limited. This is why Heartbeat expended so much effort to develop these programs.

Though there is much anecdotal or qualitative research in the field of EAT, quantitative research is lacking. Such research is needed to affirm empirically that this treatment modality is successful. This has yet to be proven to the academic and therapeutic communities.

Closing

Heartbeat's priority, since its inception, has been to serve our brave men and women of the military and their families. Our wounded warriors are particularly vulnerable, and require our highest level of service. These warriors, who were completely in control of their lives, and doing what they loved to do in serving our country, now suffer disabling physical and/or psychological conditions. That is why we at Heartbeat modified our mission to exclusively serve them. This was the impetus in developing Scuba Warriors and Back in the Saddle. At Heartbeat, we are choosing to be an answer. We are choosing to be a voice, and not just an echo.

We have served many warriors who were left on their own with no family support, homeless at a young age. That is not the way these courageous heroes should be treated. We must do more for them. After all, they have paid a very high price to keep our country free.

Warriors and their families have told us that Heartbeat has been like a family to them, not only for the help they need, but also to know that they are not alone with the struggles they face on a daily basis. For some warriors, the battle they face when they come home is almost unbearable, because the very same skills and training they utilized to keep them alive while in a war zone are now making it difficult to be at home. To be optimally responsive to the wide range of wounded warriors, and the physical and psychological conditions resulting from their military experiences, Heartbeat offers two different types of therapy programs, Scuba Warriors and Back in the Saddle; the latter is equine assisted therapy which includes hippotherapy and EAP. These programs offer not only physical healing, but also psychological healing. In fact, one warrior stated that because of his dog and the Scuba Warrior Program, he was able to face each day and grow as an individual.

These courageous and amazing warriors live "visibly" in all they do, by serving with honor, courage, integrity, and respect. They are the plum line of excellence for this country, and we cannot ever let them down.

References

Atwater, J. (1960, March 28). "Sport: Poet of the Depths." *Time Magazine. LXXV* (13).

Benjamin, J. (2000). "An Introduction to Hippotherapy." American Hippotherapy Association. Accessed at: www.americanhippotherapyassociation.org.

Borzo, G. (2002). "Horse Power: When Riding Turns Into Treatment." American Hippotherapy Association (n.d.). Accessed at: www.americanhippotherapyassociation.org.

Cabell, M. (1946). *The Horseman's Encyclopedia.* A.S. Barnes & Company, Inc.

Horse Talk Therapeutic Services. (n.d.). "Comparison of Therapeutic Riding and Hippotherapy Programs." Accessed at: http://nhhorsetalk.com/therapy-plan-mainmenu-2/riding-vs-hippo-mainmenu-10.html.

Kersten, G. (2012). "Equine Assisted History." Accessed at: www.okcorralseries.com/About.html.

Mahoney, A. (2006). *Heartbeat—Serving Wounded Warriors' Equine Riding Program: Volunteer Training Manual.* Unpublished manuscript used as manual for volunteers of Heartbeat—Serving Wounded Warriors.

Mandrell, P. J. (2006). *Introduction to Equine Assisted Psychotherapy: A Comprehensive Overview.* Maitland, FL: Xulon Press.

PATH International. (2012). Professional Association of Therapeutic Horsemanship International. Home page. Accessed at: http://www.pathintl.org/.

Sports Reference. (2012). Liz Hartel Biography. Accessed at: www.sports-reference.com/olympics/athletes/ha/lis-hartel-1.html.

Part VI

Technological and Web-Based Approaches

15 Healing Combat Trauma

The Website, the Vision, the Impact

Lily G. Casura

If I had been told in February 2006 early in the Iraq War, back when I was first starting my website, www.HealingCombatTrauma.com, that a few years later I would have published almost 1,000 articles on various aspects of one topic—what it takes to help heal post-traumatic stress from combat—I might never have begun. Today, the site encompasses 135 different categories of material, representing everything from acupuncture to yoga, with hundreds of recommended books of therapeutic interest and additional groupings of first-person narratives from every war, to help readers better understand what veterans go through in combat and its aftermath. It has been called "a Library of Congress-like site" in its comprehensive nature, and, as one reader said, seems to be the only site that takes a look at "the full 360 degrees of healing" without promoting any one agenda.

Initially, though, it was just a glimmer in its creator's eye, and the shape that it has taken since then has been a highly organic one, responsive to the readers' needs and the dictates of an ever-evolving medium. This chapter describes what happened from the beginning to establish this website, along with how HealingCombatTrauma.com has expanded into a social media phenomenon, and the many lessons learned along the way.

Initial Development of the Healing Combat Trauma Website

In early November 2005, I had a chance meeting over the Internet with a Marine officer stationed in the Sunni triangle, considered then to be the most volatile area in Iraq, filled with insurgents and with roadside bombs exploding daily. We met on a university email listserv, where he introduced himself as a Marine who was "on the ground in Ramadi, and wrote about it every day." Was anyone interested in reading what he had to say? "Not so much," I thought to myself, but then added, out of concern for how dangerous his world must be, "Stay safe."

From that simple introduction, a robust correspondence developed, with hundreds of emails ultimately exchanged, in which I had a chance to see first-hand how difficult and dangerous it could be to serve in Iraq. As this officer and I became friends, I thought about what his needs might be when he returned to the U.S., especially if his already-existing PTSD had worsened because of this tour of duty, which was not his first.

Rather than pester him with questions that he likely did not have time to answer about what his environment or the experience was like, I started reading voraciously all the first-person narratives coming back from Iraq and Afghanistan. I also found the work of Nate Fick, a Marine officer with an Ivy League background similar to his own, who had written the excellent *One Bullet Away: The Making of a Marine Officer* (Fick, 2005). Fick had also published articles in *The Boston Globe* and *The Christian Science Monitor,* detailing the troubles of homecoming for himself and his guys. Although many others were publishing first-person accounts of their service, he seemed like a good analog for the Marine officer in Iraq. They both had attended prestigious undergraduate programs, were going to or had graduated from Harvard for graduate school, and were in their late thirties. That meant to me that they likely had more (better, greater, deeper) resources than the men who served under them, and age and maturity were not the least of those.

Communicating daily, and sometimes several times a day, with the Marine officer in Iraq illustrated for me how challenging the experience was to endure. Sometimes I believed I could actually "see" him beginning to unravel before my eyes. Yes they were doing good work there, but they also were in constant danger—and from the descriptions of the bombings, the loss of comrades, the frightening situations they encountered regularly, I just began to wonder. If this older, more experienced, more seasoned and, frankly, better-resourced officer was having this difficult a time coping in real-time, how much worse would it be when he was back in the States, and how very much worse might it be for his guys, who would not have his level of resourcefulness or adaptability? These questions weighed on me. I worried that, to be a good friend, I needed to start thinking now of ways to alleviate his burden upon homecoming, and also to think of what would be useful to pass on to his men, as helpful with what were likely to be their symptoms.

From this initial introduction, I continued and expanded my reading of the first-person narratives until I had read almost all that were published at the time, including the only book of poetry to come out of the war, *Here, Bullet,* by Brian Turner (2005). Reading Jonathan Shay's work (Shay, 1994, 2002), I got turned on to several of the other authors whose work he praised, including Patience Mason (1990) and Aphrodite Matsakis, PhD (1988). Both wrote material that could be very helpful to the friends and family members of veterans suffering from PTSD. Shay had said on Amazon.com about his own work that if everyone read what they had written, he would have much less work to do. I began collecting and reading books about war trauma and PTSD, including those of Ray Scurfield (2004, 2006a, 2006b). I also chanced upon an excellent volume, now out of print, by Arthur Egendorf, *Healing from the War: Trauma and Transformation after Vietnam.* Egendorf was an Army intelligence operative in Vietnam who went on to obtain his PhD in psychology. It quickly became one of my all-time favorites. There is hardly a page in it not highlighted somewhere.

Before amassing a large collection of war trauma-related books, I began thinking constructively about what resources I had available, or tools with which I was familiar, which might be helpful in the treatment of PTSD, from my years of writing about natural medicine, also known as "integrative" or alternative medicine, though each term has a different meaning. I began to read everything there was to read and to converse with the experts I knew and would get to know—picking their brains for what they knew about, what they had tried, and what might work. In doing this, I was reproducing—even unconsciously—the method I had used years before to try to uncover the truth behind the opaque mystery of chronic fatigue syndrome (enough to recover from it personally). In the intervening years, experts I had interviewed and therapies I had learned about, or perhaps even experienced personally, all had the potential to become tools in the toolbox I was instinctively building for veterans and regarding PTSD. I also began searching the Web to determine what material was there: initially, so I could learn from it but, after I realized none was available, I found myself considering what I might also contribute.

The Importance of Conveying Hope and Empathy

Hope

It is difficult to communicate this strongly enough, but at the time I began searching for it on the Web, there was a complete absence of information online about combat-based PTSD. In light of how nebulous syndromes such as chronic fatigue and PTSD are often treated by the conventional medical community, I was concerned that stricken veterans and their families would also not be able to find any helpful information they might need; or, any constructive hope for their condition. The Bible states, "Without vision, the people perish." Another word for "vision" might be "inspiration" or hope. Hope seems central, not ancillary, to recovery. This is especially the case when suffering from an illness few acknowledge exists and fewer still understand.

Years ago, I had my own experience with this with chronic fatigue syndrome in the 1990s. I remember going through a multi-disciplinary program for its treatment, at the time the most cutting-edge program I could find. I had sought out conferences, experts, and medical journal articles in both the U.S. and England that would help me on my journey, and my New Year's resolution that year had been a vow to overcome the illness within the year. The multidisciplinary clinic belonged to a local expert I had pursued meeting: His protocol was the most highly touted in the scientific press at the time. Among the many things we tried during the program was a form of hypnosis. I distinctly remember returning to a state of conscious awareness after one hypnotherapy session, when the psychotherapist who led the session, an expert who had worked with nationally-ranked athletes, put his hand unexpectedly on my shoulder and said to me, "I know that you are going to recover from this."

At the time I was so surprised that he said this that I didn't even stop to question him about what he meant. Had he "seen" something in my hypnotized state of mind that prompted his encouragement? Ironically, I forgot his comment as rapidly as I had heard it. It did not make "sense" to my conscious mind, but he was implanting, even indirectly, a powerful suggestion that I would overcome my illness. When I eventually did recover, I remembered suddenly what he had said. And all I could presume was that, somewhere, his inquiry into my subconscious met with my very strong intention to *get* better. He must have known, somehow, that I had the full intention to recover, even if I was unaware of the methodology that would make this possible.

The irony of my situation was that, before I could get better, I first had to become whole lot worse. A reaction to a simple medication increase plunged me into immediate distress: lips and eyelids swelled uncontrollably, gigantic hives developed, along with breathing difficulties. I was making frequent trips to the emergency room, going on and off multiple courses of steroids, and generally perplexing my doctor, a specialist who shortly thereafter was said to give up the practice of medicine—but not before suggesting a series of ever more bizarre alternatives in an attempt to get my symptoms under control. It was a miserable year-and-a-half until the additional symptoms from the medication reaction finally receded, during which the series of specialists I saw did not do much more than scare me with increasingly frightening suggestions of what I really had, in addition to, or instead of, chronic fatigue syndrome (multiple sclerosis, lupus, sarcoidosis, etc.). Eventually, I did recover, but it was without reference to anything I learned—or sadly, any of the experts I consulted—during the worst phase of my health woes.

Empathy

While my intention to recover from illness might have been powerful, and the experts to whom I had access and their expertise were also impressive, it's true to say that the experience of getting much worse before I got any better was profoundly discouraging. At the time, it was extremely hard to believe that I would ever recover, or consequently to hold on to any hope that I would. Or maybe it's more accurate to say that hope was the only thing I had to hold on to, when actual progress seemed nonexistent for months at a time. This experience of struggling with illness powerfully created within me a form of sympathy—or better yet, empathy—for fellow sufferers. Combined with the personal exposure to the Marine officer in Iraq, it was hard not to get myself involved in the fight for veterans to achieve success with the symptoms of their equally baffling illness, PTSD.

Online Search

Before embarking on creating a website myself through which to offer information to veterans, I did a thorough investigation (in late 2005) about what material I could find that was published online for combat veterans with PTSD. I found that no one had undertaken this task. I repeated the search in different ways a few times over the next few weeks, wanting to assure myself that there was "no one else there first," so to speak. If I had found someone writing about it, and writing about it well—meaning, conveying good information and doing so in a helpful, understandable, way—I would have been pleased, gratified, and satisfied that the job would be under way without me, and that there would have been no need for me to also "jump in." There was plenty of material written offline, in books from the 1970s and 1980s in particular. But online there was nothing. So I decided to develop a website with the goal of offering information and hope to combat veterans diagnosed with PTSD, their loved ones, and family members.

What's in the Name, "Healing Combat Trauma?"

Choosing the name for a website is a critical task.[1] It had been my experience that *hope for recovery is actually paramount, sometimes even more important than any specific technique or information I could offer.* Without much ado, the name was chosen—"Healing Combat Trauma." Embedded in those words was the intention that the experience and the symptoms of PTSD could be overcome—hence the emphasis on the word "healing" in the name. The mechanics of "how" PTSD might be overcome, as I had learned in my own battle with chronic fatigue syndrome, might turn out to be secondary to the necessity of holding on to hope, when there seemed to be so little reason to have any. The choice of calling it "combat trauma," rather than the more commonly used PTSD, was also the result of a specific decision. On the one hand, this is somewhat of a misnomer. "Combat trauma" technically means bodily trauma, sometimes involving blood loss, stemming from combat and not necessarily from PTSD. However, it seemed clear from everything I had read that veterans, without being *traumatized* from or through their exposure to *combat*, would not be suffering the consequences of PTSD. Using those words specifically in the title seemed like a way to make the connection between war and distress most explicit. Trauma from combat causes veterans to suffer, and healing from this condition is of paramount concern to veterans and their families. And so the name and home page of my website were created, and evolved to the following.

Connecting with Counterparts and Developing a Website Identity

One of the major challenges of establishing a website is to determine to what extent the website is unique or distinctive, and to develop that "brand" over time. A few months after I created www.HealingCombatTrauma.com, a subsequent Google search turned up a website that was also being written about PTSD and soldiers by Ilona Meagher. Kathie Costos, "Nam Guardian Angel," was another friend of veterans who had written passionately and regularly about veterans' issues, and PTSD in particular, from her own experience of marriage to a Vietnam veteran. For a while, it seemed that the three of us, Meagher, Costos, and myself, dominated this topic online with similar concerns and voices, and I was concerned that we might accidentally duplicate each other's efforts or style. Over time, though, it seemed that our separate identities emerged, as our individual focuses continued to change and develop. I began to narrow my focus, moving away from my initial impulse to try to cover too much material just because no one else seemed active in the space, and moving towards material that I knew best, or could cover where perhaps no one else would. That meant more writing about natural medicine, also known as alternative medicine or integrative medicine. Consistent themes began to emerge in what I wrote about, such as catharsis, or the so-called "Tao of Healing"—how various people integrated their difficulties with the successes of healing over time. These themes came about from reading and reflection, as thinking about veterans and PTSD was now beginning to consume most of my waking hours, and much of my sleep as well.

The Word "Healing," and Connecting to the One—The Veteran with PTSD

In public speaking, you are often encouraged to think of—and speak to—an imaginary individual listener in the audience, rather than focusing on the larger mass of the assembled audience and perhaps losing your nerve or your focus. This allays fear and also helps to maintain a more conversational tone. I took the same concept into developing and writing for the website, directing it as if to an individual reader. I thought carefully about what a veteran suffering from combat-related PTSD might be struggling with, the actual emotions he or she might be experiencing because of this, and how discouraged or helpless this veteran's family members might also feel. (Here I had only to look back on my own difficult, though eventually successful, progress with chronic fatigue syndrome to empathize with their plight.) I also believed there was a need to educate peripheral people surrounding this veteran; perhaps community members whose lives overlapped, perhaps decision-makers who wondered how to treat veterans with PTSD, etc. The overall concept was to keep an actual person or people in mind, and speak to them directly—finding and conveying the material that I suspected they might not be aware existed or not be able to find, telling them what it was important to know about in their experience of the illness, and ideally, helping them to hold onto hope that they too could recover, or at the very least improve.

As it turns out, the word "healing" can be quite the litmus test as to whether or not a person even believes that a condition like PTSD can improve. Years after starting the website, and once there was a very strong presence for the site on social media (Facebook and Twitter), I often found myself defending the choice of that word. This was particularly so with any first-time visitor who just had to insist that it was not possible for him or her (usually a him) to improve or recover, because his or her healthcare provider had usually just told him so!

Eventually, that made me think very deliberately about how various words have definitions but, also, both connotative and denotative meanings. "Healing," "treating," and "curing" are all words we use when talking about the possibility of getting better. "Recovery" is also a great word, but that word has a strong association today with recovery from alcohol or substance abuse, so I tend to avoid using it. If "recovery" did not have those connotations or associations, it might have been the preferred word to use since, like "healing," it also implies a continuum of growth across which progress happens rather than a single event. But "healing" became the intentional word of choice, though it occasionally provokes frustration and even outright disbelief among some readers (typically those who do not see, or do not believe, that they are progressing yet or even at all in their own experience). Such unwanted, and often only temporary, backlash was also part of my rationale for closing off comments on the website from the beginning. I had taken pains to put all the valid information I could find on the website, being careful not to endorse any one alternative, but disseminating information about any approach that seemed to have validity.

How I chose what I considered valid approaches would take another chapter to discuss, but it drew heavily on my 10–15 years of experience in writing about natural medicine for publication, and the Rolodex/toolbox of experts, sources and therapies which I had built, which seemed to have benefit in treating the symptoms of post-traumatic stress. To this day, I read almost constantly within the field, attend conferences, talk to experts, and continue to manifest my lifetime aversion to "taking someone's word for it" when they're promoting a particular method or school of thought, unless they can support it with evidence and, ideally, embrace more than one alternative. Otherwise they appear to be, and often are, selling something. The concept of "integrative medicine"—the best of East and West—is my favored approach, because it takes the best of what is offered, from every discipline, in pursuit of the same goal: improving the patient's overall condition. Finally, journalists—I count myself as one—are trained to stay out of the story, to be neutral and impartial, and not to respond overly favorably to others' requests for promoting their particular product or service. This objectivity creates a sense of trustworthiness. Integrity is also paramount. I am not a practitioner, so I am not "selling" any particular product or service, nor do I make money from the website, which truly is a labor of love and altruism. All of these factors combine to indicate why readers might feel they could trust or be interested in what I have to say.

Breaking News

One of the many surprises of building and running the site was the ability to break news on it before the national media, or uncover relevant aspects of developing stories before other reporters did. As a journalist by nature and by training, being curious and digging behind the story are two qualities that never go away. I have never been fond of accepting the superficial read on a situation, and if something about the situation does not seem right, I do retain the investigative impulse to continue to research what is behind a story until my questions are answered.

This happened with two particular stories on separate occasions. One involved the suicide of Travis Twiggs, virtually the poster child among Marines for refreshing candor about his own struggles with PTSD. Travis was a five-combat tour Marine before he killed himself and his brother, Willard, in a murder-suicide near the Grand Canyon in Arizona. In the Twiggs case, long before his untimely end unfolded, I had sensed something was terribly wrong with the trajectory of his recovery, and reached out to him in concern. By following the developing story alertly, and putting the pieces of the puzzle together on my own, it meant that I knew he had died before his own wife had been informed. It also meant that I tried my best to humanize who Twiggs was for readers, when the media as a whole was reporting that he was "a career criminal, covered with tattoos" initially involved in a carjacking. (The carjacking part was accurate; the career criminal part was not.) Disappointingly, the national media just repeated the inaccurate information throughout the entire news cycle, pigeonholing him as someone most would not care about, instead of reporting on and highlighting the fact that he was a highly-decorated Marine with multiple tours of duty, who was struggling mightily with post-traumatic stress.

In a different news story, I uncovered the terrible truth about what a different Marine had suffered on his tour of duty in Iraq, prior to becoming a murder suspect in Texas. This was another case of scooping the national media about the true story behind a developing tragedy. In this case, the Marine Corps scrubbed the corroborating information I had dug out from their official website, a fact I later learned when a senior reporter from a Texas newspaper called me to check my sources (fortunately I had saved copies of the proof I'd found). In a third case involving a highly-decorated Marine who was now accused of attempted murder, and whose actions seemed clearly to stem from his burgeoning case of PTSD, I worked with a fellow reporter, out of our shared concern for him, to try to locate better legal counsel to represent him than his initial public defender, and to insure that the new attorney was familiar with the PTSD defense. (He was later acquitted.)

Getting Involved with Readers of the Website

One key strategic decision with the website quickly became how and to what extent to give "personal attention" to those individuals who contact me via the website. Over the years, various people have contacted me with requests for help, and I have been able to help them find resources for them near where they live, or have coordinated referrals to particular therapeutic resources or practitioners who might help them on their journeys toward recovery. Oftentimes, this might happen in person. Other times, it was at a distance, but my interventions might still manage to work. In one case, a Marine who I had known since he was injured in Iraq told me about a Marine buddy of his, another Iraq war veteran, who he was concerned was suicidal. He lived near where I did, relatively speaking—a few hours away. We connected on Facebook, and later talked on the phone, met for a home-cooked meal with him and his mother (I cooked, she didn't have to) and brought in some other people who could help with his issues, including the Injured Marine Semper Fi Fund. Contrary to his friend's initial impression, it might not have been that this Marine was technically "suicidal" so much as that he was experiencing the simultaneous collapse of everything in his life he deemed important at the time, which brought him to the brink of deep frustration and hopelessness. With the dual diagnosis of a traumatic brain injury and PTSD, he desperately needed help triaging his own problems. Months later, after successfully completing an excellent inpatient program I was able to recommend for him, and being able to resolve some of his medical, legal, and housing issues, his life appears to be successfully back on track. Without the social media connection and my Marine friend's concern for his combat buddy, it is hard to say if his friend would have made it—or been yet another casualty in the ongoing, frequently unsuccessful, "war" against suicide from PTSD.

Expanding into Social Media and the Interface with Facebook

The impact of the website grew over time, and the later advent of social media (Facebook and Twitter in particular) continued to expand its reach and effectiveness.

I joined Facebook more than five years ago, when it was still in its infancy. At first, I created just a personal profile on which, because of my never-ending interest in the topic of PTSD and veterans, I kept posting stories about veterans, PTSD, and treatment options. Then, when Facebook allowed for something called "fan pages" which were more suited to businesses and non-profit organizations, I created one for Healing Combat Trauma. Confusingly, there also was something called a "cause page" and, because "healing" combat trauma surely did appear to be a "cause" as well (and it certainly was my cause), I started one of my own. As sometimes happens in the online world, improvements are created and then later "drop off" as not sufficiently popular with enough users. This appeared to be the case with "causes" on Facebook. The "cause" page for Healing Combat Trauma has had well over 5,000 members for the past several years, but there is no real activity or engagement with the members on this particular page. The "fan" page, however, with more than 4,000 members, is a very engaged community, which waxes and wanes over time with respect to involvement, but whose numbers and impact continue to flourish. There's a certain amount of built-in redundancy to the process. You end up posting articles of interest on the fan page and then, if you have built the same sort of audience on your personal page, re-sharing material there, sometimes "branded" from the fan page of the website to the personal page. It also means that you are maintaining, simultaneously, a main website (www.Healing-CombatTrauma.com), a fan page for it on Facebook (www.Facebook.com/4PTSD), a cause page on Facebook, a personal page on Facebook where the fan page's material is often re-shared, and a Twitter account (@HealingPTSD) which, again, shares the same material. Whew. That's an awful lot of unpaid work for your obsession with the cause of your choosing. The main website, the fan page on Facebook, and the personal page on Facebook each have thousands of readers—but ironically they are not always the same individuals! Some people read the material on the website, and never venture into social media. Others become "fans" on social media, without ever journeying to the main, underlying, website. And some people become "fans" of your own personal focus on the topic, without (sadly) reading much more than the postings you make about it on social media—not delving into the substantial material on the website itself. It also means that I can write differently for the different venues, with an eye to how the readership is not always the same (though I had initially expected that it would be). When I started to really take ownership of the burgeoning fan page on Facebook, I started using it differently from how I write for the website. Every fan page on Facebook is handled differently by its creators, who are sometimes an individual, sometimes a team of people. As one of the first people to use fan pages on Facebook, I got to develop my process independently.

Initially, I just used Facebook to re-post the articles I'd written on the main website. Quickly, though, I started posting daily news articles on PTSD and veterans with the intent of generating discussion on the fan page, article by article. I post my own articles that I write for the website; the rest is articles I find that may be of interest to the fan page's readers, each introduced by me with a blurb about why they are important, a question to answer or a comment to initiate discussion. Readers of the fan page (there are almost 5,000) are drawn from a mix of combat veterans with PTSD, healthcare practitioners, family members of veterans, students who follow the topic, and interested others. This diverse mix can make for interesting discussions, and occasionally, also, conflict.

If the material I am introducing seems really meaty—given people's short attention spans, or my desire to dig into the material more deeply and integrate it with other thoughts or references—I hold off posting it and work it into an original article on the main website, which I can then post to the Facebook page. That way, it can stimulate discussion on the Facebook page, within that community, but it can also function as a fairly finished piece of work on the website. So, as I read through PTSD and veterans' news regularly, I can "pick" which venue is really best for the material, and share it accordingly. I try to post at least one relevant news item daily on the fan page, stimulating discussion, and write (at this point) fewer long pieces for the website, which I share on Facebook after they are published. A few years ago, I was concentrating more on the website, writing for that almost daily—and, sometimes, several times a day.

Creating Dialogue with Facebook Participants

Another key decision is the extent to which the website will engage participants in online interactions. When I started interacting with my own "fan page" for the Healing Combat Trauma site on Facebook, I was willing to engage in conversation with the participants and enjoy the back-and-forth discussions about the material. I wanted people to feel like they could engage in a specific, topical, discussion, but I also wanted them to come prepared by actually reading the material first. It is surprising how few people do that: many jump in to react just to the headline and never bother to actually read the article's content. You want people to feel free to say anything responsible about the material, but also to gently guide them back on track to the topic, in case they get too far afield.

It is important for discussion participants online to be able to "converse" with one another civilly and not resort to name-calling or degenerate into a political or religious discussion, which would generally be considered completely off-track. As a site administrator I want the site's participants to feel "at home," and be able to contribute freely, but I'm aware that the contribution or tone of a comment made by one individual may affect or inhibit the next contributor's ability or even willingness to join the discussion. Consequently, it's important than any one person not be allowed to dominate the discussion, or for the discussion as a whole to degenerate into inanity.

In order to do this, *you* are going to have to step in every time and guide the process, unless you are lucky enough to have a reliable and trustworthy volunteer to assist. The amount of time, effort, wisdom, objectivity and even restraint this actually requires is enormous. And all of it, of course, is unpaid; and you are finding the time for this around your real interests which might be, as they are in my case, learning more about the therapies, interviewing experts to see how valid the ideas were, and then writing about them in a way that can communicate the information to an audience that frequently might lack a significant attention span. There were times when I felt as though all I were doing was somehow related to Healing Combat Trauma.

In retrospect, what I was doing with Healing Combat Trauma on Facebook—engaging the participants in discussion about the topics at hand—is really what set the resource apart from what others were doing. I believe that I might have been the first to try this within the PTSD community. Quite a few people later commented that I was transforming the use of social media. One thing is certain: it just seemed like the need was there, and I felt drawn to making a strong attempt to engage participants.

The Challenge of Moderating the Forum on Facebook

Oddly, over time it became apparent that some of the people participating on the Facebook site were not even readers of the website, though readership of the website grew and grew. They were Facebook-centric participants who engaged on Facebook and enjoyed the camaraderie, but did not necessarily realize or care that the other, more substantial site, existed. And then there were the troublemakers who were not even interested in the healing concept at all, but had been diagnosed with PTSD and had apparently been ignored elsewhere. They came and spoke their piece vehemently to anyone who would listen.

As I worked with this new concept—essentially, how to moderate the forum on Facebook by myself—I learned a few things. One was to cut argumentative people off at the very beginning. If my sense was that they came to lash out and not to learn, it was unlikely that they were going to do anything but confirm my suspicions later. The other rule of thumb was not to allow someone to dominate the conversation who was strident and argumentative, but not part of the targeted demographic of the site— combat veterans with PTSD, usually male, who were currently being failed by the conventional system, or who at least wanted to learn more about the subject matter. If this were allowed, the intended subjects of the site (the veterans) would tune out and turn off, and their participation would ultimately be lost. Until I learned to become more decisive and trust my instincts with how people were participating, it seemed that some people took advantage of the "forum" concept by just showing up to vent about their problems, in lieu of actually seeking therapy. Their conversations were not dialogues, they were monologues, and their anger was palpable and real. They often would later admit they were there because they were between therapists or could no longer afford therapy. They might be drawn to the site's name, which mentions healing prominently—and the site is easy to find because of its popularity. But when online on the Healing Combat Trauma Facebook site, they tend to dominate the conversation, which drives others away. It is an obvious limitation of the medium, too. I am not a trained therapist; even if I were, I highly doubt that online would be the place to offer therapy. What I can do is offer impartial information to interested parties, and develop some rapport with the participants, creating a sense of community. The experience can be wonderful, but it also has its limits. It is informed compassion, but it is not therapy, nor is it ever really a substitute for therapy.

You Are on Your Own

While on the CompuServe Natural Medicine forum, back in the day, there were a few of us Systems Operators, or "Sysops" as we were called, who could moderate the discussions online. Each of us had our own area of expertise or interest; mine, not surprisingly, was chronic fatigue syndrome. I was versed in the resources and the experts and the general experience of being unwell, as well as the process I undertook to recover. While I managed the discussion board myself, there was much support from, or at least camaraderie and mutual education with, the other natural medicine discussion board leaders. The premise is the same with some volunteer organizations that support the troops, such as the excellent Books for Soldiers (www.BooksforSoldiers.com), for which I served as a volunteer in 2006 and beyond. The more experienced volunteers, who often had wonderful hearts and wisdom to share, served as unofficial mentors until those new to it learned the ropes. Sadly, on Facebook there was none of this, and no one else to rely on; hence, the necessity of learning this all on my own. Oftentimes, I wished for someone else to share the workload with, but the reality is that when you design something yourself (in this case, the original website and its intention), it's hard to find someone else who shares your exact vision and tone. It is also vital to insure that the other person's belief system and interpersonal approach are compatible. I am open to anything reasonable that looks like it might help with PTSD, so to have someone promoting their favorite discovery/therapy/brand of experience to the neglect of anything else would not work for the site.

Embracing "Everything that Works"

In the healthcare world, it certainly seems that people can be huge proponents of their own specialty area in which they are credentialed or trained. While their enthusiasm might even be warranted, an informational site like Healing Combat Trauma really is meant to embrace "everything that works," not just one person's specific background or training. So, while a yoga devotee might absolutely love yoga, and yoga might, in fact, help veterans with their experience of PTSD, so do *many* other therapies. One may not want a yoga practitioner, for example, to promote yoga continually to the exclusion of mentioning anything else that might be of help to the PTSD sufferer. What I really needed, and basically never found, was someone with a broad-minded outlook or training who was willing to consider anything that worked and not remain fixed on and consequently limited by their own area of interest or expertise. I also needed one, or even several people, who could combine this training with an ability to keep a suitable discussion going and help to nudge people back on track when they became diverted and distracted, or argumentative. Many would offer, but basically nothing ever panned out. I did, and still do, all of the work myself—not that I am suggesting this as the best alternative. It happens to be the only one that has turned out to be doable so far.

The Dynamics and Challenges of Facebook and the Absence of "Vetting" the "Experts" Own Mental Health

One of Facebook's built-in limitations, when it comes to things like "fan pages" and the communities that grow up around them, is that there is absolutely no vetting possible of actual content: whether the information is reasonable or not; who is behind the individual fan pages; and whether, if you knew the individuals, you could actually trust their expertise. Several authors of PTSD-related websites produced after mine were veterans themselves, working through their own pain and experiences, and were people I came to know over the years. To one degree or another, I encouraged their progress, although sometimes I also worried about the status of their mental health, especially when it seemed that they were experiencing significant setbacks. Several of these veterans, who I will not identify to protect their privacy, seemed to fluctuate regularly between the two poles of (mental) health and illness, promoting the one when they seemed to have it, and concernedly disappearing from view when they didn't. When they were "up" they were really "up," but when they were "down," they were truly down and out—or down for the count. My concern was that the average (veteran) reader, who might not have spent much time following their trajectory over time, might become very concerned to see this previously-considered expert now obviously flailing in public. We all have our bad and good days as human beings, but there are reasonable limits. As I watched the outward signs of several of these veterans' mental health wax and wane from month to month, I noticed that when they seemed to have their symptoms under control they were vocal fans of whatever treatment they were receiving, and they were fairly assertive or even aggressive about other people's need to try the therapies they embraced. Their apparent good mental health would go on for a few weeks or months, and then, suddenly, they might disappear from public view when they had hit their own personal wall. Often it would turn out that they had been hospitalized for suicidal ideation, and they would be gone from the Internet for weeks or months, causing many of their "followers" to wonder where they'd gone or how they were doing. Maybe they were going through intensive marital or employment woes, brought on in part by their own experience of PTSD, but without the perspective, yet, to comment on those setbacks in a manner that would help to bring healing to themselves or others. Or maybe they were back online, but spouting troubling thoughts and comments that could worry the interested bystander. (I once received a suicide note by text message from a noted veterans' advocate with a large public profile, who avoided therapy herself while advocating for others.) Quite a few times I've had the opportunity to wonder whether and how I should attempt to intervene, and this can be very distressing. I would imagine it is even more distressing to someone watching it (e.g., a fellow veteran) who has less perspective on the leader's ups and downs, and who is battling with their own, similar symptoms and getting discouraged by what he or she sees. What I want to see is not people being "fake," and pretending not to have problems; but there's a real (if unspoken) limit on how truthful it's constructive for a sufferer to be with his or her reading public, rather than with a trained therapist. Sadly, there really is no built-in system of checks and balances in place to help the casual reader get or keep perspective on the mental health of the opinion leaders in this space. It is really a case of "consumer beware," even when the "product" is the information conveyed by opinion leaders of veterans' forums online.

I readily acknowledge that a number of us are drawn to write about or work with trauma because we have some personal experience with, or understanding of, trauma to which we would like to give voice. That is acceptable, and maybe even a good idea; it can be a form of catharsis. But this needs to be balanced against the harm that can be done when a website or forum goes "dark" because the leader is struggling personally.

Certainly, life and the desire to help others is not without its attendant pain and confusion, but maybe it is better to wait until you are yourself personally less raw emotionally before attempting to offer help to other (equally raw) sufferers. On the other hand, maybe that is unlikely. Perhaps it is the very rawness of the battle that draws people into wanting to make a serious contribution, after all.

A Victory Story

Social media, though, can also be a true force for "good." Here is a story that highlights its richness, complexity and immediacy.

We roll back time to July 4, 2010, on the Healing Combat Trauma site on Facebook. Independence Day is a notoriously difficult day for combat veterans with PTSD. After combat, few enjoy being around fireworks, which frequently trigger their startle reflex and make them very unhappy and unable to enjoy the celebration with the rest of their families and friends. As July 4th approached, I was trying to think of ways to "keep the conversation going" on the Healing Combat Trauma site on Facebook: engaging the veterans with one another on the site, and hoping to keep their minds off the challenges of a night devoted to explosions.

A colleague who has some experience herself with PTSD, though not from combat, came forward—and together we came up with a writing exercise for the veterans to undertake. It was to write a simple haiku (rhyme scheme 5, 7, 5) on the topic of "fireworks." While, in typical fashion, many people could not follow directions and wrote interesting poems not at all in the haiku mode, those who disciplined themselves to produce the haiku verse came up with some pretty remarkable things. My colleague republished the best with the veterans' permission in a wider context on the Web, including in the *Huffington Post* and even an online literary journal. The veterans involved in having their verse published experienced a boost in self-esteem.

Also, as always with experiences on the Web, in addition to those who participate, there are others "lurking" who view, but do not offer, contributions to the conversation. It is their opinions that will never be known unless they come forward to offer something about their experiences some time later. That was the case with one older veteran, who had become a mind–body medicine practitioner, eager to help other combat veterans with their struggles such as PTSD. I had a side conversation with him by email and I asked him if he was a Vietnam veteran, which I suspected he might be, given his age. He said that he was, and then offered an amazing tidbit: that, until he observed the give-and-take on the site on July 4th with the veterans composing haikus about fireworks, he had never realized that he, too, suffered from PTSD. He only realized it when he understood that the symptoms he was experiencing were the same as those of other veterans who were discussing their reactions publicly! For someone 40 years removed from combat, and who had been intently trying to serve his fellow veterans for decades in the latter part of his life, it was remarkable to me that he had not noticed that until this very time. What a fortuitous experience this was, probably shared by other veterans at different times on the site, as well. Experiences like these truly reveal the "power of community." Not only did the evening's experience succeed in distracting the veterans, possibly even keeping some from self-harm, it also bonded those who shared their experiences that night, lifted the self-esteem of a few who were published because of it, and caused at least one older veteran to realize how deep his bond with other sufferers really was, since he was also one of them.

Building Rapport Among Practitioners: Creating a Community

Another important and unexpected aspect of the site has been the rapport developed among practitioners, and the support network it has inadvertently created. While the focus of the main website was initially combat veterans with PTSD and their families and loved ones, it has become clear that many who follow the Facebook site are practitioners who work with veterans. Practitioners may have lives only slightly less lonely or stressed than some of the veterans and their families, because PTSD is a condition that absolutely takes its toll on patient and practitioner alike. Some practitioners are suffering from—or soon will develop—compassion fatigue, burnout, or vicarious trauma. The social support offered on the site—in addition to the postings of relevant information and articles— lets practitioners feel they have a community of people who understand their work and what they go through. Since social support is the number one preventive for developing PTSD, it is refreshing to find that even on the Internet we are able to create a community that helps offset the rigors and loneliness of practitioners' professional lives.

Getting and Tracking Positive Feedback

There were many surprises or "firsts" from creating the site, including the surge of positive feedback received. As a writer (journalist) it is rare—or it was rare, before the Internet—to ever hear how someone liked what you wrote, or how it improved their life for the better. And frankly, most journalism does not improve people's lives for the better; it presents them with fairly unbiased information, ideally, so that they can make better decisions for themselves based on that information. Perhaps that is why I rarely heard what someone thought of something I wrote. With the site, and then later with what amounted to the "expansion" of the site through Facebook, I started having more of a personal connection with its readers and wound up receiving quite a few nice compliments.

A colleague who works as a personal coach told me years ago that it was important to keep track of the nice things people said—she suggested tracking such comments in a book or journal—so that, if you were ever discouraged, you could take out the book, read the comments, and realize how many nice things people had said to and about you over time. I liked her advice, but never really implemented it until after I had started the site on Facebook. Then I started making "screen captures" of the comments, and saving them in a file on my desktop called "Nice Words from People." Surprisingly, it was not long before that file numbered in the hundreds—a truly unexpected treat. People must feel the connection there or, at the very least, the intention behind the site, made real. Good stuff, and one of the few paybacks from an otherwise completely altruistic, volunteer endeavor.

Closing

All in all, it has been a tremendous learning experience, a clear case of following one's intention and "passion" for a topic. HealingCombatTrauma.com has been able to expand in influence, reach, and impact far beyond anything I anticipated when creating it. What Thich Nhat Hanh, quoted by Claude Anshin Thomas in his book

At Hell's Gate: A Veteran's Journey from War to Peace (2004), said is quite true: "Veterans can be a powerful force for healing in the world." And when we help veterans access healing, we become part of that experience as well.

Note

1 I joke that deciding on the title for my book on chronic fatigue, fibromyalgia, and natural medicine took almost as much time as writing it. I finally settled on *Gentle Medicine* (Casura, 2000) as an appropriate title to highlight the more subtle approaches from the world of natural medicine. I was often sorely tempted to instead title it *Getting Over It*, since this seemed to be the most pointed "call to action" sufferers needed, at the time I was writing the book.

References

Casura, L. (2000). *Gentle Medicine: Treating Chronic Fatigue and Fibromyalgia Successfully with Natural Medicine.* Seattle, WA: Self Health Press.

Egendorf, A. (1986). *Healing from the War: Trauma and Transformation after Vietnam.* Boston, MA: Shambhala Press.

Fick, N. (2005). *One Bullet Away: The Making of a Marine Officer.* Boston, MA: Houghton Mifflin Harcourt.

Fick, N. (2005, August 28). "Coming Home to What?" *The Boston Globe.* Available at: http://www. boston.com/news/globe/editorial_opinion/oped/articles/2005/08/28/coming_home____to_ what/ and http://www.healingcombattrauma.com/2006/02/great_article_b.html.

Mason, P. (1990). *Recovering from the War: A Guide for All Veterans, Family Members, Friends and Therapists.* High Springs, FL: Patience Press.

Matsakis, A. (1988). *Vietnam Wives: Women and Children Surviving Life with Veterans Suffering Post-Traumatic Stress Disorder.* Bethesda, MD: Woodbine House.

Scurfield, R. M. (2004). *A Vietnam Trilogy: Veterans and Post Traumatic Stress 1968, 1989, 2000.* New York, NY: Algora Publishing.

Scurfield, R. M. (2006a). *War Trauma: Lessons Unlearned, From Vietnam to Iraq* (HC) (Volume 3 of *A Vietnam Trilogy*). New York, NY: Algora Publishing.

Scurfield, R. M. (2006b). *Healing Journeys: Study Abroad With Vietnam Veterans* (Volume 2 of *A Vietnam Trilogy*). New York, NY: Algora Publishing.

Shay, J. (1994). *Achilles in Vietnam: Combat Trauma and the Undoing of Character.* New York, NY: Scribner.

Shay, J. (2002) *Odysseus in America: Combat Trauma and the Trials of Homecoming.* New York, NY: Scribner.

Thomas, C. A. (2004). *At Hell's Gate: A Veteran's Journey from War to Peace.* Boston, MA: Shambhala Press.

Turner, B. (2005). *Here, Bullet.* Farmington, ME: Alice James Books.

Further Reading

Fick, N. (2005, August 28). "Coming Home . . . to What?" http://www.powells.com/essays/fick. html.

Fick, N. (Undated). "The Making of a Marine Officer." http://www.powells.com/essays/fick. html.

Herman, J. (1992). *Trauma and Recovery: The Aftermath of Violence, from Domestic Abuse to Political Terror.* New York, NY: Basic Books.

Nicosia, G. (2001) *Home to War: A History of the Vietnam Veterans' Movement.* New York, NY: Three Rivers Press.

16 SimCoach

An Online Intelligent Virtual Human Agent System for Breaking Down Barriers to Care for Service Members and Veterans

Albert (Skip) Rizzo, Eric Forbell, Belinda Lange,
J. Galen Buckwalter, Josh Williams, Kenji Sagae,
and David Traum

Introduction

Over the last 15 years, virtual reality (VR) has emerged as an innovative tool for addressing numerous issues in clinical research, assessment, and intervention. Technological advances in the areas of computation speed and power, graphics and image rendering, display systems, tracking, interface technology, haptic devices, authoring software, and artificial intelligence have supported the creation of low-cost and usable PC-based Virtual Reality (VR) systems. At the same time, an expanding group of researchers and clinicians have not only recognized the potential impact of VR technology, but have now generated a significant research literature that documents the many clinical targets where VR can add value over traditional assessment and intervention approaches (Bohil, Alicea, & Biocca, 2011; Holden, 2005; Parsons & Rizzo, 2008; Powers & Emmelkamp, 2008; Rizzo, et al., 2011; Riva, 2011; Rose, Brooks, & Rizzo, 2005). This convergence of the exponential advances in underlying VR-enabling technologies with a growing body of clinical research and experience has fueled the evolution of the discipline of Clinical Virtual Reality. This state of affairs now stands to transform the vision of future clinical practice and research in the disciplines of psychology, medicine, neuroscience, physical and occupational therapy, and in the many allied health fields that address the therapeutic needs of those with clinical disorders.

These shifts in the social and scientific landscape have set the stage for the next major movement in Clinical VR. With advances in the enabling technologies allowing for the design of ever more believable context-relevant "structural" VR environments (e.g. homes, classrooms, offices, markets, etc.), the next important challenge will involve *populating* these environments with Virtual Human (VH) representations that are capable of fostering believable interaction with *real* VR users.

This is not to say that representations of human forms have not usefully appeared in Clinical VR scenarios. In fact, since the mid-1990s, VR applications have routinely employed VHs as stimulus elements to enhance the realism of a virtual world simply by their static presence. For example, VR exposure therapy applications have targeted simple phobias, such as fear of public speaking and social phobia, using virtual contexts inhabited by "still-life" graphics-based characters or 2D photographic sprites (Anderson, et al., 2005; Pertaub, Slater, & Barker, 2002; Klinger, 2005). By simply adjusting the number and location of these VH representations, the intensity of these anxiety-provoking VR contexts could be systematically manipulated with the aim of gradually habituating phobic patients and improve their functioning in the real world. Other clinical applications have also used animated graphic VHs as stimulus entities to support and train social and safety skills in persons with high functioning autism (Rutten, et al., 2003; Padgett, Strickland, & Coles, 2006) and as distracter stimuli for attention assessments conducted in a virtual classroom (Rizzo, et al., 2006). Also, VHs have been used effectively to conduct social psychology experiments, essentially replicating and extending findings from studies with real humans on social influence, conformity, racial bias, and social proxemics (Blascovich, et al., 2002; Bailenson & Beall, 2006; McCall, et al., 2009).

In an effort to further increase the pictoral realism of such VHs, Virtually Better, Inc. began incorporating whole video clips of crowds into graphic VR "fear of public speaking" scenarios. They later advanced the technique by inserting bluescreen-captured video sprites of individual humans into graphics-based VR social settings, when creating social phobia, public speaking, and cue exposure substance abuse treatment and research applications (Virtually Better, Inc., 2011). The sprites were drawn from a large library of bluescreen captured videos of actors behaving or speaking with varying degrees of provocation. These video sprites could then be strategically inserted into the scenario with the aim to modulate the emotional state of the patient by fostering encounters with these 2D video VH representations.

However, working with such fixed video content to foster this form of faux interaction or exposure has significant limitations. For example, it requires the capture of a large catalog of possible verbal and behavioral clips that can be tactically presented to the user to meet the requirements of a given therapeutic approach. Also, this fixed content cannot be readily updated in a dynamic fashion to meet the challenge of creating credible real time interactions between VHs and live users, with the exception of only very constrained social interactions. This process can only work for clinical applications in which the only requirement is for the VH character to deliver an open-ended statement or question to which the user can react, but is lacking in any truly fluid and believable interchange following a response by the user. Consequently, the absence of dynamic interaction with these virtual representations, without a live person behind the "screen" actuating new clips in response the user's behavior, is a significant limiting factor for this approach. This has led some researchers to consider the use of artificially intelligent VH agents as entities for simulating human-to-human interaction in virtual worlds.

Intelligent Virtual Human Agents

Clinical interest in artificially intelligent agents designed for interaction with humans can trace its roots to the work of MIT AI researcher Joe Weizenbaum. In 1966, he wrote a language analysis program called ELIZA, which was designed to imitate a Rogerian therapist. The system allowed a computer user to interact with a virtual therapist by typing simple sentence responses to the computerized therapist's questions. Weizenbaum reasoned that simulating a non-directional psychotherapist was one of the easiest ways of simulating human verbal interactions, and it was a compelling simulation that worked well on teletype computers (and is even instantiated on the internet today: see http://www-ai.ijs.si/eliza-cgi-bin/eliza_script). In spite of the fact that the illusion of ELIZA's intelligence soon disappears, due to its inability to handle complexity or nuance, Weizenbaum was reportedly shocked upon learning how seriously people took the ELIZA program. This led him to conclude that it would be immoral to substitute a computer for human functions that involves "interpersonal respect, understanding, and love" (Weizenbaum, 1976).

More recently, seminal research and development has appeared in the creation of highly interactive, artificially intelligent (AI) and natural language-capable VH agents. No longer at the level of a prop to add context or minimal faux interaction in a virtual world, these VH agents are designed to perceive and act in a 3D virtual world, engage in face-to-face spoken dialogues with real users (and other VHs) and, in some cases, they are capable of exhibiting human-like emotional reactions.

Previous classic work on VHs in the computer graphics community focused on perception and action in 3D worlds, but largely ignored dialogue and emotions. This has now changed. Artificially intelligent VH agents can now be created that control computer-generated bodies and can interact with users through speech and gesture in virtual environments (Gratch, et al., 2002). Advanced VHs can engage in rich conversations (Traum, et al., 2008), recognize nonverbal cues (Morency, deKok, & Gratch, 2008), reason about social and emotional factors (Gratch & Marsella, 2004) and synthesize human communication and nonverbal expressions (Thiebaux, et al., 2008). Such fully embodied conversational characters have been around since the early 90s (Bickmore & Cassell, 2005), and there has been much work on full systems to be used for training (Kenny, et al., 2007a; Rickel, et al., 2001), intelligent kiosks (McCauley & D'Mello, 2006), virtual receptionists (Babu, et al., 2006), and virtual patients for clinical training (Kenny, et al., 2007b; Lok, et al., 2007; Rizzo, et al., forthcoming). Both in appearance and behavior, VHs have now evolved to the point where they are usable tools for a variety of clinical and research applications.

What follows next is an overview of the SimCoach project that aims to develop VH support agents to serve as online guides for promoting access to psychological healthcare information, and for assisting military personnel and family members in breaking down barriers to initiating the healthcare process. While we believe that the use of VHs to serve the role of virtual therapists is still fraught with both technical and ethical concerns, the SimCoach project does not aim to become a "doc in box." Rather, the SimCoach experience is being designed to attract and engage military service members (SMs), veterans, and their significant others, who might not otherwise seek help. The anonymous online interaction with a SimCoach aims to create an experience that will motivate users to take the first step to seek information and advice with regard to their healthcare (e.g., psychological health, traumatic brain injury, addiction, etc.) and general personal welfare (i.e., other non-medical stressors, such as economic or relationship issues). The SimCoach experience also aims to encourage, empower, and support anonymous users to take the next step towards seeking more formal resources with a live provider, when the need is determined.

Challenges for Breaking Down Barriers to Care

Research suggests that there is an urgent need to reduce the stigma of seeking mental health treatment in SM and veteran populations. One of the more foreboding findings, in an early report by Hoge, et al. (2004) was the observation that, among Iraq/Afghanistan War veterans,

> [of] those whose responses were positive for a mental disorder, only 23 to 40 percent sought mental healthcare. Those whose responses were positive for a mental disorder were twice as likely as those whose responses were negative to report concern about possible stigmatization and other barriers to seeking mental healthcare.
>
> (p. 13)

While U.S. military training methodology has better prepared soldiers for combat in recent years, such hesitancy to seek treatment for difficulties that emerge upon return from combat, especially by those who may need it most, suggests an area of military mental healthcare that is in need of attention.

Moreover, the dissemination of healthcare information to military SMs, veterans, and their significant others is a persistent and growing challenge. In spite of a Herculean effort on the part of the U.S. Department of Defense (DOD) and Veterans Affairs (VA) to produce and disseminate behavioral health programs for military personnel and their families, the complexity of the issues involved continue to challenge the best efforts of military mental healthcare experts, administrators, and providers. Since 2004, numerous blue ribbon panels of experts have attempted to assess the current DOD and VA healthcare delivery systems and provide recommendations for improvement (e.g., DOD Mental Health Task Force (DOD, 2007), National Academies of Science Institute of Medicine (National Academies, 2007), Dole-Shalala Commission Report (Dole-Shalala, 2007), the Rand Report (Tanielian, et al., 2008), and the American Psychological Association (APA, 2007)). Most of these reports cite two major areas in need of improvement: 1) support for randomized controlled trials that test the efficacy of treatment methodologies, leading to wider dissemination of evidence-based approaches; and 2) the identification and implementation of ways to enhance the healthcare dissemination/delivery system for military personnel and their families, in a fashion that provides better awareness and access to care while reducing the stigma of help-seeking.

For example, the American Psychological Association Presidential Task Force on Military Deployment Services for Youth, Families and Service Members (APA, 2007), which presented its preliminary report in February 2007, poignantly stated that it was "not able to find any evidence of a well coordinated or well disseminated approach to providing behavioral healthcare to service members and their families." The APA report also went on to describe three primary barriers to military mental health treatment: *availability, acceptability, and accessibility*. More specifically:

1   Well-trained mental health specialists are not in adequate supply (*availability*).
2   The military culture needs to be modified, such that mental health services are more *accepted* and less stigmatized.
3   Even if providers were available, and seeking treatment was deemed acceptable, appropriate mental health services are often not readily *accessible* due to a variety of factors (e.g., long waiting lists, limited clinic hours, a poor referral process, and/or geographical location).

The overarching goal reported from this and other reports is to provide better awareness, availability, and access to existing care, while concurrently reducing the complexity
and stigma of seeking psychological help. In essence, new methods are needed to reduce
such barriers to care.

The SimCoach Project

Advances in technology, combined with the urgency of the OEF/OIF conflicts, have fueled
the creation of new military-focused clinical assessment and treatment approaches, from
computerized prosthetic limbs to Clinical Virtual Reality applications for PTSD treatment
(Rizzo, et al., 2011). However, improvements in the DOD/VA healthcare dissemination/
delivery system are required to take full advantage of these evolving intervention methodologies, as well as for promoting standard proven intervention options. In response to the
clinical healthcare challenges that the OEF/OIF conflicts have placed on the burgeoning
population of SMs, veterans, and their families, the U.S. Defense Centers of Excellence
for Psychological Health and Traumatic Brain Injury (DCoE) funded the University of
Southern California Institute for Creative Technologies to develop an intelligent, interactive, online VH healthcare guide program, currently referred to as SimCoach. The DCoE's
primary mission is to assess, validate, oversee, and facilitate sharing of critical information
relative to the areas of injury prevention, resilience, identification, treatment, outreach,
rehabilitation, and reintegration programs, for psychological health and traumatic brain
injury. In line with this mission, the SimCoach project is DCoE's first effort to support the
development of an online embodied VH presence to serve as a guide for assisting SMs,
vets, and their significant others in their efforts to seek behavioral health information,
advice, and actual care, if needed, with a clinical provider.

Rather than being a traditional web portal, SimCoach allow users to initiate and
engage in a dialog about their healthcare concerns with an interactive VH. Generally,
these intelligent graphical characters are being designed to use speech, gesture, and emotion to introduce the capabilities of the system, solicit basic anonymous background
information about the user's history and clinical/psychosocial concerns, provide advice
and support, direct the user to relevant online content, and potentially facilitate the
process of seeking appropriate care with a live clinical provider.

It is not the goal of SimCoach to breakdown all of the barriers to care or to provide
diagnostic or therapeutic services that are best delivered by a real clinical provider. Rather,
SimCoach will foster comfort and confidence by promoting users' private and anonymous
efforts to understand their situations better, and to explore available options and initiate
treatment when appropriate. Coordinating this experience is a VH SimCoach, selected by
the user from a variety of archetypical character options (see Figure 16.1), who will answer

Figure 16.1 SimCoach archetypes: male/female civilian and service member characters.

direct questions and/or guide the user through a sequence of user-specific questions, exercises, and assessments. This interaction between the VH and the user will provide the program with the information needed to guide users to the appropriate next step of engagement with the system, or to initiate contact with a live provider. Again, the SimCoach project is not conceived to deliver a diagnosis or treatment, or serve as a replacement for human providers and experts. Instead, SimCoach will aim to start the process of engaging the user, by providing support and encouragement, increasing awareness of their situation and treatment options, and in assisting individuals who may, otherwise, initially be uncomfortable talking to a "live" care provider, in their efforts to initiate care.

Users can flexibly interact with this character by typing text, clicking on character-generated menu options, and they can have some limited natural language speech interaction during the later phases of development. The feasibility of providing the option for full spoken natural language dialog interaction on the part of the user will be explored in the later stages of the project. Since this is designed to be an easily accessible web-based system, that will require no downloadable software, it was felt that voice recognition was not at a state where it could be reliably used at the current time. The options for a SimCoach's appearance, behavior, and dialog have been designed to maximize user comfort and satisfaction, but also to facilitate fluid and truthful disclosure of medically relevant information. Focus groups and "Wizard of Oz" user studies are currently in progress in order to prepare the SimCoach interaction system for a wide range of potential dialog.

Based on the issues delineated in the initial interview, the user will be given access to a variety of general relevant information on psychology, neurology, rehabilitation, the military healthcare system, and also to other SMs and veterans by way of recommendations for a variety of social networking tools (e.g., Second Life, Facebook, Grunt.com, etc.). The SimCoach system also draws in relevant content, from established DOD and VA websites, that has been specifically designed to address the needs of this user group (e.g., Afterdeployment, Military OneSource, National Center for PTSD, etc.). As the system evolves, the user will be able to progress at their own pace over as many days, or even weeks, as they feel comfortable, as the SimCoach will be capable of "remembering" the information acquired from previous visits and building on that information in a similar fashion to that of a growing human relationship. However, the persistence of the SimCoach's memory for previous sessions will require the user to sign into the system with a user name and password, but that is optional for initial use of the system. This will require the SimCoach system to "reside" on a high security server system. This is currently being addressed for the future implementation of SimCoach.

Interspersed within the program is the option of allowing the user to perform some simple neurocognitive and psychological testing to inform the SimCoach's creation of a model of the user; the purpose of this is to enhance the reliability and accuracy of the SimCoach output to the user, and, thereby, to support user self-awareness and better guide the delivery of initial referral options. Users will also have the option to print out a PDF summary of the computerized session. This is important for later personal review; for access to those links to relevant web content that the SimCoach provided in the session; or to enable users to bring information with them when seeking clinical care (this would potentially enhance users' comfort levels, as they would feel armed with knowledge when dealing with experts). We are also creating software-authoring tools that will allow other clinical professionals to create SimCoach content to enhance the likelihood that the program will evolve based on other care perspectives and emerging needs in the future.

SimCoach Use: A Case Example

The following is an example of how SimCoach will interact with a potential user.

Maria was the 23-year-old wife of Juan, an OIF Veteran who had completed two deployments before leaving the service. After his return, she noticed something different. He had become distant, never discussed his experiences in Iraq, and, when asked, he would answer, "that was then, this is now, case closed." He also wasn't particularly involved with their two children (the youngest one was born while he was in Iraq), only playing with their oldest boy after hours of begging. For the most part, Juan stayed home, and had yet to begin to look for a civilian job. He didn't sleep much and, when he did manage to fall asleep, he would often wake up after an hour, highly agitated and claiming that he heard someone trying to get into the bedroom window. When this happened, he would sometimes sit till dawn, peering through slits in the closed blinds, watching and waiting for the "intruder" to return. He seemed jumpy when not drinking and watching TV. He drank heavily during the day and, when she got home from her job after picking the kids up from her mother's house, Maria would often find Juan asleep or passed out on the couch. She told her mother that it felt like she was living with a ghost, but that she still loved him. She just wanted the "old Juan" back. However, each day things got worse, until Maria felt that she couldn't live like this much more. She felt guilty for the increasing resentment that she felt, but didn't know how (or was afraid) to talk to Juan about what she was feeling. Juan also kept a pistol in the house, and one time she had moved it off the dresser while cleaning. When Juan couldn't find it, he went ballistic, and ran frantically around the house, screaming, "How am I gonna protect my family without my weapon?!"

Maria was at a loss as to what to do, when her mother mentioned hearing on a talk show about a way to find help for these kinds of problems: a thing called "SimCoach" on the internet. Maria had only occasionally "played" on the AOL games site before, and she didn't own a computer, but her older sister's son was a "computer nut" and agreed to let her come over to use his computer and try out SimCoach. She couldn't understand how a computer could help her, but she was desperate for any help she could get. Her nephew showed her how to type in the address for www.simcoach.org on his computer, and then went out with his friends to a movie.

Maria was intrigued when the screen lit up and created the illusion of standing in front of a "craftsman-like" building over which there was a sign reading "DCoE Helpcenter." Immediately, the "virtual" director of the center walked out onto the porch and beckoned her to come in. The director stated that "we are here to understand your needs and get you started on the path to help," and showed Maria a poster, just inside the door, that had images and short biographies of the staff. Pointing towards the poster, the director said, "Here is our staff. Have a look and click on the picture of who you think you would feel comfortable meeting with." Maria paused when she noticed a staff member that reminded her of a teacher she had in high school who was always helpful and kind to her. She clicked on this picture, and the program whisked her into a room where Bill Ford sat on a porch, smiled, and softly asked her how he could help. Maria knew that this was just a virtual human but, for some reason, she felt comforted by his soft voice and kind facial expressions. She had never been to a clinician for this kind of help, and was surprised by how safe and comfortable she felt. Not knowing what to expect, she described how her husband, Juan, was having problems ever since he came back from the war. She was surprised when the doctor said in a reassuring voice, "If you want to tell me more about it, I think I can help you and your family." After requesting some basic information, Bill then asked Maria some questions that seemed like he really might "understand" some of what she was going through. Eventually, after answering a series of thoughtful questions, Bill reassuringly smiled, and then pointed to the side screen and said, "Here are some websites that have information that is available to help folks that are going through what you are feeling. We can pull up one of them and take a look at what is available, or I can find a care provider in or near your zip code that we can make an appointment with right now, so you can begin to find the help that both you and Juan could benefit from. Or, if you're not ready for that yet, we can still talk more about what you're going through now."

Maria couldn't believe that this computer character seemed so genuine in his face and his manner, and that she felt like she wanted to tell him more. Perhaps he might really be able to get her started on the road to help both her and Juan? Suddenly, she realized that she had been online for an hour and needed to go home. As she was leaving, she wondered aloud if she could think about the options that she learned about today and then come back to make a decision on what to do. Bill smiled and said, "Of course we can meet again . . . you see, I will always be here to guide you to the help you need, whenever you're ready."

Clinical Interaction Strategy

While the case presented above is fictional, it illustrates one of myriad forms of confidential interaction that a tireless and always available VH can foster. A fundamental challenge of the SimCoach project will be to better understand the diverse needs of the user base, such that appropriate individual user experiences can be delivered to promote better healthcare access. There are immense differences in the needs of SMs and their families. Further, there are likely to be large differences in the level of awareness that users will have of existing resources and in their own need/desire to engage such resources. Within the SM population, there is a high likelihood that individual users will have had very diverse combat experiences and help-seeking histories, and, consequently, will have had varying impacts on significant others. Thus, a one-size-fits-all "chat-bot" level approach, as has become relatively common on the internet (Rizzo, 2009), would likely be less helpful in addressing the diversity of needs within this population.

The net result of attempting to engage such a diverse user base is that the system needs to be able to employ a variety of general strategies and tactics, so as to be relevant to each individual user. In this regard, the SimCoach project is employing a variety of techniques to create the user experience. One relevant clinical model is the PLISSIT clinical framework (Permission, Limited Information, Specific Suggestions, and Intensive Therapy) (Annon, 1976), which provides an established model for encouraging help-seeking behaviors in persons who may feel stigma and insecurity regarding a clinical condition. In the SimCoach project, the aim is to address the "PLISS" components, leaving the intensive therapy component to the live providers to which users in need of this level of care can be referred. Another source of knowledge is social work practice. Such models take a case management approach, serving both as an advocate and a guide. The Sim-Coach development team is also leveraging knowledge from the entertainment/gaming industry. While knowledge from this community is not typically applied towards healthcare, a primary aim of this community is in the explicit attraction and engagement of individuals' attention. As this web-based VH interactive system evolves, experts in all three of these models are being consulted to achieve our goal of engaging and focusing this unique user base on the steps to initiate care as needed. Addtionally, all interactions will be consistent with findings that suggest that interventions with individuals with PTSD and other psychosocial difficulties achieve the following: 1) promotion of perceptions of self-efficacy and control; 2) encouragement of the acceptance of change; 3) encouragement of positive appraisals; and 4) an increase in the usage of adaptive coping strategies (Whealin, Ruzek, & Southwich, 2008). These principles of intervention will be implicit in all of the interactions between the SimCoach and its users.

Conclusions

The systematic use of artificially intelligent VHs in Clinical Virtual Reality applications is still, clearly, in its infancy. But the days of limited use of VHs as simple props or static elements to add realism or context to a VR application are clearly in the past. In this chapter, we have presented our general approach to the design and development of the SimCoach VH project, which was envisioned to serve as an online clinical healthcare guide or coach. The primary aim of SimCoach is to break down barriers to care (stigma, unawareness, complexity, etc.) by providing military SMs, veterans, and their significant others with confidential help in exploring and accessing healthcare content and by promoting the initiation of care with a live provider if needed. The current version of SimCoach is presently undergoing beta testing with a limited group of test-site users. Results from this user-centered testing will serve to inform the development of a Sim-Coach system that is expected to undergo a wider release in 2012. Although this project represents an early effort in this area, it is our view that the clinical aims selected can still be usefully addressed within the limits of current technology. However, we expect that SimCoach will continue to evolve, over time, based on data collected from ongoing user interactions with the system and advances in technology—particularly with improved voice recognition. Along the way, this work will afford many research opportunities for investigating the functional and ethical issues involved in the process of creating and interacting with VHs in a clinical or healthcare support context. While the ethical challenges may be more intuitively appreciated, the functional technology challenges are also significant. As advances in computing power, graphics and animation, artificial intelligence, speech recognition, and natural language processing continue to develop at current rates, we expect that the creation of highly interactive, intelligent, VHs for such clinical purposes is not only possible, but probable.

References

American Psychological Association Presidential Task Force on Military Deployment Services for Youth, Families and Service Members. (2007). *The Psychological Needs of U.S. Military Service*

Members and Their Families: A Preliminary Report. Retrieved April 18, 2007, from: http://www. apa.org/releases/MilitaryDeploymentTaskForceReport.pdf.

Anderson, P. L., Zimand, E., Hodges, L. F., & Rothbaum, B. O. (2005). "Cognitive Behavioral Therapy for Public-Speaking Anxiety Using Virtual reality for Exposure." *Depression and Anxiety, 22* (3): 156–158.

Annon, J. (1976). *Behavioral Treatment of Sexual Problems.* New York, NY: HarperCollins.

Babu, S., Schmugge, S., Barnes, T., & Hodges, L. (2006). "What Would You Like to Talk About? An Evaluation of Social Conversations with a Virtual Receptionist." In J. Gratch, et al. (Eds.), *IVA 2006* (pp.169–180). LNAI 4133, Berlin, Germany: Springer-Verlag.

Bailenson, J. N., & Beall, A. C. (2006). "Transformed Social Interaction: Exploring the Digital Plasticity of Avatars." In R. Schroeder & A. Axelsson (Eds.), *Avatars at Work and Play: Collaboration and Interaction in Shared Virtual Environments* (pp. 1–16), Berlin, Germany: Springer-Verlag.

Bickmore, T., & Cassell, J. (2005). "Social Dialogue with Embodied Conversational Agents." In J. van Kuppevelt, L. Dybkjaer, & N. Bernsen (Eds.), *Advances in Natural, Multimodal Dialogue Systems.* New York, NY: Kluwer Academic.

Blascovich, J., Loomis, J., Beall, A., Swinth, K., Hoyt, C., & Bailenson, J. (2002). "Immersive Virtual Environment Technology: Not Just Another Research Tool for Social Psychology." *Psychological Inquiry,13*: 103–124.

Bohil C. J., Alicea, B., & Biocca, F. A. (2011). "Virtual Reality in Neuroscience Research and Therapy." *Nature Reviews Neuroscience.* Published online, November 3, 2011.

DOD Mental Health Task Force. (2007). *DOD Mental Health Task Force Report.* Downloaded June 15, 2007, from: http://www.health.mil/dhb/mhtf/MHTF-Report-Final.pdf.

Dole-Shalala Commission. (2007). *Serve, Support, Simplify: Report of the President's Commission on Care for America's Returning Wounded Warriors.* Downloaded November 21, 2011, from: http://www.nyshealthfoundation.org/content/document/detail/1782/.

Gratch, J., & Marsella, S. (2004). "A Domain Independent Framework for Modeling Emotion." *Journal of Cognitive Systems Research, 5* (4): 269–306.

Gratch, J., Rickel, J., Andre, E., Cassell, J., Petajan, E., & Badler, N. (2002). "Creating Interactive Virtual Humans: Some Assembly Required." *IEEE Intelligent Systems,* July/August: 54–61.

Hoge, C. W., Castro, C. A., Messer, S. C., McGurk, D., Cotting, D. I., & Koffman, R. L. (2004). "Combat Duty in Iraq and Afghanistan, Mental Health Problems, and Barriers to Care." *New England Journal of Medicine, 351* (1): 13–22.

Holden, M. K. (2005). "Virtual Environments for Motor Rehabilitation: Review." *CyberPsychology and Behavior, 8* (3): 187–211.

Kenny, P., Hartholt, A., Gratch, J., Swartout, W., Traum, D., Marsella, S., & Piepol, D. (2007a). "Building Interactive Virtual Humans for Training Environments." Proceedings of the Interservice/Industry Training, Simulation and Education Conference (I/ITSEC).

Kenny, P., Rizzo, A. A., Parsons, T., Gratch, J., & Swartout W. (2007b). "A Virtual Human Agent for Training Clinical Interviewing Skills to Novice Therapists." *Annual Review of Cybertherapy and Telemedicine, 5*: 81–89.

Klinger, E. (2005). "Virtual Reality Therapy for Social Phobia: Its Efficacy through a Control Study." Paper presented at the Cybertherapy 2005 conference, Basal, Switzerland.

Lok, B., Ferdig, R. E., Raij, A., Johnson, K., Dickerson R., Coutts, J., & Lind, D. S. (2007). "Applying Virtual Reality in Medical Communication Education: Current Findings and Potential Teaching and Learning Benefits of Immersive Virtual Patients." *Journal of Virtual Reality, 10* (3–4): 185–195.

McCall, C., Blascovich, J., Young, A., & Persky, S. (2009). "Proxemic Behaviors as Predictors of Aggression Towards Black (but not White) Males in an Immersive Virtual Environment." *Social Influence*: 1–17.

Morency, L. P., de Kok, I., & Gratch, J. (2008). "Context-Based Recognition during Human

Interactions: Automatic Feature Selection and Encoding Dictionary." Paper delivered at the 10th International Conference on Multimodal Interfaces, Chania, Greece, IEEE.

McCauley, L., & D'Mello, S. (2006). "A Speech Enabled Intelligent Kiosk." J. Gratch, et al. (Eds.): *IVA 2006* (pp. 132–144). LNAI 4133, Berlin, Germany: Springer-Verlag.

National Academies of Science Institute of Medicine Committee on Treatment of Posttraumatic Stress Disorder. (2007). *Treatment of Posttraumatic Stress Disorder: An Assessment of the Evidence.* ISBN: 0-309-10925-6. Downloaded October 24, 2007 from: http://www.nap.edu/catalog/ 11955.html.

Padgett, L., Strickland, D., & Coles, C. (2006). "Case Study: Using a Virtual Reality Computer Game to Teach Fire Safety Skills to Children Diagnosed with Fetal Alcohol Syndrome (FAS)." *Journal of Pediatric Psychology, 31* (1): 65–70.

Parsons, T. D., & Rizzo, A. A. (2008). "Affective Outcomes of Virtual Reality Exposure Therapy for Anxiety and Specific Phobias: A Meta-Analysis." *Journal of Behavior Therapy and Experimental Psychiatry, 39*: 250–261.

Pertaub, D.-P., Slater, M., & Barker, C. (2002). "An Experiment on Public Speaking Anxiety in Response to Three Different Types of Virtual Audience." *Presence, 11* (1): 68–78.

Powers, M., & Emmelkamp, P. M. G. (2008). "Virtual Reality Exposure Therapy for Anxiety Disorders: A Meta-Analysis." *Journal of Anxiety Disorders,22*: 561–569.

Rickel, J., Gratch, J., Hill, R., Marsella, S., & Swartout, W. (2001). "Steve Goes to Bosnia: Towards a New Generation of Virtual Humans for Interactive Experiences." The Proceedings of the AAAI Spring Symposium on AI and Interactive Entertainment, Stanford University, CA.

Rizzo, A. A., Bowerly, T., Buckwater, J. G., Klimchuk, D., Mitura, R., & Parsons, R. D. (2006). "A Virtual Reality Scenario for All Seasons: The Virtual Classroom." *CNS Spectrums, 11* (1): 35–44.

Rizzo, A. A. (2009). "CyberSightings." *CyberPsychology & Behavior, 12* (5): 573–578.

Rizzo, A. A, Parsons, T. D., Lange, B., Kenny, P., Buckwalter, J. G., Rothbaum, B. O., Difede, J., Frazier, J., Newman, B., Williams, J., & Reger, G. (2011). "VR Goes to War: A Brief Review of the Future of Military Behavioral Healthcare." *Journal of Clinical Psychology in Medical Settings, 18*: 176–187.

Rizzo, A. A., Parsons, T., Buckwalter, J. G., & Kenny, P. (forthcoming). "The Birth of Intelligent Virtual Patients in Clinical Training." *American Behavioral Scientist.*

Riva, G. (2011). "The Key to Unlocking the Virtual Body: Virtual Reality in the Treatment of Obesity and Eating Disorders." *Journal of Diabetes Science and Technology, 5* (2): 283–292.

Rose, F. D., Brooks, B. M., & Rizzo, A. A. (2005). "Virtual Reality in Brain Damage Rehabilitation: Review." *CyberPsychology and Behavior, 8* (3): 241–262.

Rutten, A., Cobb, S., Neale, H., Kerr, S. Leonard, A., Parsons, S., & Mitchell, P. (2003). "The AS Interactive Project: Single-User and Collaborative Virtual Environments for People with High-Functioning Autistic Spectrum Disorders. *Journal of Visualization and Comp Animation, 14* (5): 233–241.

Tanielian, T., Jaycox, L. H., Schell, T. L. Marshall, G. N., Burnam, M. A., Eibner, C., Karney, B. R., Meredith, L. S., Ringel, J. S., & Vaiana, M. E. (2008). *Invisible Wounds of War: Summary and Recommendations for Addressing Psychological and Cognitive Injuries.* A Rand Report. Downloaded April 18, 2008, from: http://veterans.rand.org/.

Thiebaux, M., Marshall, A., Marsella, S., Fast, E., Hill, A., Kallmann, M., Lee, J. (2008). SmartBody: Behavior Realization for Embodied Conversational Agents. In L. Padgham, D. Parkes, J. Muller, & S. Parsons (Eds.), *Proceedings of the 7th International Conference on Autonomous Agents and Multi-Agent Systems (AAMAS 2008)* (pp. 151–158). Richand, SC: International Foundation for Autonomous Agents and Multiagent Systems.

Traum, D., Marsella, S., Gratch, J., Lee, J., & Hartholt, A. (2008). "Multi-Party, Multi-Issue, Multi-Strategy Negotiation for Multi-Modal Virtual Agents." In H. Prendinger, J. Lester, & M.

Ishizuka (Eds.), *Proceedings of the 8th International Conference on Intelligent Virtual Agents* (pp. 117–130). Berlin, Germany: Springer Verlag.

Virtually Better, Inc. (2011). Virtually Better Homepage. Last visited November 21, 2011, at: www.virtuallybetter.com.

Weizenbaum, J. (1976). *Computer Power and Human Reason.* San Francisco, CA: W. H. Freeman.

Whealin, J. M., Ruzek, J. I., & Southwich, S. (2008). "Cognitive-Behavioral Theory and Preparations for Professionals at Risk for Trauma Exposure." *Trauma Violence Abuse, 9:* 100–113.

Part VII

Other Creative Approaches

17 Resolving Combat-Related Guilt and Responsibility Issues

Raymond Monsour Scurfield (Vietnam) *and*
COL Katherine Theresa Platoni (ODS and OIF/OEF)

In the authors' clinical experiences with veterans of the Vietnam, Iraq, and Afghanistan Wars, one of the principal and, perhaps, most prevalent issues is the continuing anguish over feelings of responsibility about traumatic events that occurred months, years, or decades ago (Schiraldi, 2000; Scurfield, 1993, 1994, 2006). This chapter will describe the guilt and shame related to war trauma, the complicating role of adrenalin-fueling experiences while deployed, and how so many veterans come to be plagued with a severely exaggerated sense of responsibility for tragic events that occurred. The heart of the chapter describes in detail the rationale and steps of a clinical intervention procedure developed by Scurfield (1993, 1994, 2006), the Determining the Percentages of Responsibility technique, and two clinical vignettes in which this technique was applied to OEF/OIF veterans.

An OIF veteran describes how his post-war political activism is an expression of his feeling responsible for deaths in Iraq:

> A lot of what I'm doing is basically survivor's guilt. It's hard. I'm home. I'm fine. I came back in one piece. But there are a lot of people who haven't . . . I came home and read that six children were killed in an artillery strike near where I was. I don't really know if that was my unit or a British unit. But I feel responsible for everything that happened when I was there.
>
> (Goodman, 2004, p. 50)

War-Related Blame, Shame, and Exaggerated Sense of Responsibility

Typically, issues by service members or veterans[1] concerning an exaggerated sense of personal responsibility over the deaths or injuries of battle buddies, or of perceived innocent civilians, are exacerbated by the fallacious belief that "somehow I could or should have been able to prevent what happened." A related issue is survivor's guilt—"I survived when others did not"—or guilt over what actions the veteran did or did not take to survive. In essence, war-related guilt involves *feeling some degree of personal responsibility for something negative that happened during the war*. Typically, this feeling of responsibility is expressed as a continuing and overwhelming sense of guilt, remorse and/or shame over what one did or did not do. Such feelings and cognitions involving guilt are infused in memories about the event(s) and help to keep the memory and accompanying anguish very much alive. This is in spite of innumerable attempts by the veteran to "explain away" the guilt or otherwise to try, with futility, to bury or compartmentalize the memory in order to attempt not to be troubled by guilt over such responsibility. This can become an increasing preoccupation, characterized by disturbing, repetitive ruminations, in which self-blame and self-condemnation remain salient for years or decades (Scurfield, 1994, 2006).

> There seem to be two elements involved in our readiness to feel guilt. The first is our strenuous need to believe that the world makes sense, that there is a cause for every effect and a reason for everything that happens. The second element is the notion that we are the cause of what happens, especially the bad things that happen.
>
> (Kushner, 1981, p. 92)

For veterans suffering an exaggerated sense of personal responsibility for events that happened in the war zone, there has been a repetitive recycling of memories and "what if" recriminations, such as: "What if I only had not . . .?" or "What if I had reacted a split-second sooner . . . ?" Kubany and Watson (2003) refer to this as "hindsight bias." Scurfield (2006) uses the term "Monday morning quarterbacking"—the weekend game is over and, while no longer immersed in the fast-paced actions of actually playing the game, one can and does replay in slow motion, repeatedly, what happened and what might have happened if one had done something differently in those split-second moments in the action of the game. But, now that the events have long ended, one is both blessed and cursed with the passage of time and is able to sit back to analyze and re-analyze one's actions and inactions. And, if it happened to be the most important game of one's career, and a negative outcome of the game seemed to hinge on one's own judgment and behaviors, this replaying can be repeated countless times over the ensuing months and years.

This is exactly what happens with veterans who have war zone experiences that involve tragic consequences, and about which the veteran feels an exaggerated sense of responsibility. Associated memories, feelings, and self-recriminations do not go away easily over time; indeed, in too many cases, they fester and become worse as "the game" (e.g., the traumatic event) is played and replayed, over and over and over and over again, without respite or relief. Guilt and self-blame are most powerful, evocative, and defiant emotions when based on misperceived "lapses" involving injury or loss of life to another. The veteran is unable to let it go, and holds on to feeling "justified" for having such guilt and pain. But the price paid is never enough, and the guilt, self-recriminations, and/or shame continue relentlessly.

The prevalence and salience of the issue of exaggerated personal responsibility for the tragic consequences that befall others unfortunately is minimized and obscured by the absence of guilt, blame or responsibility as an inclusionary criteria for the diagnosis of post-traumatic stress disorder (PTSD) (APA, 2000). Scurfield (1988) critiqued this omission after 20 years of clinical experiences with Vietnam War veterans, and serving on a psychiatric team in Vietnam. He noticed how frequently Vietnam combat veterans experienced serious issues related to the amount of responsibility that they felt for events that had occurred during the war.

Scurfield then continued to develop and refine a clinical intervention to help address responsibility-based issues; this semi-structured intervention became known as the "Determining the Percentages of Responsibility Technique."[2] Independently,

Colonel Kathy Platoni had observed how prevalent the issue of responsibility-based issues were among Iraq and Afghanistan soldiers and Marines during and following deployment and afterwards. She had read about the technique (Scurfield, 2006), and, in her role in Combat Operational Stress Control, started applying it to OIF and OEF service members. She has continued to use it in her clinical practice.

It should be noted that the technique, while not subjected to evidence-based research, *has* been subjected to decades of application by Scurfield and, more recently, by Platoni and a number of other clincians. The results in the preponderance of applications have been amazingly quick and impactful by significantly reducing the amount of psychological pain and turmoil that have been carried for months, years, and/or, indeed, for decades. Application of the technique has never been known to result in an exacerbation or deterioration; the worst that has happened, on extremely rare occasions, is that nothing happens regarding exaggerated responsibility—the veteran does not reduce the amount of responsibility that he has assigned to himself.

What Does Not Work

In our extensive clinical experience with those war veterans who suffer from exaggerated and distorted sense of responsibility, guilt, and/or self-blame, it is very clear what *does not* work therapeutically. The typical approach that many well-meaning clinicians, battle buddies, service member and veteran peers, friends, and family members typically try to use is to "logically persuade" the veteran that he/she "should not feel" so much fault or not any fault. Unfortunately, this approach *just does not work*—no matter how persuasive "the facts" that seem to support such rationalizations.

Most veterans reject factually or logically-based persuasive approaches as being well meaning yet irrelevant. After all, many such veterans, subsequent to the traumatic event, *have been telling themselves, repeatedly, that they "should not" be feeling so responsible, guilty, or at fault—and yet, they have continued to feel so anyway.*

> When a special comrade is maimed or killed, the guilt is particularly deep. It is as if there can be no excuse for not having saved one's comrade or having somehow prevented what happened—even when there is absolutely no rational basis for such self-blame.
>
> (Shay, 1994)

Determing the Percentages of Responsibility Technique: Underlying Premises

The technique offers a distinctive approach to resolving such issues. It is based on several major premises.

Experiencing and surviving a combat-related trauma involves an extraordinarily powerful, if not overwhelming, onslaught of vivid visual perceptions that assault the senses; extremely powerful emotions that threaten to become overwhelming; searing cognitions that are unbelievably fast-paced and frenetic; and survival-honed behaviors impelled by muscle memory/instinctual responses that impel survival reactions to persevere against, and overcome, the incoming threat(s) to self and to others.

This remarkable panoply becomes imprinted in the survivor's very being, and inevitably infuses the survivor's memories and cognitions with distortions, exaggerations, extremely selective retention and associated markedly powerful emotions. This is partly due to the tunnel vision survival mode (see Scurfield, Platoni, & Rabb, this volume) in which *the veteran focuses so narrowly on surviving that it becomes impossible to see the whole picture.* Hence, it is common to markedly downplay the role of the full range of environmental factors that are present (Schiraldi, 2000; Scurfield, 1993, 1994, 2006). Oftentimes, there is a dramatic elevation during the traumatic event—and afterwards— of exaggerating one's own role while excluding or minimizing other people and factors involved in the actual event.

Every traumatic event in the war zone can be conceptualized as having a total of *100 percent shared responsibility* for all that occurs in any given event. And while at least a part of that 100 percent *inevitably resides with the individual service member* who is at the scene of the event in question, there *are additional persons and institutions, each of which deserve to at least be seriously considered as sharing in that 100 percent responsibility* for what occurred in any given event in the war zone.

A veteran struggling with issues of an exaggerated sense of responsibility will be open to fully considering *who* deserves to share in that 100 percent responsibility, and *to what extent,* provided that he or she is approached in a systematic and caring, yet challenging, way. And this way must *fully respect and, indeed, demand* that the veteran be logical in considering and fully accepting *two* very different realities: (1) what share of the 100 percent responsibility for a tragic consequence *is his or hers, that no amount of explaining away will or should eradicate;* and (2) *who else* should be included in an expanded circle of shared responsibility *and that no amount of explaining away will or should eradicate.* However, both realities will only be recognized and accepted by the veteran if such *makes sense to him or her,* regardless of what the clinician and/or peer veterans or anyone else might think or believe.

Our country, and the vast majority of its institutions and its citizens, are all too willing *not* to accept much, if any, degree of responsibility for anything that happens in the war zone—especially not to accept *any* degree of responsibility whatsoever for anything that happens during the myriad "individual" events that occur on a daily basis in a war zone. *Indeed, our country, and its citizens, are all too content to let 100 percent of the responsibility for what happens in those myriad daily events in the war zone fall completely on the shoulders of the troops who are deployed* (Scurfield, 1994, 2006).

Contrary to the above premise, there is the perspective that an extensive array of people and institutions "share," to varying degrees, *some* responsibility for *all* that occurs in the war zone. As Scurfield has said:

> I must admit that I have a very strong conviction about civilians during a war being fought by our country. I contend that when a nation goes to war, *every adult in that nation* bears a piece of the responsibility for each and every single traumatic incident or result that occurs.
>
> (Scurfield, 2006, p. 142)

This technique facilitates such a recognition and acceptance by the veteran of an expanded circle of responsibility; this, in turn, frees up the veteran to more realistically reappraise what his or her share of responsibility for the tragedy is. It should be noted that there is an opposing exaggerated sense of responsibility by some veterans. *They accept little or no responsibility whatsoever* for their behaviors and, instead, place the blame or responsibility onto others or the environment—even if, and when, facts indicate that they had much more responsibility than they are willing to acknowledge or accept. Due to space considerations, this will not be discussed. However, such an exaggerated lack of responsibility also is very amenable to this technique (see Scurfield, 2006, for a detailed case vignette of a Korean War veteran).

Cognitive Reframing

There is a long-established psychological intervention known as "cognitive reframing." Cognitive reframing is based upon the premise that, to understand more accurately the reality of something, it may be necessary to view it in a "fresh" or "reframed" way. This can allow a veteran who is manifesting an exaggerated sense of responsibility to be able to more fully understand and consider a more complete range of factors, e.g., to reframe such in a much more balanced way (Schiraldi, 2000). This intervention has been widely utilized by military mental health providers (see, for example, Weinraub, 2003).

Scurfield (1993, 1994, 2006) has found that cognitive reframing is substantially enhanced if the clinician is able to transpose the veteran survivor *from* sitting in the position of being a critical observer looking back at an event historically (e.g., as a Monday morning quarterback) and to, instead, facilitate the veteran *to* re-immerse him or herself back into "reliving" the memory *as if it were happening in the now.* Gestalt and existential therapies have very effective therapeutic techniques to accomplish this, including having the veteran speak in the first person present tense ("I am . . .") when describing what happened.[3] By doing so, the veteran is able to more fully "re-experience" the event—versus "talking about" it in the past tense, as a historical event—and is able to make fresh or new discoveries that were not possible when he or she remained fixated in the perspective of a Monday morning quarterback.

The Eight Steps: Determining the Percentages of Responsibility Technique

It is essential to re-emphasize that this technique is *not* an attempt to help a surviving veteran to absolve him or herself of *all* personal responsibility for what happened during a particular traumatic event. This caveat is in line with Kushner's (1981) contention that there always is a degree of personal responsibility involved in causing and/or contributing in some way to trauma and suffering, and that such ought to be accepted. Conversely, an excessive sense of guilt or responsibility fuels self-blaming more than the reality would merit.

This technique is structured to help the veteran to reconsider a much wider range of persons who might bear varying degrees of responsibility for what happened in that traumatic event, and, by doing so, it has been the authors' clinical experience that the veteran will become willing to recognize that others deserve their share of responsibility for what happened (Schiraldi, 2000; Scurfield, 1993, 1994, 2006). Consequently, by coming to the realization *of how much others might* deserve a share of the responsibility for what happened, the veteran is freed to be able to recognize and accept that he or she "deserves" *commensurately less* of a share of the responsibility (typically, *much* less) than the share that he/she has been holding onto, and that, subsequently, has bound him or her psychologically to this event.

There are eight steps in this technique. These can be followed in a strict order as described below. Alternatively, the clinician can be more flexible in which steps are applied, and "paraphrase" rather than rote recitation of these steps. This choice is dependent upon (1) clinical assessment of what will be most appropriate and effective with a given veteran; and (2) what variation is most comfortable for the clinician. Below, these eight steps (Scurfield, 1994, 2006) are identified, following which there are clinical vignettes that describe the process as applied to OEF/OIF veterans.

Step #1: Obtain a clear description of the event and the veteran's perception and rationale for the degree of self-responsibility assumed

This account by the veteran provides a "baseline" of how he or she perceives, remembers, and interprets the traumatic event. The veteran should only be interrupted or queried for the purpose of enhancing clarity if there is confusing or seemingly contradictory information being provided.

Step #2: Challenge the veteran's exclusion or minimization of the role of others who were at the immediate scene of the trauma

The clinician systematically reviews what responsibility each and every other person in the geographical vicinity who was on duty at that time might have had. This includes fellow military on duty at the time, or with the veteran, other unit/military personnel in the relatively immediate area, the enemy who were involved, and lastly the person(s) who was killed or injured in the incident. What percentage, if any, of the 100% responsibility can be assigned to each of these persons by the veteran?

Step #3: Challenge the veteran's exclusion or minimization of the indirect responsibility of others who were not at the immediate scene of the trauma

There are two additional groups of people to help the veteran consider: (1) *others in-country*, e.g., senior military officials in higher echelons of leadership, and those in command positions over forces in the region and within the country itself—those responsible on the ground for the war strategy, for troop selection for deployment, and for which specific locations, etc.; and (2) persons and institutions *back in the United States*, e.g., Congress, the President, U.S. citizens (to be discussed later).

Step #4: Re-challenge the veteran's sense of his or her own percentage of responsibility for behaviors and consequences

By this point, typically, the percentages that have been assigned are well over 100 percent. This is almost always the case, as the veteran began the process with an exaggerated percentage of responsibility assigned to him or herself while also minimizing or denying the percentages that could be assigned to others. Hence, the veteran is challenged to reframe what his/her percentage is vis-à-vis others, and in order for all of the resulting assigned percentages to total no more than 100 percent. The clinician has the choice of asking the veteran to do a rough recalculation of the percentages now that he or she has come to this realization. Alternatively, the clinician or a group member keeps track of all of the percentages assigned by the veteran and informs the veteran that there will be an opportunity later, or after the group, to calculate a percentage readjustment so that all of the percentages add up to a total of +/– 100 percent.[4] Arriving at definite or absolute percentages *during* the session are not necessary (unless the veteran is bothered by the lack of precision) and, perhaps, may not even be possible, as the veteran usually needs to have time to reflect on what are always dramatically different thoughts and perceptions about the percentages of responsibility assigned.

Step #5: Challenge the veteran to consider if he or she has been "punished enough" for his or her personal share of the (recalculated) responsibility for what happened

Inevitably, veterans holding onto, or plagued by, an exaggerated sense of responsibility will feel strongly that they "deserved to be punished" for what their responsibility was, based on their exaggerated sense of responsibility. Even so, typically, they will feel that they have not yet been punished sufficiently, but this is now at a reduced level.

An effective "legal" analogy can be to point out to the veteran (at whatever point in the process seems appropriate) that he/she has been acting as *both* the judge and jury over this perceived transgression—but *without* allowing him or herself to have a defense attorney to plead the veteran's case. In other words, *the jury* (the veteran) has decided the verdict—*guilty*—and the *judge* (also the veteran) *will not allow* any defense or evidence to be considered as relevant or sufficient—*and* will not allow any appeal. And so the veteran him or herself has done it all—been judged, tried, found guilty, and sentenced to a life imprisonment with no possibility of appeal or parole, because of the heinous nature of the transgression.

Step #6: Explicate a non-self-destructive plan to provide additional "payback" (if any more payback feels warranted) for the veteran's share of the (recalculated) responsibility

It is essential *not* to try to convince the veteran that he (or she) *should or should not feel like* he still deserves to be punished more; rather, once, and if, the veteran has decided that he still "deserves" to be punished more for his recalculated share of responsibility, help him to come up with a plan of payback that is not self-destructive or harmful, i.e., being a mentor for younger service members returning from deployment, or volunteering for a cause in which he believes. A very effective analogy, here, is to explore with the veteran if he "deserves a life sentence" for his perceived transgressions, versus if a "finite" sentence might be appropriate, with a payback plan *that fits the modified percentage* of responsibility.

Step #7: Conceptualize and commit to a homework assignment

So much therapeutic work will have happened during the application of this technique that the veteran will have gone through a major change in those perceptions that he had been holding onto for a very long time. Hence, it should be assumed that he might revert back, somewhat, to this long-held perception and, therefore, he must solidify what has been learned in the session today, as well as commit to a specific homework assignment. Typically, the homework assignment involves (1) reflection about this session; and (2) further deliberation about whether or not the percentages of responsibility assigned to himself and others need to be adjusted in any way. (If this technique has been conducted within a peer group, a member or two of the group are asked to volunteer to work with the veteran on this assignment before the next group session.)

Step #8: End the session in a way that recognizes and confirms the "work" that the veteran has accomplished today

The veteran might be so distracted or preoccupied by the many new perceptions and conclusions that he has attained that memory of much of the session might become hazy. Hence, it might be helpful to help the veteran to summarize where he had started and how the veteran had arrived at his ending point for this session, and to acknowledge the hard work that was accomplished, etc.

The Clinician's Stance During Application of the Technique

As mentioned earlier, it is vital throughout the session that the clinician assumes a "neutral" stance in terms of supporting the veteran's particular assignment of percentages of responsibility to anybody—to especially include what the veteran assigns him or herself. Scurfield has found it important *to act as a devil's advocate* each time the veteran assigns or adjusts a percentage of responsibility to himself or to anyone else. For example:

Clinician: What, you just reassigned yourself 70 percent of the responsibility for his death, and yet, all these years, you said you felt you were 95 percent responsible. Are you sure that 70 percent feels like an appropriate percentage? Is it too high? Is it too low?

Or:

Clinician: Wait a minute. You have just assigned that enemy who detonated that IED (roadside bomb) 10 percent of the responsibility for your buddy's death—and yet you have reassigned yourself 70 percent. Could you please explain how the person who actually detonated the roadside bomb bears 10 percent of the responsibility—yet you deserve 70 percent?

Clinician: Let me ask you something first. *Just how skilled and determined* were the insurgents at hiding such bombs and detonating them at just the right moment?

Veteran: They were good at doing that.

Clinician: Just how good were they?

Veteran: Well, they were *really, really,* good.

Clinician: And were they *so* good at hiding and detonating IEDs, that that a significant number of those bombs, realistically, *were never going to be found in time* to prevent their detonation—*no matter how vigilant and skilled* you or any other American was at being alert for just such IEDs?

Veteran: Well, yes, of course some of those bombs would never be found until it was too late.

Clinician: And yet, you are only willing to give that insurgent 10 percent of the responsibility for hiding and detonating that bomb?

Veteran: Well, putting it that way, I guess maybe his percentage of responsibility for the death of my buddy should be about 50 percent.

Clinician: Wait a minute—you just jumped from 10 percent to 50 percent. That is a big jump—a much higher percent of responsibility than you had been assigning him. Are you sure you now have not gone *too* high with this percentage, perhaps just to let yourself more off the hook? Could you explain your justification for doing so?

Discussion

Note that, in the above sequence, the clinician:

- Alerts the veteran to consider one or more persons whom he had *not previously considered* as having any percentage of responsibility (or whom he had considered as having a very small or very large percentage), and whether any or all of those persons "deserved" to have specific percentages of the responsibility.
- Alternates between confronting the veteran as to why and how he has or has not assigned any particular percentage of responsibility to a person or persons, and then, if the veteran does assign a percentage, the veteran is confronted to justify that particular percentage and why it is not higher or lower.

This same process is repeated with every other person at the immediate scene—*including the person(s) killed or wounded in action.*

Clinician: I notice that you have not assigned any percentage of responsibility to Tony—the very person who was killed, and about whom you have been agonizing over your responsibility for his death all these years. [Or, the veteran had recognized Tony, but had assigned him a very small—or a very large—percentage of the responsibility.]

In either case, once again the clinician assumes the devil's advocate role as to why the veteran killed or wounded does not deserve more—or less—than that which the veteran is assigning to him or her, and any recalculation and reassessment of percentages can take place. For example:

Clinician: Did you have any responsibility for convincing Tony to join the military in the first place, or any responsibility for his having been deployed?

Clinician: How much were you responsible for Tony being assigned his particular duty that day?

Clinician: How much were you responsible for the location to which Tony was deployed or sent, during that mission in which he was killed?

Clinician: How much were you responsible for deciding where in the vehicle Tony was assigned to sit?

Clinician: How much were you responsible for how well or how poorly the vehicle was designed to withstand the effects of an IED blast? etc.

And then this process is repeated for persons *beyond the immediate scene, but elsewhere in the war zone*—the next higher level commanding officer and senior NCO, other forces in the surrounding areas that had any responsibility for reconnaissance, security, calling in reinforcements, etc.

Finally, most veterans have *not considered, in any way,* what percentage of responsibility *anyone outside of the war zone* legitimately bears *specifically for any individual traumatic incident that occurs while deployed.* Thus, when this subject is introduced for consideration, it usually is necessary to suggest possible persons/institutions *so that the veteran can actively consider whether or not to assign any such people or institutions a piece of the responsibility,* e.g., the Congress that declared war; the President who is the Commander in Chief of all U.S. Armed Forces; his cabinet who assists in the process of forming national policies; the DOD and military officials at the Pentagon; and those John and Jane citizens who continued on with their daily lives as if our country was not actually at war.

Clinician: Does or does not each, indeed each and every U.S. citizen of voting age, deserve some portion of the responsibility for everything that happens in a war zone of a country that the U.S. has decided to deploy troops to—to include this particular incident? (Scurfield, 1993).

Scurfield, oftentimes, will interject the following statement at an opportune moment:

Do you agree at all or not with this statement: "The government sends us off to war, the military uses us in war, and society forgets us after war."

(Scurfield, 2006, p. 186)

Clinician: And so, how does your response/reaction to this statement effect what percentage of responsibility that you think our government deserves—if any at all—*for everything that happens to service members while they are deployed?* Does our President, his cabinet, our senators and congressmen, the DOD—do *any* of them deserve *any* such responsibility for what has happened *during the war*—and do they deserve *any* such responsibility for what happened *that specific day* back in 2004 in Iraq? (Scurfield, 2006).

The same line of questioning is continued regarding the military leaders' share of the responsibility, and our nation's citizens' responsibility. For each group, the clinician vigilantly challenges whatever percentage of responsibility that the veteran now assigns or does not assign to each such group that was back safely at home on American soil in the U.S.—until the veteran arrives at an assigned percentage (from zero on up) with which he or she feels comfortable. If yes or no, why or why not? And the same with each of the other potentially responsible parties.

Ultimately, *it does not matter one iota* what the clinician, or any other veterans present, believe or think about who should or should not be assigned what percentages of responsibility. Rather, it is our role to:

- Be neutral, and *not* to pressure the veteran unduly in one direction versus another, in terms of the percentage of responsibility that he or she assigns to self and to others.
- Help the veteran to *fully consider* the *complete range of persons and institutions* who could be considered to have some degree of responsibility.
- Bring new considerations to the veteran and to challenge the veteran's thinking all the way along.

Our opinions are just that—our opinions. *The veteran, and only the veteran, is the ultimate judge and jury* to:

- Assign the percentage of responsibility he/she and anyone else might deserve to bear for the trauma that occurred while deployed.
- Decide how much he/she has been punished.
- Decide how much more, if any, that he/she deserves to be punished.
- Determine what forms a non-self-destructive punishment might take.

And, 25+ years of applying this technique, and systematically going through the process of determining the percentages of responsibility, *almost inevitably* results in facilitation of a significant reconceptualization of the entire event, issues of responsibility and the veteran's part in it. This usually and quickly (in one to three sessions) leads to the veteran carrying a much lighter and more realistically-based load, as well as developing a healthier "payback" plan for any punishment that the veteran might feel that he or she still deserves. Finally, it is prudent to allow a full 90 minutes (in case it is needed) for the initial facilitation of applying the technique.

Application of the Technique to OEF/OIF Veterans

Ryan's Story: An OIF Veteran with a Post-War Civilian Trauma[5]

Background

Ryan is a young combat veteran in his late twenties, having served one tour in Iraq in support of Operation Iraqi Freedom several years ago. During our first few therapy sessions, he mentioned very little about his experiences as an infantryman and his active duty career. This was revealing in itself as, by virtue of his MOS (military occupational specialty), combat exposure is inherent. It was not until he completed his military obligation and was discharged back to the civilian world that the issue of survivor guilt rose to the surface of his awareness, in living color . . . but with an unexpected course. It was long after the incident (a period of at least two years) that survivor guilt came to be a prominent theme that intruded into his work and home lives. Please note that the issue of his survivor guilt is unrelated to Ryan's military service. However, his ability to completely reframe the tragic incident has excellent utility in the law enforcement and other civilian arenas. Finally, this vignette is included to illustrate how the technique is equally relevant and helpful with veterans (and non-veterans) who experience traumas that have nothing to do with their military service or deployment.

The Trauma and Its Aftermath

Ryan began his career as a law enforcement officer in a small-sized northeastern city sometime after his redeployment from the war. As a rookie cop he was assigned the night shift, though there was some personal choice in the matter. This allowed him greater latitude with the visitation schedule with his two young children. It was early in the summer of 2008 that the tragic event occurred that changed his life path, and agonizingly so.

While patrolling the streets several hours before dawn, an older model sedan traversed the otherwise empty streets at high speed and ran a red traffic light directly in front of his cruiser. There was not even a millisecond available to apply his brakes or swerve. "It just happened that fast." The passenger in the errant vehicle was killed instantly. Ryan lost consciousness and awoke in ICU the following morning with no memory for any of the events involving or surrounding the motor vehicle accident.

Ryan was informed at that time that the passenger had been killed instantly as a result of the high speed collision and that the driver was highly intoxicated, had no driver's license, possessed no automobile insurance and was not wearing a seatbelt. The driver, who had a very long history of substance abuse, was charged with responsibility for the accident and for the death of his passenger (involuntary manslaughter). Though Ryan was cleared of all charges by the IAB (Internal Affairs Board), *he continued to hold himself 100 percent responsible for the young passenger's demise.* The fact that he had lost consciousness did not permit either cognitive storage or retrieval of any elements involved in the accident scene, yet his enormous guilt and self-blame were palpable and enduring over a period of four long years. In fact, his survivor guilt intensified over time, which is what finally propelled him into treatment that was long overdue. His first therapist formally diagnosed him with PTSD; he discontinued treatment, after only a few sessions, for unexplained reasons.

It became readily apparent that Ryan's primary symptomatology involved nightmares of the few details of the accident that he was able to recall (many of these details were memories formulated from other witnesses' testimonies and their written reports). Even more significantly, survivor guilt escalated with the passage of time and the ensuing accident investigation. His survivor guilt began to consume his waking moments and to foster Ryan's questioning of his ability to continue his law enforcement career.

The Intervention

It was at the time of our second treatment session that we entertained the notion of the Percentages of Responsibility Technique; the goodness of fit for this treatment approach appealed to Ryan, and certainly addressed the crux of the matter for him. In a joint endeavor, Ryan was able to list all of the specifics of the case documented through the accident investigative reports. The facts of the case were very clear in his mind, and he swiftly and enthusiastically processed his causative role in this tragic motor vehicle accident.

The application of the technique lasted about twenty minutes, during which various steps were applied. The following, for illustrative purposes, is a very brief excerpt of one clinician–veteran interchange that took place:

Ryan: I live with the terrible fact that if I hadn't "t-boned" that vehicle, the passenger would be alive today. I know that I still can't remember any details about the accident, but it was my cruiser that hit that car.

Therapist: If you were to assign a percentage of responsibility for your role in this fatal accident, given all the facts uncovered as the result of the formal police investigation, what would your best estimate be?

Ryan: It's all mine. I caused the accident. The facts don't change that at all. I caused that life to be taken.

Therapist: On the other hand, when you take into account that the driver was intoxicated, had a long rap sheet with an extensive history of serious traffic violations, that he was not only speeding but ran a red light at high speed, and otherwise acted extremely irresponsibly in every possible way, does this alter your assessment of your responsibility in any way?

Ryan: I know. I have fought myself about this for years already. I don't want to drag this burden around with me any longer. I can't be an effective police officer if I don't. I know the guy was a sleaze bag and that he took all the risks in how he drove that vehicle and that he was high on coke when he made that decision in the first place. I didn't cause any of that.

Therapist: And so, how is it that you get 100 percent of the responsibility for the accident having occurred, and this driver of the other car gets zero percent? Please explain your logic.

Ryan: Well, if I really think about it like that, I can't blame myself for *any* of that accident. I'm going to do a recount here. In reality, if I'm completely objective here, I would have to give myself zero percent responsibility.

Therapist: Let's reassess this. You went from giving that driver zero percent to giving him 100 percent, and you went from giving yourself 100 percent to giving yourself zero percent? How does that make any sense? Are you sure that you don't deserve *at least some* of the responsibility for what happened—after all, you were driving one of the two cars.

Ryan: Well, I'm not the one who made all the bad decisions that the other driver made that ended up in a life being taken . . . none of it.

Discussion

In retrospect, and looking back after the completion of this intervention, the therapeutic interchange could have included additional exploration of the degree of responsibility that might have been assigned *to the passenger*. The interchange might have been pursued in the following manner:

Clinician: Okay, as we continue on, just remember that you might still find that you want to change the percentages assigned to you and the driver. For example, does *the passenger who was killed* have any responsibility at all for having been in that car in the first place? Unless he was forced by the driver (or by you) to be a passenger, it seems fair to assume that he was a passenger of his own volition in a car being driven by someone who was highly intoxicated and with such a long rap sheet, and the passenger chose not to wear a seat belt. Does he deserve any percentage of responsibility for having been in the car in the first place, and putting himself in harm's way, even more, by not wearing a seat belt—or does he have zero responsibility?

If the veteran comes to a new conclusion that the passenger also "deserves" any percent of responsibility, then that percentage naturally would reduce by "X" percent what the veteran might still be assigning to himself and/or to the driver. Also, there could have been exploration of the possible "indirect" responsibility of others *not at the scene*; for example, drug traffickers who make it possible for illegal drugs to be available in the first place; family members and friends who "enable" substance abusers to abuse drugs; a judicial system that can be lenient on legal consequences for such usage and for chronic offenders driving while under the influence, and so forth.

Essentially, Ryan was able to assign complete responsibility to the driver who had caused this accident and taken the life of his passenger because of recklessness and negligence. In rapid succession, yet with precise consideration, he was able to reassign his percent of responsibility from 100 percent at the beginning of the session to zero percent responsibility for the accident having occurred in the first place or for the death of the unbelted passenger. It is rare that this (or any, for that matter) technique brings the veteran to a reframing in which he reduces his or her share of responsibility to zero percent and does so within thirty minutes; however, this was the actual and favorable outcome in Ryan's case.

In almost all cases, recalculation by the veteran that he/she has at least *some* (yet a significantly reduced) degree of responsibility is an expectable and actual outcome of applying this technique. In this case, any reasonable assessment of the event by an objective outside observer would lead to the conclusion that the veteran had *literally no opportunity to react any differently than he did*, and that he had no responsibility for the reckless driving of the other driver or for the fact that the passenger was in the car, or for the death of the passenger. Alternatively, he might have concluded that he "deserved" some percentage of responsibility *simply because he was driving one of the two cars that was involved in the collision*. However, this would only be a valid conclusion if it were *his* conclusion in response to going through this technique. Further exploration by the clinician could focus on whether Ryan had been *preoccupied* at the time of the collision (i.e., had he been adjusting the radio volume or changing the station, or was he talking on his cell phone or on the two-way police transmitter, or was his attention diverted because he had been preoccupied with ruminations about, say, an argument earlier that day with his spouse)? If so, it would be understandable for him to assign himself some amount of responsibility. And, if he did, it would be a dramatically smaller percentage than 100 percent.

Sean's Story: An OEF/OIF Veteran with a Combat-Related Trauma

Inexplicable horrors are the daily diet in the wartime theater. From these, there is more often little respite. There are no front lines from which to escape, no safe haven of the rear echelon. Sean's story began long before January 3, 2010, but this pivotal day is when life as he knew it changed abruptly and tragically.

The Trauma and Its Aftermath

As a radio telephone operator (RTO), this young enlisted soldier's job was to facilitate communication between maneuvering elements on the battlefield and higher head-quarters. His personal holocaust began in the small village of Ashoque, with two enormous explosions. He only heard the first one, though these IEDs may have been ignited simultaneously. Two soldiers assigned to his platoon were instantaneously blown into the canal by the second explosion. It was then that Sean discovered "that we couldn't find anything of Josh," his very best friend since they had served together in support of Operation Iraqi Freedom in 2006. "I had to call him up as MIA" (missing in action).

It was at this point that the platoon was pinned down by small arms fire from almost all directions (AK 47 and medium machine gun fire), while Sean was also trying to call in medevac helicopters. Also at this time, Josh's body was located from a distance, and four volunteers were solicited to retrieve his remains. The volunteers had no choice but to jump down into the canal and to climb up and onto the other side. Sean was then second in line to run across the road to avoid becoming another target for the Taliban. "I went straight for Josh's body, and that's when I realized he didn't have any legs, and his left arm was missing, and he was missing the back of his head." Sean requested assistance to lift Josh's limp body onto his shoulders, but it was awkward and difficult to lift and carry him. All four soldiers ran back in the same direction they had come from, Sean lowering Josh's body to another of his fellow soldiers, then jumping back into the canal. By the time he climbed back out, two of the volunteers had grabbed what remained of Josh's body and attempted to move him to the CCP (Casualty Collection Point). Sean ran back to the radio and called in to ask where their QRF (Quick Reaction Force) was, and when they expected to arrive on scene. Then the third IED detonated. This is when Sean saw the other two soldiers, who had assisted him in carrying Josh's remains, lying dead and "torn up." All of the survivors suffered mild traumatic brain injuries and additional physical injuries that necessitated medevacuation to Kandahar airfield and hospitalization. The body count for the day: four killed in action and multiple wounded.

The Interventions

Many of the injured were later formally diagnosed with PTSD (by Platoni, who treated the survivors in the months following this horrific event). Sean was treated on an almost nightly basis for an extended period of time, when not "outside the wire" on mission, as the severity and intensity of his PTSD symptomatology and the degree of his suffering called for rigorous and exhaustive interventions. It was also determined by his clinicians that medevacuation out of theater would have clearly been more damaging than managing his symptoms in theater. This assessment was based on recognizing that the support and presence of his fellow soldiers provided him with a foundation, and the belief system that his life, in spite of this tragic event, nevertheless continued to have value, meaning, and purpose in his roles as infantryman and RTO.

The most striking and pervasive symptom experienced by this combat veteran was his immense survivor guilt. He was haunted unmercifully by images of the exploded remains of his friends killed in action. And he was unable to accept his own survival, coupled with the very fact that those who had wives and children, including Josh, had met their demise far too soon. Sean, instead, was left behind to grieve and to suffer the torment of living on. Night after night, while in session, he would rub his hands together until they were raw, in a frenzied attempt to "wash the blood off his hands." There was always a pile of dead skin on the floor under the folding chair in which he sat. His anguish, his desperation to end suffering, was palpable.

It was determined that the Determining the Percentages of Responsibility Technique might have great utility in Sean's case, survivor guilt having become a plague upon his soul and his very existence. He was motivated to engage in any intervention that might offer a miniscule modicum of relief. Though Sean did not blame himself for the deaths of the four soldiers killed on that ill-fated day in early January, he did hold himself fully accountable *for his own survival* in their place. He did not consider this thought irrational or unfounded in any way, but held decisively to the belief that real heroes died in combat. He could not be dissuaded from this.

Subsequent to a full and detailed description of the events of January 3, 2010, which Sean was only able to confront following two to three months of intensive treatment, Platoni began to assess his readiness to exclude and minimize the role of others present at the scene of the trauma. Selected excerpts of this intervention follow.

Clinician: I know that you are convinced that you should not have survived the four IED blasts that took the lives of four of your closest buddies, and that no amount of discussion over the last several months has permitted your own self-forgiveness. You have convinced yourself that you somehow are at least 90 percent responsible for their deaths. If you were to rethink this by reviewing the events of that horrific day, could you conceive of others playing a role in the dreadful outcome?

Sean: I don't know. If we hadn't been there in the first place, all of them might still be alive today. We didn't read the obvious signs correctly. We shouldn't have listened to our Platoon Sergeant, who basically led us into the Valley of Death that day. There was that eerie silence. There were no children playing outside. There was no livestock around. We should have known better. The signs were obvious. We're trained to look for the obvious, and that, when the streets are empty, we're about to get hit with an attack . . . which usually means an IED blast is about to happen.

Clinician: So, it wasn't your decision to be there in the village of Ashoque. You were also following orders, not just of your Platoon Sergeant, but of your Platoon Leader, your Company Commander, and even the Battalion Commander. That means that, as a soldier, it was your responsibility to carry out the orders passed down by your chain of command. If you consider these very facts, are you willing to assign yourself a lesser percentage of responsibility for the losses of life, as the decisions were *not* yours?

Sean: That's really hard for me at this point. My friends are dead. They had wives and children. It shouldn't have been their time. I just can't get there yet.

Clinician: Well, what about the Taliban then? Can you hold them responsible to implanting four huge IEDs, designed to maim and kill? You had nothing to do with that decision; none of it. In your way of thinking, should they bear any degree of responsibility for the losses of life?

Sean: If I look at it that way, the enemy would have to be at least 70 or 75 percent responsible. It's their goal "to take us out." They place no value on human life. They're subhuman.

Clinician: Is it possible, then, that you bear a lesser degree of responsibility for the events of that day, given that the Taliban implanted those IEDs and others "above your pay grade" gave the orders to place you where you possibly should not have been sent?

Sean: If I really thought about it, then I guess I would have to do a recount. Maybe I was only 25 percent responsible for what happened that day; maybe even less. I really have to study this issue to get to the place where I can accept that.

In the weeks that followed, and with much commitment to task, Sean was able to reduce his percentage of responsibility to 10 percent (leadership was assigned 20 percent, and the Taliban 70 percent), particularly when he was able to attend to the challenge of considering that he had already endured more than sufficient punishment for perceived misdeeds and that the measure of self-blame that he had assigned himself had, indeed, been grossly exaggerated. We would revisit this issue many times throughout the duration of his treatment. Although Sean remained unable to relinquish responsibility fully (which, in any case, is *not* the intent of applying this technique), he became accustomed to accepting a significantly reduced, and what appeared to be a much less exaggerated and more realistic, percentage of the responsibility (which *is* the intent of applying this technique).

Discussion

It is important to note that Platoni did not proceed to systematically explore several other persons and institutions who Sean might have concluded bore some of the shared responsibility for those killed and wounded that day; this was due to the multiplicity of other symptoms that required considerable attention, and the movement of Sean's company to another outlying combat outpost to which his therapist could only travel once weekly. This, otherwise, would have included the possible shared responsibility of *each or all of the men who had been killed or wounded* that day; *higher-level senior military officials* in the theater; and the possible shared responsibility of *people and institutions back in the United States*—our President, as Commander in Chief, his cabinet, Congress, the DOD, and the American people. If any or all of these had been systematically explored, and only if *Sean* had decided that any such people or institutions deserved "X" percentage of the responsibility for every event that occurs in the war zone—and what happened that day in the village—then the percentages of responsibility that he ended up assigning to the Taliban (70 percent), local military leadership (20 percent), and to himself (10 percent) would have required further adjustment to keep the total shared responsibility at 100 percent.

The bottom line, ultimately, is to have the service member or veteran *fully consider the complete range of people* (at the immediate scene, elsewhere in-country/theater, and back in the U.S.) who might bear some of the shared responsibility for that event and, consequently, how the veteran's percentage of the shared responsibility might well require further adjustment. Such an adjustment would, then, also impact on the "amount of punishment" that the veteran might feel that he or she "deserves."

Finally, there is an intervention that Scurfield has found to be particularly effective in getting veterans to reassess how they have perceived their behavior and accountability.

When it appears to be clinically relevant to do so, the veteran can be asked something like the following:

Clinician: You *were not perfect* that day, in your judgment and actions, were you?
Veteran: No, of course not, I wasn't perfect.
Clinician: And so, "of course not" means you were "not perfect" that day, correct? But were you *any good at all* that day, in terms of your thinking and behaviors?
Veteran: Well, I was not perfect, but I was pretty damned good . . .

This interchange might continue along the lines of one or more of several comments:

Clinician: Was *anyone* "perfect" in what they did, day in and day out, while in the war—or in what they did or did not do that day . . . Does it make sense that you would have not been perfect . . . We are human beings, after all, are we not—and not perfectly functioning robots, correct . . . Oh, that we were perfectly functioning—to include Josh and the others who went into the water to retrieve his body.

Typically, such a line of querying and commentary facilitates the veteran to *acknowledge two critical truths: that, while not perfect, his or her behavior was "pretty good"* (or another descriptor) that day *and/or that his selfless motivation to "save," or otherwise intervene, was focused on the other person's welfare* which, in turn, perhaps clouded his judgment; *and that perhaps no one else that day had functioned perfectly, either—except possibly the enemy.* And so, do any of these factors mitigate, in any way, the percentage of responsibility that should be his or hers, versus assigned to anyone else?

Closing

> The past is never dead. It's not even past.
>
> (William Faulkner, *Requiem for a Nun,* 1951)

Despite its absence as an inclusionary criteria for a diagnosis of PTSD in the *DSM-IV-TR* (APA, 2000), extensive clinical experiences over several decades have revealed that issues of exaggerated personal responsibility, guilt and/or shame regarding the deaths and/or wounding of fellow and sister service members (or innocent civilians), while deployed is one, if not the most pervasive, agonizing, and durable issues that plague veterans—oftentimes, for years and decades. Such an exaggerated sense of responsibility typically is impervious to attempts at "logical persuasion" by others and, indeed, by the veterans themselves, designed to convince the veteran that he or she "should not feel this way." Clinicians and veterans have nothing at all to "lose" (except for an hour or two of time and effort) in applying this technique with relevant cases. The authors welcome feedback about your experiences with this technique.

Our veterans deserve any opportunity available that might help them co-exist more peacefully with the memories of the unforgettable tragedies that occur during war, and about which they have been burdened for years or decades and, in many instances, for the remainder of their lives. There will be many days ahead in which self-forgiveness and the wiping of blood from one's hands will be the greatest obstacle faced by many of our service members and veterans. Provision of a meaningful forum that allows for recognition and acceptance of a more realistic recomputation of one's own role, or the lack thereof, in circumstances of great tragedy, cannot change the outcome of the event. However, application of the Percentages of Responsibility Technique very frequently does greatly reduce the degree of suffering, guilt, and self-blame—and thereby can alter, in a most positive way, the entire course of the lives of such suffering souls. Our service members and veterans truly do deserve to rest in peace—while they are still living.

Notes

1 The contents of this chapter applies to both service members and to veterans. However, to avoid unnecessary repetition, the word "veteran" will be used.
2 It was described by Scurfield (1993, 1994), then in *The PTSD Sourcebook* (Schiraldi, 2000) and then, in even more detail, in the third volume of his *Vietnam Trilogy, War Trauma: Lessons Unlearned from Vietnam to Iraq* (Scurfield, 2006). Development of the steps and strategies utilizing this technique owe much to a number of Vietnam veteran peer counselors with whom Scurfield co-led numerous trauma focus groups when he was Director of the Post-Traumatic Stress Treatment Program, American Lake VA Medical Center, Tacoma, WA (1985–1992). These counselors included Steve Tice, Art Owens, Rico Swain, Nelson Korbs and Bob Swanson.
3 For a description of how Scurfield had adapted Gestalt therapy techniques to war trauma focused therapy, see the companion monograph for the video, *Journey of Healing*: Scurfield, R. M. and Powch, I. (1997) *Journey of Healing*. Honolulu, HI: Department of Veterans Affairs National Center for PTSD.
4 Lori Daniels, long-time colleague and friend of Ray Scurfield, has creatively utilized a pie chart, generated from dialogue with the veteran, to visually separate the different percentages that the veteran had been assuming at the beginning of the intervention. Then, another pie chart is created later, based upon the more "objective" perspective that takes into account an expanded set of persons sharing the 100% responsibility.
5 The name and some facts have been changed to insure confidentiality.

References

American Psychiatric Association. (2000). *The Diagnostic and Statistical Manual of Mental Disorders, IV-TR*. Washington, DC: American Psychiatric Association.

Goodman, D. (2004, October 10). "Breaking Ranks." Accessed at: http://motherjones.com/politics/2004/10/breaking ranks.

Kubany, E., & Watson, S. (2003). "Guilt: Elaboration of a Multidimensional Model." *Psychological Record*, 53 (1): 51–90.

Kushner, H. S. (1981). *When Bad Things Happen To Good People*. New York, NY: Schocken Books.

Schiraldi, G. (2000). *The Post-Traumatic Stress Disorder Source Book*. Los Angeles: McGraw-Hill.

Scurfield, R. M. (1988, April). "A Critique of the Rationale to Delete Survival Guilt From the *DSM-III-R* Criteria For PTSD." National Center on PTSD, Department of Veterans Affairs, *PTSD Quarterly Newsletter*, 5 (2): 3.

Scurfield, R. M. (1993). "Treatment of PTSD among Vietnam Veterans." In J. P. Wilson & B. Raphael (Eds.), *The International Handbook of Traumatic Stress Syndromes* (pp. 879–888). New York, NY: Plenum Press.

Scurfield, R. M. (1994). "War-Related Trauma: An Integrative Experiential, Cognitive and

Spiritual Approach. In M. B. Williams & J. F. Sommer (Eds.), *Handbook of Post-Traumatic Therapy* (pp. 180–204). Westport, CN: Greenwood Press.

Scurfield, R. M. (2006). *War Trauma: Lessons Unlearned from Vietnam to Iraq.* New York, NY: Algora.

Shay, J. (1994). *Achilles in Vietnam.* New York, NY: Atheneum.

Weinraub, B. (2003, April 6). "Nation at War in the Field/V Corps: Therapy on the Fly for Soldiers Who Face Anxiety in the Battlefield." *The New York Times.* Accessed at: http://www.nytimes.com/2003/04/06/world/nation-war-field-v-corps-therapy-fly-for-soldiers-who-face-anxiety-battlefield.html.

18 Slogging the Bog of War to Return to the World of Work

Mary Beth Williams

Most approaches to healing from war describe clinical mental health interventions that focus on psychological and cognitive issues and dynamics. The approach described herein has a different focus: how to help veterans impacted by war successfully enter or re-enter the civilian workforce. Veteran transition and employment services are identified, to include a description of the purpose and methods of an innovative approach to facilitate veterans to seek, find, and retain meaningful post-war employment.

The Costs of War

By January 19, 2012, 6,351 U.S. service members and DoD civilians had been killed in Iraq and Afghanistan, and 46,484 wounded (Department of Defense, 2012). In 2010, suicides for the first half of the year had increased 12 percent over 2009 (Zoroya, 2010a). As of December, 2010, 650,000 Iraq and Afghanistan veterans had been treated in VA hospitals, nearly 500,000 of whom were receiving compensation, and 150,000 disability claims have languished in the VA system for more than 125 days (Watson Institute, 2011). The Rand Corporation (Tanielian & Jaycox, 2008) study reported that approximately one-fifth of returnees had reported symptoms of PTSD or major depression, but only half had sought treatment. Thus, over 300,000 persons have combat-related mental health problems, with an extensive human cost, and a $6.2 billion cost in direct medical care and lost productivity in the first two years after their return.

In addition, there are negative career consequences for returning veterans who have lost opportunities for promotions or even positions. According to COL Scott Marrs (Dingfelder, 2009), only 3 percent of those who referred themselves for mental health treatment encountered a negative career impact, in comparison with 30 percent who had been referred for treatment by their commanders. And Borchard (2010) notes that approximately 40 percent of homeless veterans suffer from some type of mental illness. Many veterans do not "end up" with PTSD or post-war symptoms, yet war does alter the psyche of those who participate or witness its horror.

Returning service members frequently fear that seeking mental health help will impact their careers and obstruct/pose obstacles in their progress toward attaining rank. Other veterans, as they leave active duty service or return home to civilian life, typically desire re-entry into the lives they left behind, in a seamless manner, without directing attention to themselves. However, for many, a smooth transition is not possible, and the development of a personalized Comprehensive Transition Plan becomes necessary. The individual then is aided through a process of intake, assessment, goal setting (remain in or transition from military service), review of transition goals, and rehabilitation (if necessary), which includes issues related to employment and career, pre-transition and post-transition.

The Disabled Veteran: The Challenges and Benefits of Returning to (Civilian) Work

While many veterans seek compensation for their disabilities, and enter into an often extremely frustrating VA system, others wish to return to the workforce and, oftentimes, to their previous jobs. Why is the return to work such a desirable activity? According to Morin (2004), work

> can serve as a tonic for personal identity in that it helps boost self esteem. When an individual does meaningful work, he actually develops a sense of identity, worth, and dignity . . . and even actualizes his full potential . . . work is . . . an activity through which an individual fits into the world, creates new relations, uses his talents, learns and grows, and develops his identity and a sense of belonging.
>
> (p. 3)

For many, military service fulfills such goals.

Any disability a service member might have, such as PTSD or mild traumatic brain injury, can hinder the accomplishment of desired career and job goals, or prevent him or her from obtaining future gainful employment. According to the Department of Labor (Zoroya, 2010b), young Iraq and Afghanistan veterans had an unemployment rate of 21.1 percent, compared to a 16.6 percent rate for young non-veterans, and a national unemployment rate for all individuals of approximately 9.3 percent.

Can a disabled veteran return to a pre-war civilian job? There are three primary requirements to consider with respect to meaningful work for the disabled veteran:

- *Significance*: it has value from the veteran's perspective.
- *Direction*: it fits with the veteran's orientation to work, as well as the goals he or she is seeking and the intents that guide them.
- *Coherence*: the fit between the veteran's expectations and values and the daily actions of the work he or she does (Morin, 2004).

Tasks for Military Returnees Desiring Return to the Civilian Workforce

Part of assessing whether a return to work is feasible for the veteran means examining whether or not there is a risk of harm to either the veteran or the general public if such a return to work were to occur. Any disability, such as PTSD or mild traumatic brain injury, is likely, to varying degrees, to complicate if not prevent gainful employment. This can be a daunting process for veterans with disabilities, particularly if they have lost mental or physical function, or are plagued by traumatic reminders of the war.

Another task for returnees who desire to return to the workforce outside of military service, is to examine their capacities, including physical and emotional strength, levels of endurance, flexibility, and the ability to sustain a certain activity level and degree of both acute and chronic pain. A third task is assessment of the ability to be able to handle sustained work or activity at a specific level (Talmage & Melhorn, 2005).

Legal Protections Regarding Employment

The Americans with Disabilities Act was amended in December 2008 and its provisions went into effect in January 2009. Title 1 of the ADA prohibits companies (private, state, and local government) with 15 or more employees from discriminating against individuals on the basis of disability, and requires those companies to make reasonable accommodations for them to be able to work. The U.S. Equal Employment Opportunity Commission (EEOC) enforces Title l. Veterans are also provided protection by the Uniformed Services Employment and Reemployment Rights Act (USERRA), enforced by the Department of Labor; the re-employment rights of returnees are protected and employers are required to make reasonable efforts to help veterans to become job qualified, with or without service-connected disabilities.

Veteran "MP" was awarded a 70 percent VA service-connected disability rating in 2009, retroactive to separation from military service in 2008. Numerous public sector mental healthcare providers attested that he was qualified for a 100 percent disability rating. His service included tours in Kosovo (2001–2003) and Iraq (2003–2004; 2006–2007). His therapist presented him with a copy of *The PTSD Workbook* (Williams & Poijula, 2002) and he has corresponded with me.

MP's story is similar to that of many veterans who have had repeat deployments. He receives treatment from a therapist for "intellectual grounding;" a "shrink" for medication management of sleep, concentration, stress reactions and mood; and a marriage counselor to try to save his marriage "in the 11th hour." None of his providers is a PTSD expert. He has found the VA system to be personally useless.

MP's question is, *what happens when someone with PTSD gets PTSD, and then gets it some more and then some more?* He wonders if "combat PTSD" is, in many ways, similar to complex PTSD (Williams & Poijula, 2002). He cannot identify which of many war incidents causes him the most serious of his psychological problems, but can clearly describe "the incident that took my Christian faith from me . . . (as well as) any dozen or so events that contribute to one of three recurring nightmares." He can also describe how "personally killing people face to face" makes him feel. His story illustrates the severe impact of war upon the self, which must be taken into account in providing services related to seeking, finding, and retaining employment.

Veterans' Transition and Employment Services

There are various programs that have been created to assist veterans, to include those with disabilities, to become gainfully employed. For example, in Virginia, the Virginia Wounded Warrior Program offers several services for returning veterans, as does the

Virginia Air National Guard Yellow Ribbon Program. One event hosted by the latter was a 60 day post-deployment event for 150 Air National Guard service members and their families, to provide them with resource and benefit information.

War as a Bog: The US Vet Source Veteran Transition Program

An illustration of a program that will be national in scope—a program with which I, personally, am very familiar—is the US Vet Source Program initiative. Founded in April 2008, Mais, parent of US Vet Source, is a verified service-disabled-veteran owned small business that serves as an umbrella organization through which a variety of veteran-based services are offered. The mission of the program is to support returning veterans as they re-enter and transition to the civilian workforce in particular, and civilian life in general. These veteran returnees have been, for the most part, highly trained, motivated, and disciplined through their military service, and through exposure to high risk environments in which failure can mean death. Trained to work under duress, they have relied upon the military for direction and life focus.

The US Vet Source Veteran Transition and Employment Program provides an integrated service-oriented approach to support the recruiting requirements of various corporations, including a two-and-a-half day proprietary healthcare reintegration program within the structure of acculturation and training; ongoing mentoring capability to support the veterans and employers post-hiring; human resource/capital services; and evidence-based research. The hiring and recruiting aspects of this program are the result of years of human resource consulting experiences, in the assessment and selection of veterans' needs, by James G. Masland, Jr., CEO and co-founder of the organization. He served as an Air Force pilot in the Strategic Air Command for six years, and had extensive combat time in Vietnam as he piloted refueling aircraft for the USAF. It is now on the internet as usvetsource.com.

The training program focuses on the metaphor of war as a bog. There are eight specific topics/strategies to assist veterans in dealing with the demons trapped in this bog, using a peer-reviewed group-oriented workbook that is based on military values and culture. A transition workshop is offered to companies who are hiring returning veterans, which will be incorporated into their training programs. It can also be offered independently by instructors who have extensive experience with military organizations and the field of trauma. The ongoing mentoring program uses IT technology and a web-based site that supports veterans during their first year of transition into civilian employment and life. The entire program has a very strong research component (described later). Recruits complete a series of instruments online prior to beginning the training, and complete a smaller number of instruments as part of the mentoring, in order to monitor progress in belief change, resilience, hardiness, and coping skills.

US Vet Source offers private sector employers a national database of carefully screened veterans who are seeking employment. These veterans have been identified and initially interviewed at various job fairs and veteran-oriented events. It also ensures that all veterans being hired by the selected companies will complete the training program, which focuses on the effects of combat trauma, and those skills and knowledge "bytes" that can facilitate a smoother transition and improve the chances for successful employment.

Constructing a New, Non-Military/Non-War, Reality

Any program that helps veterans to integrate within new or familiar work settings, and to re-establish a sense of identity, should include a focus on their disabilities and emotional and physical changes within a context of retraining, accommodations, and assistance. The veteran, often, must identify new world views learned in deployment (e.g., that there is no such thing as absolute safety, or that it is not always possible to trust one's immediate perceptions of what is real) and deal with challenges to previously held military values and moral principles (e.g., that personal sacrifice and honoring one's duty to fellow service members are primary). Aspects of a new reality must be constructed that are not based on core values of military service, such as "one's employer does not always have the best interests of the employee as a central focus." This also means looking at ways to extricate the self from "the Bog of War," within which the returnee can be stuck, while challenging inappropriate negative beliefs, such as "it is now impossible to trust anyone."

> "DA" is a returning OEF veteran who witnessed the aftermath of a helicopter crash that killed several of his fellow Marines. This occurred shortly after deployment. He lost other buddies, and now believes that, if he gets close to anyone at all, now that he is home, that person will have harm come to him or her. He is beginning to work on trust issues in his therapy sessions.

US Vet Source seeks corporate sponsorship from organizations interested in hiring veterans who have returned from deployment and wish to enter civilian life and the workforce. These corporations will support the Veteran Transition and Employment Program by sponsoring and funding workshops, and by committing to hiring veterans and service-disabled veterans. US Vet Source helps organizations to understand and appreciate the positives inherent in hiring veterans; for example, that veterans want to work hard to ensure that the American way of life is not destroyed. These organizations will have access to highly trained and motivated men and women who have been exposed to discipline in a high risk work environment, and who ascribe to military core values that are complementary to the work roles for which those veterans might be hired. For example, a core value that translates well to the civilian employment marketplace is that of loyalty to one's organization and employer.

In addition, individuals completing the workshop component of the training will have access to ongoing web-based mentoring and monitoring during the first year after training. Corporations will have access to the incentives of the WOTC (Work Opportunity Tax Credit), which is a federal tax credit for private sector businesses, encouraging them to hire individuals from 12 targeted groups that are facing significant barriers to employment. One such group is veterans. Thus, the MAIS Program, depending on the specific employment scenario, offers private sector businesses an opportunity to reduce federal income tax liability.

The Selection Process

US Vet Source has developed a national network of referral sources that reaches within military programs, such as the Warrior Transition Command and National Guard transition programs, to identify veterans who are seeking employment. These veterans may send resumés to, and schedule interviews with, specific companies that are hiring; additionally, US Vet Source may also organize its own training program. In 2008, Congress passed the Yellow Ribbon Program, funded by the Department of Defense, with the expressed purpose of supporting National Guard and Army Reserve returnees. Contacts with Yellow Ribbon Program directors have led to a viable source for job candidates, as have contacts with Wounded Warrior project representatives throughout the Commonwealth of Virginia. www.usvetsource.com is now a 501(C)(3) non-profit entity.

The Metaphor of War as a Bog

Re-experiencing traumatic events can keep a survivor stuck in a personal bog. A bog is generally made from dead plant material. Some individuals envision a bog as a tar bog that traps them and holds them down. Bogs can be described in a number of ways: as places that are murky, mucky, and slimy, rather than beautiful and easily traversable; as part quicksand, part solid, part liquid. Bogs also support life as land and plant communities that foster the development of peat, a precursor to coal. Thus, they are essential to human life and, through the creation of greenhouse gases such as carbon dioxide, allow energy to be retained on earth to prevent climate change.

The veteran transition workshop, developed by this author, challenges participants to explore their personal bogs to discover exit points, positive aspects, the meanings that might arise while in the bogs, and the challenges they can overcome as they improve their abilities to extricate themselves from those bogs. Bogs can be envisioned in several ways. One veteran describes his bog as "endless muck from which there is no escape at the present time." Another describes it as "a series of unstable lily pads that he must jump between, depending on the circumstances of life."

Repeated deployments and exposures to multiple traumatic events can keep the service member stuck in a personal military-based cultural bog that does not provide strategies for disengagement or a return to a productive civilian life, i.e., the collectivistic nature of military service, with the value of selfless service and primacy of duty to the mission, can prevent help-seeking and undermine reintegration into the civilian world.

"R" returned as a recognized "warrior" from Iraq, and was told he would start back in his pre-deployment job as a town employee doing landscaping and maintenance. His expectations about being honored for his personal sacrifice and selfless service in Iraq were not met. His boss placed him into a position of less authority than he had when he left. His "buddy," who had had a similar position when R left, was now his supervisor, and had no consideration for R's PTSD, his triggers, his need for space when experiencing a flashback, or for what it meant to be a returning warrior. R eventually quit his job and sought compensation for PTSD.

In general, the bog is viewed in a negative light because it holds veterans back from establishing and successfully accomplishing their goals. However, in the course of the veteran transition workshop, after learning/discussing each of the skill areas, attendees are directed to recreate/redraw their bogs and see the changes that have occurred, identifying any items/ideas/persons who have helped them to try to move out of the bog and to heal.

US Vet Source Workshop Components

The two-and-a-half day workshop is centered on the creation and conceptualization of each participant's bog and how that bog changed with the introduction of work. Eight modules examine various ways for veterans to remove themselves from the bog. Each of the eight modules includes a knowledge content base and expands into discussion, group exercises, personal activities, and skills to help them transition into civilian life and the world of work. After completing each module, the participant is redirected to vision his or her bog, and to determine whether or not it has been challenged or altered.

Challenging War-Related Belief Systems

One of the eight modules is *Work with Challenging War-Related Belief Systems*. This brief introduction to that module provides the reader with an indication as to how the technique can be utilized by a clinician, or by others, in a real-world setting.

According to Rosenbloom and Williams (2010), in their book, *Life After Trauma: A Workbook for Healing*, veterans who are attempting to return to work, if they are to improve functional outcomes, must consider their beliefs about five basic psychological needs: safety, trust, power/control, esteem, and intimacy. Additionally, they must take into account whether or not those beliefs have been significantly impacted by wartime experiences and whether or not these belief systems need to be challenged, modified, changed, or maintained if these veterans are to be successful as they transition home. CSDT (Constructivist Self-Development Theory) combines object relations, self psychology, and social cognition theories, and is founded upon the constructivist view of trauma (McCann & Pearlman, 1999).

This model indicates that an individual's unique (including military) history shapes his or her experiences of the traumatic events and defines how s/he adapts to that trauma (ibid). For example, a veteran who has been exposed to multiple deaths, has killed, and has witnessed the aftermaths of atrocities, will have a different experience of war than an individual who remains in a compound doing IT work and does not venture out into the countryside or "outside the wire," and who has not witnessed terrorist activities.

Beliefs that veterans have formed and are maintained after one or more deployments are quite likely to be different from those held prior to deployment (as described below). This is particularly true if the veterans have had experiences with the taking of lives or borne witness to the carnage of war.

Beliefs Related to the Five Basic Psychological Needs

Military service and exposure to war-related incidents greatly influence those deployed, and are designed to help the service member survive in a hostile environment. However, many of the beliefs related to the *five basic psychological needs of safety, trust, power/control, esteem, and intimacy of self, others, and the world* do not serve the veteran well in a civilian environment. The assumptions, interpretations, and principles learned while at war can, in fact, prevent acculturation. Furthermore, many civilian organizations and groups do not adhere to the sacred values of the military that service members "hold dear."

In the following section, there are brief descriptions of how the five critical psychological needs can be problematic in the transition from the military to the civilian world.

Safety

The most important psychological need upon of a returning veteran is that of safety. Disabled combat veterans need to feel reasonably protected from harm inflicted by the self, others, and the environment. They also need to believe that their significant others are reasonably protected from harm that might be inflicted by the self and also by other sources, including co-workers and the environment.

Returning veterans typically uphold many beliefs that contribute to, or detract from, a sense of safety. For persons who have been embedded in a war zone, the world is no longer a safe and predictable place. Earlier beliefs about safety may have changed, if not been challenged. Every corner might have a car ready to ram one's own car; every road may have an IED hidden, ready to explode.

When these veterans return home, they often feel no sense of safety or predictability. For example, several veterans have stated that their driving patterns have been so impacted that they cannot drive on busy highways in rush hour traffic because it simply is not safe. A terrorist may be in any car just waiting to blow them up. If they try to return to previous jobs, they feel out of place and out of touch. They may no longer feel a sense of environmental safety, and do not believe that they have the ability to exit safely when a situation turns dangerous, unless they are near to an exit or, in an office setting, have their backs to the wall so they are able to scan their surroundings at all times. They may need to develop a safe place, in reality, to which they can go in times of danger; they may also find it helpful to develop a safe place or sanctuary in their minds.

Teaching veterans a variety of behavioral techniques to help build a sense of safety may also be indicated; among these are muscle relaxation, deep breathing, mindfulness techniques (see Muzuki, this volume), creation of an internal safe place, creation of an external "cave" or safe place, and "Cook's Hookup," a specific exercise that involves crossing the midline and using deep breathing. They may also develop cues or words to use as a signal for the need to undertake a safety "check-up" or intervention when they are stressed, anxious, or uncomfortable in a situation or conversation. The questions that veterans may ask of themselves in this endeavor include: What does being "safe" mean to you? With whom do you feel safest? How safe are you "really?"

First, the veteran needs to assess presently-held beliefs regarding each of the five psychological needs. Once a belief has been identified ("I am not safe on the highway"), then the veteran must evaluate whether or not the belief is useful or destructive to the self by identifying three pieces of evidence:

1. Evidence that supports the presently-held belief *as* accurate. For example: "Anyone might be carrying a weapon in their vehicle." "I don't have the ability to see into every vehicle near me and this may be a recipe for disaster." "If there are too many cars near me, I don't have clear access to escape."
2. Evidence that the belief may *not* be accurate. For example: "I drive defensively and keep a good distance between myself and other cars." "I am carrying a weapon and have a concealed weapon's permit and could defend myself if I need to." "There have been no instances of terrorist attacks on this road at all."
3. Identify the place along a line graph where the presently held belief lies. Is it:

Accurate	Inaccurate
Helpful	Harmful
Calming	Anxiety Producing
Safety Producing	Danger Warning
Leading to Self Understanding	Self Confusing
Essential to Survival	Non-Essential
Fostering Active Coping	Non-Fostering
Meaning Sense	Meaningless
Leading to Good Decisions	Non-Productive

Depending on the responses to these questions and statements, the veteran may choose to challenge and try to alter these beliefs. For example, if the major of responses indicate that the belief is inaccurate and negative to the self ("I am not safe on this highway; this means I cannot drive to work, and there is no other mass transportation, so I have to quit and find a job closer to home"), then the individual can postulate one or more alternative beliefs that might be more useful or appropriate or desired.

A new, revised, more positive, set of beliefs might include the knowledge "that bad things can happen at any time (e.g., wrecks), but I am a good driver and pay attention to my surroundings and remain hypervigilant. These traits will help me develop a better internal locus of control over my driving, and what happens to me while driving, if I maintain a safe distance and don't weave, swerve, or speed."

It is important to remember that the alternative belief needs to be more positive, serving as a "transitional" belief until it can be evaluated, examined, and considered from a multitude of perspectives. Is it helpful? Does it give a different, more flexible or relevant picture of reality? Does it help the veteran to cope with traumatic experiences and relationships, and assist in re-entering a work environment? This format can be utilized with any of the psychological need-related beliefs (Rosenbloom & Williams, 2010).

Trust

The second psychological need for returning veterans who have chosen to enter or re-enter a workplace is trust. Trust is the need to rely on personal judgment, as well as the need to rely upon others at home, in the workplace, or in the world at large. When Reservists or Guardsmen return to pre-deployment jobs, others must also believe that they are able to trust these returnees' decision-making skills and ability to handle responsibility in the workplace. However, an employer needs to realize that he or she cannot expect the veteran to reintegrate immediately or unconditionally. The creation or re-creation of trust requires a commitment of time.

What beliefs about trust does the returning veteran have? Have those beliefs changed or have they been modified? Do those beliefs need to be challenged? It may be necessary for a mental health professional to work with these veterans to assume the role of advocate and to make contacts and referrals if veterans are unable to do so themselves. If a veteran is placed in a position of influence and authority, and does not (yet) have trust in his own judgments or ability to analyze a situation, it might be important to have someone to whom that veteran can go in order to"bounce off" ideas: a mentor. The online support aspect of the US Vet Source program can also serve to provide such support.

In order to build trust with a returning veteran, counselors and therapists alike must understand the language and culture of the branch of the military to which the veteran belong(ed). It is very critical to appreciate and understand their values, while recognizing the role of the military culture (rank, chain of command, mission, unit cohesion) upon each individual veteran. Military personnel have been taught that "rank has its privileges," and to honor those with higher rank and more experience. If they are put into a work situation in which there is little or no respect for experience, service, or position, this could lead to a conflict between values and performance.

Power and Control

Returning veterans have necessarily had to rely upon themselves and their battle buddies for safety. The trust between buddies is very powerful and durable, and often cannot be replicated in a civilian setting. Seeking ways to control some aspects of their lives may readily become a preoccupation with them. However, if those returning veterans have suffered serious injuries, brain trauma, or PTSD, they may believe that they are no longer in control, or in charge of their own bodies, actions, or destiny. They may be strangers to themselves, and no longer feel competent within their own skin. Soldiers with impacted vision, ambulation, or lessened brain functioning, may no longer believe they are able to control the environment in which they live. As their identities change, as their bodies change, as their beliefs about power and control change, so also may their body image and control of bodily functioning change.

While walking along a busy street in Atlanta, GA, a veteran and his family walked by me. I had noticed that the Redskins football team bus was beginning to load for the game. When the veteran walked by, it was obvious that the back of his head was indented and had large scars. I then noticed he was wearing an Army shirt, and had a cane in the hand that was not holding onto his spouse. His two elementary age children were accompanying the family. They turned and came back toward the bus. Automatically, I walked up to him and thanked him for his service. He explained that he and his family were in Atlanta to "see" the Skins play the Falcons. He was blind, however. I asked where he had served, and he said, "Baghdad," and added, "I just wish I could go back and finish what we started." This soldier's world has been forever changed by an IED, as he explained. Still, he wanted to continue on fighting.

To regain a sense of control of the environment, it is important to begin on a small scale. What exactly are the veterans' beliefs about control and power? What will the veteran realistically be able to control, both at home and on the job? If the veteran needs assistive devices (i.e., wheelchairs, canes, prosthetic devices), work modification (i.e., special seating arrangements, noise protection, visual assistance devices), or a service animal, in order, for example, to complete work tasks or to feel safe in the work environment, what will be the impacts of these needs in the work setting? The need for modifications may affect decisions as to what type of work it might be feasible for the veteran to embark upon, and what coping strategies are achievable, no matter how seemingly insignificant.

Among the questions veterans may ask of themselves, in order to identify their beliefs about control and power, are the following: Do you believe you are out of control? Are you a stranger to yourself? What active coping strategies do you utilize?

Esteem

Many returning veterans need to re-establish a sense of self worth within the civilian world. Their own thoughts, feelings, and beliefs are important elements of their personal self-evaluation. If the veteran is trying to develop work-related skills (a vital aspect of self-esteem), it is also important to help the veteran learn to value himself in that arena as a productive citizen. The veteran may ask herself the following questions, and then challenge beliefs those beliefs, as noted in the "Safety" section: What is your self-value? What do you value in others?

For example, many returning veterans believe they had great value as soldiers or warriors. However, when they return home, they find that their children may not know or listen to them; their spouses have taken over duties that were once theirs. Yet, they want things to be "as they once were." When this is not the case, they may begin to question their own worth and belonging. They may become angry at those around them who have "taken over" or changed their lives, whether such was done unintentionally or not.

Intimacy

The fifth, and final, psychological need is that of intimacy toward the self, others, and the environment. Intimacy is the need to know and accept personal feelings and thoughts, while also being accepted, known, and loved by others. The key factor involving intimacy is self-acceptance and emotional attachment to the self. This must be accomplished before trying to build attachment to others, both in interpersonal and workplace relationships.

Relationships built on the job are generally not the same as relationships between members of a cohesive military unit. For example, the close "battle buddy" system of warriors who understand one another does not necessarily occur on the job, unless other employees are also veterans. Also, if veterans have been exposed to horrific war experiences that have left them changed in body, mind, and spirit, their intimate relationships at home often become challenged, strained, or broken, because their capacity to be intimate has been changed as well. If these veterans have been diagnosed with PTSD, they may feel even more alienated, different, isolated, and removed from society. Changes in belief systems that have come about as the result of one's wartime experiences may also impact relationships with co-workers who may be uncomfortable dealing with returning veterans, or even if, or how, they might initiate discussion about wounds of war, including traumatic brain injury or PTSD. If the veteran's world has been completely changed by the experiences s/he has had during deployment, priorities also may have changed, and the ability to return to a former work setting may be less than feasible. Among the questions that veterans may ask themselves about intimacy are: How do you connect with yourself? Do you feel alienated or different from others?

Mentoring Support Services in the First Year of Employment

Our website has been designed to offer a portal for veterans to support the selection, workshop, and mentoring activities in which they have participated. This site also supports employers who have become corporate sponsors. The website, when operational, will allow veterans to register and seek employment opportunities; remain in touch with workshop cohorts/graduates; have access to professional support; have access to updates and news about work, PTSD, TBI, and other topics; provide access to ongoing research opportunities and measurements of personal adjustment and growth; and provide descriptions of measures to support their hiring and work processes. The support services are password protected, with various levels of security and confidentiality.

Research Focus

The US Vet Source Program offers an evidence-based research component designed to assess veterans' experiences, present level of functioning and symptoms, and the impact of the various support programs. The author has created a very comprehensive War Stressor Inventory (Williams, 2011) that can be used with permission of the author. All persons attending the workshop complete this inventory, and several other instruments, prior to attending the workshop. Among them are the Post-Traumatic Checklist, Military Version (Weathers, 1993), Combat Experiences Scale (Keane, et al., 1989), Penn Inventory (Hammarberg, 1992), Connor-Davidson Resilience Scale (Burns & Anstey, 2010), and others. Persons who complete the workshop and join the online mentoring and support groups will have follow-up research opportunities provided to them at six and twelve months post-completion, to determine whether or not their PTSD symptoms have decreased and their resilience has increased.

MP's Suggestion for Ways to Cope with his Bog

The veteran mentioned earlier in this chapter ("MP") described some of the interventions that he has used to try to cope with his PTSD. However, these counseling sessions did not offer him "the adrenalin rush of battle" or provide means to find a similar rush in a non-destructive way. Therefore, he wrote that:

> I have been a bit checked out . . . but am trying to claw back into guiding my own future . . . (I believe I must) fake it until I find a place to start till I make it. But what am I trying to make it to? I can't go back, the demon can't come out, not here, not

anymore . . . Then, one evening, I find myself standing at the midfield line on a soccer pitch . . . I could feel oxygen flowing through my blood, charging my muscles, endorphins racing about making everything feel . . . good.

He continues that he prepared to participate in a soccer game:

working out, going to practice, thinking about the game plan. All the while feeling edgy, getting a little pulse of adrenaline with every thought . . . nothing else matters, the demon races about kicking the crap out of a little leather sphere. I focus completely on the match, the ball . . . I feel the weight of nothing . . . I just feel good.

He flashes back:

The bad guys died or quit and they didn't hurt any I care about. Man, this feels good . . . Wow. I felt something, something good. So it can happen. The demon came out and played safely and it felt good . . . Knowing I can feel something without the demon taking control is a place to start.

We could ask him.

Closing

As MP's story illustrates, and as the US Vet Source Program attempts to put into practice, there is more than one way to help veterans heal and return to some semblance of a normal life. Scurfield (2011) noted, in his rationale for the creation of this book, that "The reality is that our government never will have sufficient resources to do full justice to the legitimate needs of our service members, veterans, and their families" (p. 15).

Creating training programs that are utilized within the workplace, and which are sanctioned by employers, whether standing alone or integrated into other training experiences, can help to lessen the burden on the government. The alternative ways for veterans to clear the demons and monsters with which they live and, thereby, diminish the pressures of war upon them (for example, through organized sports such as soccer, or through exercise, participation in cohort groups, or intensive workshops) can also double as excellent avenues for healing and recovery.

Any program that aids veterans in the integrating process within new work settings also assists them in re-establishing a new sense of identity that incorporates disabilities, emotional changes, and physical changes within a context of retraining, accommodations, and assistance. The veteran must identify new world views, and challenge previously-held values and moral principles, as well as other aspects of a new reality. This also means looking at ways to extricate the self from what this author terms "The Bog of War," while challenging inappropriate negatively-held belief systems.

References

Borchard, T. J. (2010). "Beyond Blue: A Spiritual Journey to Mental Health." Blogpost dated November 11, 2010. Accessed at Beliefnet.com/beyond blue.

Burns, R. A., & Anstey, K. J. (2010). "The Connor-Davidson Resilience Scale (CD-RISC): Testing the Invariance of a Uni-Dimensional Resilience Measure that is Independent of Positive and Negative Affect." *Personality and Individual Differences, 48* (5): 527–531.

Department of Defense. (2012). "U.S. Casualty Status." Accessed at: http://www.defense.gov/news/casualty.pdf.

Dingfelder, L. (2009). "War on Stigma." *Monitor on Psychology, 40* (6): *52.* Accessed at: http://www.apa.org/monitor/2009/06/stigma-war.aspx

Hammarberg, M. (1992). *Penn Inventory for Posttraumatic Stress Disorder (Penn Inventory).* Accessed at: http://www.ptsd.va.gov/professional/pages/assessments/penn-inventory-ptsd.asp.

Keane, T. M., Fairbank, J. A., Caddell, J. M., Zimering, R. T., Taylor, K. L., & Mora, C. A. (1989). *The Combat Experiences Scale.* White River Junction, VT: Department of Veterans Affairs.

McCann, I. L., & Pearlman, L. A. (1992). "Constructivist Self-Development Theory: A Theoretical Framework for Assessing and Treating Traumatized College Students. *Journal of American College Health, 40* (4): 189–196.

Morin, E. M. (2004). "The Meaning of Work in Modern Times." Paper delivered at the 10th World Congress in Human Resource Management, Rio de Janeiro, Brazil, August 20, 2004.

Rosenbloom, D., & Williams, M. B. (2010). *Life After Trauma: A Workbook for Healing* (2nd Edn.). New York, NY: Guilford Press.

Scurfield, R. M., & Platoni, K. T. (2012). *War Trauma and Its Wake: Expanding the Circle of Healing.* New York: Routledge.

Talmage, J. B., & Melhorn, J. M. (2005). *A Physician's Guide to Return to Work.* Washington, DC: APA Press.

Tanielian, T., & Jaycox, L. H. (2008). "Invisible Wounds of War: Physiological and Cognitive Injuries, Their Consequences and Services to Assist Recovery." Rand Corporation. Accessed at: http://www.rand.org/pubs/monographs/MG720.html.

Watson Institute. (2011). "Costs of War: Caring for U.S. Veterans." Accessed at: http://costsofwar.org/article/caring-us-veterans.

Weathers, F. (1993). *PTSD Checklist (PCL).* White River Junction, VA: National Center for PTSD. Accessed at: http://costsofwar.org/article/caring-us-veterans.

Williams, M. B. (forthcoming). *Slogging the Bog of War.* Warrenton, VA: Author.

Williams, M. B., & Poijula, S. (2002). *The PTSD Workbook.* Oakland, CA: New Harbinger Publications, Inc.

Zoroya, G. (2010a). "Army Reports Record Number of Suicides for June." *USA Today.* Accessed at: http://www.usatoday.com/news/military/2010-07-15-army-suicides_N.htm?csp=34news.

Zoroya, G. (2010b). "Joblessness Hits Male Vets of Current Wars." *USA Today.* Accessed at: http://www.usatoday.com/news/military/2010-04-06-vets_N.htm.

19 Spirituality in Facilitating Healing from War Trauma

Stephanie Laite Lanham and
Joyce Hartwell Pelletier

This chapter explores emotional healing from trauma, utilizing the application of spiritual interventions. Spiritual approaches are presented as well as positive coping strategies and specific options for engaging the often emotionally-guarded veteran. Quotes have been included from those who have had their lives, and the lives of their families, negatively impacted by the trauma of military service, both on and off the battlefield. There is a discussion about reconnecting with "spiritual roots" and integrating one's renewed spirituality with the reality of the past; this may result in a "new normal" for emotional stability and improvement in quality of life. Written from a Judeo-Christian perspective, the authors have included quotes from those who have made the conscious decision to add spiritual interventions into their healing experience.

The Impact of Military-Related Trauma

Veterans suffering from war trauma may experience multiple symptoms, such as poor concentration, intrusive memories, anxiety, depression, anger or rage, loss of interest in pleasurable activities, lack of motivation for life, flashbacks of traumatic events, sleep disturbances, hypervigilance, poor self-esteem, problems with trust, and communication disruption with family and friends. (See "Post Traumatic Stress Disorder (PTSD)" in the *Diagnostic and Statistical Manual of Mental Disorders, IV-TR* (APA, 2000).) While the *DSM-IV-TR* does not specify spiritually-related problems following trauma exposure, a number of clinicians and veterans report post-trauma issues that are related to spiritual and religious beliefs, such as anger towards God, confusion regarding such beliefs, and for some, a strengthening of their religious or spiritual beliefs and convictions (Sippola, et al., 2009; Scurfield, 1994, 2006). The angst that impacts many veterans and their families may reflect common themes and related concerns when they begin to openly communicate their painful and traumatic experiences of wartime service and deployment. These are illustrated by some of the poignant comments we have heard from veterans or the family members of those who have served in time of war.

From the wife of a veteran: He spends time with the children, but I see him looking into space. Even when he's looking right at the children, it's as if they aren't there, although they are standing right in front of him.

From a soldier diagnosed with PTSD: I was just driving to the store the other day and all of a sudden I didn't know how I got there. It's like time passes and I miss it. I sort of blank out, but keep living. It's disturbing.

From the spouse of a soldier: She was over there for almost a year. We kept in touch. I didn't think it would be like this when she came home. I was wrong. The first month or so was okay, but now things are falling apart. The kids notice she's not the same. I think she wants to go back! Sometimes we wouldn't mind if she did . . . she's not the same.

As these individuals returned home from war, symptoms of trauma were readily noticed by close family members. It has been said that the deepest pain leads to the road of transformation. For returning veterans, emotional pain may be experienced silently for a considerable period of time following redeployment. This is commonly referred to as the "Honeymoon Period." It is then that cracks in the armor begin to appear. Symptoms of trauma become disruptive to varying degrees, and are typically experienced as anger, depression, irritability, dissociation, denial, disturbed sleep, memory problems, trauma re-lived (flashbacks), anxiety, guilt, sexual trauma, isolation, and/or low self-esteem.

Most often, a loved one first notices there is something "not quite right" with their veteran as symptoms begin to emerge (Lanham, 2007). Trauma symptoms vary in their presentation, and do not necessarily "look" the same on everyone. Remember that our brains are as varied as our faces. Recognition of symptomatology may provide the impetus for the individual to seek psychological support. As therapeutic connections are made, all involved may begin to feel a sense of hope, which can be wonderfully contagious!

Attending to Religious Beliefs and Spirituality

The Book of Psalms beautifully expresses the alternating emotions of sorrow, despair, hope, and peace. Troubled veterans may find encouragement in the Psalmist's words: "Why are you downcast, O my soul? Why so disturbed within me? Put your hope in God, for I will yet praise him, my Savior and my God" (Psalm 42:5). (All biblical passages are from the International Bible Society (1978, 1984) *The Holy Bible*, New International Version.)

Studies indicate that people with religious beliefs—those who believe in God and participate to some degree in the religious practices of many different faiths—are in the cultural majority (Neilson, Johnson, & Ellis, 2001). Most of the world's peoples are believers in some type of religious tradition; the vast majority of Americans acknowledge a belief in God and an afterlife, with varying levels of religious commitment (ibid.). Not all maintain a strong spiritual life, but many possess a worldview based upon the belief that God exists and holds people responsible for their behaviors (Barna Group, 2011). They embrace moral values with some degree of consistency, and have found a measure of spiritual assistance in their past lives. Others are strongly invested in religious practices and following perpetual lives of faith. Religion and spirituality may be an integral part of a client's life and worldview, and their belief systems will play a significant role in their understanding of the purpose of having suffered and the restoration of emotional safety.

Therefore, religious beliefs need to be addressed in therapy as an important aspect of any client's treatment. Clinicians and caregivers who hold no religious traditions, or are uncomfortable addressing spirituality, are at a distinct disadvantage, as exploration of religious issues may be an appropriate part of comprehensive treatment planning. "Spirituality and religious involvement must be considered in each clinical case . . . it contributes to the treatment process and the course of therapy will influence its expression. We therefore advocate for the practice of psychotherapy that is sensitive to spirituality" (Sperry & Shafranske, 2005, pp. 18–19).

Trauma is especially unsettling to one's worldview and spiritual life. If not explored in the therapeutic context, this may lead the individual to question their pre-existing core beliefs regarding a just God and the ability to trust others. Common signs of spiritual or religious-related issues reported by those who experience trauma include an altered worldview about God's plan, his ways of working in the world, and God's personal protection. Those who believed in God before the trauma occurred, but had not clearly defined their spiritual views or theology of suffering beforehand, may wrestle with existential questions about suffering, evil, forgiveness, justice, purpose, and God's divine order. They may ask, "Where is God?" "Why did God allow this to happen?" "Does God still care about me?" There may be a loss of the sense of meaning of life and troubling doubts that bring about discouragement and hopelessness. Feelings of disconnection from God, isolation, and the shattering of spiritual beliefs may cause a veteran to withdraw from social support or the faith-based community at the very time this is most needed. How could a God allow such evil as befalls the soldier in time of war?

When such a spiritual disconnection is evident, the therapist may assist the client by encouraging social and spiritual support in a loving, caring congregation of welcoming believers, and by gradually exploring the client's personal theology of suffering, as well as the many existential questions asked. Veterans suffering from symptoms of PTSD must come to terms with the reality that life will likely not return to "the way things were" prior to deployment. War experiences of violence, death, isolation, fear, and other catastrophic life events alter a person emotionally. They may confront the emotional anguish that is secondary to the traumatic experience, such as grief, depression, anxiety, anger, intrusive memories, times of panic, sadness, or feelings of disorientation and loss. With the support of a caring and compassionate professional, who will assist the wounded heart in revisiting memories within a *safe* place and in working through a lessening of the pain, distressing memories can be accepted and assimilated into the present. The veteran will need to adjust to the multiple changes that have occurred personally, interpersonally, and spiritually following his or her wartime service, and learn to live within a context referred to as a *new normal*. Finally, the individual may learn effective coping skills which incorporate those strategies for redirecting emotions, in order to repair relationships and fulfill lives which have been altered by traumatic experiences (Parkinson, 2000). The trauma victim may feel very much alone and isolated. From a spiritual perspective, however, there is a God who fully understands the struggles of those who have been traumatized, and directs the wounded to those who are able to provide much needed assistance. "The Lord himself goes before you and will be with you; he will never leave you nor forsake you. Do not be discouraged" (Deuteronomy 31:8).

A veteran may be referred to a skilled professional who is trained to supply both spiritual and psychological interventions. The key is to assist the veteran in obtaining the best care for both heart and soul—only then will the spiritual, emotional, and physical healing take hold (Lanham, 2007). "I will take away sickness from among you" (Exodus 23:25). "Pray for each other so that you may be healed. The prayer of a righteous man is powerful and effective" (James 5:16, 17).

It has often been said by veterans that atheists are never found in foxholes. Perhaps this oft-repeated phrase simplifies the idea that some must be at the most desperate moment of their existence in order to cry out to a Higher Power for help and comfort. Trauma may blind, disrupt, or distort veterans' thinking about many aspects of life, including their spirituality. A world once lived in color may now be lived in shades of gray because of the symptoms so often internalized, such as anxiety, the desire to isolate, dissociation, flashbacks of trauma that may occur at any moment, and more.

A veteran, clinician, peer, or family member may gracefully and respectfully seek or suggest a spiritual pathway as a primary treatment modality. A skilled and sensitive clinician will know when the topic of spirituality is unwelcome, and will, if indicated, withdraw, yet maintain their supportive stance without pressure. When that moment presents itself, perhaps there will be a warm welcome, a smile, a slip of the hand into theirs, a nod of the head or pat on the back, or any other offer of encouragement that allows the sufferer, as well as the helper, to know that the time is right to grasp support of a spiritual nature.

Sharing with someone who is suffering from emotional pain as a result of trauma, that there is a living God who cares, is available to them, and is able to ease their suffering, may be as comforting as any of the many other treatment modalities. The appropriately matched individual psychotherapist may work alongside collaborative therapies such as acupuncture, biofeedback, groups such as Alcoholic Anonymous (AA), and other modalities. These require sensitivity and an assessment as to how suitable each might be for the veteran client. Treatment may also include prescribed and closely monitored psychotropic medication(s) following comprehensive medication evaluation.

It is crucial to recognize that spirituality in a person's life may build the inner soul confidence, faith, and grace that are able to transcend all aspects of one's life experience. Believing in a Higher Power who offers strength, healing, wisdom, and guidance to face one's life when circumstances seem formidable, can be a powerful, positive force for change. The differences between those who incorporate spirituality into their healing experiences and those who do not are exceptional. Spiritual experiences that allow a person to feel God's presence, to sense the healing intervention of the Holy Spirit, and to gain reassurance that God cares for them, may be truly transformational.

Incorporating Spiritual or Religious Elements into Evidence-Based Treatment with War Veterans

Cognitive-Behavioral Therapy (CBT) and Rational-Emotive Behavioral Therapy (REBT)

Many evidence-based treatments can be effective in working with spiritually-oriented clients, such as Cognitive-Behavioral Therapy (CBT), and Rational-Emotive Behavioral Therapy (REBT). CBT and REBT focus on clients' belief systems and the alteration of those beliefs to facilitate emotional relief and behavioral change. This clinical framework is complementary with religious values of accountability for personal behavior. Most major religions are congruent with the following REBT therapy goals: acceptance of human worth, acceptance of uncontrollable situations beyond one's control, and acceptance of life's inevitable discomforts (Neilson, Johnson, & Ellis, 2001). Those who hold commitment to God at the center of their lives can be challenged through scripture to refute those negative beliefs that elicit emotions of sadness, depression, guilt, hopelessness, anger, or fear, and to learn to release their lives into God's care, changing what they can and accepting things they cannot fully understand, such as lingering memories of trauma. Actively incorporating scripture into the therapeutic intervention may assist individuals in perceiving their life difficulties in a broader, more philosophical and spiritual context (Neilson, Johnson, & Ellis, 2001), and in looking beyond themselves to a higher source of strength. Clients can be presented with their own tendencies towards selectively choosing to believe certain elements of their religion, such as promises of joy and happiness, but excluding other helpful principles, such as the character benefits of suffering (Sperry & Shafranske, 2005).

Therapists with an understanding of scripture may assist clients in taking a more consistent, comprehensive view of spiritual principles they might not have previously considered, and to understand suffering as a means to the development of resiliency, strength, and growth. Religious scripture is filled with admonitions to tolerate hardships with patience, to have faith in God's ability to strengthen and provide assistance, and to believe in the soul's eternal significance and purpose in this life.

A Christian approach to CBT may include the following (Tan, 1987; Sperry & Shafranske, 2005, pp. 82–83): emphasizing the importance of "agape" love as divine, unconditional, self-sacrificing, active, volitional, and thoughtful; developing an empathic relationship with the client; praying for inner healing, and the healing of the negative emotional impact of memories; discussing the meaning of spiritual and experiential aspects of life and faith as shown in scripture; learning Biblical truth to promote cognitive restructuring; facilitating dependence on the Lord and the Holy Spirit for lasting change; using the Church and the spiritual community for support resources; and the reaffirming of spiritual perspectives on suffering, character, love, and grace. One example of learning Biblical truth to promote cognitive restructuring is through the utilization of religious imagery. Such imagery may be used in therapy in conjunction with prayer and relaxation techniques. As the client learns to calm his or her body by focusing on rhythmic breathing and by noticing the air flowing gently in and out of the lungs, the client can be taught to bring the body into a state of relaxation. The clinician may instruct the client to choose a peaceful image from scripture, such as the green pastures of Psalm 23, the descriptions of Jesus in Isaiah 6:1, or Jesus praying for the little children in Matthew 19:13–14.

The client may find it beneficial to learn to breathe deeply, and to generate feelings of relaxation and peacefulness while embracing mindful pictures of a kind and loving God. Words congruent with scripture, such as "breathe in peace, breathe out worry," "breathe God," and the words of Jesus in Matthew 6:27–34 ("Who of you by worrying can add a single hour to his life? Your heavenly father knows what you need . . . Do not worry about tomorrow"), may be used as a point of focus to refute negative or anxious self-talk. The client may be taught how to pray for God's help and healing, to pray with the clinician in session, as well as to pray regularly outside therapy sessions. Relaxation techniques, together with spiritual imagery, are powerful interventions for reducing anxiety, fear, guilt, and anger. They invite the client to experience

God's presence and the inner strength that comes from the Holy Spirit. Worshipful music with scriptural words can also be used as a form of meditation, especially verses from the Book of Psalms.

Interpersonal Therapy (IPT)

ITP with spiritually-oriented clients allows for the healing of emotions through insight and the renegotiation of one's interpersonal context (Miller, in Sperry & Shafranske, 2005). ITP is a widely used treatment modality for depressive symptomatology, and for the improvement of interpersonal and social functioning. When spiritual growth is seen as the most fundamental human path and purpose, IPT can assist the wounded veteran by helping him or her to work through interpersonal problems within the context of the veteran's own spiritual beliefs.

From a Christian perspective, scripture passages about loving others, living life sacrificially, understanding strife and suffering, and growing to be Christ-like, allow the individual to address four interpersonal "problem areas" that arise as a result of the emotional upheaval of trauma. These areas of conflict in IPT are seen as interpersonal disputes, life transitions, grief, and interpersonal deficits.

During therapy, the spiritual view of relationships as divine and ordained by God is explained as an opportunity for growth and change. Arguments and disputes with others represent our "blind spots" and unhealthy habits. Life transitions are an opportunity for spiritual evolution and development, and need not be feared with God on our side. Our deficits and strengths teach us spiritual lessons and allow us to share with others in our lives.

Those who experience trauma often undergo multiple losses of friends and loved ones; some have observed the tragic deaths of their fellow veterans in combat, or witnessed the slaughter of innocent civilians. Using IPT, the client and therapist work together to understand suffering from a spiritual perspective, to embrace life as imperfect, to instill hope, and to build character strengths that will carry into enriched relationships, with the expected outcome of reduced depressive symptomatology.

Group-Based Interventions

Group-based modalities, such as group therapy, group support, Marriage Encounter, and AA, can be very complementary with religious or spiritually-oriented interventions. In considering the utilization of group therapy or group support as a therapeutic modality, common integrative spiritual interventions may include group educational topics—such as coping with stress, improving marriage, and parenting effectively—along with available spiritual supports in the community, such as prayer groups, Bible studies, or faith-based addiction recovery groups. For veterans prone to isolating themselves and who may mistrust others, as well as for those who may be addicted to substances, such initiatives can be invaluable.

Clinicians may encourage the memorization of scripture, meditation, prayer, worship music, and regular church attendance within a positive, supportive congregation. Faith-based education in communication skills and anger management help to provide essential life and coping techniques for veterans who remain in the throes of anger and rage, lack self-control in the family environment, have failed relationships, experience despondency and discouragement, or hold a perpetually negative self-image. Marriage retreats, interactions with couples' groups through marriage classes and marriage events, Sunday school classes, children's programs, and camping retreats may also help to model effective partnering and family-building skills.

One couple in the process of trauma recovery, who were working to rebuild their relationship, described their experience with Marriage Encounter:

> We attended with other married couples. Some were military, but not all. It was amazing. We had been "alone" for so long, in different continents . . . it was the best thing we ever did for our marriage, our kids, and for ourselves. I don't think we would have stayed married if we hadn't gone. It was a time of meeting each other again, setting the stage for our life after war.

Another older veteran, like so many, indicated that he found AA to be his "long term lifesaver" and to be the support his family so needed for education, support, and guidance:

> I still attend meetings once a week, and my sponsor is integral to my life. I'm a sponsor to a young man just back from Iraq. The kids learned a lot when they needed it from Al-Anon, and my wife still goes to meetings sometimes. I had to get clean and every day stay clean. The group is my community.

Faciliating Coping and Healing Using Scripture Verses

Clients may elect to read or memorize verses from scripture to alter their negative, fear-producing, self-talk to positive, encouraging, words. Clinicians familiar with scripture verses can facilitate this process. Below are examples of confidence-building verses and principles that have been selected because of their emphasis on God's help, God's ability to change a life, the character benefits of suffering, and the growth potential that may follow. During times of crisis, the voice of fear and disillusionment may overwhelm good judgment. A negative inner dialogue may be at the core of anxiety and depression. A veteran who has experienced life-threatening situations, or has witnessed death and destruction, may be saying, "God doesn't care about me. Nothing works out right in my life. More disasters are likely to happen to me." Under stress, clients may fall into irrational, exaggerated, thought patterns that further discourage growth and change. Christians believe that the Bible, the precepts of the Lord, offer insight and bring happiness to the heart, as stated in Psalm 19:8: "The precepts of the Lord are right, giving joy to the heart. The commands of the Lord are radiant, giving light to the eyes." Joy speaks of happiness and renewed peace; light symbolizes vision, understanding, direction, and spiritual guidance for whatever frightening situation is faced. When reading, digesting, and memorizing scripture, the words may become an encouraging dialogue to be referenced during the storms of life, so that inner strength is not shaken, but made strong, to be able to fight against fear, terror, discouragement, hopelessness, and depression.

Pairing Symptoms with Scripture Readings

Trauma-related symptoms may be paired with an appropriate scripture reading. During the session, the clinician may read aloud a selected scripture, in order to assist the clinician with becoming more comfortable with this practice, particularly if it is new for them. The client may also choose to read verses out loud and then reflect upon their meaning within the context of the therapy session, as well as reading them outside the therapy session.

The authors have identified nine principles, in conjunction with scripture verses from the New International Version of the Bible, which may help to reframe spiritual understanding and to rebuild confidence. Below is *a set of guidelines* for utilizing these nine principles, and their accompanying relevant scripture verses:

- Reproduce these scripture principles and verses as handouts to provide to veterans.
- Ask clients to choose their own verses, through Bible readings outside of the session, as a form of homework.
- Present these verses as pocket-sized laminated key rings to retain in visible places for ready access.
- Suggest the incorporation of these verses as part of an ongoing safety plan.
- During therapy sessions, have the client first read the principles, and then read the scriptures paired with them.
- Engage in a dialogue with the client regarding their personal interpretations of these readings. For example, "What does that first principle and scripture verse mean to you? How does it relate to your life at this time? How can you apply this verse to encourage you throughout the day?"

Scripture verses may help clients to renegotiate their ways of thinking, to refute discouraging and negative thoughts, and to open their souls to God's insight, spiritual power, and emotional healing. If veterans are willing to take the time to learn Bible verses that relate to them, and to allow God's words to change the fear they are feeling inside, then they may find their inner negative dialogues changed into a more positive voice of faith. As Romans 12:2 says, "Be transformed by the renewing of your mind."

The Nine Principles and Accompanying Relevant Scripture

1 God Loves Me and Always Will, No Matter What

This principle is vital for veterans who might bear guilt for having done "bad" things during the war, such as the aking of human lives. They may believe that God will reject them because of their actions while at war. They must learn to reframe those negative self thoughts in a way that will make it possible to move forward toward emotional healing. The Bible teaches that God loves, forgives, is gracious and merciful. These verses will help to restore the understanding of God's acceptance and forgiveness.

> "I have loved you with an everlasting love; I have drawn you with loving-kindness." (Jeremiah 31:3b)

"Who shall separate us from the love of Christ? Shall trouble or hardship or persecution or famine or nakedness or danger or sword? No, in all these things we are more than conquerors through him who loved us. For I am convinced that neither death nor life, neither angels nor demons, neither the present nor the future, nor any powers, neither height nor depth, nor anything else in all creation, will be able to separate us from the love of God that is in Christ Jesus our Lord." (Romans 8:35–39)

II God Is My Strength and My Helper

For veterans who are struggling with anxiety, depression, intrusive thoughts, interrupted sleep, anger, feelings of fear, helplessness, and hopelessness, and the steadfast belief that they will never be "normal" again, this second principle may assist them in remembering that God sees and understands their plight. The verses listed below may offer spiritual help in their efforts to heal.

"The Lord is my light and my salvation—whom shall I fear? The Lord is the stronghold of my life—of whom shall I be afraid?" (Psalm 27:1)

"God is our refuge and strength, an ever-present help in trouble." (Psalm 46:1)

"When I am afraid, I will trust in you." (Psalm 56:3)

"I will lie down and sleep in peace, for you alone, O Lord, make me dwell in safety." (Psalm 4:8)

III God Answers Me When I Call

Veterans may feel that their prayers go unanswered and that God no longer hears their desperate requests. In therapy, they may be encouraged to consider the unexpected ways in which God answers prayer and how God's timetable in answering prayer may be dissimilar to their own. They may be asked to explore the various means by which God has answered their calls for help in the past, and what He may be telling them during times of "silence."

"When I called, you answered me; you made me bold and stouthearted." (Psalm 138:3)

"Call to me and I will answer you and tell you great and unsearchable things you do not know." (Jeremiah 33:3)

"Call upon me in the day of trouble; I will deliver you, and you will honor me." (Psalm 50:15)

IV With God's Help, I Have What I Need to Succeed

For veterans who are feeling discouraged and consumed with negatively-impacted interpersonal relationships, a host of unresolved psychological symptoms, times of intrusive and unresolved anger, and/or a lack of progress and resolution to their issues, the application of these verses may help to rally and expand their self-talk in encouraging ways, and to promote acceptance of their "new normal."

> "I have learned the secret of being content in any and every situation, whether well fed or hungry, whether living in plenty or in want. I can do everything through him who gives me strength." (Philippians 4:12b–13)

> "And my God will meet all your needs according to his glorious riches in Christ Jesus." (Philippians 4:19)

> "Those who hope in the Lord will renew their strength. They will soar on wings like eagles; they will run and not grow weary, they will walk and not be faint." (Isaiah 40:30–31)

V There Is Something Special and Unique About Me

For veterans who feel insignificant in God's eyes, and who feel hopeless and worthless, unable to find meaning or purpose in life due to psychological wounds and/or physical injuries received as the result of their military service, these verses reveal the importance of each person to God. God regards the internal life of faith as more significant than outward accomplishments. Scripture helps to reinstate feelings of self-worth and emphasize the importance of the inner spiritual life.

> "You created my inmost being; you knit me together in my mother's womb. I praise you because I am fearfully and wonderfully made; your works are wonderful, I know that full well." (Psalm 139:13–14)

> "The Lord does not look at the things man looks at. Man looks at the outward appearance, but the Lord looks at the heart." (1 Samuel 16: 7b)

VI My Strengths and Weaknesses Are Helped by Others

Veterans are trained to be strong and self-sufficient and may therefore reject psychological assistance or any form of help from others within the community of faith. These verses help the individual to understand that each of us needs a network of support and a "hand up" at some time in our lives. In addition, each and every person has something invaluable to contribute to others.

> "Now you are the body of Christ, and each one of you is a part of it." (1 Corinthians 12:27)

> "We have different gifts; according to the grace given us . . . share with God's people who are in need." (Romans 12:6, 13)

> "Praise be to the God and Father of our Lord Jesus Christ, the Father of compassion and the God of all comfort, who comforts us in all our troubles, so that we can comfort those in any trouble with the comfort we ourselves have received from God." (2 Corinthians 1:3–4)

VII God Has Good Plans for My Life

Those suffering from PTSD or other psychological conditions stemming from trauma exposure may feel life no longer has anything purposeful to offer. They may believe that their lives are forever darkened, and that constructive goals and hopes will now elude them. The following verses offer encouragement for an alteration in painful affect from emotions of sadness, depression, self-doubt, and despair.

> "For I know the plans I have for you," declares the Lord, "Plans to prosper you and not harm you, plans to give you hope and a future." (Jeremiah 29:11)

> "Surely goodness and love will follow me all the days of my life, and I will dwell in the house of the Lord forever." (Psalm 23:6)

> "I can do everything through him who gives me strength." (Philippians 4:13)

VIII When Bad Things Happen, God Works Through Them for Good

Those returning from wartime service are inclined to question the presence/availability of God's protection, of justice, of unrestricted evil in the world, and the reasons for the torment of such misery and anguish. A thorough exploration of the theology of suffering as an expected part of spiritual life, and the building of resiliency and character that arise from these struggles, may help to bring about hope and insight. These verses address positive outcomes of injurious events.

> "And we know that in all things God works for the good of those who love him, who have been called according to his purpose . . . If God is for us, who can be against us? He who did not spare his own son, but gave him up for us all—how will he not also, along with him, graciously give us all things?" (Romans 8:28, 31b–32)

> "And the God of all grace, who called you to his eternal glory in Christ, after you have suffered a little while, will himself restore you and make you strong, firm, and steadfast." (1 Peter 5:10)

> "We also rejoice in sufferings, because we know that suffering produces perseverance; perseverance, character; and character, hope. And hope does not disappoint us, because God has poured out his love into our hearts by the Holy Spirit, whom he has given us." (Romans 5:3–5)

IX I Am Focusing on the Good Things in My Life

An essential component of CBT and RET is the importance of positive internal talk, and the disputing of negative, often irrational or exaggerated, thought patterns. The Bible addresses the necessity for mindfulness and focus on the noble and virtuous aspects of life. These verses can be offered to help in taking note of everyday successes and life's blessings.

> "Whatever is true, whatever is noble, whatever is right, whatever is pure, whatever is lovely, whatever is admirable—if anything is excellent or praiseworthy—think about such things . . . and the God of peace will be with you." (Philippians 4:8–9)

"The Lord is my shepherd; I shall not be in want. He makes me lie down in green pastures, he leads me beside quiet waters, he restores my soul." (Psalm 23:1, 2)

Scripture for Carrying with You

God Loves Me and Always Will, No Matter What

"I have loved you with an everlasting love; I have drawn you with loving-kindness." (Jeremiah 31:3b)

"Who shall separate us from the love of Christ? Shall trouble or hardship or persecution or famine or nakedness or danger or sword? No, in all these things we are more than conquerors through him who loved us. For I am convinced that neither death nor life, neither angels nor demons, neither the present nor the future, nor any powers, neither height nor depth, nor anything else in all creation, will be able to separate us from the love of God that is in Christ Jesus our Lord." (Romans 8:35–39)

God Is My Strength and My Helper

"The Lord is my light and my salvation—whom shall I fear? The Lord is the stronghold of my life—of whom shall I be afraid?" (Psalm 27:1)

"God is our refuge and strength, an ever-present help in trouble." (Psalm 46:1)

"When I am afraid, I will trust in you." (Psalm 56:3)

"I will lie down and sleep in peace, for you alone, O Lord, make me dwell in safety." (Psalm 4:8)

God Answers Me When I Call

"When I called, you answered me; you made me bold and stouthearted." (Psalm 138:3)

"Call to me and I will answer you and tell you great and unsearchable things you do not know." (Jeremiah 33:3)

"Call upon me in the day of trouble; I will deliver you, and you will honor me." (Psalm 50:15)

With God's Help, I Have What I Need to Succeed

"I have learned the secret of being content in any and every situation, whether well fed or hungry, whether living in plenty or in want. I can do everything through him who gives me strength." (Philippians 4:12b–13)

"And my God will meet all your needs according to his glorious riches in Christ Jesus." (Philippians 4:19)

"Those who hope in the Lord will renew their strength. They will soar on wings like eagles; they will run and not grow weary, they will walk and not be faint." (Isaiah 40:30–31)

There Is Something Special and Unique About Me

"You created my inmost being; you knit me together in my mother's womb. I praise you because I am fearfully and wonderfully made; your works are wonderful, I know that full well." (Psalm 139:13–14)

"The Lord does not look at the things man looks at. Man looks at the outward appearance, but the Lord looks at the heart." (1 Samuel 16:7b)

My Strengths and Weaknesses Are Helped by Others

"Now you are the body of Christ, and each one of you is a part of it." (1 Corinthians 12:27)

"We have different gifts; according to the grace given us . . . share with God's people who are in need." (Romans 12:6, 13)

"Praise be to the God and Father of our Lord Jesus Christ, the Father of compassion and the God of all comfort, who comforts us in all our troubles, so that we can comfort those in any trouble with the comfort we ourselves have received from God." (2 Corinthians 1:3–4)

God Has Good Plans for My Life

"For I know the plans I have for you," declares the Lord, "Plans to prosper you and not harm you, plans to give you hope and a future." (Jeremiah 29:11)

"Surely goodness and love will follow me all the days of my life, and I will dwell in the house of the Lord forever." (Psalm 23:6)

"I can do everything through him who gives me strength." (Philippians 4:13)

When Bad Things Happen, God Works Through Them for Good

"And we know that in all things God works for the good of those who love him, who have been called according to his purpose . . . If God is for us, who can be against us? He who did not spare his own son, but gave him up for us all—how will he not also, along with him, graciously give us all things?" (Romans 8:28, 31b–32)

"And the God of all grace, who called you to his eternal glory in Christ, after you have suffered a little while, will himself restore you and make you strong, firm, and steadfast." (1 Peter 5:10)

"We also rejoice in sufferings, because we know that suffering produces perseverance; perseverance, character; and character, hope. And hope does not disappoint us, because God has poured out his love into our hearts by the Holy Spirit, whom he has given us." (Romans 5:3–5)

I Am Focusing on the Good Things in My Life

"Whatever is true, whatever is noble, whatever is right, whatever is pure, whatever is lovely, whatever is admirable—if anything is excellent or praiseworthy—think about such things . . . and the God of peace will be with you." (Philippians 4:8–9)

"The Lord is my shepherd; I shall not be in want. He makes me lie down in green pastures, he leads me beside quiet waters, he restores my soul." (Psalm 23:1, 2)

In the Words of Veterans and Their Partners

Spiritual interventions have been used as successful and powerful therapeutic tools to refute negative thought patterns; to strengthen, support, and encourage military personal and veterans to re-engage positively in life; and to assist them in rebuilding family, social and professional relationships. Veteran clients have commented about the impact of spiritual interventions in their lives (names have been changed):

- Mary stated, months after returning from a second tour: "I didn't feel comfortable in groups, but, somehow, going to a smaller group of people in a Bible study helped me. They loved me and I hadn't felt accepted like that in a long time."
- A couple, who has received marriage counseling from a therapist sensitive to the needs of clients with a military background, now attends worship services regularly. The husband commented: "My wife waited until I felt that I could go without feeling like I would run out, and we sat in the back. It helped that people were friendly without crushing me. Now I look forward to going. It's a safe place. I need safe places . . . "
- A statement from a soldier who is again attending his place of worship: "I feel stronger for going back to services, and I need to feel strong."

- Brad is a soldier who believed that he had lost his marriage when he first returned from war having fired his weapon "at people I couldn't even see. For a while I thought they were following me, the people I killed." Brad's visits to the local veterans' center helped him regain his psychological footing. Returning to his religious roots with his family has been a restorative experience for them. "It's one of the things we do as a family. We have become better for going to church together."
- Many veterans find strength in attending 12-step programs. One young man indicated that "Going to AA has helped me find a Higher Power and rekindled my faith. I might go back to church someday. It's all good."
- David expressed gratitude for unconditional acceptance, an appreciation often repeated by those who are open to religious support. "I am stronger now than before I went to war. I was a mess when I came home. I can say that now. My synagogue, people at shoal, held me up, never looked at me like I was anything less-than."
- Selecting a pastoral counselor brings the religious experience directly into the counseling or therapy session. "I went to a pastoral counselor who prayed before and after our therapy sessions. I didn't know that was something a therapist did. It was really comforting. I am beginning to feel stable again."
- Kevin returned from war and struggled with every aspect of his life. His therapist, his family, and a very few friends offered him support. Slowly, he began to find some stability and found his way back to church when a co-worker invited him to a Christmas service. It was then that he says his life really turned around. "I am a different Christian now. Before I was shallow and went to church because it was my tradition. Now I have trouble with those who say they are believers but don't take their faith seriously. I don't mean to judge. I need the Lord every day of my life."

Closing

The post-trauma recovery period is an exceedingly stressful time for veterans and families alike. It is vital for therapists, and those working with them, to evaluate and align with the client in a manner that assures the veteran and his or her family that they are being cared for and supported in every way possible on their journey. Too often, it seems a veteran returns from war and is celebrated . . . then forgotten. It is, perhaps, particularly the case that, during this "forgotten" period, various psychological symptoms or emotional problems may arise. Violence, substance abuse, and divorce are not necessarily popular topics of conversation in the community of faith; however, many are experiencing these heartbreaking concerns.

Spiritual communities must reach past any prejudices they may have concerning these complex topics in order to support one another. We must extend help to traumatized veterans for them to experience the opportunity to be welcomed into a community of spiritual support. Apostle Paul writes, "As we have the opportunity, let us do good to all people, especially those who belong to the family of believers" (Galatians 6:10).

Love and acceptance, perhaps especially when combined appropriately with spiritual interventions such as those discussed in this chapter, may enable traumatized individuals to receive the therapies needed to recover from post-trauma illnesses, and to arrive at their personal best "new normal," as they return all the way home.

References

Barna, G. (2001). "Barna Examines Trends in 14 Religious Factors Over 20 Years (1991–2011)." Accessed at: http://www.barna.org/faith-spirituality/504-barna-examines-trends-in-14-religious-factors-over-20-years-1991-to-2011.

International Bible Society (1978, 1984). *The Holy Bible.* New International Version. Colorado Springs, CO: Biblica, Inc.

Lanham, S. L. (2007). *Veterans and Families' Guide to Recovering from PTSD.* Annandale, VA: Military Order of the Purple Heart.

Lanham, S. L., & Pelletier, H. J. (2010). *Recovering from Traumatic Stress: A Guide for Missionaries.* Pasadena, CA: William Carey Library.

Miller, L. (2003). "Interpersonal Psychotherapy from a Spiritual Perspective." In L. Sperry & E. Shafranske, *Spiritually Oriented Psychotherapy* (pp. 153–175). Washington, DC: American Psychological Association.

Nielson, S., Johnson, B., & Ellis, A. (2001). *Counseling and Psychotherapy with Religious Persons.* London: Lawrence Erlbaum Associates.

Parkinson, F. (2000) *Post Trauma Stress.* Cambridge, MA: Dacapo Press.

Scurfield, R. M. (1994). "War-Related Trauma: An Integrative Experiential, Cognitive and Spiritual Approach." In M. B. Williams & J. F. Sommer (Eds.), *Handbook of Post-Traumatic Therapy* (pp. 180–204). Westport, CN: Greenwood Press.

Scurfield, R. M. (2006). *War Trauma: Lessons Unlearned from Vietnam to Iraq.* New York, NY: Algora Publishing.

Sippola, J., Blumenshine, A., Tubesing, D., & Yancey, V. (2009). *Welcome Them Home, Help Them Heal: Pastoral Care and Ministry with Service Members Returning from War.* Duluth, MN: Whole Person Associates.

Sperry, L., & Shafranske, E. (2005). *Spiritually Oriented Psychotherapy.* Washington, DC: American Psychological Association.

Tan, S. Y. (1987). "Cognitive Behavior Therapy: A Biblical Approach and Critique." *Journal of Psychology and Theology,* 15: 103–112.

Further Reading

American Psychiatric Association. (2000). *The Diagnostic and Statistical Manual of Mental Disorders, IV–TR.* Washington, DC: American Psychiatric Association.

Bourne, E. (2002). *The Anxiety and Phobia Workbook.* Oakland, CA: New Harbinger Publications.

Dees, R. F. (2007). *The Combat Trauma Healing Manual.* Newport News, VA: Military Ministry Press.

Herman, J. (2002). *Trauma and Recovery.* New York, NY: Basic Books.

Headington Institute (n.d.). *Spiritual Symptoms of Trauma.* www.headingtoninstitute.org/ Online training.

Kushner, H. S. (1981). *When Bad Things Happen to Good People.* New York, NY: Anchor Books.

Afterword

War Trauma Resources

Raymond Monsour Scurfield (Vietnam) *and*
COL Katherine Theresa Platoni (ODS and OIF/OEF)

We, the editors, are hopeful that *Healing War Trauma* has provided a meaningful array of creative approaches to healing war trauma. These approaches, of course, are only a sampling. We hope that there will be other books that describe yet additional creative approaches. Some that come quickly to mind include:

- Mantra-based meditations.
- Yoga and massage therapy.
- Sports for physically disabled veterans.
- Gardening/farming for veterans.
- Non-chemical approaches for chronic pain management, such as acupuncture.
- Retreats in Buddhist monasteries or other spiritual places.
- Veterans returning to former battlefields (Scurfield, 2004, 2006).
- Veterans meeting and engaging with veterans of other countries, such as the number of interchanges between Soviet Afghani veterans and Vietnam veterans in the 1980s and 1990s (Scurfield, 2004).

Unfortunately, our nation's history, and current and projected government resources, make it crystal clear that our government will never be willing or able to provide a sufficient range of therapeutic and other support services for our nation's service members, veterans, or their families. Even if our government had an exponentially increased amount of funding and resources, there would still be major obstacles. Government bureaucracy and politics engender most bureaucracies to be conservative in accepting or promoting innovative, traditional, non-evidence-based approaches. Thus, it is in the best interests of service members, veterans, and their families for there always to be an abundant array of non-governmental and innovative resources to complement the "mainstream" services provided by government.

A perpetual challenge is how providers and targeted consumers can be informed about such resources. Over a number of years, Ray Scurfield had recognized, in his many presentations to service providers, veterans, and their families, that they, oftentimes, simply were unaware of many of the available resources. In 2008, he decided to compile a two-page handout to complement his presentations. This handout quickly and inexorably morphed into what has become a resource listing of approximately 100 pages, and which includes some 500 resources. Scurfield posts and periodically updates this listing on his University of Southern Mississippi website (http://www.usm.edu/socialwork/scurfield/). It includes a plethora of both public and private resources and is designed to be very user friendly, accessible to any provider or consumer seeking knowledge and contact information about services and programs that are specifically developed for, or have particular relevance to, service members, veterans, and their families. It should be noted that the War Trauma Resources list is not a "vetted" or "endorsed" listing. There are annotated descriptions provided, excerpted directly from each website. For a small number of the websites, those about which Scurfield has personal knowledge, he provides additional comments.

This listing illustrates the incredible expanding circle of healing, and the innovative approaches that have evolved from the hearts and minds of so many dedicated people and organizations to help address the multiple needs of our service members, veterans, and their families. However, as impressive as this listing is, it also reflects the enormous work there is to promote knowledge about these various resources, facilitate possible coordination among them, and avoid duplication and gaps—as well as the ongoing demands upon many such organizations and resources to maintain or develop adequate funding, people, and material resources to remain viable.

Selective Excerpts from the War Trauma Resources Listing

The listing is divided into seven sections; resources within each section are in alphabetical order. One fully annotated example (for illustrative purposes) is listed within each of the eight sections. (Excerpts are as of February, 2012.)

Active Duty Military, Reserve and Guard Resources (pp. 2–9)

An entry:

Resources for Military Children Affected by Deployment

(http://www.armymwr.com/cys-images/Deployment%20A%20Compendium%20of%20Resources.pdf). Compilation by U.S. Army Family and Morale, Welfare and Recreation Command, Children and Youth Services. January, 2008. Includes links to books for children, deployment kits for children and families, deployment/resources for parents and staff, and websites for children, parents, and teachers.

Other DOD and Governmental Resources (pp. 9–11)

An entry:

DCOE (Defense Centers of Excellence) For Health Professionals

(http://www.dcoe.health.mil/). Information and resources on traumatic brain injury, psychological health issues, and combat stress, specifically tailored to healthcare professionals.

Here one can learn about treatment options for PTSD and review tips for civilian healthcare professionals treating military patients. Visit the resources page to access evidence-based clinical practice guidelines, as well as relevant web sites and reports. TBI Information, PTSD Treatment Options. Tips for Civilian Healthcare Professionals Treating Chronic Symptomatic Mild Traumatic Brain Injury and Post-Traumatic Stress Disorder, Joining the TRICARE Network: How do I become a TRICARE-accepting provider? DCoE Outreach Center.

U.S. Department of Veterans Affairs (pp. 11–14)

An entry:

My HealtheVet

(https://www.myhealth.va.gov/index.html). My HealtheVet (MHV) "is the VA's gateway to veteran health benefits and services. It provides access to trusted health information; links to Federal and VA benefits and resources; the Personal Health Journal; and online VA prescription refill. In the future, MHV registrants will be able to view appointments, co-pay balances, and key portions of their VA medical records online, and much more! My HealtheVet is a powerful tool to help you better understand and manage your health."

State Department of Veterans Affairs (pp. 14–15)

The mission and services of some state DVAs, as well as specific programs, are described. An entry:

Illinois State Department of Veterans Affairs

(http://www.illinoiswarrior.com/) "The Illinois Warrior Assistance Program . . . provides confidential assistance for Illinois veterans as they transition back to their everyday lives after serving our country. Our health professionals are here to help. In the military, you are trained to be physically, mentally and emotionally tough. But our service members need to know that mental and psychological wounds can be just as debilitating as external, physical injuries and they need to seek help for these wounds. We all need to do everything we can to help our warriors when they return home—we owe it to them." Confidential Phone Line for counseling assistance: 866.554-IWAP (4927).

Surfing the Web (pp. 15–85)

400+ resources (mostly non-governmental). An entry:

Farmer-Veteran Coalition

(www.Farmvetco.org). "Farmers helping veterans; veterans helping farmers." Helps returning veterans find jobs, training, and places to heal on America's farms. It's a way to help veterans and also replace the aging population of farmers and ranchers as they die or retire. "Our mission is two-fold. We need and want more young people going into agriculture and, secondly, we want to create healthy and viable futures for America's veterans by helping them find employment or careers in agriculture," said Michael O'Gorman, founder and executive director of the Farmer-Veteran Coalition.

Videos (pp. 85–95)

Sampling of non-governmental videos/movies related to military deployment, readjustment, veterans, families, and communities. An entry:

Soldiers Surprising Their Loved Ones: Video, Part 1

Just one of over two million (!) viewer comments: "If you don't have tears in your eyes from the very start of this video then I don't know what to say—I know I did. This video shows—and you can see if in the little girls eyes at the beginning of this—that it's not only our fine men and women who serve that sacrifice and display bravery each and every day for all of us but also their family and friends who wait for them to return." Note: Simple yet very emotional concept of filming unsuspecting family members being surprised by the unannounced return of their servicemembers from deployment captures several really special moments on camera. http://www.youtube.com/watch?v=hkGzqpGx1KU.

Canadian Military/Veterans' Resources (pp. 95–96)

An entry:

Operational Stress Injury Social Support Program (OSISS)

"The Operational Stress Injury Social Support program is a national peer support network to support those suffering from operational stress injuries as a direct result of military service." See the OSISS website at: www.osiss.ca.

In closing, the above sampling does not begin to do justice to the remarkable diversity and number of creative websites that are listed. We salute the remarkable litany of people who are behind these many resources, as well as the countless individual practitioners, clinicians, volunteers, and the informal and ad hoc responses of so many other caring people. We truly are blessed; these folks epitomize the attitude of "paying it forward"—and the "can do" attitude of the Seabees.

Ray Scurfield   Kathy Platoni

References

Scurfield, R. M. (2004). *A Vietnam Trilogy: Veterans and Post-Traumatic Stress Disorder, 1968, 1989 & 2000.* New York, NY: Algora.

Scurfield, R. M. (2006). *Healing Journeys: Study Abroad with Vietnam Veterans.* New York, NY: Algora.

Index

310   *Index*